'Race' and Ethnicity in Canada

For Linda and good old Lucy and Jack
Vic Satzewich

For Manos and Vera, hoping they will make a difference
Nikolaos Liodakis

'Race' and Ethnicity in Canada
A Critical Introduction

**Vic Satzewich
and Nikolaos Liodakis**

OXFORD
UNIVERSITY PRESS

OXFORD
UNIVERSITY PRESS

70 Wynford Drive, Don Mills, Ontario M3C 1J9
www.oup.com/ca

Oxford University Press is a department of the University of Oxford.
It furthers the University's objective of excellence in research, scholarship,
and education by publishing worldwide in

Oxford   New York

Auckland   Cape Town   Dar es Salaam   Hong Kong   Karachi
Kuala Lumpur   Madrid   Melbourne   Mexico City   Nairobi
New Delhi   Shanghai   Taipei   Toronto

With offices in

Argentina   Austria   Brazil   Chile   Czech Republic   France   Greece
Guatemala   Hungary   Italy   Japan   Poland   Portugal   Singapore
South Korea   Switzerland   Thailand   Turkey   Ukraine   Vietnam

Oxford is a trade mark of Oxford University Press
in the UK and in certain other countries

Published in Canada
by Oxford University Press

Copyright © Oxford University Press Canada 2007

The moral rights of the author have been asserted

Database right Oxford University Press (maker)

First published 2007

Library and Archives Canada Cataloguing in Publication Data

Satzewich, Vic, 1961–
Race and ethnicity in Canada : a critical introduction / Vic Satzewich & Nikolaos Liodakis.

Includes bibliographical references and index.

ISBN 978-0-19-542131-6

1. Canada—Emigration and immigration—Textbooks. 2. Multiculturalism—Canada—Textbooks.
3. Canada—Race relations—Textbooks. Canada—Ethnic relations—Textbooks.
I. Liodakis, Nikolaos, 1963– . II. Title.

FC104.S295 2007   305.80'0971   C2007-901182-9

Cover Design: Brett J. Miller

Cover Image: © stockbyte: Education

1 2 3 4 – 10 09 08 07

This book is printed on permanent (acid-free) paper ∞.

Printed in Canada

Contents

List of Boxes, Figures, and Tables

Boxes

Figures

Tables

Acknowledgements

We would like to thank Lorne Tepperman and the late James Curtis for initially inviting us to contribute a volume to this series. A number of individuals at Oxford University Press have been both patient with us and very helpful in seeing this book through the publication process. In particular, we want to thank acquisitions editor Lisa Meschino, development editor Marta Tomins, managing editor Phyllis Wilson, and Dorothy Turnbull, copyeditor extraordinaire, for their varying roles in the process of publication. The three referees who read and commented on an earlier draft of this book provided valuable critical comments, and this book is better because of the time they took to review our work. We would also like to thank our students, who over the years have been the unknowing collaborators with us on this project. They have provided us with valuable informal feedback on the particular take on ethnic relations and immigration that we offer in this book. Vic Satzewich would also like to thank Jackie Tucker, Olga Cannon and Corinne Jehle of the Department of Sociology at McMaster for the valuable support that they provide to faculty members in a busy and dynamic scholarly environment. Nikolaos Liodakis would like to thank Tom Chmielewski for his assistance in recoding 'classless' Canadian census data.

Preface

For students of immigration, Aboriginal/non-Aboriginal relations, and wider patterns of 'race' and ethnic relations, Canada is a sociological garden. Our country offers an extraordinarily rich and complex environment for examining some of the central issues associated with indigenous/settler relations, why people migrate, how they integrate into society, how they retain aspects of their cultures and identities, and how racism, discrimination, and multiculturalism work. Part of the reason that Canada is such an interesting country to study is that patterns of immigration and of 'race' and ethnic relations defy simple description and explanation. Moreover, there seem to be so many paradoxes.

Many individuals around the world are interested in moving to Canada in order to find a better life for themselves and their children. Canada allows more than a quarter of a million immigrants per year into the country so that they can pursue these dreams. It also makes the acquisition of Canadian citizenship relatively easy. If you have lived in the country for three years and can pass a fairly basic multiple-choice test, you get a Canadian passport, earn the right to vote in elections, and have the same rights as a person who was born here and whose ancestors came to this country centuries ago. However, even though Canada needs and wants permanent immigrants, thousands of farm and domestic workers are admitted into the country to live and work on only a temporary basis and are denied basic citizenship rights. In other words, we need and want immigrants, but at the same time, some people are considered good enough to work in Canada but not good enough to stay, form families, and pursue the Canadian dream. What makes an individual a good immigrant, and what makes another individual a good worker but not a good potential future citizen?

Economically speaking, some immigrants in Canada do spectacularly well. We have Frank Stronach, who came to Canada as a young and virtually penniless Hungarian immigrant and subsequently built one of the world's largest auto parts empires. We have Michael Lee-Chin, the child of Jamaican immigrants, who is now the CEO of one of Canada's largest wealth management funds. While some may dismiss these examples as isolated Horatio Alger stories that have little relevance for the majority of immigrants to Canada, it is the case that many other immigrants and their descendants earn high incomes, own businesses, run corporations, live in palatial homes, and have lifestyles that many of us would envy. At the same time, however, some immigrants do spectacularly poorly in Canada and face a lifetime of poverty, hard work, and sometimes no work. Some immigrants end up cleaning toilets at Pearson Airport. Moreover, stories of overseas-educated doctors, lawyers, nurses, and engineers who are unable to practise their professions in Canada and end up driving taxis in Ottawa, Hamilton, or Saskatoon because of sticky professional licensing requirements or demands for 'Canadian experience' are not simply urban legends.

Canadians of different origins generally get along well with each other. Even though the characterization of Canada as a multicultural society that celebrates and tolerates diversity is a cliché, it is true that compared to residents of many other countries, Canadians of different backgrounds do not generally and routinely go around hurting or killing other people because of who they are. Canadians are encouraged to celebrate and maintain their ancestral identities, cultures, and religions. Intermarriage rates have increased over the past three decades. Many cities have multicultural festivals, and so-called 'ethnic' restaurants do not just cater to members of their own communities but also have diverse clienteles. Some say that these phenomena are superficial indicators of tolerance and diversity, more a reflection of symbolic ethnicity than anything else, but the fact remains that we do not have large-scale ethnic, 'racial', or religious violence.

Yet we do have instances of racism and discriminatory treatment. Many institutions in this country have been accused of racism. Some Canadians, including people in some of Canada's most powerful institutions (like the police) are deeply suspicious of the commitment of certain religious and ethnocultural communities to Canada and to Canadian values. Homeland politics and controversies sometimes play themselves out in this country with tragic consequences. The bombing of the Air India flight from Vancouver in 1985 is thought to be related to Sikh struggles for an independent homeland. In some quarters, the Muslim religion is considered fundamentally at odds with Canadian values such as equality and tolerance and as a breeding ground for terrorism.

Many of our national symbols and coveted cultural artefacts are derived from Aboriginal cultures. Many Canadians enjoy canoeing as a way of communing and reconnecting with nature, and our quirky national symbol, the beaver, is in some ways a tribute to the complex relations of economic and cultural exchange that early Europeans and First Nations engaged in during the course of the seventeenth and eighteenth-century fur trade. Yet First Nations standoffs, blockades, and protests over unfilled treaty promises and land grabs are all too common in this country. And as we have seen in the case of the shooting of Dudley George at Ipperwash Provincial Park in Ontario in 1995, these standoffs do not always have happy endings.

The aim of this book is to help students analyze and understand some of the complex patterns of immigration, Aboriginal/non-Aboriginal relations, and 'race' and ethnic relations in Canada. These patterns, as will be clear from this book, are full of ironies, contradictions, and tensions. In the book, we adopt a position of methodological and theoretical pluralism. We want to encourage students to think critically about these issues and not to accept certain claims made in the media, by other academics—or even by us—as unquestionable truths. Rather than attempting to review, summarize, and synthesize what is now a massive body of scholarly and activist knowledge in these areas, this book deals with major approaches to and explanations of a number of issues that are central to the field.

Chapter 1 discusses some central concepts and theories in the field of 'race' and ethnic relations. Concepts and theoretical perspectives are important because they help define our subject matter and offer lenses through which we can begin to understand and make connections among various issues.

In chapter 2, we argue that history matters when it comes to understanding contemporary patterns of immigration, French/English relations, 'race' and ethnic relations, and Aboriginal/non-Aboriginal relations. While we are not simple historical determinists who argue that history explains everything, we do believe that in order to understand issues like land claims disputes and allegations that the Canadian immigration system is racist, we need to have an understanding of the past.

Chapter 3 discusses issues associated with the contemporary immigration system. It considers the question of why Canada has immigration and discusses a number of controversies over different immigration categories. These questions include but are not limited to: Are family class immigrants a 'drain' on the Canadian economy? Do new safe third country rules put refugees at risk? What is the social impact of the business immigration program on Canada?

Chapter 4 discusses the issue of economic inequality among immigrants, non-immigrants, and 'racial' and ethnic groups. Even though there is evidence that the vertical mosaic in Canada is being recast along 'racial' lines, we propose an alternative perspective to understanding inequality. Our alternative suggests that social scientists also need to study the internal class and gender differences within basic ethnic and 'racial' categories.

In chapter 5, we examine issues of ethnic identity and multiculturalism. In particular, we consider some of the factors, such as institutional completeness, that allow immigrants and ethnic communities to maintain themselves and individual identities. We also consider issues associated with segmented assimilation and different pathways to integration among immigrants. We also conduct an extensive and critical discussion of the Canadian federal government's policy of multiculturalism. As we show, multicultural policy is a favourite whipping boy for Canadians, with some claiming that it encourages too much diversity and others that it does not promote genuine diversity.

Chapter 6 focuses on the issue of racism. We outline a number of definitions of racism and critically evaluate several sociological explanations for racism. We question whether racism is a 'whites only' phenomenon as well as claims that there is a new kind of racism that characterizes many Western societies. We provide examples of institutional racism and extensively discuss 'racial' profiling in policing and whether safe schools policies put black and other minority youth at a disadvantage.

In chapter 7, we turn our attention to contemporary Aboriginal/non-Aboriginal relations. We examine the political constitution of Aboriginal identities and categories and some of the controversies associated with how First Nations are defined. We then examine how social scientists explain differences in health status and socio-economic achievement between Aboriginal and non-Aboriginal peoples. In doing so, we critically evaluate biological, cultural, structural, and historical explanations of these differences. We conclude the chapter with a discussion of an alternative way of thinking about Aboriginal peoples' position in Canadian society—a way of thinking that focuses, once again, on the internal divisions within a group. We suggest that Aboriginal communities are fractured by gender, class, and political power.

Finally, in chapter 8, we extensively discuss two new approaches to the study of immigration and ethnic relations. The concepts of 'diaspora' and 'transnational' are introduced, explained, and critiqued in this chapter. We provide a number of examples of what researchers mean when they describe a community as either transnational or a diaspora. We argue that while these two concepts provide a useful lens through which patterns of immigration and of 'race' and ethnic relations can be understood, many of their proponents' claims are not entirely new or novel.

Chapter 1

Theories of Ethnicity and 'Race'

Learning objectives

In this chapter you will learn that:

- The meanings of the terms ethnicity and 'race' are historically specific—i.e., they mean different things to different people in different places at different times.
- Ethnicity and 'race' are important bases for the formation of social groups. Historically, they have shaped the formation of real or imagined communities of people.
- Ethnicity and 'race' are relational concepts. They are social relations. As such, they represent the lived experiences of individuals and groups and are important dimensions of social inequality.
- Ethnicity is usually associated with people's cultural characteristics, mostly symbolic, such as their customs, beliefs, ideas, mores, language, history, folklore, and other symbols that hold the group together and assist others to recognize them as separate.
- 'Race' is an irrational way of dividing human populations into groups based on the members' physical characteristics. 'Racial' categories have their roots in nineteenth-century Western pseudo-science, supported and justified ideologically by the Enlightenment. Colonization, exploitation, and slavery have warranted the material subordination of non-Westerners over the centuries.
- Over time, material conditions and racist ideologies reproduce patterns of inequality among and within ethnic and 'racial' groups. Social scientists recognize that ethnic and 'racial' groups are not homogeneous entities; they differ in terms of their social class composition, gender, age, place of birth, and so on. Along with class and

gender relations, ethnicity and 'race' constitute the fundamental bases of social inequality.

- Most states, like Canada, are not homogeneous. They are multi-ethnic, multicultural and 'multi-racial'. They are characterized by class and gender divisions. It is important to study the ways that such divisions overlap and interact.

INTRODUCTION

On 27 October 2005, in the outskirts of Paris, police chased two French teenagers of African origin to their deaths. Bouma Traore (15) and Zyed Benna (17) were playing soccer with other teenagers in a middle-class neighbourhood, close to La Pama where they lived—a small apartment complex where French citizens predominantly of African and Arab descent reside. The two boys, trying to avoid the usual police chase and questioning ('Where are you from?' 'What are you doing here?' 'Show me your papers.'), ran into and hid in an electrical substation where they were electrocuted by a transformer (*Toronto Star* 2005). Their undeserved deaths sparked riots that lasted for two weeks and 'necessitated' the imposition of a state of emergency in Paris and many other French cities. The last time a state of emergency was imposed in France was in May 1968, when the French government put down student uprisings. Before that, the last time was during the Second World War.

Many French people of African and Arab origin and members of other ethnic groups took to the streets of France and demonstrated against police brutality, the high unemployment rates experienced by immigrant groups, poverty, discrimination and outright racism, the imposition of a policy of 'Frenchness', and its corollary of their arguably forced assimilation into the dominant French culture. There was destruction. Thousands of cars were burned. Personal property was destroyed. Demonstrators and police officers were injured. The conservative government crumbled. Jacques Chirac, president of the French republic and well-respected European Union leader, and Minister of Public Order Nicolas Sarkozy scrambled to find a quick resolution of the problem. And they did: a short-term resolution that involved more police repression. A second, more long-term solution involved promises that the liberty/equality/fraternity mantra, with some further economic and social policy tinkering, would eventually bear fruit for France's mainly black, Muslim, immigrant underclass.

'Cast aside by France', read the headlines (*Toronto Star* 2005). Who cast whom aside? Why and how? What is the problem here? Is it the fact that the police routinely chase 'illegal-looking' blacks in France? Is it that immigrants face increased levels of poverty? Is it that people became fed-up and had to do something about their social conditions? Is it that over the years, policies of assimilating 'foreigners', the 'not true Frenchmen', had not produced any concrete results for minorities? Is it that assimilation policies do not work and that policies of multiculturalism should be pursued instead? It appeared that France's history of colonization and continued practice of discrimination against minorities had come back to haunt it.

How do we, as social scientists, explain the events that unravelled in France not so long ago? After all, we live in a country that is also multi-ethnic and, unlike France, we take pride in our policy of multiculturalism, not assimilation. No American-style melting pot here. No French forced assimilation either. Could such a riot take place in Toronto? In Montreal perhaps? In any other multi-ethnic and multi-'racial' Canadian metropolis? Was it a problem of ethnicity/'race'? One of social class? Gender, perhaps? Is it a French problem, not a Canadian one? Have we solved our problems of ethnic/'racial' inequality? These are both pressing and complex questions that require a simplified start. We suggest that in order to understand and explain social phenomena of conflict, as in the case above, we must begin from theory.

This chapter begins with a discussion of early historical and philosophical theories of ethnicity and 'race'. The work of Max Weber is examined next to show how an early sociological approach differed from historical and philosophical perspectives. We then go on to provide a brief history of the concept of 'race' and suggest a particular way of defining and understanding this much-used and misused concept. We conclude the chapter with an extended discussion of some influential schools of thought in the field, including the Chicago School, cultural theory, political economy, and intersectional analysis.

ETHNICITY: HISTORICAL ORIGINS AND APPROACHES

The term 'ethnicity' has its roots in the Greek word ἔθνος (*ethnos*) and means 'people'. In proto-Christian times, it was used to differentiate people who were not Christians. They were called *ethnics*. In ancient Greece, the standard term used to refer to cohesive social groups formed on the basis of kinship was φυλή (*phyle*), which some today tend to associate with tribe or 'race'. *Phylai* (plural) were larger in size than those covered by the less-inclusive term 'House of' (Οἶκος), such as the House of Heracleidae, Atreides, Alcmaeonidae. *Phylai* were larger groups of people who were related by real blood ties or could trace their ancestry back to an often-perceived bloodline. But *phylai* were subdivisions of ethnic groups. The latter social groups shared a common language and worshiped the same or similar deities. They did not necessarily reside in the same geographical area, but they could claim common biological ancestry. They had the same customs, eating habits, dress codes, and historical symbols. They shared what we call today a sense of belonging together (συνανήκειν).

In Herodotus, their first historian, we find early accounts of ethnic groups. His *Histories*, in which he gave detailed accounts of the Persian wars against the Greeks, contain many passages mentioning innumerable ethnic groups and describing their ways: their languages, their gods, some of their customs, their 'idiosyncrasies', their geography, and their contacts with other groups, as well as their history, politics, social arrangements, and economies (Herodotus, Books I–IV). He also provided a definition that was applicable to all ethnic groups. Speaking of the Greeks, recognizing that they were geographically and politically fragmented, he argued that they constituted an ethnic group because they were of common descent and had a common language, common gods, sacred places, sacrificial festivals, and customs, and common *mores* or ways of life, as well as 'the common character they bear' (Herodotus, Book VIII).

His stories, some based on real historical facts, some imaginary, show that from early on there had been extensive cultural contacts and exchanges among groups, primarily through peaceful coexistence, trade, and exogamy among the upper classes but also through war, colonization, and conquest. Even though he recognized the influences of Egyptian, Phoenician, and Mesopotamian civilizations on Greece, Herodotus did not hide his ethnocentrism. For example, he considered the Assyrians a warlike people, who wore 'helmets upon their heads made of brass, and painted in a strange fashion which is not easy to describe. They carried shields, lances, and daggers very like the Egyptian; but in addition, they had wooden clubs knotted with iron, and linen corselets' (Herodotus, Book VII). He went on to meticulously describe (among others) the war costumes of the Bactrians (who dressed like the Medians), the Scythians, the Indians, the Arians, the Parthians, the Chorasmians, the Sogdians, the Gandarians, the Dadicae, the Caspians, the Pactyans, the Utians, the Arabians, the Ethiopians, the Libyans, the Paphlagonians, the Phrygians, the Lydians, and the Phoenicians (Herodotus, Book VII). We are familiar with some of these ethnic groups even today. Groups that still identify themselves as Assyrians and Chaldaeans can be found in Detroit, Montreal, and Toronto (in ancient times, the Chaldaeans, a group related to the Assyrians, served under them in Xerxes's war against mainland Greece). Others have disappeared.

In addition, Herodotus was able to differentiate among subgroups within the same, more broadly conceived ethnic group. For example, he distinguishes between eastern and western Ethiopians, Amyrgians and other Scythians, Padaeans and other Indians, and Asiatic versus European Thracians. Among the Greeks, he distinguishes Athenians, Lacedaemonians (Spartans), Thessalians, Macedonians, Argians, Locrians, Thebans, Pylians, Naxians, Cretans, Rhodians, Salaminians, and Plataeans, among many. In terms of blood or kinship ties, he mentions that Lacedaemonians are of Doric blood, whereas Athenians are of Ionic blood. Finally, he often makes associations between ethnic groups and their perceived social, mental, and behavioural characteristics. For example, his work operates from the assumption that there is a hierarchy in terms of the desired characteristics of groups. He distinguishes between Greeks and barbarians, but his hierarchy is not a 'racial' one. Instead, it is based on the notion of freedom (Goldberg 1993). The Greeks were free, and the barbarians were not. The former had desired characteristics, often deemed superior (a better language, being clever, brave, adventurous, pious, clean, favoured by their gods) to those of the barbarians (lacking in intellectual capacity, dressing strangely, dirty, cowardly, tricky, irreverent, bloodthirsty, raw meat eaters, and so on).

According to Goldberg (1993), explanations for these ethnic hierarchies tended to be environmentalist: that is, they were products of the history and shared physical environment in which these groups evolved. As we will see later, this is a major theme in the development of naturalist accounts of group characteristics, from Locke to Hume and Kant. Modern versions of environmentalism naturalize the similarities and differences and make them seem virtually unalterable (Goldberg 1993,

77), just as did Herodotus, who wrote that the Hellenes had never, since their origin, changed their speech (Book I).

Herodotus, of course, is not alone in discussing similarities and differences among ethnic groups, associating them with moral, behavioural, and intellectual traits and trying to account for these traits in terms of their physical environment. Many centuries later, one of the most prominent British historians, Edward Gibbon, who studied the Roman and Byzantine empires exhaustively, also employed environmentalist explanations. Writing in 1776, he argued in an attempt to study the differences between the Arabs and the Europeans that

> [t]he separation of the Arabs from the rest of mankind [*sic*] has accustomed them to confound the ideas of stranger and enemy; and the poverty of the [Arabian] land has introduced a maxim of jurisprudence which they believe and practice to the present hour. They pretend that, in the division of the earth, the rich and fertile climates were assigned to the other branches of the human family: and that the posterity of the outlaw Ismael might recover, by fraud or force, the portion of inheritance of which they had been unjustly deprived. (1998, 788).

Commenting on their perceived lawlessness, violent character, ill-temper, vindictiveness, and contempt for human life, and juxtaposing these qualities with European standards, he wrote from an ethnocentric perspective that

> [i]n private life, every man, at least every family, was the judge of its own cause. The nice sensibility of honour, which weighs the insult rather than the injury, sheds its deadly venom on the quarrels of the Arabs; the honour of their women and of their *beards* [emphasis in the original], is most easily wounded; an indecent action, a contemptuous word, can be expiated only by the blood of the offender; and such is their patient inveteracy that they expect whole months and years for revenge. A fine or compensation for murder is familiar to the barbarians of every age; but in Arabia the kinsmen of the dead are at liberty to accept the atonement, or to exercise with their own hands the law of retaliation. The refined malice of the Arabs refuses even the head of the murderer, substitutes an innocent to the guilty person, and transfers the penalty to the best and most considerable of the 'race' by whom they have been injured (1998, 789).

Notice how Gibbon uses the term 'race' here: he means enemy 'family' or tribe. Does this remind you of present-day discourses and depictions of Arabs in North American mass media, especially since the events of 11 September 2001 in the United States, the war in Afghanistan, and the subsequent invasion of Iraq by the US and some of its allies? Does Gibbon's description of Arabs have any parallels to the way the US State Department constructs the notion of 'Arab terrorists' today? Remember that Gibbon wrote the above in 1776, several centuries before the West invented 'the Arab terrorist'.

SELF AND OTHER IN THE ENLIGHTENMENT

Notions of Self and Other, of civilized and savage, of superiority and inferiority were already flowing among philosophical circles in Europe long before the economic, ideological, social, and political ascendancy of the bourgeoisie. The ideological seeds of racialization and racism (see chapter 6) were already present in the Enlightenment in the works of John Locke, Gottfried Leibniz, David Hume, Immanuel Kant, and Voltaire, among others. The Utilitarians, Jeremy Bentham, James Mill, and John Stuart Mill, followed in the era of capitalism. In his *Two treatises on government* (1960), written in the late seventeenth century, John Locke, who had assisted in the drafting of the constitution of Carolina, specified conditions under which wars were justified and 'Negro' slaves captured. He considered the slave expeditions of the Royal Africa Company as just wars and that the captured 'Negroe' slaves 'forfeited their claim to life'. In his epistemology, rationality was a 'nominal essential property', a prerequisite for the constitution of humans as such. In his eyes, people of colour were associated with lack of rational capacity. This was a ground for excluding 'Negroes' from humanity and for enslavement; they could be justifiably treated as chattel property, as brutes and animals.

Leibniz, a rationalist also writing in the seventeenth century, commented on the 'unacceptability' of the customs of Native Americans, writing that 'one would have to be as brutish as the American savages to approve their customs which are more cruel than those of wild animals' (in Goldberg 1993, 28). David Hume distinguished between national and 'racial' characteristics and between moral and physical determinants of the 'national character'. Mind and nature, in his theory, are correlated in various ways. Following environmentalist thinking, he believed that climate and air are the determinants of perceived human differences. Moral causes, such as customs, economic conditions, government, and external relations, also influence the minds and manners of people. National characters are the result of moral causes. In *The philosophical works* (1960), writing 'On national character', he branded Jews as 'fraudulent', Arabs as 'uncouth and disagreeable', modern Greeks as 'deceitful, stupid and cowardly', unlike their 'ingenious, industrious and active' ancestors and certainly unlike the Turks who had 'integrity, gravity and bravery'.

Superior among all national characters was, of course, the English. Hume's views echoed earlier descriptions by Francis Bacon and George Berkeley, who believed that the inhabitants of the far north and the tropics, because they lacked industrial habits and sexual moderation, were inferior to those of more temperate European regions. But for Hume, whereas national differences were social, 'racial' differences were biological and inherent. All other 'species of humans' were considered naturally inferior to whites. His justification was empirical: only whites, he argued, had produced arts and science; 'Negroes' had not. Like Locke, he believed that the difference was one of 'breeds'. Goldberg quotes Hume as saying that '[i]n Jamaica they talk of one negroe [*sic*] as a man of parts and learning; but tis likely he is admired for very slender accomplishments, like a parrot, who speaks a few words plainly' (1993, 31).

Immanuel Kant, writing in the late eighteenth century and following Hume, proceeded from 'national character' to 'race'. Not surprisingly, he held that Germans were superior to all others in terms of national character because they represented a synthesis of English 'intuition for the sublime' and French 'feeling for the beautiful'.

Discussing oriental 'races', which he often called Mongolians, he found the Arabs most noble, being 'hospitable, generous and truthful', although 'with an inflamed imagination that tends to distort'. Persians were 'good poets, courteous, with fine taste', and the Japanese were resolute but stubborn. Indians and Chinese were considered lower because of 'their taste for the grotesque and monstrous'. Indians, in particular, were 'committed to the despotic excess of *sati*'. 'Negroes', on the other hand, were found the most lacking of all 'savages', whereas the American 'Indians' were 'honourable, truthful and honest' and were the least lacking of the 'savages' (Goldberg 1993, 32). For Kant, 'racial' subordination was an a priori principle. He thought that the differences between whites and 'Negroes' were so fundamental that skin colour was the causal explanation of assumed differences in 'mental capacities': '[t]he blacks are in vain in the Negro way, and so talkative that they must be driven apart from each other by thrashings' (Kant 1960, 11). Later, describing a black male, he remarked that 'the fellow was so black from head to foot, a clear proof that what he said was stupid' (Kant 1960, 11). The proof was in the colour.

Voltaire, a prominent figure in French philosophy and politics and for some the European voice of equality par excellence, was also a proponent of polygenism, i.e., the idea that humans evolved from different groups independently of each other. In 1734, writing against monogenism—the idea that humans evolved from a single human group—he explained that 'Bearded whites, fuzzy Negroes, the long-maned yellow races and beardless men are not descended from the same man . . . [Whites] are superior to these Negroes, as the Negroes are to apes and the apes to oysters' (Voltaire 1734, in Poliakov 1974, 176). He argued that 'only a blind man is permitted to doubt that Whites, Negroes and Albinos . . . are totally different races' (Voltaire 1754, in Poliakov 1974, 176). For Voltaire, differences in the observable physical characteristics of groups were rooted in 'racial' difference. For him, there was no one, single, unified human race.

Bentham, James Mill, and John Stuart Mill also shared racist views, although they rejected Voltaire's polygenism. James Mill worked for the British colonial service of the East India Company and bequeathed his office to his son John Stuart. The elder Mill was the most powerful administrator of India. Goldberg (1993, 34–5) notes that in Mill's *History of British India* (1820) we find attacks on the 'hideous state of Hindu and Muslim civilizations'. The Chinese, but especially the Indians, were said to be 'tainted with the vices of insincerity, dissembling, . . . treacherous . . . disposed to excessive exaggeration . . . cowardly and unfeeling . . . in the highest degree conceited . . . and full of affected contempt for others. Both are, in a physical sense, disgustingly unclean in their persons and houses.' His son, John Stuart Mill, despite his principles expressed in *On liberty*, did discriminate between civilized and uncivilized peoples, although he believed that there was nothing in the nature of Indians to prevent them from self-determination and good government. They simply needed to be directed, as children do, administratively, legislatively, pedagogically, and socially (Goldberg 1993, 35). This is reminiscent of modern theories of development, the policies of the World Bank and the International Monetary Fund, and recent European and US 'efforts' to democratize Afghanistan, Iraq, and other 'rogue' states.

WEBERIAN APPROACHES

Do social scientists explain ethnic phenomena differently from the way historians and philosophers do? How do we define ethnic groups? How do we account for their similarities and differences, their interactions, and the social relations prevalent within and among them? Processes in the formation of social groups are of central concern to sociologists. Group formation is associated with social practices of inclusion/exclusion, which in turn are important in the production and distribution of scarce valuable resources such as wages, social status and status symbols, economic and political power, equality, voting rights and citizenship, access to social programs, human rights, self-determination, and autonomy. These practices constitute the basis upon which decisions about rewards/sanctions are made.

Max Weber (1864–1920) was one of the most eminent sociologists to study ethnic groups, albeit superficially. His definition, you will notice, is not that different from the definition Herodotus used to describe ethnic groups. Nor is Weber far from environmentalism. According to Weber (1978), common descent, tribe, culture (including language and other symbolic codes), religion, and nationality (a product of the Enlightenment) are important determinants of ethnicity. In distinguishing between kinship and ethnic groups, Weber wrote:

> [w]e shall call 'ethnic groups' those human groups that entertain a subjective belief in their common descent because of similarities of physical type or of customs or both, or because of memories of colonization and migration; this belief must be important for the propagation of group formation; conversely, it does not matter whether or not an objective blood relationship exists. Ethnic membership differs from the kinship group precisely by being a presumed identity, not a group with concrete social action, like the latter (1978, 389).

Weber used the term 'race' to denote the common identity of groups based on heredity and endogamous conjugal groups. He argued that 'racial' heredity had historically been a basis for delineating social groups. Customs as well as visible similarities and differences, however minor, could serve as potential sources of affection and appreciation or repulsion and contempt (Dreidger 1996, 5). Weber wrote, 'Almost any kind of similarity or contrast of physical type and of habits can induce the belief that affinity or differences exist between groups that attract or repel each other' (1978, 386). Cultural differences, both symbolic and material, produced and reproduced over time, also constituted the foundations upon which a 'consciousness of kind' could be built.

Such cultural traits, in turn, 'can serve as a starting point for the familiar tendency to monopolistic closure' (Weber 1978, 386). Monopolistic closure simply means processes and practices, often institutionalized, whereby members of the in-group have access to the scarce valuable resources mentioned above, whereas non-members (the out-group) are excluded. The former monopolize; the latter are left out. Social boundaries have thus been set. From the often minor but not inconsequential 'small differences' that are 'cultivated and intensified' comes monopolistic closure. Cultural differences may become apparent 'due to the peaceful or warlike

migrations of groups that previously lived far from each other and had accommo-
dated themselves to their heterogeneous conditions of existence' (Weber 1978, 388).

Weber makes clear that these differences may indeed be minor, but what matters is the (group) belief in them. Commenting on the early experiences of people
who immigrated as part of the great labour migrations under industrialization and
colonization, Weber suggested that even if these cultural differences are superficial
or do not really exist, belief in their existence 'can exist and can develop in group-
forming powers when it is buttressed by a memory of an actual migration, be it colonization or individual migration. The persistent effect of the old ways and of
childhood reminiscences continues as a source of native-country sentiment among
emigrants even when they have become so thoroughly adjusted to the new country
that return to their homeland would be intolerable' (Weber 1978, 388).

The use of term 'tribe' is derogatory today. What is it that makes 30 million
Kikuyus in Kenya a 'tribe' and 10 million Swedes a 'nation'? Why do some consider
the Iroquois people a tribe and not a nation? In the recent past, however, the term
has been used as analogous to the broader Greek word *phyle*, mentioned above. For
Weber, tribe is the historical predecessor of the ethnic group. A characteristic of the
tribe is the formation of extended kinship groups. As families of people banded
together to produce and share resources, protect themselves, survive, wage war, and
migrate, they formed the basis for the emergence of a common historical memory,
mainly through oral histories, as well as the notion of the 'people' (*volk* in German).
Weber argued that this often-assumed common memory of the people had a 'vague
connotation that whatever is felt to be distinctly common [among ethnic group
members] must derive from common descent' (Weber 1978, 395).

Further, the *volk*-feeling eventually gave rise to the notion of nationality, a concept that emerged during the Enlightenment. Later, during the time of the French
Revolution, the idea of 'nation-state' became prominent. There appeared to be a
progressive-at-the-time call for the formation of states on the basis of nations. Until
then, large political entities were multi-ethnic and multinational. The Roman,
Byzantine, Ottoman, and Chinese empires—even the Austro-Hungarian Empire
and the Holy Roman Empire—were multi-ethnic. Initial notions of nationality
based the concept on a common language. Weber has suggested that 'in the age of
linguistic conflicts, a shared common language is pre-eminently considered the normal basis of nationality' (Weber 1978, 395). The term nation-state had become synonymous with a state based on a common language. Today of course, modern states
are seldom unilingual. Nevertheless, in eighteenth- and nineteenth-century Europe
there was a push for the formation of nation-states on the assumption that there
were ethnic groups that had become large enough in size and had some historical
claim to nationhood and by extension to the right to form their own state—a
nation-state.

Capitalist competition and bourgeois ideology, as well as the requirements of
colonialism, necessitated the formation of strong states. Unification of feudal estates
under a king had already taken place in the British Isles and in some parts of Europe.
By the late nineteenth century, most of western and southern Europe, as well as parts
of eastern Europe, comprised full-fledged nation-states. Here, the relationship

between people, culture, and nation-state appeared to be linear, inevitable, and historically complete. It was the great era of 'nation-building'. As globalization is demonstrating today, this teleology was tenuous at best, and the processes of state formation and national realignment and reconfiguration are far from over. As Hobsbawm (1990, 5) has argued, nation is a very elusive term, and objective criteria for nationhood are hard to find. Joseph Stalin, not exactly famous for 'nation-building', argued that a nation is 'a historically evolved, stable community of language, territory, economic life and psychological make-up manifested in a community of culture' (in Hobsbawm 1990).

The links of ethnicity to nationality and the state are comprehensive and totalizing. But Weber, like Herodotus, also included religion in his definition of ethnic groups. Religion, seen as an ideological system of symbols, is an essential part of culture. As such, common religion is a strong source of group (self-)identification and solidarity. Religion constitutes the basis upon which group values, ideas, customs, morality, and 'world outlook' (*Weltanshauung*) are formed. As part of ideology, religion can have important material consequences. For example, Weber argued that we could not understand the development of capitalism without a comprehensive analysis of the 'Protestant ethic' (Weber 1958).

A SHORT HISTORY OF 'RACE'

While ethnicity is usually defined in terms of the cultural characteristics of group members, 'race' has been historically defined in terms of physical or genetic characteristics. We use quotations around the term 'race' to denote that the term is a socially constructed category for classifying humans, with no real biological referent and, as we will argue below, with little analytical, *sui generis* value in the social sciences. In the past, the physical characteristics of humans that have been used to classify groups have included skin colour, eye colour, hair type, nose shape, lip shape, body hair, and cheek-bone structure (Hooten 1946, in Driedger 1996, 234–5).

When we ask our students how many 'races' there are, the usual answer is that there is only one, the human 'race'. But when we begin to discuss the legacy of colonialism or issues of inequality among social groups, it is hard to avoid using terms like white, black, visible minorities, and Aboriginals, among others—terms that connote 'race' as something that is real. According to Banton (1987, 1), the term appeared in written English for the first time in a poem by William Dunbar in 1508. It is associated with the voyages of European 'discovery', exploration, expansion, domination, colonization, and imperialism.

With colonization, Europeans 'discovered' and came into contact with the peoples that inhabited the lands they conquered. 'Races' implied population groups of different roots, in different geographic areas. It meant lineage, or line of descent, and it was attributed to social groups with a common history (Banton 1987, xi). It was used to refer to what we consider ethnic groups today. For example, in eleventh-century Britain, reference was made to the 'alien Norman race' that had conquered the Saxons (Banton 1987, 12–13). In pre-revolutionary France, the term 'race' had a legal sense, and it referred to people with a common lineage (Guillaumin 1995). Among the aristocracy, 'race' was used for self-identification in order to differentiate themselves, their ancestors, and their offspring from others who did not share the same glorious lineage. Aristocratic families had become 'races' by virtue of their common blood and descent (Satzewich, 1998a, 27). But from its inception, the term 'race' entailed both natural and social qualities (Goldberg 1993, 62).

In the late eighteenth century, there was an apparent shift in the meaning of 'race'. Processes of definition of Self (European/dominant) and Other (non-European/subordinate) had already taken shape. Banton (1977) argues that European science was genuinely preoccupied with the explanation of the physical and cultural diversity of the newly 'discovered' social groups. The concept of 'race' was increasingly used to explain physical, social, moral, and intellectual variation among peoples. Under conditions of colonialism, the 'racialization of the world', a scientific error, took place. Guillaumin (1995), on other hand, has argued that in France, changes in the class structure after the revolution gave rise to changes in the meaning of the term 'race'. Offering a materialist account of these changes, she has suggested that the social content of 'race' was altered. Before the advent of capitalism, 'race' was used in a legal sense to describe people with common lineage and as a self-identification label for the aristocracy. However, with the emergence of the bourgeoisie in France, the term was used to define a range of 'others', including 'Negroes', 'Jews', 'Arabs', and 'Asiatics'. It became an externally imposed label.

In addition, the process of categorization of certain groups as 'races' was coupled with negative evaluations of their members' biological and social characteristics. The French bourgeoisie lacked the pedigree, privilege, divine right, or royal approval of the aristocracy. Without access to an ideology of superiority, they slowly began to characterize others without the economic and political power that they were now enjoying as 'races'. 'Race' also had a class content. It applied not only to non-French 'others' but also to the manual working class and the peasantry (Guillaumin 1995). We will return to the discussion of 'race' and class later in this chapter.

MODERN STRUGGLES OVER, AND WITH, 'RACE'

Beginning in 1950, the United Nations Educational, Scientific and Cultural Organization (UNESCO) held a series of conferences at which it invited world-renowned scholars to address issues of 'race'. UNESCO was responding largely to the horrors of Nazism and its concerted efforts to exterminate people of Jewish descent, communists, the Roma, and homosexuals to 'preserve German purity'. It attempted to discredit the racist doctrines that posited the existence of 'races' and emphasized the biological superiority of 'Aryans' over a variety of others. As a result, efforts were made to deracialize the world and reject racist ideas and practices (Montagu 1972).

Despite these efforts, however, the idea of 'race' as a legitimate, 'scientific' basis for classifying human populations is alive and well. Moreover, the idea tends to inform the overall *problematique* of many contemporary social scientists, as well as state discourses and policies. Driedger (1996, 234), for example, has argued that using Hooten's criteria (Hooten 1946, in Driedger 1996, 234–5), human populations can be divided into 'Caucasoid', 'Mongoloid', and 'Negroid' 'racial types'. In fact, he proceeds to describe the physical characteristics of the three categories:

The Caucasoids have the fairest or lighter colour of skins and eyes, while the Negroids have the darkest, with the Mongoloids falling in between. The nose and lip shapes of the Caucasoids are the narrowest, while the Negroids have the broadest and the thickest. The Mongoloids have the straightest and coarsest hair texture, while the Negroids have the woolliest hair. The Mongoloids have also the most visible cheek-bones, while these are the least prominent among Caucasoids. Caucasoids have the most hair on the body, and the Negroids the least (Driedger 1996, 234–5).

When human populations do not 'fit' this schema, attempts are made to classify them by 'proximity'. Driedger has written that

[t]he Aboriginals of North and South America . . . seem to fit between the Cauca-soid and Mongoloid types, but are usually classified as Mongoloid. The peoples of the Pacific Islands, having somewhat darker skins than the Mongoloids, seem to fit between the Mongoloid and Negroid categories . . . It is for reasons as these that many scholars have created more than three 'racial' types, but Hooten suggested that we begin with these three basic types, and then subdivide into more groups as considered necessary (1996, 236).

'Considered necessary' by whom and why? In this conceptualization, the cate-gories are biological subspecies, based on a common (assumed) genetic constitu-tion. The phenotypical/genotypical characteristics of 'races' (visible, biological, and objective) are often associated with the behavioural, moral, and intellectual capaci-ties and/or 'abilities' of the populations they purport to describe. As we will see, these capabilities/abilities, in turn, are often used to 'explain' the socio-economic performance of members of these objectified categories.

On the other hand, van den Berghe has argued that we should use the term 'social races' instead in order to emphasize that they are not based on objective geno-types but rather are socially constructed (1981, 216–18). They are illogically con-structed, and they do not (and cannot) correspond to genetic typologies (Li 1999, 8). Reacting to the dominant paradigm of 'race' and 'race relations', sociologists like Miles (1982, 1984, 1993), Miles and Torres (1996), and Banton (1979, 1987), among many, have opted for the concept of racialization. Banton argues that ethnicity tends to reflect positive tendencies of identification, whereas 'race' usually represents the negative tendencies of exclusion and disassociation (1979). Miles (1982) argues that in the processes and practices of categorization of individuals and groups, both cul-tural and phenotypical characteristics are used. As a result, we cannot reduce our definitions of ethnicity and 'race' to sets of cultural characteristics for the former and phenotypical traits for the latter (see also Dunk 1991). Instead, we must exam-ine processes whereby both sets of criteria are used in order to identify social groups. Racialization, then, can be defined as sets of social processes and practices whereby 'social relations among people [are] structured by the signification of human bio-logical characteristics in such a way as to define and construct differentiated social collectivities' (Miles and Brown 2003, 99–102).

It could also be argued that the signification of cultural characteristics has been, and still is, used to identify social collectivities. We could, then, also speak of ethnicization or of minoritization in general. Goldberg has used the term *ethnorace* to denote the similarities that the terms racialization and ethnicization share and how they have been used in the literature, as well as by minoritized populations as a form of *resistance* to dominant population classifications. According to his argument, the social content of both concepts share: a) a history of being so named; b) similar processes as well as criteria of boundary construction; c) a rhetoric of genesis; d) conflictual and exclusionary relations with other groups (Weber's 'closure'); and e) terms of self-identification and self-ascription (Goldberg 1993, 76–7)

With respect to 'race', Miles and Torres have made the case that there is a discrepancy between the popular, everyday, common sense use of the term and its social-scientific content. In criticizing 'race' as an analytical category, they have argued that social scientists ought to jettison the idea of 'race' and refuse to use it as a descriptive and explanatory concept (Miles and Torres, 1996, 32). The reason is simple. Social scientists tend to reify 'race', 'insofar as the outcome of often complex social process is explained as a consequence of something named "race" rather than of the social process itself' (ibid).

How do we resist the temptation to use racist language and 'explanations' and terms that are without scientific foundation? There is a major theoretical and practical difficulty here. Although, as we argue, 'races' do not have a social referent—that is, the biologically constructed categories do not correspond to real social groups—we lack a language, both academic and colloquial, that can capture the historical development and different, contextualized uses of 'racial' terms. We must indeed reject the racist-inspired classificatory terms ('white', 'black', 'mongoloid', etc.) and seek social-scientific definitions and explanations of social inequalities. But we still lack the appropriate language. Goldberg argues that

> [t]he discourse promoting resistance to racism must not prompt identification with and in terms of categories fundamental to the discourse of oppression. Resistance must break not only with *practices* of oppression, although the first task is to do that. Resistance must oppose also the *language* of oppression, including the categories and terms of which the oppressor (or racist) represents the forms in which resistance is expressed (1990, 313–14).

In the following pages, we present a brief historical account of the development of theoretical frameworks that deal with the social issues of ethnicity and 'race' in the social sciences.

THE CHICAGO SCHOOL

So what happened when certain European states like Britain, France, Germany, the Netherlands, Spain, Portugal, Belgium, Italy, and Russia and non-European states like Japan and China colonized America, Africa, Oceania, and parts of Asia through war and conquest? We know what happened to indigenous cultures in these areas. Some were completely destroyed; few survived intact. Most of their natural resources were plundered, and indigenous people were enslaved. Slave labour constituted one of the bases upon which early capitalist accumulation flourished.

Human beings, not just human labour power, became commodified: they were bought and sold. Social inequalities among and within ethnic groups deepened. Early capitalist accumulation led to the Industrial Revolution.

In North America, French-British wars and diseases brought over from Europe decimated the then-thriving populations of Native peoples. British and French settlers took over their land. Missionary Christianity forcefully 'replaced' their local religious traditions. Natives in other parts of the world suffered similarly. The American Revolution brought about the establishment of the United States as an independent country, while Canada remained a part of the British Empire. Once independent, the US proceeded to take over and populate vast lands with new immigrants from European countries, mostly from the British Isles. The age of great labour migrations had begun on an unprecedented scale, with millions of people streaming into the new nation. The early southern United States economy was dominated by slavery: basically a huge plantation system in which black slaves toiled for the benefit of their white masters.

By the mid-1800s, industrialization of the northeast and midwest US had commenced. Increased numbers of new European immigrants flocked to the urban industrial centres of New York, Detroit, Chicago, Boston, Pittsburgh, and Cleveland. By the late nineteenth century, the resource extraction, manufacturing, and transportation sectors of the US economy were booming. Starting in the 1880s and continuing until the 1920s, large numbers of southern and eastern European immigrants rushed to the US. The end of slavery in the South brought a sizable unskilled black labour pool from southern plantations to the urban, industrialized settings of the North. 'Taylorism' had revolutionized production methods, and great capitalist fortunes were being made. The feeling grew that everyone was entitled to access to a piece of the pie. The American Dream took shape, quickly spreading to the minds of the propertyless masses. The ideology held that if you worked hard enough, you could make it, despite your ascriptive characteristics of ethnicity, culture, colour, religion, language, nationality, or pedigree. Ascription was rejected as a thing of the past, a relic of the old continental European tradition that had no place in the new and economically vibrant 'land of the free'. Achievement was what counted in the US, so it was thought.

The First World War brought a temporary end to large-scale immigration, but it also pointed to ostensible problems of ethnic competition and conflicts, which culminated during the Great Depression. The presence of large numbers of German immigrants in Pennsylvania, for example, led to concern among Americans of British descent about these immigrants' patriotism: the process of Anglo-Americanization had already begun, and some called for curtailing immigration from 'undesirable' countries in order maintain the 'American' character of the land. Such restrictions actually came into effect in the 1920s.

Sociologists at the University of Chicago, writing in the early twentieth century, well understood this broad historical context. They studied the processes by which different ethnic groups came into contact with each other, the forms their contacts assumed, the nature of their competition, and the processes by which groups either maintained or lost their ethnic characteristics. Two sociologists of the Chicago

School are especially important: W.I. Thomas, whom you may know from his famous dictum, 'What is real in people's minds is real in its consequences', and Robert Park, who developed the theory of 'the race relations cycle'.

Thomas was influential in introducing the study of 'race' and ethnicity to sociology (Persons 1987), studying the adjustment of recent immigrants to the host society. With Florian Znaniecki, he published *The Polish Peasant in Europe and America*, a five-volume study that analyzed the experiences of Polish peasants after they had left their homeland and immigrated to major US cities like Chicago. They theorized that there should be a change in the experiences of Polish peasants after they had left the rural community settings of their country to seek a better life in a more 'advanced', complex, and more competitive society like that of Chicago. In essence, they were studying transitions and adaptations from feudal agrarian to industrial capitalist settings. Logically, they expected a social *reorganization* on the part of the peasants. The family unit, both a unit of production and consumption and a source of solidarity and support back home, suffered greatly in the competitive capitalist and individualistic environment of the tough Chicago labour markets. With few or no skills, the Polish peasant was competing not only with other ethnics but also often with compatriots for jobs, higher pay, and better opportunities. This internal and external competition often led to community disorganization, despair, and disarray, all characteristics of advanced industrial societies. In addition, they found that in subsequent generations, the family form changed to a smaller, less supporting structure (Driedger 1996, 18). The experiences of Polish peasants, as analyzed by Thomas and Znaniecki, were not that different from the experiences of thousands of Canadian immigrants who came to our industrial centres of Toronto, Montreal, or Hamilton.

As pressures for the Americanization of immigrants increased, Thomas argued against the forced abandonment of ethnic cultures, languages, religions, or other bases of ethnic identity. He did not support immigrants' fusion into the American melting pot. Instead, and against the current of the time, he called for the maintenance of ethnic languages and press, identities, institutions, communities, and organizations, tolerance of ethnic differences, and reconciliation. Driedger suggests that he was among the first to preach cultural pluralism, although Thomas never used this term (1996, 19). We can detect in his work the early seeds of multiculturalism, a Canadian value we recognize with pride and often use to differentiate ourselves from our neighbours.

Robert Park had a different focus. He studied the seemingly more complex processes through which 'racial' groups come into contact and interact. He had considerable experience working with black people in the American South and represented the interaction of whites and blacks in terms of a cycle, his now famous 'race relations cycle', which is also applied to ethnic relations. The cycle included several stages and two different routes but one outcome: assimilation, in which the subordinate minority groups assimilate into the dominant majority group. Initially, there is contact between the two groups, creating competition for access to and acquisition of scarce and valuable resources. This competition can lead either to accommodation and eventually fusion/assimilation or to conflicts that in turn lead to accommodation and then fusion/assimilation. Underlying the cycle is the tenet that the 'new' culture emerging from the fusion is good for both and certainly good for the 'nation'. Fusion also implies social harmony, even equality. This, in short, is the melting pot theory of ethnic and 'race' relations in the US (Park 1914).

Lieberson (1980, 68) argued, however, that there are different types of contact between groups, depending on existing conditions prior to initial contact. For example, there is a difference between contact involving the subordination of indigenous populations by a migrant group, as has been the case in black/white relations in South Africa, and contact involving the subordination of a migrant population by an indigenous 'racial' or ethnic majority group—for example, the Japanese immigrant experience in the US. In Canada, we have witnessed both types of contact: under colonialism, the British and French subordinated Canadian Aboriginals, became dominant, and later subordinated Chinese and Japanese immigrants to Canada (not to mention others) through discriminatory institutional controls and policies (Ujimoto 1999, 264). Park's cycle, then, does not take into account the socio-economic and political conditions under which initial contact takes place or the configuration of power under which conflicts over resources occur and distributional outcomes are shaped.

CULTURALISM AND ITS LIMITATIONS

Earlier, we mentioned that there is a tendency within the social sciences to reduce explanations of groups' behavioural, moral, and intellectual capacities/abilities and socio-economic characteristics to environmentalism and naturalism. Briefly restated, the argument goes as follows: ethnic and 'racial' groups share common values, beliefs, sentiments, ideas, languages, historical memories, symbols, religions, historical leadership, a past, and often ecological territories. They have specific ways of responding to their external conditions that vary and are shaped by their own environment. In other words, they have a common culture. Culture, then, is the key to understanding their behavioural differences. Moreover, if we want to explain their differential socio-economic achievements, we should look into their culture. Culture is the *explanans* (that which explains) rather than the *explicandum* (that which must be explained). Cultural values and biological characteristics affect the psychological composition of their members and produce, it is claimed, 'differences in cognitive perception, mental aptitude, and logical reasoning' (Li 1999, 10). In turn, these differences affect subsequent educational and economic achievements. Thus, some groups do better than others in school and in the labour market.

Here is an early example cited by Vlassis (1942), referring to Greek Canadians: Greeks have a 'national character' moulded by the sea (presumably applicable even to those coming from rural areas of Greece who had never seen the sea before boarding the ship that brought them to Canada). Further, Greeks are 'adventurous, endeavouring to marry within their own race', 'desire to attain the full status of Canadian citizenship', 'possess an innate respect for law and order', 'have an innate proclivity for education', are 'thrifty and enterprising', 'proud and independent, hard working, courageous, persevering, and usually successful in business (mostly restaurants, confectioneries and hotels) despite the fact that they begin with very meagre resources and with no experience, and are characterized by individuality and exclusiveness' (1942, 7, 8, 10, 13–14, 17, 23, 25).

It could be argued that this list of group traits represents a special version of the mobility dream in which presumed success in business and education is not based solely on individual effort in a free market or an equal opportunity society. In fact, it is often recognized that the playing field is not level at all. Not all groups begin with the same resources and experience in either the education system or the labour market. Success, therefore, is often explained as being based (also) on or attributable to the 'national character' of the group in question. To be fair to Vlassis, this argument is used in reference to many ethnic groups and is not exclusively applied to Greeks (Herberg 1989).

In summary, some 'cultures' have been seen as fostering values conducive to economic achievement, while others have not. Members of cultures that foster these values do well; members of those that do not are helpless. For example, Rosen (1956; 1959) studied the relative upward social mobility of six groups—Greeks, Jews, white Protestants, French Canadians, Italians, and blacks—and 'found' that the first three groups had higher mobility rates than the latter three because of what he claimed were differences in achievement motivation, achievement values, and educational aspirations. He did not, of course, examine or show differentials *within* these groups. Did all Greeks score high on his scales? Did all French Canadians score low? Were there not any highly motivated Italians in his sample? How could we explain, based on culture alone, French Canadians with high educational credentials? Presumably, if they all share the same culture and have the same achievement motivation, values, and educational aspirations, there should not have been any differences within the groups.

Chimbos (1974) has studied the social mobility of Greek immigrants compared to that of Slovaks in London, Ontario. He showed that despite the fact that the Greeks in the study had been in Canada for fewer years than the Slovaks, they exhibited higher levels of upward mobility. Greeks moved upward through the avenue of small business (1974, 66). The difference, according to Chimbos, was due to the 'individualistic competitive commercialism observed among the Greeks', which is 'a long established cultural value which aids their upward movement in Canadian society' (ibid.). Chimbos, following Rosen (1959), suggested that cultural values explain the motivation for economic gain and competition, portraying Greeks as individualistic, foresighted, competitive traders (Rosen 1959, 55). Moreover, Chimbos relied on early-century accounts from the US to illustrate the stages of Greeks' upward mobility, quoting Ross, who wrote that 'once his foot is on the first step, the saving and commercial-minded Greek climbs. From curb to stand, from stand to store, from little store to big store, and from there to the branch stores in other cities—such are the stages in his [*sic*] upward movement' (1974, 58–9).

This account, of course, does not explain why the 'commercial-minded' Greek Canadians tend to be overrepresented in the working class and have earnings as low as and often lower than those of 'visible minorities' (see chapter 4). If the above account represents a special case of the mobility dream ideology, we must ask what the actual socio-economic conditions of Greek Canadians are. What is the reality? All the ideology and wishful thinking in the world cannot—alone—change the structural conditions within which people find themselves and operate in society.

Despite the 'affinity for hard work and socio-economic advancement' displayed by Greeks in Canada (Chimbos 1980, 43), as we show later, not all 'competitive-minded' Greek Canadians necessarily win in the economic 'game'. We cannot and should not generalize and apply what appear to be 'characteristics' exhibited by petty bourgeois male, immigrant Greek Canadians to the whole ethnic group.

Box 1.1 *The Ethnic Myth: Race, Ethnicity, and Class in America*

Stephen Steinberg's 1981 book, *The ethnic myth: Race, ethnicity, and class in America* (Boston: Beacon Press), is a powerful analysis of the material conditions that account for why some ethnic groups do better than others in American society. It is also a powerful critique of cultural explanations of ethnic achievement and under-achievement. Here are a few excerpts from the book:

On culture:
By its very nature, ethnicity involves ways of thinking, feeling, and acting that con-stitute the essence of culture . . . The problem, however, is that culture does not exist in a vacuum; nor is it fixed or unchanging. On the contrary, culture is in con-stant flux and is integrally a part of a larger social process. The mandate of social inquiry, therefore, is that ethnic patterns should not be taken at face value, but must be related to the larger social matrix in which they are embedded. (ix)

On the Horatio Alger theory of ethnic success:
The classical expression of the American success legend is found in the hundred or so novels that Horatio Alger wrote in the late nineteenth century, a time when immigration was at a historic peak. Alger's heroes typically do not reach great fame or fortune, but in the unravelling of the novel they overcome obstacles placed in their way, correct their errant impulses, and by the final pages are resolutely headed down the road of success. Alger's unmistakable message was that, what-ever the obstacles, the individual can triumph by living an exemplary life and piously observing all the middle-class injunctions concerning hard work and moral rectitude. (83)

Jewish economic success: A matter of culture or material conditions?
In terms of their European background, Jews were especially well equipped to take advantage of the opportunities they found in America. Had Jews immigrated to an industrial society without industrial skills, as did most other immigrants, their rich cul-tural heritage would have counted for little. Indeed, a parallel situation exists today in Israel, where Jews immigrating from underdeveloped countries in North Africa typi-cally lack the occupational and educational advantages of the earlier settlers, and despite the fact that they share the same basic religion, the recent immigrants find themselves concentrated at the bottom of Israeli society. Thus, in large measure, the Jewish success in America was a matter of historical timing. That is to say, there was a fortuitous match between the experience and skills of Jewish immigrants, on one hand, and the manpower [sic] needs and opportunity structures, on the other.

This is not to deny the Jews possessed values that served them in their quest for social and economic advancement. But one would not expect an urban proletariat to exhibit the same values as peasants emerging from folk societies and semi-feudal conditions. Nor would one expect a group on the threshold of a dramatic economic breakdown to exhibit the same attitudes and values as groups that were destined to remain indefinitely poor. If Jews set high goals, it is because they had a realistic chance of achieving them. If they worked hard, it is because they could see the fruits of their labour. If they were willing to forgo the pleasures of the moment, it is because they could realistically plan for a better future, for their children if not for themselves. In short, there was much in the everyday experience of the Jewish immigrants to activate and sustain their highest aspirations. Without this reinforcement, their values would have been scaled down accordingly, and more successful outsiders would today be speculating about how much further the Jews might have gone if only they had aimed higher. (103)

Others, such as Lewis (1959, 1966), in attempting to explain the persistence of poverty among certain groups, resorted to a similar argument: his *culture of poverty thesis*. Living in poverty over extended periods of time becomes a culture within which generations are nurtured and that they cannot easily escape. Wagley and Harris (1959) used 'adaptive capacity' as an explanatory device. According to this line of thinking, some groups are able to adapt to their new external conditions better and more readily and perform better in education and the labour market than others because their own cultural values prepared them to do so. They argued that the French-Canadian and Jewish cultures had higher adaptive capacity than those of Canadian Natives and 'blacks'. Hence, the former groups enjoyed higher socioeconomic status than the latter.

In his well-known *The Vertical Mosaic* (1965), John Porter, although he emphasized structural conditions in explaining income inequalities, could not resist the temptation to rely on cultural explanations as well. He distinguished between behavioural assimilation (acquiring dominant group values) and structural assimilation (integration into the economic, social, and political life of the country). He argued that ethnic affiliation was a determinant of social class membership and prevented the upward mobility of certain groups, partly because they had not *assimilated culturally* to the new conditions of capitalist development in Canada. This was his famous *blocked mobility thesis*.

Vernon (1984), a researcher studying Natives and 'Asians' in North America, argued that that the two groups showed profound differences on 'intelligence' tests. Asians exhibited 'remarkable abilities and achievement', and he attributed this to the traditional values preserved in their family structures. Natives, on the other hand, exhibited no achievement because of the destruction of their culture by the colonizers. What do these 'tests' measure? Could they be culturally bound, class and gender-based tests? Could they express dominant ideologies? Could differences in *average* scores in 'intelligence tests' be the result of unequal educational opportunities between and within the groups? How do we explain educational and economic differentials within the same group?

According to Li (1999, 10–13), there are some fundamental flaws in cultural approaches. First, he argues, there are too many unquestioned assumptions about culture and the linkage between culture and ethnicity. There is no simple correspondence between people, culture, and 'nation': ethnicity cannot be equated with culture; the link is tenuous at best (Li 1988). Second, as Wallerstein (1979) has demonstrated, centuries-old processes of international migration and colonialism and the development of modern capitalism have resulted in cultural heterogeneity among and within social groups and nations. There is no cultural homogeneity based on territory, no common culture, tradition, ancestry, and so on. People with claims to common origins do not necessarily share the same experiences or culture. Even in ethnically/'racially' homogeneous societies—if they ever really existed— there were cultural differences among different gender groups, social classes, age cohorts, regions, and so on. We argue that culture is not static, monolithic, uniform, or homogeneous. It is a set of social processes and practices; it is a dynamic response of socially constituted individuals to their *ever-changing* external conditions (both material and ideological), largely determined by pre-existing social conditions and structures. Culture needs to be explained; it cannot be a tautology—that which explains and must be explained at the same time (Valentine 1968).

This insistence on the simplistic understanding and use of culture as the single or most important explanatory concept is associated with what is often called *essentialism*. Essentialism refers to the belief that social groups and individual members of these groups have a true *essence* that is 'irreducible, unchanging, and therefore constitutive of a given person or thing' (Fuss, in Jhappan 1996, 28). Two issues are important here. First, we are not denying that culture does play a role in the educational and earnings potential of ethnic groups. Within every culture there undoubtedly exist dominant (and subordinate) beliefs and ideas about the importance of education, wealth, prestige, and power. There also exist customs and other social practices that may be conducive to social/economic advancement. But not all members of ethnic groups share them—at least not equally. Individuals from different regions, generations, social classes, gender groups, or professions, albeit members of the same ethnic group, may have different cultural values. Second, the symbolic culture of immigrants alone—even if it is 'compatible' with the dominant values of a host society, without reference to the material elements of culture, i.e., the structural economic, political, and social conditions within which culture is formed and constantly changing—cannot explain why some groups do better than others or some members of the same group do better than others. The often-celebrated Jewish success in the US and Canada is instructive (as we show in chapter 4, not all Jewish-origin Canadians are successful; see also Box 1.1).

In Canada, Breton et al. have shown that Jewish-origin Canadians tend to score high in the ethnic cultural identity index (1990, 51–83), along with the Chinese and the West Indians. This index uses indicators like individuals' views on obligatory endogamy, their use of in-group language, use of in-group media, consumption of ethnic foods, and so on. This is particularly important, since most Jewish respondents in the Breton et al. study were second and third-generation Canadians, unlike the two groups that also scored high. This may suggest, then, that groups can resist behavioural assimilation and still do well in education and earnings. The cases of the Chinese and West Indians in the US illustrate this. Also, native-born Chinese Canadians, both male and female, are doing well in education and earnings (Li 1988, 1992; Liodakis 2002).

In the US, challenging the contemporary American image of Asian Americans as the quintessential immigrant success story—a success often explained in cultural terms—Louie (2004) conducted extensive interviews with second-generation Chinese Americans attending Hunter College, a humble learning institution, and Columbia University, an elite Ivy League school. All of the Hunter respondents came from 'urban enclaves' like Manhattan Chinatown and ethnically mixed neighbourhoods in Flushing and Brooklyn. Most respondents at Columbia grew up in middle-class suburbs. Louie found large within-group differences in both groups in terms of income, neighbourhood, and parents' occupation. She concluded that 'race', gender, and class do matter in opportunities and choices. Though most Chinese immigrant families value higher education and see it as a necessary safeguard against potential 'racial' discrimination, she found that class differences do indeed shape the students' different paths to university education. Students whose parents had graduate degrees from elite universities back home or advanced degrees in America, had worked as engineers, doctors, or lawyers, and had houses in gated communities were more likely to attend the Ivy League school. Students whose parents had only grade-school education back home, had to work long hours in ethnic restaurants or in garment factories, and could only afford to rent apartments in ghettoized neighbourhoods went to tough schools that were 'a waste of time' or changed schools frequently, often struggled academically, and witnessed their siblings and friends drop out of school, end up in jail, or die.

CRITICAL POLITICAL ECONOMY

Partly in response to some of the problems associated with cultural approaches—but also parallel to it—the critical (as opposed to liberal) political economy perspective analyses have emerged in order to explain both the historical development of the terms ethnicity and 'race' and the social inequalities among and within such social groups. The critical political economy perspective is a wide and varied corpus of literature that tends to share the following characteristics: a) it tends to be rooted in the conflict theories of Marx and Weber and their contemporary variations and proponents; b) as such, it focuses on the study of differential allocation of economic, political, and ideological power among individuals and groups in society; c) in turn, it examines social relations based on the ownership and control of private property, as well as the historical development and manifold ideological and social manifestations and/or embodiments of these social relations; d) its approaches have as a central premise that people, in their relations to the means and objects of their labour and in the processes of the production and reproduction of their daily lives, engage in meaningful social action and practices. Critical political economy is fundamentally concerned with social change.

The critical political economy perspective begins with the tenet that individuals belong to inherited social structures that enable but also constrain their social actions. These structures include those built on the social relations of class, gender, 'race'/ethnicity, age, sexual preference, physical ability, and mental health/illness. Societies are characterized by the differential distribution of property, power, and other resources, both natural and socio-political. Who owns and controls what, when, why, and how are central concerns of critical political economy (Satzewich 1999, 314). Analysis of intergenerational endowment of these resources is also imperative to the understanding of relations of social inequality. To paraphrase Marx, individuals are born into a web of unequal social relations, inherited from the past and beyond their immediate control at least until they understand them and try to change them. Although these social relations are malleable—it takes concerted social action—it takes social *praxis* to bring about social change.

With regard to ethnic and 'race' relations, then, we must begin by trying to understand what processes have historically brought about the differentiation and classification of human populations, their social impact, and their conditions. Hence, critical political economy approaches question, for example, who has historically defined certain human populations as superior and others as inferior and on what basis. Li (1988) has argued that skin colour, for example, is a characteristic of classifying human populations only if it is deemed as socially important. What makes it socially important? Why not use people's shoe size as a socially or culturally 'necessary' criterion for a demonstrably different classification of human populations? We must look into the legacy of colonialism and slavery in order to understand the historical roots of the social construction of the term 'race' as well as the racialization/ethnicization or minoritization of social groups by dominant groups and their hegemonic ideologies. Historically, under capitalism in the West, the 'white' (see how we cannot escape racialized language?), male capitalist class has been in control of the means of production and reproduction as well as the political and ideological tools of domination. This domination has by and large been a catalyst in creating and sustaining the coupling of people's cultural and physical characteristics with presumed behavioural, moral, and intellectual traits (see chapter 6). As Brown (1995) argues, the assignment of significance to biological or physical attributes (and arguably cultural ones) is *itself* a cultural ethnocentric choice.

The critical political economy approach perceives 'race' and ethnicity as *relational* concepts. Goldberg has argued that 'race' (and, we argue, ethnicity as well), has been used as social status both in the Weberian sense and in the Marxist sense. As status, it is an 'index of social standing or rank reflected in terms of criteria like wealth, education, style of life, linguistic capacity, residential location, consumptive capacity, or having or lacking respect. Status has to do with one's ranking in a social system *relative to the position of others* [emphasis ours], where the ranking involves criterial complex of self-conception and (de)valuations of others. Those who are conceived as "acting white" will be considered "white"' (1993, 69). At least historically, 'race' and ethnicity have been defined as and often overlapped with class—class being both a fundamental economic relationship between groups and a structural condition within which these relations take place. The social composition of dominant classes corresponded with the dominant 'racial'/ethnic groups. Although 'race'/ethnicity cannot be reduced to class, they are nevertheless connected to it.

'Race' and ethnic conflicts tend to be rooted in the competition among and within groups for valuable scarce resources such as jobs (Bolaria and Li 1988; Li 1988). Li (1998b, 7) has argued that 'race' (and also ethnic) 'problems' begin as labour problems. Although racism predates capitalism, it is associated with it. In capitalism, capital and labour are the two fundamentally opposed social classes. In this conflictual relationship, workers must sell their labour power—i.e., their ability to work—to the capitalists in exchange for wages and/or salaries. Capitalists make profits by paying workers less than the value of the products of workers' labour. Capitalists extract surplus value and surplus labour from workers. They have an economic and political interest in keeping workers' wages low. The lower workers' wages are, the higher the capitalists' profits will be.

Workers' exploitation leads to capital accumulation. How do capitalists keep workers' wages down? They create economic structures in which there are differentials in the price of labour. In North America, for example, under conditions of competition among workers for jobs—as in the case of the Polish in the US (mentioned above) or the Irish, the Chinese, and more recently other people of 'colour' in Canada—their ethnic/'racial' identities, or the labels that have been applied to them, coupled with processes of minoritization, have led to the devaluation of their labour (Bonacich 1979).

But racism and the interests of capitalism do not always correspond. In Canada, migrant labour has been considered a threat by Canadian-born workers, not employers, and it has been often excluded from employment and/or unionization. Historically, for example, the labour of Chinese immigrants was cheaper than the labour of British-descent unionized workers in the late nineteenth and early twentieth centuries. It is well documented that in British Columbia, Chinese labour was worth about half the price of the labour of 'white' Euro-Canadian workers doing the same kind of work (see Phillips 1967; Creese 1984; Li 1988). This led to calls by labour organizations to employers as well as to the federal and provincial governments to restrict the entrance of Chinese immigrant workers. The Coal Mines Regulation Act of 1903 was passed, and a head-tax was imposed on Chinese immigrants (Li 1979; 1988). Racist legislation was also directed at people from India (Continuous Passage Regulations, 1908).

The critical political economy approach recognizes that social reality is complex. We cannot digest the social world in one sitting. For analytical purposes, we do make the necessary theoretical distinctions between 'race'/ethnicity and class or gender, but social relations based on these structures are interconnected, as are the individuals who are the *agents* of these social relations. In response to mono-dimensional understandings of social reality, and monocausal explanations of social inequality, a number of researchers in the critical political economy perspective have attempted to integrate 'race'/ethnicity with class and gender in order to provide multi-dimensional analyses of social inequality.

INTERSECTIONAL ANALYSIS

Today, many researchers are proponents of the *integrationist* or *intersectional* approach (Stasiulis 1990; 1999). This perspective recognizes the multi-faceted nature of social inequality and seeks to understand and explain the dynamic inter-action of class, gender, and ethnic/'racial' forms of domination and subordination, as well as the different ways in which each dimension is experienced by people—separately as well as through the other dimensions. It is claimed that although these dimensions are necessarily treated as analytically distinct, their conceptualization as interlocking, mutually determining, and reinforcing categories, as well as their inter-connections, have now become central to social analysis (Fleras and Elliott 1999, 148). Despite the disagreements on the meanings and significance of class, gender, and 'race'/ethnicity, the trio is the new mantra of Canadian social researchers, as Agnew has suggested (1996, 3). Researchers now advocate the need to take into account all three when examining social inequality. For example, some researchers in the qualitative tradition have mainly examined the experiences of immigrant women (of 'colour') and the way in which they experience racism, compared to those of non-immigrant women (Ralston 1991; Agnew 1996). The central argument of this approach is that 'race'/ethnicity, along with class and gender, are bases affect-ing individual and/or group identity, life experiences, and position in society. Ralston (1991), interviewing immigrant women, has found that 'race', class, and lan-guage are interconnected and their combination has a significant (negative) impact on the determination of the 'actualities' of everyday life. Class, gender, and 'race' are bases of the 'multiple jeopardies' that confront minorities. This combination is the cause of the differential work experiences of immigrant and non-immigrant women (1991, 131). Agnew (1996), interested in the feminist movement in Canada, has examined the compounding effects of 'race', class, and gender on the lives of immi-grant women from Asia, Africa, and the Caribbean. She has suggested that the 'trio' provides different bases for the political mobilization of immigrant women, which is necessary for social *praxis* and social change.

Unfortunately, there is no agreement on which of these bases of social inequal-ity has the greatest impact on individual or group identity, life experiences, or social position. Stasiulis (1990; 1999) for example, has suggested that some black feminists see 'race' rather than gender as the primary basis of their oppression. Gender is seen as more important than 'race' among 'white' feminists. Marxist and neo-Marxist scholars see class as the primary basis of social inequality. Stasiulis has argued recently that the intersectional theorizing of class, gender, and 'race'/ethnicity is by no means dominant within the 'white' feminist tradition. References to differences among women along class and 'race' lines are, according to Stasiulis, 'token mention'. We must avoid 'race' and gender essentialism, she urges (see also Jhappan 1996). Most of these approaches are guilty of ignoring one or more of the simultaneous and interlocking axes of 'racial', class, and gender power within the matrix of domi-nation (Stasiulis 1999, 348).

The main conceptual anchor for a new intersectional theorizing ought to be the understanding of the simultaneity of racism, sexism, and class exploitation and the fact that they are interrelated systems of privilege and oppression (Stasiulis 1999,

349). Notably absent from some analyses, however, is class. Despite calls for the analysis of all three dimensions of social inequality and for relational definitions of culture (Stasiulis 1999, 378), few offer a theoretical or operational definition of class, relational or otherwise. Many recognize the importance of class in the abstract, but few have a good way of integrating it empirically into their work. Few analyze the 'experiences' of different classes within gender and 'race'/ethnic groups. They often do not explain how exactly class intersects with gender and 'race'/ethnicity and tend to conflate 'race' and class. The typical focus is the nativity dimension of gender and 'race'/ethnicity (immigrant women of 'colour'), and either it is assumed that all immigrant women are members of the working class or the experiences of other classes of women are not analyzed. As Jhappan reminds us, not all 'white' women are middle-class (1996, 38); not all non-'white' women are working-class either. There also exist petty bourgeois immigrant women (of 'colour' or not), capitalist immigrant women, and immigrant women professionals or managers and supervisors whose life experiences and positions in society are different from those of working-class immigrant women, but these groups of women are not always analyzed. As Jhappan suggests, to argue that racism is more important in the lives of women of 'colour' (than class?) 'is at least questionable, given the very different *class positions* of women, and the different degrees to which they are exposed to the dominant society' (1996, 32; emphasis ours).

Quantitative studies of the interconnections of 'race'/ethnicity with class and gender are difficult to find (with the exception of Li 1988, 1992; Nakhaie 1999, 2000). Data on the actual class composition of the gender and nativity segments of 'racial'/ethnic groups are usually not reported. Any reference to class, to paraphrase Stasiulis, may be a 'token mention'. Even those who incorporate class into their intersectional (qualitative) analyses do not analyze all classes (see Ng 1986, 1991; Calliste 1991, 1996). It is now accepted that most analyses of the gender dimension of social inequality demonstrate that gender relations cannot be subsumed under or be fully captured by (Marxist) class relations (Stasiulis 1990, 1999; Boyd 1992; Li 1992; Krahn and Lowe 1993). The gender and 'race'/ethnic dimensions themselves do not capture the class dimension either. However, we must be faithful to an important sociological principle: the specificity of phenomena within social systems (McAll 1990, 216). The dilemma of whether to assign theoretical primacy to one or another dimension of social inequality is false and misleading. All class, gender, and ethnic inequalities are manifested in the Canadian social formation. All dimensions, then, should be analyzed. The Canadian social type is not only based on gender and ethnicity/'race'; it is not only racist and sexist. It is also capitalist.

Summary

We began this chapter by posing a number of provocative questions about how to understand a specific incident of what appeared to be 'racial' conflict in France. These questions, we think, are intrinsically interesting. At the same time, the questions are conceptually and theoretically loaded. Many of the terms that we use to describe events in the world have both common sense and scientific meanings. Further, many of the explanations that social scientists offer for events in the world seem to be part of common sense. A phrase like 'racial conflict', though seemingly simple and obvious, is both theoretically and conceptually loaded.

We have begun this book from the point of theory—not because we are necessarily fans of or cheerleaders for theory but because theories and concepts are necessary for the analysis of social events and social processes. They shape how we define, explain, and sometimes even try to predict events in the world. In the remaining chapters, we offer a number of explanations of, debates on, and approaches to a variety of contemporary and historical issues related to understanding immigration, Aboriginal relations, and broader patterns of 'race' and ethnic relations in Canada.

Questions for Critical Thought

1. What does a French person look like? If you were a journalist with a sociology degree in the midst of the Paris riots of 2005, how would you explain the root causes of the civil unrest? Would you attribute it to the physical characteristics of the protesters? To Islamophobia? To high levels of unemployment and poverty within Arab minorities in France? To their age? To the policies of assimilation of the French government? Are these causes mutually exclusive?
2. Some of the ethnic groups mentioned in Herodotus's *Histories* are still around today, most with the same name. Choose a group with which you are familiar, and try to examine the changes that their culture, both material and symbolic, has undergone over the millennia. Do they have the same language? Dress today as they did back then? Have the same symbols? Produce and exchange goods the same way? What has changed? What appears to persist? Remember that culture is a dynamic process.
3. Do 'races' exist? If so, how many are there, and what are the criteria for dividing human populations based on physical characteristics? Why do we not categorize humans by their shoe size or height?
4. Why is it that historically, claims for nationhood and/or the formation of states have been made only by ethnic groups (not 'racial' groups)? What is the relationship between ethnicity and nation-state? Does the latter help to forge the former?
5. Let us reverse the metaphors: Can you think of any 'melting pot' social processes and/or government policies that homogenize minorities in Canada? Conversely, even though there is no official policy, doesn't multiculturalism exist in American society?

Annotated Additional Readings

Gellner, Ernest. 1983. *Nations and nationalism*. Oxford: Blackwell. The author links ethnicity to nation and traces the historical formation of nation-states.

Goldberg, David Theo. 1993. *Racist culture: Philosophy and the politics of meaning*. Oxford: Blackwell. Goldberg is the director of the University of California Humanities Research Institute. This book provides a sustained critique of the racialized discourse of modernity and post-modernity.

Hobsbawm, Eric. 1990. *Nations and nationalism since 1780: Programme, myth, reality*. Cambridge: Cambridge University Press. An historical analysis of nationalisms that links ethnicity in modernity with the state and a prophetic look at the future of ethnicity and nationalism in post-modernity. States create imagined communities like ethnic groups, their language, and their (wrong) history—i.e., their myth.

Jablonski, Nina. 2006. *Skin: A natural history*. Berkeley: University of California Press. This nuanced work provides a fascinating and comprehensive account of the biological and cultural aspects of human skin. Jablonski begins with a look at skin's structure and functions and then tours its 300 million-year evolution, delving into such topics as how the skin reflects and affects emotions and how environmental conditions have influenced its colours.

Steinberg, Stephen. 1989. *The ethnic myth: Race, ethnicity, and class in America*. 2nd ed. Boston: Beacon Press. The author argues that cultural 'traits' that are often considered 'ethnic' may be more directly related to class, locality, and other social conditions. A caustic commentary on the conditions of recent immigrants and a penetrating reappraisal of the black underclass in the United States.

Taylor, Paul. 2003. *Race: A philosophical introduction*. Cambridge: Polity Press. This book is a philosophical introduction to the field of 'race' theory and to a non-biological and situational notion of 'race'. The book explores the many complex issues surrounding the concepts of 'race', 'racial' identity, and 'race' thinking. It addresses such topics as 'mixed-race' identity, white supremacy, the relationship between the 'race' concept and other social identity categories, and the impact of 'race' thinking on our erotic and romantic lives.

van den Berghe, Pierre. 1981. *The ethnic phenomenon*. New York: Elsevier. The author interprets ethnic and 'racial' phenomena in terms of the primordial origins of groups and the 'selfishness of the genes'. It is a controversial sociobiological argument. For this author, ethnicity and 'race' are extensions of kinship elements. Ethnocentrism and racism are seen as extended forms of nepotism. Nepotism is supposedly grounded in the evolutionary 'struggle of the genes' to perpetuate themselves.

Related Websites

The 2005 riots in Paris, France: http://en.wikipedia.org/wiki/2005_Paris_suburb_riots.
Herodotus on-line: http://classics.mit.edu/Herodotus/history.html.
Max Weber on-line: http://cepa.newschool.edu/het/profiles/weber.htm.
The Chicago School: http://en.wikipedia.org/wiki/Chicago_school_(sociology).
Glossary of political economy terms: http://www.auburn.edu/~johnspm/gloss/.
Canadian heritage: http://www.canadianheritage.gc.ca/.

Chapter 2

The Dynamics of Nation-Building: French/English Relations, Aboriginal/Non-Aboriginal Relations, and Immigration in Historical Perspective

Learning objectives

In this chapter, you will learn that:

- The historical accommodations that English and French-Canadian elites made in the late eighteenth and the nineteenth century continue to have implications for contemporary Canadian society.
- Quebec society in the first half of the twentieth century was characterized by an ethnic division of labour in which 'capital spoke English and workers spoke French'.
- The provincial government in Quebec has control over its own immigration policy.
- Quebec's policy of immigrant integration is called 'interculturalism', whereas in the rest of Canada the policy is called 'multiculturalism'.
- Many of the contemporary issues faced by ethnic communities and Aboriginal peoples have their roots in historical processes and decisions made by policy-makers in the past.
- The historical patterns of Aboriginal/non-Aboriginal relations in Canada were structured by a complex of factors, including racism, economic expansion, and the process of state formation.
- Decades-old treaties with Aboriginal peoples still have contemporary relevance.

- The federal government's policy of assimilation had a variety of negative consequences for Aboriginal peoples.
- A variety of factors has shaped historical patterns of immigration control in Canada.
- A racialized hierarchy of desirability ranked potential immigrants to Canada until the 1960s.
- Movements to exclude immigrants from certain countries were not motivated by a psychological distrust of the other but by wider economic considerations.
- Canada abandoned 'racial' discrimination in immigration policy in the 1960s, and this was the result of a combination of ideological, political, and economic factors.

INTRODUCTION

In Canada, many of the issues and struggles that ethnic groups and Aboriginal peoples face today are rooted in the political and economic decisions, individual actions, and government policies and practices of many years ago. Let us take just three examples. First, in the past 20 years, more than 600 'specific claims' have been filed by various First Nations against Indian and Northern Affairs Canada in Ottawa (Frideres and Gadacz 2001, 202). These claims revolve around decades-old disputes over unfilled treaty promises and the loss of reserve land through government negligence or malfeasance. In fact, the ongoing dispute in Caledonia, Ontario, between members of the Six Nations and developers has its origins in differing interpretations of a lease agreement between the British Crown and the Six Nations in 1841.

Second, growing support in Quebec for the Parti Québécois (PQ) in the late 1970s led to dramatic changes in the social and political landscape of Canada. In 1977, the PQ government of René Lévesque passed Bill 101, the Charter of the French Language. The legislation made French the official language of Quebec, in the courts and in the legislature. It also restricted access to English language schooling to children who had at least one parent educated in English in Quebec. The rationale for the charter was that francophones were a minority within both Canada and North America more generally and that active measures needed to be taken to protect the French language and culture in the province (Denis 1999, 189). Three years later, the PQ government held a referendum, asking Quebeckers to give the provincial government a mandate to negotiate sovereignty-association—a form of separation—with the federal government. Even though 60 per cent of Quebeckers voted 'no' in the 1980 referendum, the PQ nevertheless continued its push towards separation. A second referendum was held in 1995, with a slight majority voting against separation. As many as 120,000 English-speaking Quebeckers left the province between 1976 and 1986 (Rudin 1993, 345) as a result of the passage of Bill 101 and the first referendum in 1980. Many of those who left the province moved to Toronto, as did the headquarters of many major Canadian corporations, such as Canada's largest insurance company at the time, Sun Life. Corporations moved their head-quarters from Montreal to Toronto out of fear that as anglophone-owned compa-nies, they and their employees would face a hostile business climate in the province. These and other conflicts surrounding language and culture have long and compli-cated historical roots related to the founding of Canada.

Third, members of a number of ethnic communities in Canada are currently lobbying the federal government to apologize or provide compensation for events that occurred generations ago: Japanese Canadians successfully lobbied for redress over the internment of members of their community during World War II (Omatsu 1992); Ukrainian Canadians have pressed for an apology and redress over the internment of Ukrainian Canadians during World War I (Luciuk 1994); Chinese Canadians have just recently secured an apology from Prime Minister Stephen Harper and compensation for the head tax that was imposed on Chinese immi-grants to Canada between 1885 and 1923 (Li 1998a); and Italian Canadians are pressing for an apology and compensation for the internment of members of their community during World War II (Iacovetta and Ventresca 2000). These cases raise interesting sociological questions about why ethnic groups pursue the correction of historical wrongs and the role that historical memories of victimization play in con-temporary community organizations. Box 2.1 asks you to consider some of these questions with reference to the case of Italian Canadians.

For the purposes of this chapter, however, these three examples illustrate the importance of an historical perspective in understanding contemporary issues and patterns of 'race' and ethnic relations. They also point to the ways in which broader issues of 'race' and ethnic relations have been central to Canadian nation-building. The first section of this chapter focuses on French-English relations; the second focuses on broad patterns of Aboriginal/non-Aboriginal relations; the third focuses on historical patterns of immigration control.

FRENCH/ENGLISH RELATIONS IN HISTORICAL PERSPECTIVE

The 'two founding nations' metaphor has been called into question as an accurate description of the historical forces that founded Canada. As critics have noted, a third nation, consisting of Aboriginal peoples, also played a significant part in nation-building, as did immigrants from nations other than Britain and France. At the same time, however, it is clear that the French presence in Quebec and subse-quent patterns of relationships between French and British settlers and their descen-dants have had a profound influence on the shape of Canada. These historical patterns continue to shape issues of 'race' and ethnic relations in this country.

The conquest
When the British won control of New France from France in 1763, they inherited both a problem and an opportunity. With France out of the way, Britain could further exploit the economic possibilities that the New World held; settlement and colonization would also be easier. But what would become of the some 70,000

**Box 2.1 The Internment of Italian Canadians during World War II:
What Is to Be Done?**

When Italy entered the war on 10 June 1940, Canadians from coast to coast were in the grips of panic and hysteria about the 'fifth column'. In the two short months of April and May 1940, the Nazis had conquered all the democratic countries in continental Europe. In Canada those extraordinary military successes made ominously real the words that Francisco Franco's general Emilio Mola Vidal (1887–1937) uttered early in the Spanish Civil War in the course of his 1936 offensive against Madrid. When asked which of his four columns would take the city, the general responded that it would be his fifth, made up of supporters inside the city. Obsessed by the 'enemy within' in the wake of Nazi victories in Europe, Canadians across the country provided the Mounties with a mass of information about saboteurs, spies, and enemy agents. As a result, on 13 June, the dominion minister of justice, Ernest Lapointe, announced in the House of Commons: 'The very minute that news was received that Italy had declared war on Great Britain and France I signed an order for the internment of many hundreds of men whose names were on the list of RCMP as suspects. I cannot provide the House with the exact number; the RCMP has asked me not to divulge this information because it might create an obstacle to their work'. Among those arrested were several hundred Italian Canadians. (Angelo Principe. 2000. 'A tangled knot': Prelude to 10 June 1940'. In Franca Iacovetta et al. (Eds), *Enemies within: Italian Canadians and other internees in Canada and abroad*. Toronto: University of Toronto Press)

The above description is an account of some of the events leading up to the internment of Italian Canadians during World War II. By the end of the war, some 17,000 Italian Canadians had been placed on enemy aliens lists in the country. In the 1990s, the National Congress of Italian Canadians, along with a number of other Italian Canadian organizations, launched a campaign of 'redress' to correct this historical wrong.

This and other cases of redress pursued by Ukrainian Canadians, Japanese Canadians, and Chinese Canadians raise interesting and important sociological and historical questions in the field of 'race' and ethnic relations:

• Why and how do groups become politically mobilized around redress campaigns?
• How do narratives of victimization contribute to the formation of historical memory?
• Why do members of ethnic communities think it is important to remember and seek compensation for past wrongs perpetrated by the government?
• What obligations do current governments have to compensate groups for past wrongs?
• How does a government sort through the legitimacy of claims for redress?

French-speaking inhabitants of Quebec? Much of the French-speaking political and economic elite left as a result of the British conquest, but peasants, Catholic church officials, and many large landowners stayed (Beaujot and McQuillan 1982, 10–11). When the Quebec Act was passed by the British Parliament in 1774, British authorities were worried about an impending war with the American colonies. As a result, the British attempted to secure control over Quebec by legally recognizing the seigneurial system of landholding, by granting the Catholic church the right to collect tithes, and by allowing French civil law to prevail. The hope was that these measures would satisfy the French-Canadian elite of landlords and Catholic church representatives and that they would in turn act as agents of social control over the much larger French-Canadian peasantry. American colonists tried to incite Canadians to join struggle for independence from Britain, but few Canadians, including the newly conquered French Canadians, were willing to join their cause.

Racialized understandings of French/English relations

Britain lost the war with the American colonies in 1783, but it managed to retain control over the northern half of North America. The accommodations that the British made to French-Canadian society in 1774, however, came back to haunt them as a variety of conflicts arose within Quebec and between Quebec and the rest of Canada (Whitaker 1993, 20–1). During the nineteenth and early twentieth centuries, conflicts between English and French populations of the country were commonly constructed in 'racial' terms. Lord Durham, who was sent by Britain to investigate the rebellions in Upper and Lower Canada in 1837, succinctly described the nature of 'the problem'. He stated that before he began his investigation,

> I expected to find a contest between a government and a people: [Instead] I found two nations warring in the bosom of a single state: I found a struggle, not of principles, but of races; and I perceived that it would be idle to attempt any amelioration of laws or institutions, until we could first succeed in terminating the deadly animosity that now separates the inhabitants of Lower Canada into the hostile divisions of French and English. (Durham 1963, 22–3)

Lord Durham's construction of the 'race' problem in Quebec did not put equal blame on both groups. Even though he thought that the French 'race' had some quaintly redeeming qualities, he nevertheless saw them and their way of life as 'hopelessly inferior' (Durham 1963, 216). André Siegfried (1966), who wrote *The race question in Canada* nearly 60 years later, tended to spread the blame around. The problem was not the inferiority of the French 'race' but rather their profound cultural and linguistic differences from the English 'race'.

Confederation to the Quiet Revolution

With Confederation in 1867, control over major economic institutions tended to remain in English hands. On the other hand, French was recognized as an official language in Quebec, and provincial governments, including that of Quebec, were given considerable authority over culture and education. The Catholic church retained control over educational and religious matters and many other aspects of civil society. Political scientist Reginald Whitaker (1993, 22) described Quebec society in the first half of the twentieth century as one in which 'capital speaks English and labour speaks French'. By the early 1960s, however, the Catholic church's control over civil society began to erode, and the old elite consensus began to break down. The 1960s witnessed a 'Quiet Revolution' that involved dramatic changes to the social structure of the province. Some of those changes included secularization of the educational system, reform of the civil service, and nationalization of sectors of the Quebec economy. It also entailed a cultural and linguistic renaissance (Whitaker 1993, 23–4).

The Quiet Revolution had a number of sources and a number of consequences (Whitaker 1993). One consequence was growing support for more independence for the province of Quebec within Confederation and growing support for some form of independence. The majority 'no' vote in the 1995 referendum on sovereignty settled the issue of separation for the time being. However, the spectre of another sovereignty referendum always seems to lurk in the background of provincial politics and of wider federal-provincial relations. One consequence of the growing influence of the sovereignty movement in the 1970s has been Quebec's ability to negotiate successfully for more powers. This is important for understanding contemporary patterns of immigrant and 'race'/ethnic relations in at least two ways.

Immigration and interculturalism in contemporary Quebec

First, while provincial governments have always had some authority over matters related to immigration, Quebec is the only province that has its own control over this policy field (Black and Hagen 1993). In 1978, the Quebec government negotiated an agreement with the federal government that gave it some influence over immigration. By 1991, Quebec had its own immigration policy and complete control over the selection of independent immigrants as well as language training and adaptation programs for immigrants (Black and Hagen 1993, 280). Quebec uses a modified version of the points system to admit workers to the province (the points system used in Canada outside of Quebec is discussed in detail in chapter 3). The Quebec version includes 20 possible measures of assessment pertaining to education, occupation, experience, language, and adaptability. Two of the central aims of Quebec immigration policy are to increase the number of French-speaking immigrants in the province and to advance economic development. The Quebec government maintains nine overseas immigration offices in places like Paris, Brussels, Hong Kong, and Damascus for recruiting immigrants and processing applications.

Second, as we will discuss in more detail in chapter 5, Quebec, like the rest of Canada, also has an official policy designed to facilitate the integration of newcomers to the province. Outside of Quebec, Canada's policy of immigrant integration is known as multiculturalism, but in Quebec the province's policy is termed 'interculturalism'. According to Kymlicka (1998), although it is similar in objectives to multiculturalism in the rest of Canada, Quebec's approach to managing diversity is different insofar as its encouragement of diversity operates within three important limits: (1) recognition of French as the language of public life; (2) respect for liberal democratic values, including civil and political rights and equality of opportunity;

and (3) respect for pluralism, including openness to and tolerance of others' differences. According to Kymlicka, 'these three principles form the bedrock of the "moral contract" between Quebec and immigrants which specify the terms of integration.'

ABORIGINAL/NON-ABORIGINAL RELATIONS IN HISTORICAL PERSPECTIVE

Some argue that Europeans came to North America with racism and ethnocentrism their bones and that these were the main factors shaping their dealings with Aboriginal peoples (Miles and Brown 2003). In many ways, this is a persuasive argument. The assumption underlying European incursions into North America was that since the existing inhabitants were not organized into states, they could not have legal title to land (Dickason 1992, 100). Furthermore, racism was pervasive in early Canada and took a variety of individual and institutional forms. The early explorers, merchants, military officials, government representatives, police, and members of the wider public construed Aboriginal peoples as non-Christian savages who would benefit from the guidance of a superior people. Institutional forms of racism also resulted in the unequal treatment of Aboriginal peoples; government policies and practices regulated their activities and shaped their life chances in ways that prevented their full participation in society.

While a focus on racism provides a powerful explanation of how and why Aboriginal peoples were defined as a problem population in early Canada, it is really only one part of the puzzle. Expressions of racism and policies based on racist assumptions are always shaped by historical context, structural realities, practical considerations, and class-based as well as other material and symbolic interests. Therefore, it is important to understand the ways by which wider social conditions and historical contexts shaped the meaning of racism. After all, there were variations in the ways that Europeans regarded Aboriginal peoples as problem populations who needed to be transformed into a people that would emulate European values and culture. Thus, even though there may have always been a basic level of racism characterizing Europeans' actions and attitudes towards Aboriginal peoples, the meaning and consequences of those expressions of racism have not been the same throughout history.

In the case of Canada, the wider context for the understanding of Aboriginal/non-Aboriginal relations involves processes of colonial expansion and state formation. Before Confederation, a number of European powers had interests in Canada, and those interests were varied. Some were attracted to the plentiful stocks of fish that could be found in the waters off the east coast of the country; others were interested in timber, while yet others were interested in animal pelts. Eventually, among the European powers, the French and the English came to be the dominant contestants over Canada. Both were interested in the vast resources that the lands and waters contained, but they initially differed in how they pursued the exploitation and extraction of those resources.

In simple terms, the French initially chose to exploit the resources by encouraging the permanent settlement of French nationals on the land, mainly around the upper reaches of the St. Lawrence River. The English, on the other hand, chose to exploit the resources through the establishment of fur trading posts along major waterways and other bodies of water. These posts were staffed by English, Scottish, and Welsh labourers and traders. Initially, the settlement of colonists on the land was not a high priority for the English.

As a number of historians have noted, early relationships between Aboriginal peoples and European settlers, government representatives, missionaries, and fur traders were complex. While Europeans did possess what would now be regarded as racist attitudes toward First Nations peoples, those attitudes and the policies based on those attitudes were moderated by two factors. First, various Aboriginal groups acted as important military allies of the French and the English (Allen 1993). Second, there were relationships of mutual economic interdependence between Europeans and First Nations. Thus, negative attitudes and attempts at the social transformation of Aboriginal peoples were muted by the fact that these peoples were central to the success of the fur trade and the extraction of other resources from the environment and helped European powers in their efforts to establish military supremacy over North America.

Europeans had a more powerful material interest in treating Aboriginal peoples well during the fur trade period than they did after the fur trade declined. Besides being important military allies, Aboriginal peoples were central to the reproduction of the social relations of the fur trade through their role as suppliers of food, clothing, and other goods that sustained European fur traders, through their supply of valuable trade commodities, and through the teaching of survival and transportation techniques that had been honed over the course of the centuries. The fact that Aboriginal peoples were not only useful military allies but central to the operation of the fur trade created a strong incentive for Europeans to treat them with care and perhaps even some grudging respect.

The significance of the 1763 Royal Proclamation

When the English won the contest for Canada in 1763, French Canada and French Canadians became subordinate to British rule. At the same time, their control of North America led British authorities to articulate a more systematic policy for dealing with Aboriginal peoples in their newly consolidated territory. This policy, which some legal scholars regard as more of a negotiated treaty (Borrows 1997), was articulated in King George III's Royal Proclamation of 1763. Why should we pay attention to this proclamation? According to legal scholar John Borrows (1997, 169), the reason is that from 1763 to the present, the 'principles derived from the Royal Proclamation have provided the procedural rules which govern the treaty-making enterprise in Canada' (see also St. Germain 2001, 1). Thus, the proclamation shaped the kinds of strategies, structures, and options that subsequent government decision-makers faced in their dealings with Aboriginal peoples. In turn, the decisions that followed from the principles laid out in the Royal Proclamation continue to carry social and political weight today.

For our purposes, there are three significant aspects to the Royal Proclamation. First, it recognized Aboriginal peoples' rights to land in 'Indian territory' west of the Appalachian mountains in the United States and in that part of Canada outside

Rupert's Land and the old colony of Quebec (Frideres and Gadacz 2001, 169; Borrows 1997, 159–61). British subjects were not allowed to settle on or acquire so-called 'Indian lands'. Second, the proclamation stated that no lands were to be taken from Aboriginal peoples without their consent. If land was to be given up by Aboriginal peoples, the authorities had to seek the agreement of the Aboriginal peoples, and there had to be compensation. Third, agreements to give up land could not be made between individual Aboriginal peoples and Europeans. Rather, land was to be surrendered to the government, which could then keep it as Crown land, give it away, or sell it to someone else (Borrows 1997, 159–60).

In light of British priorities of the time, the principles outlined in the proclamation made sense. The British were concerned about the monetary cost of maintaining peace between colonists and Aboriginal peoples on the western frontier of European settlement. By outlawing European incursions on 'Indian lands', the British hoped to reduce the potential for conflict on the frontier (St. Germain 2001, 1–2). And while lands in eastern North America were already becoming filled with settlers, lands in western North America were still seen as important for the fur trade. As a result, the proclamation helped to prop up the economic status of the fur trade by emphasizing that Aboriginal peoples should remain 'undisturbed' on the lands of western North America so that they could continue to supply furs and other commodities to the traders.

The War of Independence undermined the status of the Royal Proclamation in the United States. The newly independent American government did not feel bound to this colonial document, and so they selectively rejected or maintained aspects of the proclamation that suited their interests. Thus, after 1776 the American approach to dealing with Aboriginal peoples began to depart from the British/Canadian approach (St. Germain 2001, 2–3).

In Canada, as the fur trade declined and pressure for settlement grew, the guarantees contained in the Royal Proclamation eventually became more and more problematic for the authorities. Recognition of Aboriginal title to the land became a constraint on further westward expansion, economic development, and the process of state formation. The proclamation did, however, provide the broad outline of an approach to solving this problem, and the solution came in the form of land surrender treaties.

From the British/Canadian point of view, treaties were about how to extinguish Aboriginal peoples' title to the land in order to provide a legal basis for settlement, economic expansion, and the eventual formation of the Canadian nation. These motives were clearly articulated by the Canadian government, for example, in its approach to Treaty 8, which was agreed to by the Cree, Beaver, and Chipewyan Indians and the government in 1899. As one government official explained, it is 'Her [Majesty's] desire to open for settlement, immigration, trade, travel, mining, lumbering and such other purposes as to Her Majesty may seem meet' the lands in much of what is now northern Alberta, British Columbia, and the southern Northwest Territories (Canada 1993, 291).

In Canada, land surrender treaties tended to take two forms. In southern Ontario, for instance, much of the land was surrendered in exchange for one-time cash payments, but on occasion groups like the Six Nations of Grand River had reserve land provided to them. For example, between 1790 and 1792, the Odawa and Potowatomi people sold the government some five million acres of land between Lake Erie and the Thames River for approximately 2,400 British pounds (Dickason 1992, 190).

As pressures for the settlement of western Canada grew following Confederation, the government's treaty-making strategy changed. The government felt that one-time cash payments were too costly and that smaller payments, to be made in perpetuity, would be a more economical way of acquiring Aboriginal lands. Beginning in 1871, the government embarked on an ambitious treaty-making process that when concluded in 1930 covered northern Ontario, Manitoba, Saskatchewan, Alberta, and the present day Northwest Territories. The 11 treaties that were agreed to between 1871 and 1930 are often referred to as 'the numbered treaties'. For a variety of reasons, treaties were not agreed to between government authorities and Aboriginal peoples in most of present day British Columbia and the Yukon (see Figure 2.1).

While the specific terms of the treaties varied, they generally included the setting aside of reserve lands, cash annuities, and the provision of agricultural implements. For example, Treaty 8 provided for the creation of reserves, with one square mile allocated to each family of five in a band. Chiefs were to receive $25 per year, while other band members would receive $5 each year in perpetuity. Chiefs were to receive a 'suitable suit of clothing' every three years, and upon signing the treaty they received a medal and a flag (Canada 1993, 292). Provisions were also made to supply hoes, spades, pitch forks, and other farm implements to bands that had taken up or were willing to take up farming.

The treaties also mentioned certain rights and obligations, which still have important implications today. For example, Treaty 6, which was agreed to in 1876 in southern Saskatchewan, contained a provision for a 'medicine chest' at the Indian agent's office, while other treaties contained provisions for the supply of teachers in support of the education of Indian children (Dickason 1992, 282). Indian people were also given the right to hunt, fish, and trap on Crown land.

The continuing relevance of treaties

These decades-old treaties are still relevant to the understanding of contemporary patterns of Aboriginal/non-Aboriginal relations in a number of ways. First, Aboriginal peoples and the federal government currently disagree over the interpretation of the terms of the treaties. The federal government tends to favour narrow, literal interpretations of the obligations outlined in the treaties. Thus, in many reserve communities in western Canada, a 'treaty day' is still held at which a five-dollar payment is made to each band member. First Nations, however, tend to see the treaties as living documents that need to be reinterpreted in light of changing times and social standards. For example, the commitment to provide teachers is interpreted by some First Nations leaders in western Canada as a long-term provision to support aspirations for the higher education of Aboriginal youth (Satzewich and Wotherspoon 2000). This is why some claim that government support for post-secondary education is in fact a 'treaty right'.

Figure 2.1   Historical Treaties of Canada

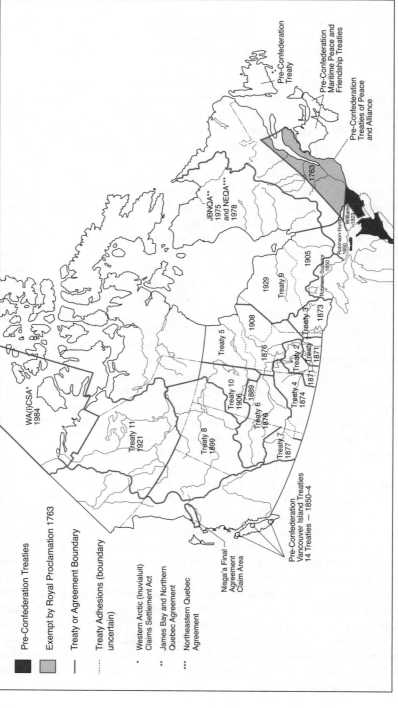

Source: Canada. Indian and Northern Affairs Canada. 'Historical treaties of Canada'. http://www.ainc-inac.gc.ca/pr/trts/hti/mps/eng/htoc–e.pdf.

Second, there have been instances of government negligence, malfeasance, or simple incompetence that resulted in Aboriginal communities not being given the amount of land they were entitled to as specified in the treaties. In some cases, federal government officials deliberately under-counted the number of people in a band in order to reduce the size of the reserve allotment; in other cases, they were simply sloppy in arriving at a proper tally because they did not bother to include individuals who were away from the community at the time of the count. Some First Nations communities are currently seeking ways of addressing these kinds of historical wrongs or oversights through the courts.

Third, even though reserve lands were supposed to be provided to Aboriginal peoples in perpetuity, on many occasions Indian people were coerced or tricked into giving up portions of their reserve land. In western Canada, government officials often responded positively to pressure from land-hungry white farmers who wanted access to the good-quality land that fell within the boundaries of reserve communities (Carter 1990, 185–8). These 'surrenders' of portions of reserves are now the subject of legal dispute, with government representatives of the time accused of failing to act in a responsible manner to protect the interests of Indian peoples and lands under their tutelage (Frideres and Gadacz 2001, 205).

Fourth, treaties gave Indian people the right of access to and to hunt and fish on Crown land. Currently, there are disputes about what the limits (if any) to those rights should be and whether they extend to the Métis and non-status Indians who did not agree to treaties with representatives of the federal government.

Assimilation policy

From the government's perspective, treaties solved the problem of acquiring land so that the process of economic development and state formation could take place on a sound legal footing. However, treaties did not really resolve the question of how Aboriginal peoples were to be transformed into facsimiles of Europeans. That is, how could First Nations be transformed into a group of people with European values, attitudes, and orientations to life, work, and property? This is where government policies of assimilation came into play.

When the fur trade began to decline in the mid-1800s in western Canada and as pressure for settlement grew, Aboriginal peoples became more and more superfluous to economic development. While their skills and associated lifestyles were good for the fur trade, European authorities felt that their culture did not translate well when economic priorities shifted to the requirements of commercial agriculture and capitalist industry. Indeed, their presence as occupants of the land, along with their traditional lifestyles, constituted obstacles to further socio-economic development. Thus, while European settlers, fur traders, missionaries, colonial administrators, and government officials may have always harboured racist and ethnocentric attitudes about Aboriginal peoples right from the days of early contact, only in the mid-nineteenth century do we really see the more systematic articulation of racist ideas and the emergence of government legislation and policies aimed at socially transforming Aboriginal peoples into something resembling white Euro-Canadians.

The titles of the mid-nineteenth century pieces of legislation that were precursors to the 1876 Indian Act are telling indicators of the ways that those in power regarded Aboriginal peoples at the time. For instance, the 1857 Act for the Gradual Civilization of the Indian Tribes of Canada clearly suggested that Indian people were in need of careful guidance to transform them from their uncivilized state. In not very subtle terms, the legislation implied that there was something faulty about Aboriginal peoples and their cultures but that these faults could be corrected through the mindful and benevolent actions of missionaries and the Canadian government.

Following on these assumptions, the federal government developed a variety of policies, strategies, and programs to transform Indian people into Christians and to civilize and assimilate them. The government's resocialization strategies and techniques varied depending on the gender and age of the Aboriginals. Among the many efforts undertaken to accomplish these ends from the late nineteenth century to the early 1960s, when the official rhetoric of the federal government changed from 'assimilation' to 'integration' (a subtle and some say meaningless difference), were policies and practices designed to eradicate traditional cultural and religious practices—including the residential school system.

The eradication of traditional cultural and religious practices was a major preoccupation of the Department of Indian Affairs between the late nineteenth and the middle of the twentieth century (Pettipas 1994; Backhouse 1999). Egged on by missionaries offended by religious rituals involving body mutilation, the worship of non-Christian symbols and objects, and a seeming lack of respect for the notion of private property (Titley 1986), ceremonies such as the sun dance on the prairies and the potlatch on the British Columbia coast became objects of government surveillance and repression (Pettipas 1994). An amendment to the Indian Act in 1895 made participating in or assisting in the organization of the following kinds of events indictable offences:

> any Indian festival, dance, or other ceremony of which the giving away or paying or giving back of money, goods or articles of any sort forms a part, or is a feature, whether such gift of money, goods or articles takes place before, at, or after the celebration of the same, and every Indian or other person who engages or assists in any celebration or dance of which the wounding or mutilation of the dead or living body of any human being or animal forms a part or is a feature (cited in Backhouse 1999, 63).

Simple persuasion was not always successful in convincing Indian people not to engage in these practices, and so jail terms and the denial of political positions and economic resources to participants were also used in the attempt to eradicate them (Backhouse 1999; Satzewich and Mahood 1994).

It is worth noting that Indian peoples were not passive victims in these instances of state and missionary-led repression. They continued to engage in the practices surreptitiously, and they modified them in ways to get around prohibitive legislation. Sometimes, in co-operation with whites in local communities (particularly merchants who wanted to include 'exotic' Indian dances at local country fairs), they challenged the legislation in the courts (Backhouse 1999; Pettipas 1994).

While prohibitions against religious and cultural practices were directed against adult Indians, the government used other age-specific resocialization strategies. Industrial schools were established for Indian children in eastern Canada in the 1840s, but what became known as the residential school system in Canada was established following Nicholas Flood Davin's 1879 investigation into industrial school education in the United States. One of the features of the American model that impressed Davin was the use of a subcontracting arrangement in which the government gave per capita grants to churches to operate the schools (Titley 1986, 75). Churches were eager to take on this responsibility because it gave them a source of revenue as well as a captive audience of potential new recruits to their version of Christianity.

The residential school system was premised on what sociologists see as a 'classical' approach to resocialization. As is the case with resocialization in the military or in religious cults, government, religious, and educational officials recognized that the transformation of Indian children was best accomplished in a setting where contact with their previous way of life was reduced to a minimum. That is, contact with friends, family, and previous customs and habits was severely curtailed. In taking children out of their homes and family environments, isolating them in schools often several hundred kilometres away from their communities, and discouraging contact between children, parents, and other relatives, the government and missionaries were attempting to minimize conflicting messages about appropriate forms of behaviour coming from home. Officials felt that this kind of educational environment would give them a relatively free hand to erase old patterns of culture, behaviour, and identity and to create in Indian children new, European, Christian attitudes, behaviours, and identities.

At the peak of the system in the 1930s and 1940s, approximately one-half of all Indian children enrolled in school in Canada were enrolled in residential schools (Titley 1986). The other children were enrolled in day schools and lived at home. Residential schools were phased out in the 1950s and 1960s.

Unfortunately, many of the children in the residential schools received more than just an education in the '3 Rs'. Boys and girls in the schools also had to perform hard physical labour: chopping wood, washing clothes, and growing food. Some were subject to physical, emotional, and sexual abuse, and many First Nations individuals and communities continue to carry the scars associated with the residential school system. Given that they never experienced a normal family life while they were young, many First Nations individuals who attended residential schools feel that they now lack proper parenting skills (Schissel and Wotherspoon 2003).

As with its approach to treaties, the strategies, policies, and practices that the government adopted in the past in an attempt to civilize and assimilate Aboriginal people continue to reverberate today. The residential schools were more often than not unsuccessful in their efforts at resocialization. Many children managed to retain their identities and attachments to their communities; others who went through the system eventually became leaders in their communities and are now pressing the federal government and churches for compensation for the wrongs that were committed at the schools. By January 2001, 6,700 residential school survivors had launched lawsuits, and it was expected that another 15,000 suits would be filed in the future. In response, the federal government at the time established a resolution framework that included an alternative dispute resolution process, health supports, commemoration, out-of-court settlements, and litigation. More recently, the Assembly of First Nations and Indian and Northern Affairs Canada concluded an agreement that provides for compensation, healing, commemoration, and a truth and reconciliation process associated with First Nations attendance at residential schools (Assembly of First Nations 2006).

Chapter 7 deals in more detail with contemporary patterns of Aboriginal/non-Aboriginal relations in Canada. However, it should be clear from this discussion that past decisions, practices, and policies continue to exert pressure on present-day patterns of Aboriginal/non-Aboriginal relations.

IMMIGRATION IN HISTORICAL PERSPECTIVE

Aboriginal peoples occupied an ambiguous place in the minds of decision-makers in post-Confederation Canada. They and their cultures were regarded as inferior, but at the same time they were also regarded as capable of being moulded into something resembling an ideal/typical 'European'. Economic and political elites in Canada understood, however, that it was unrealistic to expect that the further development of capitalist industry and commercial agriculture could occur solely by using 'assimilated' Aboriginal peoples as labourers and by encouraging them to become commercial farmers. As a result, elites realized that the non-Aboriginal population would have to increase dramatically in order for Canada to develop economically, socially, and politically.

There are two ways for a country to increase its population. One is to encourage its citizens to have more children. Natural population growth within the existing European population of Canada solved part of the dilemma associated with where future citizens, workers, and farmers would come from. Indeed, when France lost control of New France, the Catholic church in Quebec encouraged the formation of large families as a way of solidifying the status of the French in the context of growing British immigration. In the province, the average number of births per marriage was more than seven, and families with 10 or 12 children were not uncommon (Beaujot and McQuinlan 1982, 13). As can be seen in figure 2.2, the other way to increase population in Canada has been through the promotion of immigration. That story is the focus of this section.

Understanding immigration control in the early twentieth century

British elites in Canada realized from a fairly early date that individuals and families would have to be recruited from abroad in order to increase the size of the population and for Canada to prosper as a white settler society. The process of immigration, like the patterns of Aboriginal/non-Aboriginal relations, was therefore part of the process of state formation. Immigrants were not simply seen by decision-makers as economic agents whose main value was their contribution of brawn. Immigrants were also expected to become permanent settlers, to bring and/or form families, and to eventually take up the rights and responsibilities of citizenship. As a result, there has always been an inherent tension within immigration policy—which

Figure 2.2   Canada – Permanent Residents, 1860 to 2004

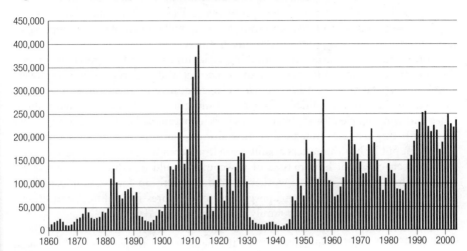

Historical highlights

- 1896 to 1905: the settlement of the West with an offer of free land results in large numbers of immigrants from the United Kingdom, Europe and the United States
- 1906: *Immigration Act*
- 1910: *Immigration Act*
- 1913: 400,000 immigrants arrive in Canada
- 1914 to 1918: immigration slump during World War I
- 1928: opening of Halifax's Pier 21, the Atlantic gateway to Canada
- 1930s: extremely low levels of immigration during the Depression years
- 1940s: during and after World War II, approximately 48,000 war brides and their 22,000 children arrive in Canada
- 1950s: Canada receives about one and a half million immigrants from Europe
- 1952: *Immigration Act*
- 1956 and 1957: Canada accepts 37,500 Hungarian refugees
- 1962: new immigration regulations are tabled to eliminate all discrimination based on race, religion, and national origin
- 1967: the government amends Canada's immigration policy and introduces the point system for the selection of skilled workers and business immigrants
- 1968 and 1969: Canada takes in 11,000 Czechoslovakian refugees
- 1972: Canada resettles more than 6,175 Ugandan Asians
- 1973: Canada accepts more than 6,000 Chileans
- 1975 to 1978: Canada resettles almost 9,000 Indochinese
- 1976: *Immigration Act*
- 1979 and 1980: 60,000 Vietnamese, Cambodian and Laotian 'boat people' arrive in Canada
- 1999: Canada accepts more than 7,000 Kosovars
- 2002: *Immigration and Refugee Protection Act* (IRPA)

Source: Canada. Citizenship and Immigration Canada. *Immigration overview, 2004.*
http://www.cic.gc.ca/english/pdf/pub/facts2004.pdf.

is still with us today—between seeing and using immigrants as a convenient means of solving short-term labour market problems and seeing them as individuals and members of families and larger communities who will contribute to the reproduction of wider social and political relations in our society.

Over the years, a variety of competing social forces and ideologies have shaped the process of immigrant recruitment, selection, and control. Some employers wanted cheap labour, regardless of where it came from; social purity advocates focused on the moral qualities of potential immigrants; politicians thought about votes and winning elections; police forces were concerned about maintaining order and combating real and imagined crime among certain immigrants; doctors worried about public health matters arising from immigration; government bureaucrats were concerned about how masses of newcomers could be educated, assimilated, and transformed into citizens; workers feared competition for scarce jobs; immigrants themselves wanted to escape poverty and oppressive political conditions, build new lives, and bring other family members to Canada.

Furthermore, broad cross-sections of Canadian society were concerned about the 'racial' and ethnic characteristics of the newcomers, their 'foreign' languages, customs, and ideas, and whether the admittance of newcomers from unfamiliar parts of the world was good for the long-term interests of Canada. Immigrant recruitment, selection, and control was therefore a site of conflict between a variety of competing social forces and ideologies. Thus, social definitions of class, gender, sexuality, and ethnic/'racial' capacities shaped decisions, policies, and practices about who should be allowed in, the conditions under which they should be let in, and who should be kept out.

Some commentators have focused on the racist nature of immigration control and immigration policy in the post-Confederation years (Henry and Tator 2005). This focus is not wrong, but broader considerations such as class, gender, health, and sexuality as well as political security also played important roles in regulating the flow of immigrants to Canada in the twentieth century. These factors speak to the importance of looking at international migration in light of the process of state formation.

Class background, broadly defined, was an early focus of concern in post-Confederation immigration policy. For example, Canadian politicians, concerned that Canada was being used by Britain as a dumping ground for its poor, unemployed, and unemployable surplus population, introduced legislation in 1879 to prevent the arrival of British paupers and destitute immigrants (Knowles 1992, 47). Further, at the turn of the twentieth century, immigration officials were specifically interested in recruiting immigrants with agricultural backgrounds so that they could more easily take up homesteads on the Canadian prairies. At the same time, railroad, mining, and lumber companies were eager to recruit immigrants who were both tough and desperate enough to work in a variety of physically demanding jobs for relatively low pay (Avery 1995, 30–1).

Women who were perceived to be of doubtful moral character were not permitted as immigrants. The Immigration Act of 1910, for example, prohibited the entry of 'prostitutes and women and girls coming to Canada for any immoral purpose and pimps or persons living on the avails of prostitution . . . [and] persons who procure or attempt to bring into Canada prostitutes or women or girls for the purpose of prostitution or other immoral purpose' (Roberts 1988, 12–13). For a time, the definition of coming to Canada for 'immoral' purposes extended to couples who had eloped to Canada (Roberts 1988, 17).

Notions of physical and 'mental' fitness also shaped immigration admissions. The 1910 Immigration Act prohibited the entry of: 1) 'the mentally defective', which included those defined as 'idiots, imbeciles, feeble-minded, epileptics and the insane'; 2) 'the diseased', which included those afflicted with 'loathsome, contagious or infectious diseases'; and 3) 'the physically defective', which included 'the dumb, blind, or otherwise handicapped' (McLaren 1990, 56).

Perceived political loyalty was also an important criterion of immigration control. A 1919 amendment to the Immigration Act defined the following behaviours as grounds for deportation from Canada:

> Every person who by word or act in Canada seeks to overthrow by force or violence the government of or constituted law and authority in the United Kingdom of Great Britain and Ireland, or Canada, any of the provinces of Canada, or the government of any other of His Majesty's dominions, colonies, possessions or dependencies, or advocates the assassination of any official of any of the said governments or of any foreign government, or who in Canada defends or suggests the unlawful destruction of property or by word or act creates or attempts to create any riot or public disorder in Canada, or who without lawful authority assumes any powers of government in Canada or in any part thereof, or who by common repute belongs to or is suspected of belonging to any secret society or organization which extorts money from or in any way attempts to blackmail, or who is a member of or affiliated with any organization entertaining or teaching disbelief in or opposition to organized government shall, for the purposes of the Act, be deemed to belong to the prohibited or undesirable classes, and shall be liable to deportation (cited in Roberts 1988, 19).

Assessments of those who constituted political threats to Canada changed depending on the circumstances. At times, people falling into the loosely defined category of 'labour radicals' were barred from entry, and during the early post-World War II years, Canada was obsessed with preventing the arrival of Nazis, war criminals, communists, and communist sympathizers (Avery 1995, 126–43).

'Race' and ethnicity were also critical. The first 60 years of the twentieth century saw sustained efforts by the government to control the immigration of people who were defined as unsuitable because of their 'race', ethnicity, or country of origin. The social evaluation of immigrants was based on a racialized hierarchy of desirability in which some groups were seen as both good workers and desirable future citizens and should be encouraged to come; some were regarded as 'racially' unsuitable for life in Canada and should be prevented from coming; and some were 'in-between' people who, while perhaps posing certain long and short-term problems for Canada, could be admitted as a last resort.

Generally, British, white American, and northern European immigrants were at the top of the hierarchy of desirability. J.S. Woodsworth, an influential early twentieth-century commentator on immigration matters, once asked whether white Americans were 'desirable settlers'. Answering his own question, he had no doubts:

> Yes. Most of them are 'well-to-do' when they come, and are bound to 'make things go.' The majority of them average up pretty well with our own Canadians. Of course, they are not British subjects, and some of them rather object to acknowledging allegiance to King Edward VII. But the King lives away in England. They soon become good Canadian citizens. Their children will be loyal British subjects (Woodsworth 1972, 65).

But immigrants from 'preferred' countries were not necessarily given blanket 'free passes'. African-Americans were actively discouraged by Canadian officials from moving north of the border (Shepard 1991, 30–1). And at times, a disadvantaged class background could trump the privileges of ethnicity/'race'. Woodsworth, for example, had this to say about the English working class:

> Generally speaking, the Scotch, Irish and Welsh have done well. The greater number of failures have been among the English. This is due partly to a national characteristic which is at once a strength and a weakness—lack of adaptability. Someone has said that 'the English are the least readily assimilated of the English-speaking nationalities.' But the trouble has been largely with the *class* of immigrants who have come. Canada has needed farmers and labourers, and these should be resourceful and enterprising. England has sent us largely the failures of the cities. The demand for artisans in our cities is limited. In any case many of the immigrants are culls from English factories and shops. These cannot compete with other English-speaking people and often not with non-English, despite the latter's disadvantage in not knowing the language (Woodsworth 1972, 47–8; emphasis in original).

Eastern and southern Europeans were 'in-between peoples' in the racialized hierarchy of desirability. Even though broad 'racial' distinctions seem rather obvious and self-evident today, during the late nineteenth and early twentieth centuries it was not at all clear where 'Europe'—and by implication 'whiteness'—began and ended. In Canada and in the United States as well (Roediger 1991), assessments of the social desirability of European immigrants became more ambivalent and harsh as their origins approached the southern and eastern edges of Europe (Satzewich 2000; Petryshyn 1991).

Like other immigrants, immigrants from eastern and southern Europe had both their supporters and detractors in Canada. Railroad companies were keen on eastern European immigrants because they helped settle the West and provided a market for more rail traffic between eastern and western Canada. Among the better known supporters of eastern European immigrants at the turn of the last century was Clifford Sifton, editor of *The Winnipeg Free Press* and minister of the interior in the early 1900s. Anxious to populate the Canadian West with farmers, Sifton saw in eastern European men, women, and families a unique and seemingly 'racial' ability to work hard on the land.

Others, however, were less than enamoured with the prospect of admitting immigrants from the southern and eastern fringes of Europe. They spoke unfamiliar languages, and some people were offended by their real and imagined customs and habits. Referring to immigrants from southern Europe, one Ontario member of Parliament stated in 1914 that 'we do not want a nation of organ-grinders and banana sellers in this country' (McLaren 1990, 49). Another commentator argued even more grandly that

> a line drawn across the continent of Europe from northeast to southwest, separating the Scandinavian Peninsula, the British Isles, Germany, and France from Russia, Austria-Hungary, Italy, and Turkey, separates countries not only of distinct races but also of distinct civilizations. It separates countries of representative institutions and popular government from absolute monarchies; it separates lands where education is universal from lands where illiteracy predominates; it separates manufacturing countries, progressive agriculture, and skilled labour from primitive hand industries, backward agriculture, and unskilled labour; it separates an educated, thrifty peasantry from a peasantry scarcely a single generation removed from serfdom; it separates Teutonic races from Latin, Slav, Semitic, and Mongolian races (cited in Osborne 1991, 84).

Bloc settlements of eastern Europeans on the prairies were of particular concern to some critics (Lehr 1991; Kaye 1964). Rather than move to areas that might have better land but were some distance from family members and co-ethnics, many eastern European immigrants preferred to settle close to one another for social, economic, and psychological support. In some ways, bloc settlements made government settlement work easier; teachers who knew the ethnic language dominant in the area could be sent to schools and help to transform the children into 'Canadians', and the provision of certain government services could be ethnically streamlined (Kaye and Swyripa 1982, 46). However, critics saw bloc settlements as giving immigrants the opportunity to maintain their language and customs. In some people's minds, the formation of these ethnic colonies was also deterring the settlement of better-quality immigrants on the prairies. In 1899, *The Winnipeg Telegram* wrote of the difficult predicament this posed for British settlers:

> The unfortunate settler finds himself hemmed in by a whole horde of people little better than savages—alien in race, language and religion, whose customs are repellent and whose morals he abhors. Social intercourse is impossible, all hopes of further British settlement in the neighbourhood vanishes; he becomes an alien in his own country. There is nothing left for him but a galling life-long exile on British soil equivalent to deportation to a Siberian settlement (cited in Lehr 1991, 40).

The newspaper argued that the formation of bloc settlements should be actively discouraged as an obstacle to assimilation. In some ways, these concerns are not unlike today's reservations about immigration—namely, that too many immigrants are settling in places like Toronto, Montreal, and Vancouver, which prevents their assimilation into the larger society.

At the other end of the scale of social desirability were non-European, non-white groups, who were defined as unassimilable and unsuitable as permanent settlers. Pre-World War II immigration legislation is full of examples of efforts to keep various 'visible minority' groups out of the country and to limit the civil, political, and economic rights of those 'undesirable' immigrants who did manage to find their way in and stay.

Chinese males were initially encouraged to come to Canada in the 1880s by labour-hungry contractors looking for cheap and disposable workers to help build the transcontinental railroad. Between 1880 and 1884, approximately 15,700 immigrants from China arrived in Canada, mainly in British Columbia, to work on railroad construction. These workers and those who came after them were soon caught in the crossfire between business-based pro-Chinese immigration sentiments and working class-based anti-Chinese immigration sentiments. Nativists, labour unions, and other working-class organizations were concerned about competition in the labour market and the dilution of the white and British character of the province of British Columbia and were opposed to capitalists who continued to want access to Chinese labour (Roy 1989).

Caught between these competing forces, the government tried to resolve the conflict by keeping the door open to Chinese immigration but at the same creating obstacles that would reduce the rate of migration. The government needed to appear to be 'doing something' to placate the politically influential anti-Chinese forces but at the same time did not want to alienate business owners in British Columbia and elsewhere by cutting off a valuable source of labour. Its preferred solution was the creation of the infamous 'head tax', which amounted to a bounty that Chinese male and female workers and family members had to pay the government when they arrived in Canada. The first head tax, introduced in 1885, was pegged at $50 per person. In 1900, the tax was increased to $100, and in 1903, it was raised to $500 per person. The head tax might have slowed the rate of immigration to Canada from China, but it did not put a stop to it; indeed, the federal government collected approximately $23 million in revenues from the head tax during the time it was in effect (Li 1998a, 42). Eventually, the Chinese fell victim to exclusionary pressures that prevented further immigration to Canada and limited their employment opportunities in this country. By 1923, restrictionist forces were able to win the contest over Chinese labour migration, and the government introduced the Chinese Immigration Act, which barred further Chinese labour migration until after the Second World War (Li 1998a, 89).

As with other immigrants, class background and gender were also important in regulating Chinese immigration to Canada. Chinese immigrants with wealth and capital who were interested in investing or establishing businesses in Canada were exempt from the head tax and the exclusionary provisions of the Chinese Immigration Act; merchants of Chinese origin could still come to Canada after 1923, as could members of the diplomatic corps, students, and children born in Canada 'to parents of Chinese race or descent' (Li 1998a, 35).

Chinese women, on the other hand, were the object of special concern, entangled in contradictory discourses and government practices. Some government officials feared 'racial inter-mixing'. They felt that the absence of women within early

Chinese communities in Canada would inevitably lead men within these communities to 'debauch white women'. Furthermore, intermarriage between Chinese men and white women would eventually lead to white 'race' degeneration (Dua 2004). Thus, for some, the migration of women from China should be encouraged because Chinese men would form families with them, preventing future 'racial inter-mixing'. At the same time, however, the presence of women from China was also seen as leading to the reproduction of 'alien' cultures in Canada. Some Canadian immigration officials feared the creation of a second generation and tried to discourage the migration of Chinese women to Canada. The expectation was that once in Canada, they would marry men of 'their own kind', have children, 'propagate the race' here, and undermine the status of Canada as a white settler society (Dua 2004).

Immigrants from India were also the object of concern during the early twentieth century. Some of the dynamics of Indian immigration to Canada were the same as those of Chinese and southern/eastern European immigration. Poor peasants were looking for ways to escape from their dire circumstances at home, and Canada was seen as an attractive option. By 1908, a rather modest 5,000 immigrants from India had arrived in Canada. Upon their arrival, Indian immigrants became the object of widespread anti-immigration sentiments. However, like the Chinese, Indian immigrants had some champions within the business community of British Columbia. The owners of steamship companies made money from the fares they paid to reach Canada, and lumber and mining companies were always in search of cheaper and more exploitable sources of labour (Basran and Bolaria 2003).

However, international political considerations introduced a wrinkle that made the regulation of Indian migration to Canada more complicated than it was for the Chinese. Whereas anti-Chinese legislation was blatantly 'anti-Chinese', anti-Indian legislation was more subtle because of India's link with Canada through the British Empire. In theory, one of the official principles of the British Empire was that it 'makes no distinction in favour of, or against any race or colour' (Bolaria and Li 1988, 169). The Canadian government was concerned that blatantly anti-Indian immigration legislation would publicly embarrass the British and jeopardize their authority in India. As a result, it opted for legislation that appeared to be 'racially' neutral but in fact was specifically designed to prevent the further migration of Indians to Canada. An order-in-council, passed on 9 May 1910, contained what is now known as 'the continuous journey stipulation':

> From and after the date here of the landing in Canada shall be, and the same is hereby prohibited of any immigrants who have come to Canada otherwise than by continuous journey from the country of which they are natives or citizens and only through tickets purchased in the country or prepaid in Canada (cited in Basran and Bolaria 2003, 99).

On the surface, the wording of the order-in-council appeared to have nothing to do with Indian immigration. But despite the seemingly ethnically neutral language, its intent was to curtail further Indian migration to Canada. It was no coincidence that at the same time that the legislation was passed, the Canadian government persuaded Canadian steamship companies to stop making direct sailings between

Canada and India. Thus, Indians who wanted to make the trip to Canada had to do so via Hong Kong, Hawaii, or some other location, which according to the terms of the order-in-council was not a continuous journey and was therefore not an allowable means of getting to Canada.

Indians saw through the discriminatory intentions of the legislation and knew that it was specifically directed at them. In 1914, a Sikh businessman chartered a ship named *Komagata Maru* in Hong Kong to bring 376 Indian passengers to Canada, which was in direct contravention of the continuous journey stipulation (Basran and Bolaria 2003, 100). On its arrival in Vancouver, the ship was refused permission to disembark its passengers. After a standoff that lasted for two months, the ship was escorted out of the harbour by the Canadian naval ship *Rainbow* and forced to return to India.

Dimensions of the early vertical mosaic

During the first half of the twentieth century, racism and ethnic stereotypes not only regulated who was deemed a suitable immigrant but also played a role in allocating immigrants to different kinds of jobs and occupations. Ethnic and 'racial' stereotypes contained bundles of beliefs about the kinds of work that immigrants from different parts of the world were suited for in Canada (Porter 1965, 66). Writing in the mid-1960s, sociologist John Porter (1965, 63) referred to this as part of the 'vertical mosaic' in Canada, where a 'reciprocal relationship between ethnicity and social class' developed. Porter sketched the broad dynamics of the formation of the vertical mosaic in Canada in the following terms:

> A given ethnic group appropriates particular roles and designates other ethnic groups for the less preferred ones. Often the low status group accepts its inferior position. Through time the relative status position, reinforced by stereotypes and social images . . . harden and become perpetuated over a very long time. In the general scheme of class and status that evolves with economic growth and immigration there exists an 'entrance status' to be assumed by the less preferred ethnic groups. Entrance status implies lower level occupational roles and subjection to processes of assimilation laid down and judged by the charter group. Over time the position of entrance status may be improved or it may be a permanent caste-like status as it has been, for example, with the Chinese in Canada. Thus, most of Canada's minority groups have at some time had this entrance status. Some, but not all, have moved out of it (Porter 1965, 63–4).

There are many concrete examples of the dynamic that Porter outlined. Eastern Europeans were deemed to be 'racially' suited for the backbreaking labour associated with farming in western Canada. In an often-quoted speech, minister of the interior Clifford Sifton defended eastern European immigration in this way:

> When I speak of quality I have in mind something that is quite different from what is in the mind of the average writer or speaker upon the question of immigration. I think a stalwart peasant in a sheep-skin coat, born on the soil, whose forefathers had been farmers for generations, with a stout wife and half-a-dozen children, is good quality (cited in Porter 1965, 66).

Italians, on the other hand, were stereotypically viewed as having special capacities for hard manual labour in cities (Iacovetta 1992, 8).

Restrictions placed on economic opportunities for immigrants were not just the result of informal sanctions based on ethnic and 'racial' stereotyping. During the early part of the twentieth century, a variety of legal mechanisms were used to restrict employment opportunities for certain groups of immigrants and Canadian citizens and to limit their civil and political rights. Individuals of Chinese origin, in addition to facing severe restrictions at the border, faced equally severe restrictions in a variety of other spheres of life. In 1912, the government of Saskatchewan passed a law preventing the employment of white women in businesses owned or managed by any Japanese, Chinese, or 'other Oriental' person (Backhouse 1999, 136). Chinese Canadians could not vote in provincial elections in British Columbia and Saskatchewan until after World War II. Violation of other rights was also common. Black people were not allowed to sit in certain areas of movie theatres in Nova Scotia, were denied positions on the Canadian Pacific Railway, and faced segregated schools.

Explaining exclusionary movements

There is ongoing debate about the social sources of this kind of hostility and the exclusionary movements that sought to prevent the arrival of what were defined as undesirable immigrants. Was it simply the 'racial otherness' of certain immigrants that provoked opponents? Did 'racial' ideas mask deeper concerns about labour market competition? Or did deeply held racist attitudes interact with economic considerations to produce exclusionary movements?

Some argue that racism directed against groups like Indian and Chinese immigrants in Canada at the turn of the twentieth century was an expression of a deep-seated social/psychological antipathy on the part of white people towards non-whites. Reflecting a primordial approach to the explanation of racist hostility and social exclusion, Ward (2002) argues that 'white British Columbians yearned for a racially homogeneous society'. The 'psychological tensions derived from white society's desire for racial homogeneity, a drive continually stimulated by the racially plural condition', led members of that society to resolve their tension by trying to prevent further migration of Chinese and other 'racial others' to the province.

The problem with this explanation is that it leaves open the question of where the desire for 'racial homogeneity' comes from; rather than seeing 'racial preferences' as socially constructed and socially derived, the approach seems to assume that 'preferring one's own kind' is a basic human need. If it is a need, however, it does seem to be socially malleable. Further, the explanation assumes that 'white society' is an undifferentiated mass with the same material and psychological interests in maintaining 'racial purity' (Anderson 1991, 19). However, as we have seen, there were deep differences of opinion within 'white society' about the desirability of non-European immigrants.

Other interpretations focus on 'capitalism' more generally as the source of conflict and hostility. Working within the theoretical framework of political economy, Bolaria and Li (1988, 7) argue that 'race problems begin as labour problems'. They argue that racism is inherently connected to the dynamics of capitalism and the search by employers for cheaper, more exploitable sources of labour. As outlined in chapter 1, this approach focuses on the economic interests of capitalists in having a socially divided working class. They argue that 'racial' ideologies and divisions are promoted and encouraged by capitalists as a strategy to divide and rule the working class. In their terms, a 'racially' divided working class is easier to control and exploit if there is in-fighting between workers of different origin. In-fighting conveniently deflects workers' attention away from the 'real' source of their economic problems, which is exploitation by employers.

This view is persuasive but not entirely convincing. The capitalist class in Canada did have its share of racists, and capitalists did likely benefit from intra-working-class hostilities. Furthermore, racism did contribute to the social and political marginalization of non-white immigrants. That marginalization further contributed to their economic vulnerability and made them more exploitable than other immigrants and the Canadian-born, who were on a more secure social and political footing. One of the problems with this explanation, however, is that in many cases, racism in post-Confederation Canada eventually resulted in the exclusion of those immigrants, thus making it difficult or impossible for employers to exploit the labour power of immigrants from places like China and India. Furthermore, many of the exclusions that arose out of racism prevented immigrants from gaining employment in certain industries. For instance, an 1890 law prevented Chinese workers from working underground in coal mines (Li 1998a, 51). Thus, if racism was self-consciously propagated by capitalists for their own economic interests, then this was a decidedly short-sighted plan that badly backfired.

Another perspective, also focusing on labour market dynamics, is the theory of the split labour market (Bonacich 1979). Instead of focusing on capitalists as the source of ethnic and 'racial' tensions, this perspective suggests that the economic competition among workers who sell their labour power at different prices is the source of tension, conflict, and eventual forms of exclusion. According to this view, historical circumstances led immigrants from places like China and India to sell their labour power cheaper than Canadian-born workers and European immigrants did. Some of these circumstantial factors included extreme poverty and few economic options in their place of origin, the fact that many men were single or came to Canada without their families, and the fact that they did not necessarily handle their own negotiations over wages. In British Columbia at the turn of the century, wage differences between Chinese and white workers were significant. According to the 1902 *Report of the Royal Commission on Chinese and Japanese Immigration*, Chinese workers in a variety of industries could be hired for as little as one-third of the wages paid to white workers doing the same work (Li 1998a, 48). According to split labour market theorists, these wage differences produced tensions between the high and low-priced workers and led to efforts by the higher-priced white workers to prevent employers from having access to cheaper Chinese and Indian workers. Thus, members of the white working class in British Columbia are seen as responsible for exclusionary immigration policies and for policies that prevented Chinese and Indian workers from taking certain jobs.

American sociologist Edna Bonacich sums up the broad contours of this argument as follows:

> The real division is not between white and non-white, but between high priced and cheap labour. This distinction, because of historical accident, happens to have been frequently correlated with the white/non-white distinction, hence 'race' comes to be the language in which the ensuing conflicts are expressed. When a split labour market . . . falls along other lines, other idioms are used. In other words, the underlying issue is a class issue (price of labour), not biological differences (Bonacich 1979, 20).

Perhaps the answer to the question of where ethnic and 'racial' hostilities originate lies somewhere in between. It is not clear, for example, whether differences in the price of labour were simply the result of historical accidents or whether they themselves were a consequence of racism and hostility. Capitalism and capitalists may not necessarily have created 'racial' ideas and 'racial' distinctions, as some versions of political economy theory have suggested. Given the historical evidence, it is clear that understandings of fixed, biological human difference predated capitalism, as did the use of the word 'race'. However, the development of capitalism did infuse racist ideas, distinctions, and understandings with new meanings and new social consequences.

Post-World War II migration

While efforts were made after World War II to moderate some of the more discriminatory aspects of immigration policy, the basic philosophy behind immigration control remained the same: namely, that immigration to Canada was a privilege and not a right; that immigration needed to be carefully controlled; that the promotion of non-white immigration was not in the best long-term interests of the country; and that the economic benefits of immigration needed to be balanced by its 'social' costs. The philosophical framework for the early postwar immigration program was laid down in prime minister Mackenzie King's speech in the House of Commons in 1947:

> The policy of the government is to foster the growth of the population of Canada by the encouragement of immigration. The government will seek, by legislation, regulation and vigorous administration, to ensure the careful selection and permanent settlement of such numbers of immigrants as can advantageously be absorbed in our national economy (Canada. 1947. *Debates of the House of Commons*. 1 May, 2644–6).

At the same time, Mackenzie King recognized that economic priorities needed to be balanced by social considerations stemming from the logic of state formation:

> There will, I am sure, be general agreement with the view that the people of Canada do not wish, as a result of mass immigration, to make a fundamental alteration in the character of our population. Large scale immigration from the orient would change the fundamental composition of the Canadian population. Any considerable

oriental immigration would, moreover, be certain to give rise to social and economic problems of a character that might lead to serious difficulties in the field of international relations. The government, therefore, has not thought of making any change in immigration regulations that would have consequences of the kind (Canada. 1947. *Debates of the House of Commons.* 1 May, 2644–6).

Admittedly, Canada did get rid of some of the more noxious and blatantly racist immigration legislation after the war, but many of the changes were largely symbolic. The Chinese Immigration Act was officially repealed in 1947, but the door still remained more or less closed through the application of other rules that restricted Asian migration to Canada more generally (Li 1998a, 89–92). In a concession to Commonwealth solidarity, the continuous journey stipulation was repealed, and the door to immigration from India opened ever so slightly: in 1952, immigration from India was set at a quota of 150 per year, and five years later the quota was raised to 300 per year (Basran and Bolaria 2003, 104). Small numbers of black women were allowed to enter Canada to work as domestics, typists, and nurses. Thus, despite the changes, the focus of the postwar immigration program remained on white immigrants from Europe and the United States.

Postwar immigration policy continued to give the Department of Citizenship and Immigration a tremendous degree of leeway to prevent the arrival of what it defined as undesirable and unassimilable immigrants. According to the 1952 Immigration Act, the government could prohibit the entry of people for any of the following reasons:

i)   nationality, citizenship, ethnic group, occupation, class or geographical area of origin;
ii) peculiar customs, habits, modes of life or methods of holding property;
iii) unsuitability having regard to the climatic, economic, social, industrial, educational, health or other conditions, or requirements existing temporarily or otherwise;
iv) probable inability to become readily assimilated or to assume the duties and responsibilities of Canadian citizenship within a reasonable time after their admission.
(Satzewich 1991, 124–5).

If anything, the list is comprehensive in terms of the number of criteria for exclusion and for the flexibility it gave immigration officials to prevent the arrival of the 'unsuitable immigrant'. However, one variable notably absent from the list is 'race'. This was not accidental. In fact, in previous incarnations of the Immigration Act, 'race' was a ground for exclusion. Why did it disappear from the books after the Second World War? Did it indicate that 'race' did not matter in the selection of immigrants?

Part of the reason that the 'race' category was taken out of the postwar Act was that Canada and Canadians had gone to war in part to fight a regime that had committed terrible atrocities against Jews and others in the name of 'race'. Hitler and his National

Socialist party had exterminated six million Jews because they believed that Jews were 'racially' inferior. As more and more of the wartime atrocities flowing from 'racial' ideology came to light in the immediate aftermath of the war, many countries around the world felt deeply uncomfortable about having official social and immigration policies that were based on the same underlying assumptions of Nazi 'racial' doctrine. Thus, it would have been politically embarrassing for Canada to leave the category of 'race' on the books as a ground for exclusion and risk unfavourable references and comparisons between Canada and the Nazi regime. By taking the 'race' category out of the Immigration Act but leaving in a wide range of apparently 'non-racial' grounds for possible exclusion, the 1952 Immigration Act gave the government and its officials a certain degree of deniability when it came to public criticisms of immigration policy.

One area where this deniability came in handy was in the way that federal immigration officials dealt with the 'problem' of immigration from the Caribbean. After the war, representatives of a number of Caribbean governments and Canadian employer organizations lobbied the federal government to open the door to black immigration from the Caribbean. Employers such as fruit and vegetable farmers in Ontario were having trouble finding and keeping European immigrants and Canadians as employees and became particularly interested in recruiting workers from the Caribbean. Newly independent Caribbean governments were also interested in finding opportunities for their nationals to migrate in order to ease unemployment problems and lobbied Canadian officials to permit more immigration from their countries (Satzewich 1991, 148–9).

Federal government officials, however, were reluctant to admit black workers from the Caribbean, in part because of the old-style racist concerns that characterized pre-World War II immigration policy and control: namely, black people could not assimilate into life in a fast-paced, competitive, capitalist society; they were unsuited to climatic conditions in Canada; and their presence would cause the emergence of 'race relations' problems. In 1952, the minister of immigration explained the position of his department on the issue of black migration to Canada:

> . . . in light of experience it would be unrealistic to say that immigrants who have spent the greater part of their life in tropical countries become readily adapted to the Canadian mode of life which, to no small extent, is determined by climatic conditions. It is a matter of record that natives of such countries are more apt to break down in health than immigrants from countries where the climate is more akin to that of Canada. It is equally true that, generally speaking, persons from tropical countries find it more difficult to succeed in the highly competitive Canadian economy (cited in Satzewich 1991, 127).

In 1964, the Department of Citizenship and Immigration explained that

> . . . although Canada may not discriminate racially in its immigration policies we cannot deny the right of a state to decide its own social and racial composition and refuse to accept immigrants whose presence would cause severe disruptions or drastic change (cited in Satzewich 1991, 134).

What is interesting about these statements is the disjuncture between the reality of immigration control, which was saturated by a concern over preserving the existing 'racial' makeup of Canada, and the reluctance of Canadian government officials to admit publicly that 'race' was a factor shaping whom they would allow into the country.

It took a decade and a half after the Second World War for the Canadian government to take the first genuine steps toward eliminating racist assumptions and practices from its immigrant admission criteria. In 1962, the federal government finally came clean and publicly admitted what most critics knew all along: that racist criteria were being used to select immigrants but that these criteria would no longer be in operation (Avery 1995, 176). In 1967, further measures were taken to rationalize immigrant selection and make it fairer through the introduction of the points system. That system, which has evolved and changed over the years and which will be discussed in more detail in chapter 3, involved the selection of immigrants on the basis of a combination of largely objective criteria such as age, educational background, English and French language abilities, and job skills and experience. As can be seen in table 2.1, it opened the door to a greater proportion of immigrants from Asia, Africa, the Caribbean, and South America coming to Canada.

Explaining the deracialization of immigration control

Why were racist selection criteria publicly abandoned by the government in the mid-1960s? Three explanations have been offered.

First, some argue that the deracialization of immigration control in Canada was largely the initiative of liberal, enlightened, and forward-thinking bureaucrats in the immigration department who increasingly found 'racial' discrimination distasteful (Hawkins 1988). This bureaucratic-centred approach is problematic in that it assumes that there was a genuine interest on the part of these officials to eliminate 'racial' discrimination in the early 1960s. Again, perception and reality collide: at the same time that the federal government was claiming it had eliminated racist selection

Table 2.1   Percentage of Immigrants to Canada by Major Source Area, 1950–5, 2000–4

Area	1950–5 %	2000–4 %
Africa and the Middle East	0.4	19.1
Asia and the Pacific	3.6	50.3
South and Central America	1.5	8.3
United States	6.3	2.6
Europe and the United Kingdom	88.0	19.7
Other/not stated	0.2	0.0

Source: Figures for 1950–5 compiled from Canada. Department of Manpower and Immigration. *Immigration statistics.* Figures for 2000–4 compiled from Citizenship and Immigration Canada. 2004. *Facts and figures 2004: Immigration overview.* <http//:www.cic.gc.ca/English/pub/facts2004/permanent/12.html>.

criteria, racist attitudes within the bureaucracy continued to affect decision-making about which groups should be let into the country and their conditions of entry (Satzewich 1991).

A second, related explanation focuses on the liability that 'racial' discrimination posed for Canada's international relations. After the war, Canada was emerging as a middle power, and Canadian officials were becoming increasingly involved in mediating international conflicts. The existence of a 'racially' discriminatory immigration policy was an international embarrassment and undermined the credibility of Canada in its efforts to act as a neutral international mediator and problem-solver. Consequently, some argue that international political considerations played an important role in the public abandonment of racist immigrant selection criteria.

A third explanation focuses on the changing nature of the Canadian economy and changing assessments of where suitably qualified immigrants might come from in future. Some commentators argue that the Canadian economy was undergoing a transformation from resource extraction to a more diverse industrial base. A resource extraction-based economy requires large numbers of relatively unskilled workers who do the heavy work of logging, mining, and the like. Technological innovations had reduced the demand for these kinds of workers, and white-collar types of employment became more and more important. Further, this argument suggests that European workers, particularly skilled workers, would be harder to recruit because there was growing competition for Europeans from countries like Australia and the United States and because the rising tide of economic prosperity in Europe made it more difficult to persuade them to leave in the first place. As a result, this argument suggests, the deracialization of immigration control was not so much rooted in ideological considerations but rather in hard-headed, practical economic considerations about the kind of workers the economy needed and a recognition that the search for that kind of worker would have to be global for the country to remain economically prosperous and competitive.

SUMMARY

The recruitment of immigrants in the late nineteenth and early twentieth centuries and early measures developed to deal with the presence of Aboriginal peoples in Canada were part of the federal government's efforts to promote capitalist economic development, commercial farming, and the creation of a Canadian nation. These economic and political priorities help set the wider context for the way that immigration and Aboriginal/non-Aboriginal relations in Canada were managed. The process of state formation involves more than the creation of political boundaries, government offices, and houses of Parliament. It also involves the creation of citizens, national identities, and 'populations' willing and able to be governed. As we have seen in this chapter, the creation of a governable population in this country was a complex matter. Different classes and groups of people had different ideas of who might constitute a good worker and a good citizen, what a good citizen looked like physically, and how individuals and groups who did not initially appear to possess the right qualities of citizenship might be able to acquire those qualities. Further, some groups were defined as 'racially' unsuited to become part of the population and members of the emerging Canadian nation. As we will continue to show in later chapters, the policies and practices that emerged in this context produced outcomes that had powerful implications at the time and continue to reverberate today.

Questions for Critical Thought

1. To what extent is it accurate to describe Quebec before the Quiet Revolution of the 1960s as a place where 'capital speaks English and workers speak French'?
2. How do Quebec's immigration and interculturalism policies differ from wider Canadian immigration and multiculturalism policies?
3. Why are the treaties agreed to by Aboriginal peoples and government officials many decades ago still relevant to understanding patterns of social conflict between Aboriginal/non-Aboriginal peoples today?
4. What factors have shaped historical patterns of immigration to Canada?
5. What motivated some Canadians in the early twentieth century to want to stop immigrants from China and India from coming to this country?
6. Critically assess the various explanations that have been offered for the deracialization of immigration control in the late 1960s.

Annotated Additional Readings

Avery, Donald. 1995. *Reluctant host: Canada's response to immigrant workers, 1896–1994.* Toronto: McClelland and Stewart. An outstanding analysis of the history of immigration to Canada.

Miller, James. 2000. *Skyscrapers hide the heavens: A history of Indian-white relations in Canada.* Toronto: University of Toronto Press. A comprehensive history, including an extensive discussion of treaties and residential schools.

Satzewich, Vic. 1991. *Racism and the incorporation of foreign labour: Farm labour migration to Canada since 1945.* London: Routledge. A discussion of postwar immigration policy, with a central focus on the issue of racism.

Titley, Brian. 1986. *A narrow vision: Duncan Campbell Scott and the administration of Indian Affairs in Canada.* Vancouver: University of British Columbia Press. An excellent analysis of the federal government's policy of assimilation of Aboriginal peoples.

Related Websites

The Assembly of First Nations: http://www.afn.ca/.
Indian and Northern Affairs Canada: http://www.ainc-inac.gc.ca/.
Citizenship and Immigration Canada: http://www.cic.gc.ca/.
Pier 21, Halifax: http://www.pier21.ca/.
Multicultural History Society of Ontario: http://www.mhso.ca/.

Chapter 3

Immigration and the Canadian Mosaic

Learning objectives

In this chapter you will learn that:

- While Canada is a major immigrant-receiving country, many other countries around the world accept immigrants.
- Immigrants are admitted to Canada for a variety of economic and demographic reasons.
- Canada's adherence to the 'safe third country' principle is controversial because it may place vulnerable refugees in further danger.
- Family class immigrants are not a drain on the Canadian economy.
- Immigration officers have a tremendous amount of discretion in evaluating applications for permanent residence in Canada. Some claim that this is one of the ways that racism continues to affect the selection of immigrants.
- Many Canadians have ambivalent attitudes toward business class immigrants
- Migrant workers are subject to exploitative working and living conditions in this country.
- Illegal immigration is a growing concern in both Canada and the United States.

INTRODUCTION

Over the past five years, nearly 1.2 million new immigrants have come to call Canada home. Few other countries in the world admit more immigrants on a per capita basis than Canada. In 2001, 18.4 per cent of the population of Canada was born outside of the country. This was the highest proportion of foreign-born in Canada since 1931. In 2001, immigrants made up 43.7 per cent of the population of

Toronto and 37.5 per cent of the population of Vancouver. Other large and medium-sized Canadian cities also have relatively significant immigrant populations: 18.4 per cent of the population of Montreal, 20.9 per cent of Calgary, 17.8 per cent of Edmonton, and 21.8 per cent of Ottawa was made up of immigrants, according to the 2001 census.

At the same time, it is also worth noting that large swaths of Canada remain largely untouched by recent immigration. As figure 3.1 shows, Newfoundland and Labrador, Nova Scotia, New Brunswick, Prince Edward Island, and Saskatchewan were the intended destinations of only 2.2 per cent of the 262,236 immigrants admitted to the country in 2005. Ontario attracted 53.6 per cent, Quebec 16.5 per cent, British Columbia 17.1 per cent, Alberta 7.4 per cent, and Manitoba 3.1 per cent of all immigrants who came to Canada that year.

As noted in chapter 2, before 1962 Canada's immigration system was characterized by a distinct preference for white immigrants from Europe and the United States. While small numbers of visible minorities were allowed entry to Canada under highly restrictive quotas and other special arrangements during the early postwar years, there was a general feeling among government officials and many members of the Canadian public that non-white immigration was harmful to the long-term social, political, and economic stability of the country. In the early 1960s, the door to immigration began to open gradually to more and more immigrants from outside of the United States and the traditional European source countries. Between 1947 and 1955, Europe supplied 87.1 per cent of all immigrants to Canada, but between 1979 and 2000, Europe's share of total immigration declined to 22.5 per

Figure 3.1   **Permanent Residents by Province or Territory, 2005 (Showing Percentage Distribution)**

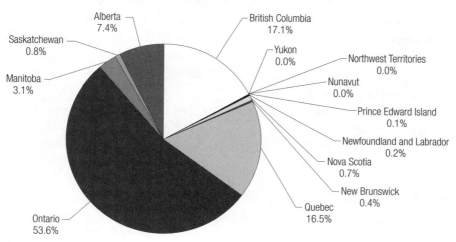

Source: Canada. Citizenship and Immigration Canada. 2005. Facts and figures, 2005.
http://www.cic.gc.ca/english/pub/facts2005/permanent/17.html.

cent. Now, as table 3.1 shows, six of the top 10 sources of new immigrants to Canada are countries in either Asia or the Middle East.

In this chapter, we consider a number of controversies and debates about the contemporary immigration system. We focus on the following questions: Why does Canada admit immigrants? Where do immigrants come from? Why are some people from other parts of the world admitted as immigrants and others admitted as migrant workers? To what extent does 'race' continue to play a role in the process of immigration to Canada?

WHY IMMIGRATION?

Why does Canada have immigration? Journalist Daniel Stoffman's answer to this question is that:

> There are the official reasons, the real reasons, and the ideal reasons. Officially, we could not survive without immigration and would be foolish not to have more of it. As no evidence exists to support the official version, Canadians are supposed to accept it on faith. They are 'un-Canadian' if they don't. The real reasons Canada has immigration are that it helps the Liberal Party stay in power; it depresses wages, thereby transferring billions of dollars from workers to employers; and it benefits certain powerful industries, including the industry the program itself has created (2002, 186–7).

Stoffman's provocative answer to why Canada has immigration is problematic, not least because it assumes that immigration is unique to Canada and that there are peculiarly political circumstances in the country that lead us to admit relatively large

Table 3.1   Top Ten Sources of Immigrants to Canada, 2005

Source countries	Number	Percentage distribution
China, People's Republic of	42,291	16.1
India	33,146	12.6
Philippines	17,525	6.7
Pakistan	13,576	5.2
United States	9,262	3.5
Colombia	6,031	2.3
United Kingdom	5,865	2.2
Korea, Republic of	5,819	2.2
Iran	5,502	2.1
France	5,430	2.1
Top 10 source countries	144,447	55.1
Other countries	117,789	44.9
Total	262,236	100

Source: Canada. Citizenship and Immigration Canada. 2005. *Facts and figures, 2005: Immigration overview.*
<http://www.cic.gc.ca/english/pub/facts2005/permanent/12.html>.

numbers of immigrants. As noted above, Canada is undoubtedly one of the world's major immigrant-receiving nations. Even though a central element of Canadian national mythology is that 'Canada is a country of immigrants', other countries can just as legitimately make similar claims. Immigrants make up 23.4 per cent of the population of Australia, 19 per cent of Switzerland, 9.8 per cent of the United States, 9.1 per cent of Austria, and 8.9 per cent of Germany. Moreover, immigration is not just a feature of advanced Western nations. Immigrants and migrant workers also make up significant portions of the population and labour force in a number of countries in Asia and the Middle East (Castles and Miller 2003, 154–77). For example, in 2000 there were 590,000 migrant workers living in Singapore, 380,000 in Taiwan, 312,000 in South Korea, and 665,000 in Thailand. Migrant workers in Singapore came from Malaysia, Thailand, Indonesia, the Philippines, Sri Lanka, and China and made up 28 per cent of the labour force in the tiny republic (Castles and Miller 2003, 162–7). In the Persian Gulf states in the late 1990s, migrant workers made up 28 per cent of the labour force in Saudi Arabia, 65 per cent in Kuwait, 65 per cent in Bahrain, 77 per cent in Qatar, and 73 per cent in the United Arab Emirates (Castles and Miller 2003, 159–60).

Since many other countries also admit migrant workers and immigrants, we should be sceptical of explanations of Canadian immigration, such as the one offered by Stoffman, that focus solely on factors unique to Canada. There are undoubtedly unique social and political circumstances that lead to immigration to specific countries, but there are also wider social and economic considerations that lead to immigration in general, regardless of national context. These broader factors need to be understood in order to fully understand why immigration occurs.

There are a number of theoretical perspectives that seek to explain international migration (Massey 1999). Some theories focus on the 'push' factors that lead groups to leave their countries of origin, while others focus on 'pull' factors that attract individuals to immigrant-receiving societies. Some theoretical traditions attempt to understand both sets of dynamics within the same framework. This chapter cannot discuss in any detail the complex push factors that lead people to leave their countries of origin. However, among the significant factors are poverty, inequality, repressive political systems, and blocked opportunity for mobility (Massey 1999).

The political economy of immigration

From the perspective of political economy, immigration has traditionally been viewed within immigrant-receiving countries as a tool in the process of capital accumulation (Castles and Kosack 1984). From this perspective, countries do not admit immigrants out of a sense of altruism or obligation to help people in difficult social and economic circumstances in their countries of origin. Instead, national immigration policies are seen as mechanisms to supply workers for various industries. Immigrants have been admitted by various countries and are of value for the role they play in the economy; they are, in the words of Castles and Kosack (1984), 'tools that assist in the process of capital accumulation'—or 'factory fodder' in the words of Australian economist Jock Collins (1988).

Despite coming from different political starting points, there is a certain affinity between the analysis of immigration offered by political economists and by commentators like Stoffman. According to some of the early claims made within the political economy perspective, there are a number of reasons that immigrants are so important to the process of capitalist expansion. First, the cost of producing educated and skilled immigrant workers is borne in another country, thus resulting in significant savings for the receiving society. That is, in recruiting and admitting individuals who are already educated, trained, and skilled in the work they do, receiving societies like Canada save considerable public expenditure that would otherwise have gone into educating and training native-born workers. For example, in 1996 immigrant men made up 22 per cent of all men in managerial occupations, 23 per cent of all men in professional occupations, and 32 per cent of all men in food and beverage services. Immigrant women comprised 20 per cent of all women in managerial occupations, 39 per cent of all women in manufacturing and processing, and 22 per cent of all women in travel and recreation-related services (Li 2003, 97). One estimate suggests that between 1967 and 1987, Canada benefited to the tune of $42.9 billion in post-secondary educational training that immigrants brought with them to Canada (Devortez and Laryea 1998; Li 2003, 98). Some analysts consider this as money that Canada would have had to spend on training Canadians to take up jobs. This is, incidentally, why some commentators argue that 'south to north' migration is contributing to the brain drain from less developed countries and that immigration is in fact a form of development aid that poor, underdeveloped countries provide to developed countries like Canada.

Second, political economists argue that because of their socio-economic vulnerability, immigrants are willing to take jobs that native-born workers avoid because they are poorly paid, difficult, dangerous, or otherwise unattractive. Immigrants, according to this perspective, do the 'dirty work' of a society.

Third, political economists suggest that immigration is used by employers as a way of disorganizing the working class. According to some versions of political economy, racism, ethnocentrism, and prejudice are mechanisms that employers use to promote disunity among workers. By promoting ideologies that identify immigrant workers as the source of native-born workers' socio-economic problems, employers are able to divide and conquer the working class and weaken efforts on the part of workers to organize collectively and pursue their wider common class interests.

Though originally developed in the 1970s, many of the broader assumptions of this classical political economy framework have been picked up by a number of Canadian scholars particularly critical of the recent 'neo-liberal' turn in Canadian immigration. According to Abu-Laban and Gabriel (2002), neo-liberalism is a set of assumptions about the proper functioning of government in the era of globalization. These assumptions include 'a more limited role for the state and, consequently, an emphasis on cutting back state policies and programs; a greater stress on individual self-sufficiency; and a belief that free markets are efficient allocators of goods and services' (Abu-Laban and Gabriel 2002, 21). Critics of neo-liberalism argue that immigration policy-making has been hijacked by business interests and more recently by an American-driven security agenda. They contend that recent changes in the immigration system are rooted in part in a desire to keep Canadian industry globally competitive. According to Abu Laban and Gabriel:

> ... large numbers of immigrants have always been selected on the basis of their ability to contribute to the Canadian economy. This is accentuated and consolidated in current developments. In response to the perceived economic imperatives of globalization, the 'best' immigrants, and by extension prospective citizens, are those whose labour market skills will enhance Canada's competitive position in a world economy (2002, 62).

There is some evidence to support some of the broad contentions about immigration made by political economists, critics of the current immigration system, and commentators like Stoffman. Generally, employers in Canada and in other countries have historically been in favour of maintaining a robust immigration program and relatively open borders in order to facilitate the arrival of immigrants. For example, at the turn of the twentieth century, business elites involved in railway construction, shipping, and mining were one of the only segments of British Columbia society in favour of Chinese immigration; trade unions as well as white women's and small business organizations opposed it because they saw Chinese immigrants as threats to their economic and social well-being and the future of BC as a 'white man's province' (Roy 1989). Employers, on the other hand, valued their relatively cheap labour power and lobbied the federal government to continue to allow Chinese workers into Canada (Satzewich 1989).

Furthermore, because of their social and economic vulnerability, some immigrants are willing to take jobs that native-born Canadian avoid. For example, farm labour, domestic labour, housekeeping, and child-minding have been jobs that Canadian-born men and women have historically avoided like the plague. Farm work is difficult, relatively poorly paid given the arduous nature of the work, and not covered under many provinces' labour standards legislation. Domestic work is also characterized by long hours, poor pay, and the intense regulation of personal lives. Canadian-born workers are keen to leave these jobs when better job offers in other industries present themselves. As a result, farmers and middle-class families in need of nannies and housekeepers have historically had to rely on the government's recruitment of immigrants to fill job vacancies in these relatively unattractive sectors (Satzewich 1991; Bakan and Stasiulis 1997). It is important to remember that this dynamic is not unique to Canada. In many Persian Gulf states, better-paying public sector jobs are reserved for citizens of the country, and poorer-paying jobs in construction, agriculture, and domestic service are filled by migrant workers from India, Pakistan, Bangladesh, and Sri Lanka (Castles and Miller 2003, 159–60).

At the same time, there is little evidence to suggest that racism is a conspiracy cooked up behind the closed doors of capitalist industry in order to disorganize the Canadian working class. Racism, as we will see in chapter 6, is not the exclusive domain of one class, nor does it necessarily have only one logical consequence. As discussed in chapter 2, racism in British Columbia society in the 1910s and 1920s eventually resulted in fewer opportunities for capitalists to bring in and exploit Chinese workers.

Nor is it the case that the presence of immigrants necessarily depresses wages. Research on the macroeconomic consequences of immigration has produced varying results, in part because of different assumptions and models used in the calculations. Research suggests, however, that immigrants make less use of the employment insurance program than native-born Canadians (Li 2003, 87), that immigrants create jobs through their demand for goods and services, and that immigrants generally pay more in taxes than they withdraw in the form of publicly funded government services (Li 2003, 86; Preston et al. 2003).

Immigration: broader considerations

The political economy perspective has certain strengths and weaknesses when it comes to explaining why Canada, along with many other countries around the world, currently needs, wants, and admits immigrants. However, even with its strengths, it is not a complete explanation. Though broadly defined economic conditions and labour market factors do drive much of the process of immigration, a number of other factors also shape contemporary immigration flows and patterns. First, demographic considerations underlie at least some of the current emphasis on the recruitment of new immigrants. Even though population aging may be somewhat exaggerated as an impending social problem (Stoffman 2002), Canada, as well as many other economically advanced Western countries, is facing the demographic reality of declining birth rates and population aging. In this context, immigration is a means of mitigating some of the negative consequences of population aging, such as increasing tax burdens and worker shortages.

Canada is not alone in its concern over the 'ticking time bomb' of demographics. Spain, for example, has one of the lowest birth rates in the European Union. In the 1960s and 1970s, Spain was a country of emigration. It supplied hundreds of thousands of workers to countries like France, Germany, and Switzerland to fuel their postwar economies (Castles and Miller 2003, 71). Spain is now turning into a major immigrant-receiving country, actively recruiting Spanish-speaking immigrants from Latin America. Moreover, every year thousands of individuals from North Africa, Latin America, and eastern Europe enter Spain illegally (Cornelius 2004). Since 1986, Spain has implemented at least five amnesties for the thousands of illegal immigrants currently living in the country in the hope that with the legal right to live there, they will settle, work, form families, have children, and thus help to offset the effects of a declining birth rate and population aging (Cornelius 2004).

Second, immigration flows are diverse, and not all immigration flows are about recruiting workers. While critics are right to be cynical about some of the claims made about the humanitarian nature of Canada's immigration program, Canada does have a record of humanitarianism in the field of immigration that it deserves to be rightfully proud of.

Third, immigration policy is also formulated out of a complex set of pressures and social relations. Though business-based interests do play a major role in shaping immigration policy, other groups like trade unions, church groups, non-governmental organizations, political parties, and bureaucrats themselves also play a role in shaping the overall direction of immigration policy (Hardcastle et al. 1994).

Finally, immigrants are more than just worker bees who create wealth that is appropriated by capitalist employers. Immigrants are human subjects with particular bundles of social, personal, and economic capabilities, characteristics, and potentials. Immigrants have been—and are—part of Canada's wider nation-building project, where the hope and expectation is that they will eventually become 'Canadians', however ambiguous the term. Potential immigrants have been—and are—evaluated on the basis of their economic capabilities as well as their wider capacity to contribute to the social reproduction of Canadian society. As a result, assessments of the ability of immigrants to 'fit in' or 'adjust' to Canada have played an important role in regulating who gets in.

The criteria for assessing how individuals might 'fit in' have changed. Even though some people feel that being Canadian is intangible and difficult to quantify, the writers of the guide to preparing for the Canadian citizenship test (part of which is excerpted in box 3.1) had little difficulty in describing who Canadians are and the kinds of values and responsibilities that Canadians have.

In sum, though simplistic, Stoffman's answer to the question of why Canada has immigration provides a useful foil to consider the broader reasons associated with why immigrants come to Canada. While there may be powerful political and economic interests behind certain recent policy changes and initiatives, immigration is a complicated process that does not lend itself to simplistic analysis.

Box 3.1 What Does Canadian Citizenship Mean?

The following is an excerpt from *A look at Canada*, produced by Citizenship and Immigration Canada for people applying for Canadian citizenship. Immigrants are selected in part on the basis of how well they will adopt the values and responsibilities of being a Canadian.

> *Canadian values include freedom, respect for cultural differences and a commitment to social justice. We are proud of the fact that we are a peaceful nation. In fact, Canadians act as peacekeepers in many countries around the world.*

Canada is a large country with a small population. We have developed a unique federal style of government that is based on compromise and coexistence. We value our **democracy**, and every citizen is encouraged to do his or her share. Our laws are based on our **democratic values**. Canadian values include:

Equality—We respect everyone's rights. Everyone has the right to speak out and express ideas that others might disagree with. Governments must treat everyone with equal dignity and respect—two other fundamental Canadian values.

Respect for cultural differences—We try to understand and appreciate the cultures and traditions of all Canadians, whether they were born in Canada or came here from another country.

Freedom—As Canadians, we enjoy basic freedoms, such as freedom of thought, freedom of speech, freedom of religion and freedom of peaceful assembly.

Peace—We are proud of our non-violent society and our international role as peacekeepers.

Law and order—We respect democratic decision making and the 'rule of law'. We promote due process so that the courts and the police treat everyone fairly and reasonably. We ensure that our elected governments remain accountable to Canadians.

As you reflect on these values, ask yourself which responsibilities you will take on when you become a Canadian citizen.

Source: Canada. Citizenship and Immigration Canada. 2002. *A look at Canada.* Ottawa: Minister of Public Works and Government Services.

CONTEMPORARY IMMIGRATION CATEGORIES: DEBATES AND CONTROVERSIES

Canada's immigration system is complex. There are a number of ways that individuals can come to Canada as legal permanent residents, but at its simplest, individuals can gain permanent residence status in Canada in four main ways: as skilled workers, as refugees, as business class immigrants, and as family class immigrants. Table 3.2 provides information on the number and proportion of immigrants in each category admitted in 2005. Each of the four mechanisms for gaining permanent resident status carries certain controversies. Debates have arisen over the philosophy and administrative practices behind each category, the hidden agendas, and the social and economic consequences of each category of admission. Though ethnic and 'racial' considerations are no longer part of the official immigration policy, there are a number of ways that ethnicity and 'race' are presumed to impinge on contemporary controversies surrounding immigration. In this section, we highlight and evaluate some of the controversies associated with specific immigration categories.

Table 3.2   Number and Categories of Immigrants Admitted to Canada, 2005

Family class		Skilled workers		Business immigrants		Refugees		Others		Total	
N	%	N	%	N	%	N	%	N	%	N	%
63,352	24.2	142,842	54.5	13,469	5.1	35,768	13.6	6,796	2.6	262,236	100

Source: Canada. Citizenship and Immigration Canada. 2005. *Facts and figures 2005: Immigration overview.*
<http://www.cic.gc.ca/english/pub/facts2005/overview/1.html>.

Refugees

In 2005, Canada admitted 35,768 refugees, who made up 13.6 per cent of the total flow of immigrants to Canada that year. There are two general components to Canada's refugee system: (1) the Refugee and Humanitarian Resettlement Program; and (2) the In-Canada Refugee Protection Process.

The first program is intended for people seeking refugee status from outside of Canada. In many cases, these people are the 'stereotypical' refugees with whom we are most familiar because of heart-wrenching media images of squalid refugee camps or columns of refugees desperately trying to flee their country in times of civil war or ethnic cleansing. There are three subcategories of refugee that Canada admits under this program. The convention refugees abroad class refers to people who are outside of their country of citizenship or habitual residence and have a well-founded fear of persecution for reasons of 'race', religion, political opinion, nationality, or membership in a particular social group. The country of asylum class includes people who are outside their country of citizenship or habitual residence and are seriously and personally affected by civil war, armed conflict, or massive violations of human rights. The source country class includes people who are still in their countries of origin but nevertheless meet the definition of a convention refugee. This subcategory also includes people who have been detained or imprisoned and are suffering serious deprivation of the right to freedom of expression, the right of dissent, or the right to engage in trade union activity. Only citizens or residents of certain countries with known records of human rights violation are eligible to come to Canada under this provision.

Canada works with the United Nations High Commission for Refugees, which determines the legitimacy of individual claims for refugee status under one of the above three subcategories. In 1995, it was estimated that there were more than 15 million refugees and asylum-seekers in need of protection and assistance around the world; another 20 million people were in refugee-like situations and also in need of protection but were not officially recognized by the UN as refugees or asylum-seekers (Castles and Miller 2003, 5). In a sense, the UN-certified refugees constitute a pool from which Canada and other countries select refugees for resettlement. In Canada, provincial governments and charitable organizations can also act as sponsors of refugees.

The In-Canada Refugee Protection Process is the refugee determination system for individuals already in Canada. In its 1985 *Singh* decision, the Supreme Court of Canada ruled that non-Canadians, if they are on Canadian soil, are covered by many of the protections of the Canadian Charter of Rights and Freedoms (Pratt 2005, 66). It also ruled that all refugee claimants in Canada have the right to an oral hearing to determine the legitimacy of their case. In that context, the federal government established the Immigration and Refugee Board (IRB) to adjudicate in-Canada refugee claims. Individuals who present themselves at a Canadian port of entry or a Canadian immigration centre in Canada can claim refugee status. Individuals qualify as a refugee if the Immigration and Refugee Board determines that the person is a convention refugee—a person outside of their country of nationality or habitual residence and unable or unwilling to return to their country because of a well-founded fear of persecution for reasons of 'race', religion, political opinion, nationality, or membership in a particular social group. Alternatively, individuals must prove that they are in need of protection because their removal from Canada to their country of origin would subject them to the possibility of torture, risk to life, or risk of cruel and unusual treatment or punishment (Canada. Citizenship and Immigration Canada 2003c).

Canada adheres to the 'safe third country' principle, which prevents individuals from making a refugee claim in Canada if they have already found a safe haven in another country. This principle is intended to deter 'asylum shopping'—situations in which individuals seek refugee status in one country even though they have already secured a safe haven in another country. However, critics argue that by agreeing to this principle, Canada is indirectly turning its back on some genuine refugees and indirectly sending them back to strife-torn situations where their lives are in danger. For example, through the In-Canada Refugee Protection Process, Canada accepts some refugee claims from individuals from Colombia. The United States government, however, generally does not accept refugee claims made by individuals from Colombia. Difficulties and double standards arise when some Colombians manage to enter the United States but subsequently try to gain entry to Canada in order to claim refugee status here. Because they are in a 'safe third country'—the United States—they are either turned back at the border or not allowed to make a refugee claim in Canada and are returned to the US. Even though the refugee claimant might temporarily have a safe haven in the United States, there is no guarantee that the US will accept their refugee claim and not return them to a dangerous situation in Colombia. Critics point out that had the refugee claimant managed to arrive directly in Canada, their case would likely have been adjudicated differently and they would have been allowed to stay.

At the same time, Canada's refugee determination system is ahead of the curve on many issues. To its credit, Canada was the first refugee-receiving country to accept gender-based persecution as a basis on which an individual can make a successful refugee claim. In a different context, American authorities criticize Canada for considering recent refugee claims by American soldiers who have refused to fight in Iraq and deserted the American armed forces. The Immigration and Refugee Board is currently hearing at least two high-profile cases of American servicemen who argue that they face persecution in the United States if they are forced to return there.

Some critics have suggested that Canada's willingness to consider in-country refugee claims through the In-Canada Refugee Protection Process is fundamentally flawed and helping to undermine the future stability and prosperity of the country. While they support efforts by the Canadian government and the international refugee protection agency to resettle bona fide refugees, they are less supportive of the system that allows individuals to apply for refugee status in Canada. They suggest that the in-Canada system is too lax and in fact encourages individuals to make bogus refugee claims as a way of bypassing the other legitimate channels for acquiring permanent resident status in Canada. According to Stoffman (2002, 154) 'most of those making refugee claims in Canada are not refugees but immigrants using the refugee system to cut to the front of the immigration line'.

Henry and Tator (2002, 113) argue that *National Post* columnist Diane Francis has undertaken a 'crusade' against the In-Canada Refugee Protection Process. Francis alleges, among other things, that 'most refugee claims are bogus', that 'refugees are "illegal" entrants to this country', that 'refugees "defraud" out [*sic*] system by hiring lawyers, using court time . . .', that 'refugees use millions in tax dollars pressing their claims through the system', that 'refugees are a health hazard to Canadians; they bring illness and even death to Canadian citizens', and that 'Ottawa's refugee determination system is flawed, expensive and unwieldy and allows too many bogus refugees into the country'.

Other critics have suggested that international criminal and terrorist organizations use the relatively generous nature of the refugee determination system to gain entry to Canada to further their criminal and terrorist objectives and to cause harm to Canada and its neighbours. Henry and Tator (2002) also argue that the *National Post* has targeted the Tamil community in Canada as a particular object of opprobrium, carrying out a campaign against this community. There are between 160,000 and 200,000 Tamil speakers in Canada, and many of them are refugees. Henry and Tator (2002) argue that the newspaper has carried out a sustained attack against some Tamil organizations, alleging that they are fronts for the Tamil Tigers—what the *National Post* terms an insurgent terrorist organization but what others term 'freedom-fighters' whose goal is to establish a state for themselves in Sri Lanka.

Other analysts have criticized the makeup and methods by which members of the Immigration and Refugee Board are appointed. The procedures undertaken by the board have changed over the years, and it remains a much-maligned body. Individuals are appointed by the cabinet, and some critics have charged that it is staffed by patronage appointees, 'refugee advocates', and 'refugee lawyers' (Stoffman 2002, 162; see also Francis 2002). Critics have questioned both the competence of IRB members and their objectivity. They have suggested that the IRB has been taken over by the so-called immigration and refugee industry that has a direct material interest in maintaining the many layers of appeal within the system. Some argue that members are too sympathetic to refugees, that some are much more likely to accept claims than others, and that some are inherently sympathetic to refugee claims.

There is no question that Canada's refugee determination system is among the most generous in the world. Compared to those of other countries, Canada's system bends over backwards to give refugee claimants a fair chance to make their case. Further, there is no doubt that some individuals who are not genuine refugees use the refugee determination system as a way of bypassing the other mechanisms to gain legal permanent residence status or use the system as a pretext to come to Canada to further terrorist or other criminal objectives. However, where critics tend to go wrong is that they exaggerate the extent of the problems. Furthermore, no country is immune to individuals intent on crossing borders in order to cause harm; international criminal and terrorist organizations are extremely clever in the way they negotiate borders, and no country has devised a perfect system for balancing considerations of justice with considerations of security.

Skilled workers

The largest category of immigrants to Canada is made up of skilled workers. As noted in table 3.2, the 142,842 skilled workers and their families admitted to Canada in 2005 made up more than one half (54.5 per cent) of the 262,236 immigrants admitted to the country that year.

Skilled workers must meet a number of criteria in order to be admitted. For example, there are minimum work experience requirements. From time to time, the federal government identifies certain types and levels of skill in demand in Canada, and applicants must have a minimum of one year of experience during the previous 10-year period in one of the predetermined skill types or levels. In addition, applicants must meet certain minimum financial requirements if they do not have arranged employment in Canada. Skilled workers who bring three family members to Canada must have a minimum of $17,286 in their possession to show that they can support themselves after they arrive in Canada (Canada. Citizenship and Immigration Canada 2003d).

Beyond these basic minimum requirements, applicants are also assessed according to a points system. The system originated in 1967 and since then has been modified a number of times. Currently, there are six selection factors, each carrying a different weight: education, official language ability, work experience, age, the existence of arranged employment, and adaptability. Table 3.3 shows an abridged version of the points system. The 'pass mark' is 67 out of a maximum 100 points. In some ways, the pass mark, along with the other minimum requirements, represents an initial entry point into the application process. Applicants who meet these minimal conditions are interviewed by a Canadian immigration officer, who can exercise both 'positive' and 'negative' discretion. Positive discretion occurs in cases in which individuals who do not earn the requisite number of points for immigration to Canada may still be granted permanent residence status because an immigration officer believes that they are likely to be 'good' for Canada. Negative discretion occurs in cases in which an immigration officer denies an application for permanent residence even though the applicant may have earned the minimum number of points (Bouchard and Wake Carol 2002).

The exercise of discretion by immigration officers is a controversial aspect of Canada's immigration system. In previous versions of the points system, immigration officers could allocate discretionary points for what was termed 'personal suitability': they could use their discretion and award points based on their perception of the applicant's adaptability, motivation, initiative, and resourcefulness (Jakobowski 1997, 20). Discretion is controversial because some analysts believe that it is one of the ways that 'racial' discrimination can creep into the immigrant selection system (Pratt 2005). Critics argue that under previous versions of the points system, it was harder for visible minority immigrants to earn discretionary points for personal suitability. In the 1980s, Anderson and Frideres argued that

> depending on the selection officer's bias (or views about racial groups), the applicant can receive zero points in this category, thus lessening the applicant's chance of entering Canada. As the saying goes, 'If you're White, you're right, if you're Brown, stick around and if you're Black, stand back' (1980, 227).

Table 3.3   Selection Grid for Skilled Workers and Business Immigrants

Selection criteria	Skilled workers	Investors and entrepreneurs
Education (maximum points)	25	25
Official language (maximum points)	24	24
Experience (maximum points)	21	
Business experiences (for investors and entrepreneurs)		35
Age (21–49 years of age at time of application, less	10	10
2 points for each year of age over 49 or under 21 years)		
Arranged employment in Canada	10	
Adaptability (maximum points)	10	6
For skilled workers:		
Spouse's or common-law partner's education	3 to 5	
Minimum one year full-time authorized work in Canada	5	
Minimum two years post-secondary study in Canada	5	
Have received points under arranged employment in Canada	5	
For investors and entrepreneurs:		
Business exploration trip to Canada within five years		
of application		6
Participation in designated joint federal/provincial business		
immigration initiatives		6
Maximum points	100	100
Pass mark for skilled worker immigrants	67	

Source: Canada. Citizenship and Immigration Canada. 2003d. *Will you qualify as a skilled worker?*
<http://www.cic.gc.ca/english/skilled/qual-1.html>.

The Canadian Race Relations Foundation (2001), Evelyn Kallen (2003, 112), and Henry and Tator (2005, 79) all claim that the exercise of discretion in the current immigration system continues to put visible minority immigrant applicants at a disadvantage.

While intriguing, the allegation that racism informs the exercise of discretion should be considered more of a hypothesis than a statement of fact. Even though immigration officers do unquestionably use their discretion to assess applicants for permanent resident status, there is no empirical evidence available to substantiate the allegation that immigration officers systematically awarded visible minority applicants fewer points for personal suitability under the old points system or that they are now more likely to subject visible minority applicants to more negative and less positive discretion than they do white applicants.

Another way that discrimination is said to continue to affect the selection and admission of skilled immigrants has to do with the distribution of immigration visa offices abroad. Currently, there are 90 immigration offices variously located in Canadian embassies, high commissions, and consulates abroad. Decisions about where these offices are located and decisions on the number of staff allocated to each office are arguably two of the ways that the federal government informally controls immigration from certain countries and regions of the world. Each immigration office has only a limited number of staff members to process applications. For example, the office in Kyiv, Ukraine, can process 2,500 successful applications for permanent resident status per year. As a result, even though there is no formal quota on the number of immigrants that Canada admits from Ukraine, the resources available for staffing the office in Ukraine act as a de facto ceiling on immigration from that country. Government resources are limited, of course, and it would be unrealistic to expect that every immigration office be provided with unlimited resources for processing applications for admission to Canada. Immigration officials claim that overseas staffing resources are allocated on the basis of where they will do the most good: not all countries in the world are defined as containing enough potential immigrants with the educational, occupational, and language skills that Canada is looking for. As a result, offices and resources are allocated on the basis of where they are likely to net the most in terms of what Canada defines as desirable immigrants (Simmons 1998, 103).

On the other hand, some critics argue that the location of immigration offices and the number of staff members allocated to these offices reflects the continuing 'racial' bias in the selection of immigrants to Canada. While overt racism has admittedly been removed from the immigration system, Jakubowski (1997, 21) argues that 'in less obvious ways, immigration law is still racist. The number and location of immigration offices outside of Canada and the discretion awarded to immigration officers in determining adaptability suggests that immigration, to some degree, is still being "controlled."'

Family class

In 2005, the 63,352 family class immigrants admitted to Canada made up 24.2 per cent of the total number of immigrants. However, family class immigration is diminishing in importance in Canada's overall immigration system. For example, in 1994, the 93,019 family class immigrants admitted to Canada represented about 42 per cent of the total number of immigrants admitted to Canada. The reasons for the decline in the size of the family class are rooted in part in government perceptions that family class immigrants make fewer positive economic contributions to Canada than skilled workers do.

Canadian citizens and permanent residents living in Canada may sponsor certain close relatives or family members who want to move to Canada. Individuals can sponsor spouses, parents and grandparents, dependent children (including adopted children), and children that they intend to adopt, as well as orphaned brothers, sisters, nephews, nieces, or grandchildren if they are under 18 and do not have a spouse. Federal immigration authorities recognized the validity of same-sex marriages even before federal legislation on this matter was passed in the summer of 2005. As a result, Canadian citizens and permanent residents may sponsor their same-sex partners under the family class. Sponsors must agree to financially support their family members for between three and 10 years so that they will not need to apply for social assistance. The length of time of the family support provisions depends on the age of the person sponsored and the nature of the relationship to the sponsor. For example, spouses (including common-law spouses) must provide financial support for three years from the date that the person becomes a permanent resident in Canada; sons and daughters, on the other hand, must provide 10 years of financial support to their parents and grandparents (Canada. Citizenship and Immigration Canada 2003b). Individuals who do not live up to these sponsorship conditions may not be eligible to sponsor further family members. With the exception of the elderly, individuals sponsored under the family class must sign an undertaking in which they agree to make every effort to become self-supporting in Canada.

Family class immigration is probably the most politicized of all immigration categories. The family class category is popular within many immigrant communities because it is an important vehicle by which immigrants may become reunited with their families in Canada. Immigrants in the family class do not face the same stringent selection criteria as skilled or business immigrants, and thus it is easier for individuals falling within one of the admissible groups to come and settle in Canada. The family class is particularly popular in urban ridings in Toronto, Vancouver, and Montreal that already have relatively large numbers of recent immigrants. As a result, members of Parliament representing these ridings are reluctant to support proposals that call for narrowing of the kinds of relatives eligible for family class immigration, reducing the overall size of the movement, or placing yearly caps on the number admitted in this category. One estimate suggests that for federal MPs in Toronto, Montreal, and Vancouver, immigration-related casework comprises between 60 and 80 per cent of all constituency casework and that these MPs annually handle up to 40,000 immigration-related inquiries from their constituents (Malloy 2003, 48). Immigration clearly matters to federal MPs in Canada's big cities, and they would be foolish not to court this segment of the electorate.

Recently, controversies have arisen over the economic performance of family class immigrants and whether they are a net drain on the Canadian economy (Frances 2002; Borjas 1999). Because they are not selected under the points system, family class immigrants are purportedly of poorer 'quality' in the sense that they bring less human capital to Canada than skilled worker immigrants, investors, and entrepreneurs. Critics of the family class argue that because they are less skilled, they do not do as well as skilled immigrants in the labour market, they are more likely to rely on social assistance than other immigrants, and they are a net drain on the Canadian economy (Stoffman 2002).

Empirical evidence challenges the claim that recent family class immigrants are declining in 'quality'. Li (2003, 93–4) shows, for example, that among family class immigrants who landed in Canada in 1996, only 0.5 per cent can be expected never to reach the earnings level of the Canadian-born. Another 0.5 per cent catch up to native Canadians' earnings in one year's time, and the average time required to reach earnings parity with average Canadian earnings is 6.8 years for men and 5.8 years for women. In fact, the average time it takes for family class men and women to reach earnings parity has improved over the past decade. For instance, among family class immigrants who landed in Canada in 1986, it took men an average of 16.6 years to catch up to the average earnings of Canadian males and 14.8 years for women to reach parity with average female employment earnings.

Furthermore, data for Toronto indicates that in 1995, both economic class (skilled workers and business immigrants) and family class immigrants were net contributors to the tax base. On average, for every $1.60 that family class immigrants paid in income tax, they collected only $1.00 in welfare and employment insurance benefits. Economic class immigrants did even better: for every $3.50 that they paid in income tax, they received $1.00 in social assistance and employment insurance benefits (Preston, Lo, and Wang 2003, 197–9).

Some critics suggest that the support conditions attached to sponsored immigrants are in fact a double-edged sword. While it may make economic sense for the Canadian government to want to limit its potential welfare liabilities for family class immigrants, the support provisions of the legislation can create economic dependency on the sponsor. This dependency is problematic and puts family class immigrants in possible jeopardy if they happen to be in abusive relationships with their sponsors. Some sponsored immigrant women may be unwilling to leave abusive relationships with their sponsors out of fear that they will be violating their initial agreement with the federal government and hence jeopardize their permanent residence status in Canada. Though Canada and other countries have provisions that relax the support provisions in cases of abusive relationships, these provisions are not well known. Furthermore, for women in abusive relationships, there is no certainty that these provisions will be applied in their specific case.

Even though it is clear that critics of the family class immigration category exaggerate the negative economic consequences of this kind of immigration, there are other reasons that such criticisms are misplaced. Evaluating family class immigration solely on the basis of economic logic is a one-sided bench mark that downplays the social benefits that accrue to other immigrants and to Canada more generally from family class immigration. For instance, a number of commentators have argued that social capital is an increasingly important aspect of immigrant integration in Canada. Social capital refers to the social relations and social networks that may provide access to resources and support (Voyer 2004). The relationship between immigrant economic success and the presence of family and ethnic networks is complex. While some argue that these networks may function in ways that reduce contact with 'mainstream' society and dominant groups and hence reduce social capital (Ooka and Wellman 2000), the presence of family members and other co-ethnics may strengthen the networks of social relations that provide support for immigrants, which may assist in the long-term integration of immigrants into Canadian society. In addition, efforts to quantify the economic contributions that family class immigrants make to Canadian society discount the social and mental health benefits associated with family reunification. Research suggests that there are long-term mental health benefits associated with having ethnic and family support (Noh and Kaspar 2003, 342).

Some analysts allege that the criticisms directed against the family class immigration category are really a smoke screen for deeper, 'racially' based concerns about Canada admitting too many visible minority immigrants. In the 1990s, the Reform Party of Canada was highly critical of the Canadian immigration program, in part because it believed that family class immigrants were a drain on the

Canadian economy. Though the Reform Party eventually changed its name to the Canadian Alliance and then merged with the Progressive Conservative Party, it continues to express concerns over the number and quality of family class immigrants coming to the country. Some analysts allege that the Reform Party's concern over family class immigration in the 1990s was a thinly veiled way of saying to Canadians that they were really concerned about too many visible minorities being admitted to Canada. According to Kirkham:

> The party's call to increase the Independent Class of immigrants and restrict Family Class entrants is . . . not as innocuous as it first appears. In 1987, 43 percent of all Family Class immigrants were from Asia. By 1992, this figure had increased to 55 percent. It is therefore possible to conclude that the party's policy would in effect bar much non-European immigration into Canada, in spite of Reform officials' protests otherwise. In this sense, the intent of the party's original statement which called for an end to immigration policy that is 'explicitly designed to radically or suddenly alter the ethnic makeup of Canada' becomes more clear, notwithstanding Reform's attempts at damage control. Yet in focusing its policy on economic criteria—something that appears neutral, fair and more important, non-racial—the party is able to mask the racialized sub-text and implications of its policy (1998, 252).

As we will see in chapter 6, this is arguably a form of 'new racism'. Racist views are expressed in 'non-racial' language, but the 'racial' meanings and consequences are still evident. Opposition to family class immigration, 57.5 per cent of which came from Asia in 2003 (Canada. Citizenship and Immigration Canada 2003a), for example, acts as a kind of code language for raising concerns about the negative changes to Canadian society as a result of visible minority immigration to Canada.

Business class

Canada's business immigration program is designed to admit individuals who can invest in or start businesses in the country. There are three categories of business immigrants: investors, entrepreneurs, and self-employed. Individuals applying under the investor category have to demonstrate 'business experience', have a minimum net worth of $800,000, and make an investment of $400,000 in the country. Entrepreneurs must have a minimum net worth of $300,000 and the intention and ability to control and actively manage a business that creates at least one new full-time job in the country. Those applying in the self-employed category must have relevant experience in cultural activities, athletics, or farm management. They must have the intention and ability to establish a business that at minimum will create employment for themselves.

Business immigrants represent a significant though declining proportion of all immigrants admitted to Canada. In 1994, the 27,404 business immigrants who came to Canada represented 12.4 per cent of all immigrants admitted that year. By 2005, however, the 13,469 business immigrants and accompanying family members represented just 5.1 per cent of all immigrants admitted. The relatively large number of business immigrants recruited from the late 1980s to the mid-1990s was in part the result of the British government's announcement that it would transfer authority over Hong Kong to China in 1997. Many wealthy business people and entrepreneurs feared the impending take-over. Concerned that the Chinese government would undermine the free enterprise environment that characterized Hong Kong society, many sought to find a safe haven for themselves, their families, and their capital in Canada.

Canada was more than willing to oblige and so ramped up the business immigration program to capitalize on the fears and anxieties of Hong Kong residents. A number of other countries are also keen to recruit business immigrants. The United States, Australia, Britain, and New Zealand, for example, all have business immigration programs that aim at recruiting wealthy individuals eager to gain permanent residence status by expressing an intention to invest at least part of their wealth in the country (Borowski and Nash 1994, 228; Wong and Netting 1992, 95). Each year, for example, the United States allocates 10,000 visas for wealthy investors, hoping to attract them and their families. Investors must create at least 10 jobs and invest a minimum of one million (US) dollars (Borjas 1999, 177). As the global competition for business immigrants heats up, the bar for admitting business immigrants may be falling progressively lower with reductions in the required thresholds for capital and investment.

In Canada, the overwhelming majority (92 per cent) of business immigrants end up in Ontario (36.1 per cent), British Columbia (33.9 per cent), and Quebec (21.9 per cent). Table 3.4 provides information on the top 10 source countries for the combined categories of investor, entrepreneur, and self-employed. It shows that the 25,422 individuals from Hong Kong admitted under the business immigration

Table 3.4   Top Ten Source Countries of Investors, Entrepreneurs, and the Self-Employed (Principal Applicants Only), 1982–2002

Rank	Source country	Number	Per cent
1	Hong Kong	25,422	31.4
2	Taiwan	11,959	14.8
3	South Korea	7,179	8.9
4	China	4,970	6.1
5	Germany	2,161	2.7
6	United Kingdom	1,986	2.5
7	Iran	1,976	2.4
8	United States	1,626	2.0
9	United Arab Emirates	1,503	1.9
10	Pakistan	1,349	1.7
Total for top ten only		60,131	74.2
Total for other countries		20,910	25.8
Total		81,041	100

Source: Canada. Citizenship and Immigration Canada. 2002. *Business immigration program statistics, 2002.* <http://www.cic.gc/engish/business/bus-stats2002.html>.

program represented 31.4 per cent of the total number of business immigrants admitted to Canada. Other major sources of business immigrants to Canada include Taiwan, South Korea, China, Germany, the United Kingdom, Iran, the United States, the United Arab Emirates, and Pakistan (Canada. Citizenship and Immigration Canada 2002a). Information collected by Citizenship and Immigration Canada indicates that between 1986 and 2002, immigrant investors have collectively invested $6.6 billion in the country and that in 2002 alone, immigrant entrepreneurs invested $122,615,713 and created 1,108 full-time and 753 part-time jobs in Canada (Canada. Citizenship and Immigration Canada 2002a).

Despite what appear to be obvious economic benefits associated with business-related immigration programs, not everyone is in favour of these kinds of programs and arrangements.

First, some critics have raised ethical issues associated with what amounts to the sale of permanent residence status and eventually a Canadian passport. Critics have suggested that putting permanent residence status and citizenship up for sale to wealthy business people and investors is consistent with a wider neo-liberal project. 'These class advantaged people embody the very spirit of neo-liberalism—they are independent, self-reliant, active, and entrepreneurial' (Abu-Laban and Gabriel 2002, 173). The priorities placed on recruiting business immigrants, in Abu-Laban and Gabriel's view (173), reflects a growing emphasis on seeing the economic contributions of a person as indicative of the sum worth of a person, which is a particularly 'superficial and narrow reading of diversity'.

Some commentators defend this approach to immigration on the grounds that immigration should benefit the country of immigration and that there is nothing inherently wrong or immoral in 'selling' immigration visas. Commenting about the United States, Borjas argues that

> if bread, butter, and the proverbial widget can be bought and sold in the open market . . . why not also sell the limited number of entry visas that the United States makes available every year? The United States . . . could announce at the beginning of each year that it is willing to sell visas at, say, $50,000 per visa. Those who want to migrate to the United States at that price would then enter the marketplace (1999, 177).

Second, many business immigrants can be characterized as 'transnationals'—individuals whose business interests as well as their identities and social and personal lives straddle more than one country (Wong and Satzewich 2006). Many business immigrants maintain homes, social networks, and business interests both in Canada and in their country of origin. They travel relatively unencumbered by national borders and move easily and seamlessly around the globe. Critics of some business and other well-off transnational immigrants have called them 'astronauts': individuals who settle their families in Canada, Australia, or the United States but continue to conduct their businesses in their home country and occasionally fly back to Canada to maintain their permanent residence status (Borowski and Nash 1994, 247). These business immigrants and other upper-middle-class immigrants have been the targets of hostility for their real and imagined transnational behaviours. Further, when the children of these astronaut families occasionally get into trouble with the law or display their wealth ostentatiously, they are often the subject of media attacks and criticism. At the extreme, questions are raised about their political loyalties and how committed they are to Canada.

Finally, some analysts argue that the business immigration program has helped to create a 'race relations' problem in places like Vancouver, a city that is a major destination for visible minority business immigrants. Vancouver in the late 1980s and early 1990s was at the centre of a number of controversies about the apparent negative social, cultural, and economic consequences of large-scale business immigration. According to Wong and Netting (1992), white residents of Vancouver blamed immigrants for driving up housing prices in the city and destroying the character of certain neighbourhoods by erecting 'monster houses' and cutting down age-old trees on their newly acquired properties because they interfered with the *feng shui* of the location. Business immigrants were also constructed by some residents as being driven only by greed and responsible for importing an organized crime problem from Hong Kong to Canada. Wong and Netting also argue, however, that class conflict underscored some of these racist attitudes in important ways. They argue that while white working-class British Columbians expressed alarm and resentment over the skyrocketing price of housing in the city, middle and upper-class white Canadians were also concerned that their neighbourhoods, their schools, and their clubs were also being negatively affected by seemingly large-scale migration and settlement of wealthy Chinese business immigrants (Wong and Netting 1992, 119; see also Mitchell 2004).

MIGRANTS ON THE MARGINS

Any discussion of Canadian immigration policy is incomplete if it does not look at individuals on the margins. Although much of Canada's immigration program is oriented toward the admission of individuals as permanent residents, other aspects of the program are devoted to the admission of temporary workers. Moreover, discussions of immigration always raise the issue of 'illegal immigration'. Both of these cases of migrants on the margins of Canadian society—temporary workers and 'illegals'—raise implications for patterns of 'race' and ethnic relations.

Migrant workers

The fact that Canada admits a relatively large number of individuals as immigrants should not blind us to the fact that Canada also admits a relatively large number of individuals as *migrant workers*. They are different from immigrants in that they do not have the right to permanent residence, they are admitted to Canada to do specific jobs for specific lengths of time, and they must return to their country of origin when their temporary work visas expire. While in Canada, they cannot quit or change their jobs without the permission of the federal government. If they do quit or change jobs without government permission, they are subject to deportation. Sometimes referred to as 'guest workers' or 'unfree migrant workers' (Satzewich 1991; Sharma 2001), they are arguably a growing part of the labour force in Canada.

Canada allows individuals to work in the country on a temporary basis through the Non-Immigrant Employment Authorization Program (NIEAP). This program, first instituted in 1973, allows individuals the right of temporary residence and temporary employment in Canada. Sharma (2001) argues that Canada is undergoing a relatively rapid transformation from an *immigrant-receiving* to a *migrant-receiving* nation. She shows that when the NIEAP began in 1973, non-immigrating workers represented 43 per cent of the total number of people destined for the labour force arriving in Canada that year. Conversely, 57 per cent of those destined for the labour force were admitted as immigrants or permanent residents. By 1993, however, the balance between migrant and immigrant workers had shifted: 70 per cent of those destined for the labour force were migrant workers, and only 30 per cent were admitted as permanent residents or immigrants. Sharma argues that a major reason for the Canadian government's admission of proportionately more migrant as opposed to immigrant workers is to provide employers with a relatively cheap and docile pool of labour that can be subject to greater degrees of exploitation than Canadian citizens and permanent residents. In Sharma's view:

> The operation of the migrant worker category can substantially enhance the ability of the Canadian government to attract and/or retain capital investment in its territory by giving employers in the country . . . access to a 'cheap labour strategy' of global competition. . . . The operation of the NIEAP enables those in the Canadian government to produce a group of non-citizens who, because of their classification as 'non-immigrants,' can legally be exempted from laws on minimum employment standards, collective bargaining, and the provision of social services and programs such as unemployment insurance, social assistance, old-age pensions, etc. (2001, 426).

It is important to note that the NIEAP allows individuals in a variety of circumstances the right to enter and work in Canada temporarily. Non-immigrant work authorizations cover a wide range of situations, so not all individuals working in Canada under an employment authorization are 'guest workers' in the traditional sense of the term. As Sharma notes, non-Canadian entertainers, sports figures, and artists who earn income in Canada require an employment authorization, as do foreign academics who are paid for giving visiting lectures, seminars, or workshops. Even when these cases are discounted from the overall program figures, Sharma suggests that her general argument still holds: namely, that a greater emphasis has recently been placed on admitting migrant instead of immigrant workers. Notwithstanding her qualification, it is still not clear whether the remaining workers who come to Canada under non-immigrant employment authorizations are migrant workers in the strict sense of the term. More research is needed on the occupational categories and employment niches for which non-immigrant employment authorizations are issued and the labour market experiences of workers in Canada under the NIEAP to determine whether they should be regarded as genuinely 'unfree labour'.

There is, however, at least one kind of migrant worker within the NIEAP that unquestionably falls within the ambit of Sharma's overall argument. Farm work is one of the single largest occupational categories for non-immigrant work authorizations. Beginning in 1966 as a small experimental movement of 264 Jamaican workers to Ontario, the program now involves more than 18,000 workers from various Caribbean countries and Mexico admitted on a yearly basis to work on farms in every province of Canada except Newfoundland and Labrador. The vast majority work in Ontario in greenhouses or in fields picking various tender fruits, vegetables, and tobacco. Some also work in food processing plants.

As migrant workers, they come to Canada under labour contracts that stipulate that they can remain in Canada for between six weeks and eight months and that they must return to their country of origin when their contract expires. Farmers must pay for the workers' accommodation. The cost of transportation to Canada is paid by the farmers, but they can recover up to $425 from the worker. Employers are also required to provide food or cooking facilities and can recover up to $6.50 a day per worker for the cost of meals.

Part of the reason that workers from the Caribbean and Mexico are so attractive to seemingly increasing numbers of employers across Canada stems from their condition of unfreedom. Since they come from countries with high levels of unemployment and poor economic conditions, the wages offered in Canada can be quite attractive compared to the alternatives in their country of origin. Given this economic dependency on Canadian wages, workers are reluctant to do anything that would jeopardize their employment situation here. As a result, migrant workers are relatively compliant workers, reluctant to complain about their living and working conditions or possible health and safety violations in the workplace. They fear that they will be sent home before their contract expires or not be invited back by immigration authorities the next year. According to Basok's analysis:

> . . . the growers realize, of course, that what makes Mexican (and Caribbean) labour so valuable is that the workers are not free to quit. If Mexican workers were to come as permanent residents, this advantage would be lost, as one grower points out: 'The disadvantage of legalizing Mexicans would be that they would be free to leave the greenhouses and go to work cutting mushrooms, for instance. Mushrooms are "hi tech" now. They are air conditioned—sixty degrees. You'll get workers there. They will be there before they'll be here . . .' [sic] (2002, 126).

Migrant worker vulnerability is further aggravated by the fact that in Ontario, they are not protected by provincial labour standards legislation. As agricultural labourers, they are able to form 'associations' but cannot bargain collectively with employers to improve wages or working conditions.

Illegal immigrants

In 1994, through Proposition 187, Californians sought to deny a variety of public sector benefits, such as welfare, education, and all but emergency medical care, to illegal immigrants. The proposition also required that teachers, police officers, and welfare workers report any knowledge of illegal immigrants to the Immigration and Naturalization Service (INS) so that it could initiate deportation proceedings (Lee, Ottati, and Hussain 2001). The proposition was initially approved by a majority of California voters but was later ruled unconstitutional and overturned by the courts. Since then, however, other federal government policies in the United States have gone a considerable distance toward addressing the underlying concerns of Californians and other Americans more generally (Rivera-Batiz 2000) who feel that their country is being taken over by an 'alien nation' of illegal immigrants (Brimelow 1995).

Even though there is less research on illegal immigration in Canada than there is in the United States, political elites and members of the general public in this country do occasionally become concerned about the issue. In the summer of 1999, the arrival of four ships containing 600 undocumented migrants from the province of Fujian, China, raised alarm bells that Canada was about to be swamped by 'hordes' of illegal immigrants who would use the in-Canada refugee determination system to gain a foothold in Canada. The feeling was that these arrivals were just the tip of a much larger iceberg of illegal immigration from China to Canada. It was feared that many more 'ghost' ships were lurking in the waters off British Columbia, waiting to disembark their human cargo in isolated bays, coves, and inlets along the coast.

Hier and Greenberg (2002, 161) argue that the Canadian media blew this 1999 incident out of proportion and succeeded in creating a moral panic about illegal immigration from China. They argue that the ensuing public debate eventually led to a 'hardening of attitudes and policies related to undocumented migratory populations'.

Even though Hier and Greenberg (2002) downplay the size of the movement and suggest that the fears about Canada being swamped with illegal immigrants were overblown, there is evidence to suggest that illegal immigrants are in fact a significant part of the social fabric of this country and that they are arguably an increasingly important element of certain sectors of the Canadian economy. One estimate suggests that there are up to 200,000 illegal immigrants in Canada. Yet, contrary to Hier and Greenberg (2002), Canadians appear to have turned a blind eye to the issue of illegal immigration. It is common knowledge, for example, that the Ontario construction industry is heavily reliant on the labour of illegal immigrants, with as many as 76,000 working in that industry alone in 2003. In Toronto, there are certain parking lots and street corners where contractors and other construction industry employers know they can go to hire illegal immigrants on a day-labour basis. Other illegal immigrants are hired on more permanent arrangements to work in factories and restaurants and on farms. Indeed, the federal government is currently considering a program that would grant undocumented workers legal status in order to help the construction business in Ontario solve its perennial labour shortage (Jiminez 2003; Soave 2006). Thus, rather than leading to a hardening of attitudes and policies related to undocumented immigration, the 1999 incident and its aftermath seems to be a distant memory in both policy-maker and public minds. It is probably more accurate to say that Canada and the United States appear to be more concerned about the initial interdiction of illegal immigrants at the border. If and when they get through the border, they are subject to a less stringent enforcement regime.

'Illegal immigration' is actually a catch-all term used to describe individuals in three different circumstances. First, some people enter Canada without official authorization. Often, these individuals come to Canada through human smuggling operations, and their final destination is the United States (Jiminez 2005). The global traffic in human beings is estimated to be a five to seven-billion-dollar per year industry. It can, for example, cost individuals from China and other Asian countries between $30,000 and $40,000 (USD) to be smuggled into the United States through Mexico (Spener 2001, 154). Human smuggling chains are often difficult to police because traffickers use sophisticated techniques to create false documents and hiding places and because they have complex networks that can be shut down or established on very short notice.

Second, some people are visa over-stayers. They enter the country legally on one particular kind of visa (a temporary work, student, or visitor visa) but stay beyond the time frame allowed in their original entry visa. Although Canada's visa-granting system is designed to prevent the arrival of individuals who mask their true intentions for wanting to come, Canada exercises very little control over people once they are legally admitted to Canada (Cox and Glenn 1994). Visa over-stayers are difficult to police because Canada does not have a mechanism to track whether individuals given the right of temporary entry ever actually leave when their visas expire.

The third stream of illegal immigration in Canada comprises failed refugee claimants. Indeed, as in other countries, there is sometimes a blurring of the distinction between illegal immigrants and legitimate refugees. One estimate suggests that in 1994, between 60,000 and 120,000 asylum-seekers were smuggled into Europe by migrant traffickers (Koser 2001, 58). Individuals whose in-Canada applications for refugee status were denied but who have not left or have not been deported may become illegal immigrants in Canada. Some individuals use the in-Canada refugee determination system to get a foot in the door and to buy time in order to go underground. It is relatively easy for individuals to disappear from the system if their intention is simply to gain access to Canadian soil and better themselves economically. Furthermore, even though the fear that terrorists are using refugee systems to gain entry to places like Canada, the United States, and Europe is probably overblown, there may very well be a small number of individuals who use the refugee determination system as a way of gaining entry for more sinister reasons associated with participation in terrorist or other criminal activities.

While it is difficult to determine which of these three streams contributes the most to the total population of illegal immigrants in Canada, experts suggests that the latter two streams likely produce the largest numbers of illegal immigrants in Canada.

Illegal immigrants are in an even more precarious social position than migrant workers. With few rights and in constant fear of being apprehended, illegal immigrants in many ways constitute an ideal workforce for employers chronically short of labour whose profit margins are tight. Commenting about the United States but with no less relevance to Canada, Gimpel and Edwards argue that

The practice of employing low wage workers in squalid sweatshop conditions is surprisingly common in certain low-profit-margin businesses. The illegitimate employers routinely dodge wage and labor laws because they know the illegal workers they employ will not go to the authorities out of fear of being discovered and deported (1999, 85).

In addition, illegal immigrants may deprive themselves and their family members of important services, such as health care or police services when they need them, for fear of apprehension (Cox and Glenn 1994, 284).

Canada and the United States have both undertaken measures to control illegal immigration. These measures range from border controls, to imposing visa regulations on certain countries deemed to produce illegal immigrants, to laws that prohibit persons from knowingly employing illegal immigrants. For example, in the 1986 US Immigration Reform and Control Act, employers who knowingly hire illegal aliens can be fined between $3,000 and $10,000 (USD) per worker or face terms of imprisonment for repeated infractions. In Canada, employers who do not carry out due diligence in determining whether an individual is legally entitled to work in Canada are subject to fines of up to $50,000 and/or two years' imprisonment. Workers found to be working illegally in Canada are subject to deportation, although if they make a claim for refugee status, they must receive a hearing before their case is disposed of. Canada also has carrier sanctions in place to help stem the flow of illegal immigrants. Airlines that board individuals without proper documentation on flights destined for Canada face 'administrative' fees of up to $3,200 and must cover the cost of the individual's return to their place of origin (Cox and Glenn 1994, 286; Canada. Department of Justice 2002).

In the United States, a minutemen militia has been established without the sanction of the American federal government. These are voluntary patrols set up by concerned Americans, located mainly along the Mexican/American border. However, minutemen militia members also patrol the United States/Canada border. They station themselves along known illegal immigrant border crossing points, the objective being to assist Immigration and Naturalization Service authorities by identifying individuals who appear to be crossing the border illegally so that they can be apprehended. Some critics see this as a form of vigilantism, but supporters argue that they are there simply to act as an extra set of eyes and ears for the chronically understaffed INS.

A number of issues relevant to ethnic and 'racial' relations emerge out the problem of illegal immigration. First, even though both Canada and the US have laws prohibiting the employment of individuals who are not legally entitled to work, the enforcement mechanisms for these laws are rather weak in both cases. Fines for knowingly hiring illegal aliens appear to be minimal; between 1994 and 1996, only 3,765 of the more than 15,000 US employers charged with hiring illegal aliens received a fine (Koslowski 2001, 352). In Canada, few employers seem to be prosecuted for knowingly hiring illegal workers. Some attribute this lack of will to enforce the law as a reflection of the political power of certain employer groups that rely on illegal immigrant labour and can exert pressure on legal and political authorities to turn a blind eye to violations. In the US since 11 September 2001, INS workplace inspections have decreased, in part because it now focuses its activities on places that might be terrorist targets, such as airports.

Second, some critics allege that there is a double standard inherent in public debate about illegal immigration. For example, while Mexico constitutes the single largest source of illegal immigrants in the United States, other countries, including Canada, also contribute significant numbers of illegal immigrants. In fact, Canada is the fourth largest contributor of illegal immigrants to the US (Stalker 2000, 28). Even though the sources of illegal immigrants in the US are diverse, the stereotypical illegal immigrant in many American minds is poor, uneducated, and of Mexican or Latin American origin. Public debate in the United States focuses almost exclusively on Mexican or Latino illegal immigrants, and the irony is that little if any public concern is expressed over the thousands of presumably 'white' Canadians living and working illegally in the United States. In Canada, Hier and Greenberg (2002, 161) argue that the moral panic surrounding the 1999 landing of 600 illegal immigrants from China was a reflection of the wider resentment that many white Canadians had towards the legally resident and upwardly mobile Chinese middle class in the country.

Third, there is evidence in the United States that laws directed against employers hiring illegal immigrants contribute to the economic disadvantage of legally resident immigrants and American citizens of Latin American and Mexican origin (Bansak and Raphael 2001). As noted previously, in that country the stereotypical image of an illegal immigrant is someone from Latin America or Mexico. According to research conducted by the US Government Accounting Office (GAO), legally resident Mexicans and Latinos face fewer job opportunities and lower wages because some employers avoid hiring individuals who appear to look like 'stereotypical' illegal aliens. The authors of the GAO report show that

> an estimated 227,000 employers report that they began a practice, as a result of the IRCA [Immigration Reform and Control Act], not to hire applicants whose foreign appearance or accent led them to suspect that they might be unauthorized aliens. Also, contrary to the IRCA, an estimated 346,000 employers said that they applied IRCA's verification system only to persons who had a 'foreign' appearance or accent. Some employers began both practices (US. Government Accounting Office 1990, 6).

Fourth, in the aftermath of 11 September, there is evidence suggesting that Muslims, South Asians, and individuals of 'Middle Eastern' appearance are being subjected to excessive scrutiny at Canadian and American border points, 'racially' profiled, and constructed as potential illegal immigrants and terrorists coming to Canada and the United States to wreak havoc. According to an Ontario Human Rights Commission report on racial profiling, one of the common complaints they receive from individuals identifying themselves as Muslim, Arab, or South Asian is that they are searched more often than or scrutinized differently from others when flying or crossing the Canada/US border (Ontario Human Rights Commission 2005, 10).

SUMMARY

This chapter shows that the Canadian immigration system is complex, with a number of economic, political, and demographic factors shaping the contemporary immigration system. Though 'race' was removed from immigration processes more than 30 years ago, critics continue to allege that there are racist overtones to many aspects of the ways that immigrants are allowed to come to Canada and in how Canadian society responds to the presence of immigrants. Some of these allegations are based on more solid empirical foundations than others.

Canada admits individuals from around the world under a variety of different categories: refugees, skilled immigrants, family class immigrants, business immigrants, and migrant workers. Each of these forms of migration carries certain controversies: safe third country provisions for refugees are said to put some legitimate refugees at risk; skilled immigrants are said to be declining in quality; family class immigrants are accused of being a drain on the economy; and business immigrants are said to be responsible for skyrocketing housing costs in places like Vancouver. Many of these accusations are without strong empirical foundation.

Even though Canada admits nearly a quarter of a million immigrants per year, it also appears to admit large numbers of migrant workers. The admittance of migrant workers raises hard questions about the unequal access to citizenship rights in this country.

Questions for Critical Thought

1. To what extent does racism continue to inform the contemporary Canadian immigration system?
2. Does Canada's adherence to 'safe third country' principles actually put legitimate refugees at risk?
3. Why does Canada admit immigrants?
4. Canada is a country of immigrants, yet it also admits thousands of migrant workers to work on only a temporary basis. How can this apparent anomaly be explained?
5. Are family class immigrants a drain on the Canadian economy? What evidence supports this claim, and what evidence questions it?

Annotated Additional Readings

Basok, Tanya. 2002. *Tortillas and tomatoes: Transmigrant Mexican harvesters in Canada*. Montreal and Kingston: McGill-Queen's University Press. Explores the role played by Mexican seasonal workers in Canadian agriculture.

Li, Peter. 2003. *Destination Canada: Immigration debates and issues*. Toronto: Oxford University Press. A thorough review of a number of debates about the social and economic consequences of immigration to Canada.

Mitchell, Katharyne. 2004. *Crossing the neoliberal line: Pacific Rim migration and the metropolis*. Philadelphia: Temple University Press. A sophisticated account of the debates and controversies about the social and economic consequences of Chinese businesses immigration to British Columbia in the 1980s and 1990s.

Sharma, Nandita. 2006. *Home economics: Nationalism and the making of 'migrant workers' in Canada*. Toronto: University of Toronto Press. A thoughtful analysis of migrant and illegal worker issues in Canada.

Stoffman, Daniel. 2002. *Who gets in: What's wrong with Canada's immigration program—and how to fix it*. Toronto: Macfarlane Walter and Ross. A highly critical account of the contemporary Canadian immigration system.

Related Websites

Citizenship and Immigration Canada: http://www.cic.gc.ca/.

International Organization for Migration: http://www.iom.int/.

Justicia for Migrant Workers-J4MW: http://www.justicia4migrantworkers.org/.

Metropolis Project—An international forum for research and policy on migration and cities: http://canada.metropolis.net/.

Understanding Social Inequality: The Intersections of Ethnicity, Gender, and Class

Learning objectives

In this chapter, you will learn that:

- John Porter's work, *The Vertical Mosaic*, has provided the groundwork for much of the current debate about social inequality in Canada.
- There is evidence that when taking occupational attainment and earnings into account, there has been a trend toward convergence among ethnic groups in Canada in relation to their socio-economic status.
- Some sociologists argue that despite this convergence, the vertical mosaic metaphor continues to be relevant to Canadian society.
- Some sociologists argue that there is a new colour-coded vertical mosaic in Canada.
- Immigrant educational credentials are devalued in Canada, and this accounts for at least some of the inequalities between immigrants and the Canadian-born and between visible minority and non-visible minority immigrants.
- Social class still is an important dividing line in Canadian society. Ethnic groups are not exclusively concentrated in one particular social class, and most immigrant groups are distributed across the range of class sites in Canada.
- Gender and nativity (place of birth), along with class, constitute bases of inequality in earnings not only among but also within ethnic and visible minorities.
- Social inequality is complex; two-tier metaphors and monocausal explanations obfuscate the picture. If we want to explain social inequality among and within ethnic groups, we must focus on their class, gender, and nativity dimensions.

INTRODUCTION

It is clear that some people in Canada do better economically than others. Some people earn high incomes, are well-respected professionals, or own businesses or large corporations. People with what are perceived to be 'really good jobs' live in big houses, drive nice cars, and do not have to temporarily do without in order to afford a winter vacation. At the other extreme, some Canadians are homeless, rely on food banks, and live in grinding poverty. Even though they may superficially appear to be comfortably well-off, many so-called 'middle-class' Canadian households include two full-time income earners struggling to make ends meet.

How do immigrants and members of racialized communities fit into this very general overall picture of Canada? Are immigrants and members of visible minority communities concentrated at the bottom of the socio-economic hierarchy? Do they do the 'dirty work' of Canadian society, characterized by low pay and poor and unsafe working conditions? Conversely, are 'white' Canadians and the historically preferred European ethnic groups that we talked about in chapter 2 concentrated at the middle and top of the rank? Do they have the good jobs, characterized by status, prestige, and high income? Are the labour market experiences and socio-economic positions of men and women within immigrant, ethnic, and racialized communities the same, or are they different? Is it possible that at the same time that Canadian society restricts opportunities for mobility and economic advancement for some immigrants and members of ethnic and racialized communities, other members of the same communities do very well for themselves and find that this country truly is a land of opportunity?

These are complex questions, and they point to a complex reality. It is tempting to look for individual or cultural-level explanations for why some individuals and groups are better off economically than others. Some people think that things like hard work, talent, and education are the keys to explaining economic success. Others think that culturally determined values explain why some groups do better than others in Canadian society. These variables, while undoubtedly important, do not tell the full story about social inequality in this country, either for immigrants, for the Canadian-born, for racialized communities, or for 'white', so-called 'non-visible' minorities. As we noted in chapter 1, it is hard to understand social inequality in this country without understanding the interrelationship between ethnicity, 'race', class, gender, and place of birth.

This chapter has three central objectives. First, it summarizes what John Porter meant when he characterized Canada in the 1960s as a 'vertical mosaic'. Second, it provides an assessment of the debates surrounding the continued relevance of the vertical mosaic metaphor for Canadian society. In doing so, it considers debates about the declining significance of ethnic origin in the vertical mosaic. It also considers the continuing significance of visible minority status—or 'race'—and immigration status in shaping the occupational distribution and incomes of individuals in Canada. In other words, it asks whether Canada is now characterized by a racialized or colour-coded vertical mosaic. Finally, the chapter provides an alternative perspective on the earnings inequalities of selected ethnic groups in Canada. In particular, we focus on the class divisions within ethnic groups. In this section of the chapter, we are particularly interested in the picture of social inequality that emerges when we start from a different analytical lens.

THE VERTICAL MOSAIC: PORTER'S LEGACY

Over the years, much of the research on social inequality in Canada has focused on the socio-economic performance of ethnic groups in order to demonstrate that Canadian society is hierarchically structured (Agocs and Boyd 1993, 337). John Meisel, in his foreword to John Porter's *The vertical mosaic: An analysis of social class and power in Canada* (1965) welcomed the timing of the publication as fortunate because it appeared 'at the very moment when our national attention and preoccupation centre *on ethnic, rather than on class differences*' (Porter 1965, ix; emphasis ours). Prior to Porter's work, declared Meisel, the attention of most politicians and researchers focused on the role of ethnicity in the operation of Canadian society, underestimating the 'importance of social status, thus concealing even more than heretofore the true nature of Canadian society' (ibid.). Porter's book was supposed to 'protect us from too exclusive a preoccupation with the ethnic facts of Canadian society . . . enriching our understanding of them by showing how, in many instances, they are linked to class and status' (ibid.). Today, this sounds ironic since most students of social inequality in Canada associate Porter's work with ethnicity, not social class. Arguably, the call for bringing class back into the analysis of social inequality in Canada is as current today as it was in 1965.

Porter stated in the preface that his book was 'an attempt to examine the hitherto unexplored subjects of social class and power in Canadian society' (1965, x). He suggested that in multicultural societies, there was some relationship between membership in a cultural group and class position (and consequently, power) (1965, xii). The title 'vertical mosaic' was originally assigned to the chapter that examined the relationship between ethnicity and social class in order to demonstrate the ethnic component of the structure of class hierarchy in Canada (1965, xiii). Porter argued that immigration and ethnic affiliation were important factors in the process of social class formation in Canada, especially at the bottom and elite layers of the stratification system (1965, 73).

His argument was based on an analysis of census data from 1931, 1951, and 1961. As the title suggests, Porter argued that Canadian society, understood as an ethnic mosaic, is hierarchically structured in terms of the differential distributions of wealth and power among its constituent ethnic groups. Examining the Canadian labour market from a Weberian perspective, Porter found that ethnic groups were unequally represented in the occupational structure. Four of his findings are noteworthy. First, the 'charter' groups (British and French) had appropriated (higher) positions of power and advantage (in the social, economic, and political realms) and had designated the 'entrance status' groups to lower, less preferred positions. Over time, reinforced by stereotypes and social images, these divisions in status were hardened and perpetuated.

Second, 'less preferred' groups that arrived in Canada later than the charter groups were relegated to an 'entrance status'. That is, they were employed in lower-status occupations and were subject to the assimilation processes laid down by the charter groups (Porter 1965, 63–4). Third, ethnic affiliation implied blocked social mobility. Upward mobility of ethnic groups depended on the culture of the ethnic group in question and the degree to which it conformed to the rules of assimilation set by the charter groups. The improvement in the position of entrance status groups over time could be determined by their 'assimilability' or their behavioural and structural assimilation (1965, 67–73).

In terms of the relative hierarchical position of ethnic groups in the occupational structure, which he regarded as a crude substitute for class, Porter found that a pattern of ethnic inequality persisted. Canadians of Jewish and British origin were at the top. They were persistently overrepresented in the professional and financial occupations (higher status and income) and under-represented in agricultural and unskilled jobs (lower status and income). The Germans, Scandinavians, and Dutch were closest to the British. Italians, Poles, and Ukrainians were next, with other southern Europeans (Greek and Portuguese) near the lower end of the spectrum (1965, 90). The French, somewhere between the northern and southern Europeans, were under-represented in professional and financial occupations and overrepresented in agricultural and unskilled jobs. Aboriginal people were at the bottom of the hierarchy (1965, 73–103).

Fourth, as far as the charter groups were concerned, the British were more powerful than the French (1965, 91–8). In fact, despite the considerable influence exerted on the political system by French-Canadians, not only in Quebec but also at the federal level (1965, 417–56), and their access to high-status political positions and the media, it was the British who dominated Canada's economic life and were overrepresented in elite positions (1965, 201–308, 337–416, 520–59).

Porter's work has been characterized as the most important book in Canadian sociology (Forcese 1997, 83). His arguments have set the stage for much of the debate on social inequality in Canada (Brym and Fox 1989, 92; Ogmundson 1993; McAll 1990, 173; Li 1988, 3).

EVIDENCE FOR ETHNIC CONVERGENCE?

Since the mid-1960s, sociologists have paid attention to the relationship between ethnic origin and class in Canadian society, and a number of significant questions have arisen regarding Porter's findings and treatment of the data. Subsequent analyses of Porter's data and methods have shown that his claims might have been exaggerated on both mass and elite mobility levels (see Brym and Fox 1989, 93–9, 103–19). Ascription, or the characteristics that you are born with, argue Cuneo and Curtis (1975), is not more important in determining status in Canada than it is in the US. Canada is not an ascriptive but an achievement society (Goyder and Curtis 1979, 229). A detailed account of Porter critiques is not our aim here (see Brym and Fox 1989; Ogmundson 1991, 1993; Ogmundson and McLaughlin 1992). However, it is necessary to place some of these criticisms in the wider context of the social inequality debate. Research on social inequality and on the lack of mass and elite mobility has been basically concerned with either supporting or refuting Porter's work. Here we only examine issues associated with mass mobility.[1]

Occupational attainment

Since the 1960s, a number of researchers have maintained that differential occupational attainment among ethnic groups is substantial and an enduring feature of the labour market. The British continued to enjoy higher occupational status than the French (Royal Commission on Bilingualism and Biculturalism 1969; Breton and Roseborough 1971; Boyd et al. 1981). Other ethnic groups, such as the Jewish and northern and western Europeans, were in advantaged positions. Southern Europeans, visible minorities, and Aboriginal people were found at the bottom of the occupational hierarchy (Porter 1985; Li 1988; Lautard and Guppy 1990; Reitz 1990). Despite a decline since the 1960s, ethnic disparities in occupational status have been seen as persistent. Lautard and Guppy (2007), for example, argue that ethnic occupational inequality is still substantial enough to justify the vertical mosaic image of Canada. As table 4.1 shows, despite a significant decline in the significance of ethnicity in determining occupational status between 1971 and 2001, 'ethnic origin continues to influence occupational inequality' (2007, 17).

On the other hand, occupational dissimilarity does not necessarily imply social inequality. Some have re-examined Porter's thesis and have argued that ethnicity does not play a significant role in occupational attainment or, more generally, in social mobility. Darroch (1979, 1–25) re-examined Porter's data and argued that Porter paid too much attention to the actual order of the ethnic hierarchy in occupational status and failed to notice the decreasing strength of the association between ethnicity and occupational level over time. In 1961, for example, ethnic occupational over and under-representation was lower than in 1931. In 1931, occupational dissimilarity was great among all non-charter groups, but by 1961, the differences had almost disappeared for Germans and eastern and other Europeans and had declined significantly for every other group except Aboriginal peoples. The blocked ethnic mobility thesis, then, had no factual foundation, and Darroch suggested that we should be 'sceptical of the idea that ethnic affiliations are a basic factor in generally limiting mobility opportunities in Canada' (1979, 16). Porter's mobility trap hypothesis, according to Darroch, is 'an exaggeration of any data available to date' (22).

Tepperman (1975) voiced even greater opposition to Porter's thesis, arguing that the privileged position of the charter groups had been effectively challenged by other European groups (149–52), and called the vertical mosaic thesis 'patently false' (156). Ethnic affiliation/cohesion and upward economic mobility are not necessarily incompatible. Canada admits immigrants at various levels of the occupational hierarchy, and all but the most recent arrivals earn more than their native-born counterparts, with the exception of the Jewish and Asians (149).

Earnings inequalities

Along the same lines as the debate about occupation, some researchers have suggested that there has been earnings equalization among ethnic groups, whereas others argue that ethnic inequalities persist in that area. Ornstein (1981) has shown that ethnicity alone does not explain much of the variation in earnings. He argued that much of what appear to be ethnic differences in earnings may be attributed to place

Table 4.1   Net Difference[a] in Occupational Status (1971) and Occupational Skill Group (2001) between Selected Ethnic Groups and the Rest of the Labour Force, by Sex: Canada.

	Male		Female	
Ethnic Group	1971	2001	1971	2001
British	0.13	0.06	0.14	0.05
French	−0.06	0.04	−0.02	0.06
German	−0.08	0.04	−0.09	0.01
Dutch	−0.09	0.05	−0.10	0.04
Scandinavian	−0.08	0.07	−0.01	0.05
Ukrainian	−0.09	0.06	−0.13	0.03
Polish	−0.08	0.03	−0.12	−0.02
Hungarian	−0.06	0.07	−0.13	0.02
Italian	−0.22	0.01	−0.35	0.00
Portuguese	−0.38	−0.15	−0.62	−0.16
Greek	−0.27	0.02	−0.48	−0.04
Yugoslav	−0.12	0.03	−0.29	−0.03
Jewish	0.36	0.34	0.24	0.24
Chinese	−0.04	0.19	−0.20	0.00
South Asian	0.26	−0.05	0.19	−0.12
Aboriginal	−0.35[b]	−0.15	−0.23[b]	−0.08
Black	NI	−0.10	NI	−0.09
Mean ($\bar{x}$)	0.17	0.09	0.21	0.06
Number of Occupational Ranks/Skill Groups	(498)	(4)	(464)	(4)

[a] A negative figure indicates a relatively low occupational status/skill group, a positive figure a relatively high status/skill group. Zero indicates equality of occupational status/skill group. The greater the absolute size of the index, the greater the inequality.

[b] Does not include Inuit.

NI: Not included.

Source: Hugh Lautard and Neil Guppy. 2007. 'Occupational inequality among Canadian ethnic groups, 1931 to 2001'. In Robert J. Brym (Ed.), *Society in question*, 5th ed. Toronto: Nelson Canada.

of birth, place of education, and language. Subsequent research (Ornstein 1983) has demonstrated that class and gender, along with labour market variables, are more important determinants of earnings than ethnicity. Weinfeld (1988), examining 1971 and 1981 census data, has argued that in that 10-year period there had been a reduction in income inequalities among ethnic groups. When sex, nativity, occupation, age, education, and number of weeks worked are statistically controlled, non-visible groups had almost the same income, whereas the earnings gap of visible minorities had become narrower. What matters, according to Weinfeld, was the percentage of the foreign-born within visible minorities and their amount and type of educational attainment (Weinfeld 1988, 603–5).

Winn (1988), using 1981 census data, argued that there is no necessary correspondence between low income[2] or low prestige and 'visibility'. Some non-'visible' groups, who presumably might have enjoyed higher prestige because of their 'white' colour, had lower incomes than 'visible' groups. In 1981, the Japanese were the third highest income group. Indo-Pakistanis and Koreans were found in the second quintile of earnings (1988, 197, table 17-2). Looking back at 1971 data, Winn argued that Asians were the second highest income group (1988, 196, table 17-1). The British in 1971 had lower incomes than lower-status groups such as the Jewish, Italians, other eastern Europeans, and other southern Europeans. Some higher-prestige groups, such as Scandinavians, Germans, and the Dutch, had incomes either below or around the national average (1988, 196–8). Therefore, argued Winn, it was plausible to suggest that there has been considerable ethnic mobility in earnings, especially as far as visible minority and lower-status groups are concerned. Winn suggested that upward mobility was experienced mostly by visible groups and downward mobility by higher-status, non-visible groups (1988, 198–200). In fact, Winn went even further, suggesting that employment equity policies were unnecessary[3] since visible minorities and low-prestige groups had made considerable economic progress.

THE NEW COLOUR-CODED VERTICAL MOSAIC?

Even though questions have been raised about the persistence of the vertical mosaic when European ethnic groups are considered, some suggest that the vertical mosaic persists in a racialized form and that Canada is characterized by a *colour-coded vertical mosaic* (Galabuzi 2006, 7).

In 1984, the Royal Commission on Equality in Employment, using 1981 census data, found that among men, visible minorities such as Aboriginal people, the Indo-Chinese, Central and South Americans, and blacks had incomes below the national average and were at the bottom of the income hierarchy. Among women, Aboriginal people, Central and South Americans, the Indo-Chinese, and Koreans had the lowest incomes (Royal Commission on Equality in Employment 1984, 84–5). These income disparities were attributed to systemic discrimination in the workplace. Visible minorities were often denied access to employment because of unfair recruitment procedures and were more likely to be unemployed. Their educational credentials, acquired outside Canada, were not recognized in the labour market or by governments. Sometimes, Canadian experience was required unduly (46–51). For Aboriginal people, the situation was even worse. Native men earned 60 per cent of the earnings of non-native men; native women earned 72 per cent as much as non-native women (33). Educational opportunities and training were seen as inadequate responses to the problem of inequality (34–5). Native people were more likely to be found in part-time or seasonal employment and less likely to move up the promotional ladder (37).

In response to Winn's argument that employment equity policies are unnecessary, Boyd (1992) demonstrated that visible minorities receive lower monetary rewards than their non-visible counterparts for similar qualifications. Using 1986 data, she showed that after controlling for age, region, place of residence, marital status, education, occupation, and employment status, the adjusted wages and salaries of visible minority men and women were lower than those of non-visible minority men and women (1992, 305–6, table 5). In the case of women (with the exception of the Chinese, who earned on average $237 more per year than other Canadian women), all visible minorities earned less than their non-visible female counterparts. West Asian women made $1,928 less than the average of $15,144 annually, and other visible minority women made between $491 and $233 less. French women earned the highest average income, $1,245 above the average for all women. However, non-visible minority women of Greek, Italian, Portuguese, other European, and Dutch descent, made less than the average.

In the case of men, all visible minorities earned substantially less than the average of $28,074 per year. Again, however, Greek men earned $3,344 less than the average (the second lowest earnings, ranking only above Filipino men), eastern Europeans $669 less, Germans $326 less, Portuguese $300 less, and other Europeans $194 less. The British earned the highest average income among men—$3,306 more than the average for all men.

Lian and Matthews (1998) examined 1991 census data and analyzed ethnic inequalities in earnings, studying the relationship between ethnicity and education and between education and income. They argue that 'race' is now the fundamental basis of income inequality in Canada. The French now earn more than the British, and there is a general trend of convergence of earnings among the European groups. Visible minorities, however, at all educational levels receive lower rewards, substantially below the national average (1998, 471, 475). Controlling for a number of variables, such as gender, age, age squared, marital status, province and place of residence, and year of immigration, Lian and Matthews suggest that in most of the 10 categories of educational level they examined, visible minorities make less than non-visible minorities (1998, 473, table 5). These findings led them to conclude that the old ethnic vertical mosaic may be disappearing, but it is being replaced by a strong 'coloured mosaic' (1998, 476; see also Pendakur and Pendakur 1996).

In a hard-hitting analysis titled *Canada's economic apartheid: The social exclusion of racialized groups in the new century*, Grace-Edward Galabuzi (2006) argues that there is substantial evidence to support his and others' claim that there is a new colour-coded vertical mosaic. Table 4.2 illustrates Galabuzi's findings, giving a comparison of the after-tax income of racialized and non-racialized persons in Canada in 2000. It shows, for example, that the average after-tax income for racialized persons was $20,627, 12.3 per cent less than the average after-tax income of $23,522 for non-racialized persons. Table 4.2 also shows that differences in after-tax income can even be found when higher education is taken into account. It shows that among university degree-holders in 2000, racialized individuals had an after-tax income of $35,617, while non-racialized individuals had an after-tax income of $38,919, an 8.5 per cent difference.

We will return to the colour-coded mosaic thesis later in this chapter. But before offering a critical perspective on it, we want to consider one more dimension of inequality that has been the subject of considerable research in Canada: inequalities between immigrants and non-immigrants.

Table 4.2   After-Tax Income of Racialized and Non-racialized Persons
              Canada, 2000

After-tax income	Total population	Racialized (a)	Non-racialized (b)	Difference $	%
Average	$23,023	$20,627	$23,522	$2,895	12.3
Median	$18,138	$15,909	$18,348	$2,439	13.3

After-Tax Income of Racialized and Non-racialized Persons with University Degree Canada, 2000

Average	$38,312	$35,617	$38,919	$3,302	8.5
Median	$32,832	$28,378	$33,230	$4,852	14.6

Source: Grace-Edward Galabuzi. 2006. *Canada's economic apartheid*, 100. Toronto: Canadian Scholars Press.

Immigrants and the vertical mosaic

Another focus of sociological research on inequality examines what happens specifically to immigrants when they arrive in Canada. In other words, how do immigrants fare in the Canadian labour market once they are here, and is there evidence that they are treated fairly by employers and licensing bodies that regulate entry to the professions in Canada? These are not, as you might expect, simply academic questions. Policy-makers, immigrant advocates, and immigrants themselves are profoundly concerned about how immigrants, particularly those with valuable skills, education, and experience, are treated in Canada. After all, as we noted in chapter 3, Canada needs, wants, and recruits skilled immigrants, but it is not clear whether the Canadian labour market fairly rewards all immigrants for the training and the talent that they bring to the country.

We examine two specific issues in this section. First, to what extent do immigrants earn the same income as native-born Canadians, even when other relevant background variables are taken into consideration? Second, what evidence is there that immigrant credentials are evaluated fairly in Canada? In other words, are immigrants who bring certain skills and educational credentials to this country fairly rewarded?

One way to assess the inequalities between different groups of immigrants and the Canadian-born is to compare data on earnings differences after other sources of variation in earnings have been statistically controlled for. Table 4.3 provides a comprehensive portrait of these differences. The net earnings of immigrants and the Canadian-born are represented as deviations from the national mean earnings of $26,521 in 1996; these differences are also subdivided by the size of the Census Metropolitan Area in which individuals live. Net differences refer to differences in earnings after a number of other individual and market characteristics are statistically controlled for. Put differently, the net differences in earnings are the differences that exist even when individuals have similar occupations, work in the same industries, have similar years of schooling and years of experience, and work the same number of weeks. The other similarities that are controlled for are given in the footnote to table 4.3.

Table 4.3 highlights a number of important aspects of social inequality. First, it shows that immigrant men and women in each of the four CMA types earn less than their Canadian-born counterparts. For example, in medium-sized CMAs, Canadian-born white males earn $5,136 above the average for all Canadians, but white male immigrants earn only $1,349 above the average. In large CMAs, Canadian-born visible minority women earn $2,722 less than average, but immigrant visible minority women earn more than $10,000 below the Canadian average. Second, table 4.3 shows that the earnings of Canadian-born and immigrant men exceed the earnings

Table 4.3   Net Earnings of Immigrants and Native-born Canadians as Deviations from National Mean Earnings ($26,521) for Four Census Metropolitan Area (CMA) Levels, 1996 Census (in Dollars)

		Net earnings after adjusting for individual and market characteristics	
		Native-born Canadian	Immigrant
Not CMA			
White:	Male	5,136	1,258
	Female	−2,901	−8,645
Visible minority:	Male	4,801	1,686
	Female	336	−5,768
Small CMA (<500,000)			
White:	Male	6,044	2,432
	Female	−3,238	−9,578
Visible minority:	Male	4,764	−2,151
	Female	−1,517	−8,250
Medium CMA (500,000–999,999)			
White:	Male	5,136	1,349
	Female	−3,813	−10,578
Visible minority:	Male	61	−6,372
	Female	−1,588	−9,823
Large CMA (1,000,000+)			
White:	Male	5,392	−314
	Female	−3,508	−10,188
Visible minority:	Male	479	−6,654
	Female	−2,722	−10,372

Net earnings are adjusted for differences in individual characteristics and differences in market characteristics. Individual characteristics include industry of work, occupation, full-time or part-time work, years of schooling, years of work experience, experience squared, number of weeks worked, official language ability, and number of years since immigrating to Canada for immigrants. Market characteristics include the level of unemployment in the person's region of residence and the size of immigrants' population as a percent of the region's total population.

Source: Peter Li. 2003. *Destination Canada: Immigration debates and issues*, 108–9. Toronto: Oxford University Press.

of comparable groups of Canadian-born and immigrant women. In small CMAs, 'white' immigrant men earn $2,432 above the average, but 'white' immigrant women earn $9,578 below the average. Canadian-born visible minority men in small CMAs earn $4,764 above the average, while Canadian-born visible minority women earn $1,517 less than the average of $26,521. Third, the table shows that 'white' Canadian-born men tend to do better than 'white' immigrant men and that visible minority Canadian-born men do better than visible minority immigrant men. Fourth, it shows that 'white' Canadian-born men do better than visible minority Canadian-born men but that visible minority Canadian-born women tend to do better than 'white' Canadian-born women. And fifth, it shows that 'white' and visible minority immigrant women have roughly the lowest levels of earnings of all groups in each of the four CMAs.

These patterns are complex, but one of the things that table 4.3 shows is that when other individual and job market-level variables are taken into account, immigrants do more poorly in every Canadian CMA than the Canadian-born. Yet if Canadian society rewarded everyone equally on the basis of the skills and training that they bring to the labour market, the net differences between groups should be minimal.

How do sociologists explain these kinds of findings? Among other things, the patterns point to the devaluation of immigrant credentials as an important part of the explanation of social inequalities between immigrants and the Canadian-born. Devaluation of immigrant credentials refers to the lack of recognition of educational qualifications earned outside of Canada (Li 2003, 113). There is evidence that shows that many immigrant teachers, doctors, nurses, and engineers find that their non-Western university degrees and diplomas are of little value in Canada (Henry and Tator 2005; Basran and Zong 1998).

For many of these professionals, the choices they face are rather stark: (1) some simply give up trying to practise their professions in Canada and face lifetimes of underemployment and status dislocation; (2) some swallow their pride and start from scratch by getting a Canadian degree in the field that they have already been trained in, even though they already have the skills and knowledge required to practise their craft; (3) some take on lengthy and expensive battles with professional licensing bodies to have their credentials recognized as equivalent to a Canadian degree; and (4) some simply give up on Canada and either return to their country of origin or move to another country perceived to evaluate immigrant educational credentials more fairly. Jeffrey Reitz (2001) argues that in 1996 alone, the combination of immigrant skill underutilization and pay inequities between immigrants and non-immigrants resulted in a $55.5-billion earnings deficit for immigrants.

A CRITICAL ASSESSMENT OF ETHNIC/ 'RACIAL' INEQUALITY RESEARCH

The research discussed above has made valuable contributions to the study of social inequality in Canada. Box 4.1 provides one particular example of an immigrant 'success story', but there are other such stories in this country. As we noted in chapter 3,

Box 4.1 An Immigrant Success Story

Farrokh Moheb

Farrokh Moheb came from Iran and channelled his passion for tennis into building a business that trains the tennis stars of tomorrow.

'This is a country that gives you the freedom to make goals and be successful,' says Farrokh Moheb, owner/operator of People's Courts in Coquitlam.

'If you roll up your sleeves and apply your own motivation, you are not going to regret it.'

And he should know, because that's exactly what he has done.

When he moved to Canada from Iran in 1999, Moheb brought with him a background in political science in international relations, a love of tennis, and a dream to own and operate a business. Putting the three together resulted in his taking over a tennis club that today turns out some of the top players in the country.

'I'm proud to say that we are now the home of the juniors,' he says. 'Our Tennis Academy Programs are becoming a major launching pad for talented players seeking provincial, national and international titles. In fact, we have produced more players on the national team than any other in western Canada.'

Moheb had qualified for immigration under the federal entrepreneur category and was provided with counselling and support by BC's Business Immigration office in Vancouver. He took this opportunity to provide a place for young tennis hopefuls to develop their skills while also providing coaching jobs for certified international professionals, as well as employment for 20 assistant coaches and other staff.

He credits his success to having the right combination of goals, motivation and sound decision-making. His management style is one of teamwork, considering the person who cleans the windows as important to the business as his coaching staff.

'I'd done a great deal of study in political leadership and teamwork effectiveness,' he says. 'I think these days the more you know about management and leadership and teamwork, it really helps you, it doesn't matter what you do for a living.'

Continuing success for Moheb means once more rolling up his sleeves and applying his business and motivational skills to developing partnerships with communities that would benefit from a similar tennis program.

'A business like this brings employment for people in the community,' he says. 'And it brings opportunities for children from six to sixteen to learn and maximize their abilities. It is our goal to help every athlete reach his or her full potential.'

Source: British Columbia. Ministry of the Attorney General.
http://www.ag.gov.bc.ca/immigration/profiles/moheb.htm.

Canada has a business immigration program, and the immigrants admitted under this category do not easily fit into the new colour-coded vertical mosaic thesis. In this section, we want to highlight a number of problematic aspects of this research.

First, ethnicity has played a prominent role in the explanation of social inequality in Canada. The 'ethnic' approach now constitutes a dominant research tradition, but there has arguably been an overemphasis on the ethnic/'racial' dimension of social inequality in Canada. Pluralist conceptions tend to reduce Canada to an amalgamation of ethnic groups (Driedger 1996): Canada, a country of immigrants, is thought to be constituted by ethnic/'racial' groups only. Our history of nation-building, our present demographic reality, and the official policy of multiculturalism, among other things, tend to lend ideological credence to this argument. In response to the question of what Canada is, the usual rejoinder is that it is an ethnic/'racial' mosaic, an amalgamation of cultural/ethnic groups. When the question of social inequality arises, ethnicity becomes the main or the only dimension of analysis: some ethnic groups are doing better than others. Ethnicity, no doubt, is a social reality. But it is not the only social reality. Demographic profiles and policies of official multiculturalism provide the empirical and ideological evidence that justifies the portrayal of Canada as being only multi-ethnic. But this is, of course, a one-dimensional and reductionist portrayal of the structure of the country, especially as far as social inequality is concerned. Canada, it is important to remember, is also a capitalist and a patriarchal society, and it is necessary to incorporate these dimensions into the analysis of social inequality.

Second, with some exceptions (Li 1988, 1992; Nakhaie 1999, 2000), the class dimension of social inequality in Canada is not adequately examined. Porter himself argued that ethnic groups have internal hierarchies and are themselves stratified (Porter 1965, 73). They are not homogeneous: they are differentiated by religion, by whether they are recent or earlier arrivals (Porter 1965, 72), and by class (Li 1988, 1992; Liodakis 1998, 2002). Porter ignored gender, but it has also been added to the dimensions of internal stratification of ethnic groups (Boyd 1992). As mentioned earlier, it is ironic that Porter's work, which was an effort to bring class back into the analysis of social inequality in Canada, has been interpreted by some social scientists as asserting the analytical dominance of ethnicity (Liodakis 2002). Class and ethnicity are important dimensions of social inequality in Canada. They may also be viewed as competing theoretical approaches to the analysis of social inequality (McAll 1990). Even if we accept that there was a period in the history of Canada during which ethnicity overlapped with class, there was never a one-to-one correspondence of the concepts. In other words, despite the fact that there was never empirical evidence to support the notion that one ethnic group is associated with one class only, ethnicity, thanks to Porter's work, became a proxy of class. Ethnic groups became statistical 'classes' that exhibited differential socio-economic performance and held differential amounts of political and economic power.

The vertical mosaic thesis should be questioned, not because we now have more ethnic equality but arguably because inequality in Canada is still very much based on social class, and ethnicity and 'race' serve as sources of division within the broader class structure (Li 1992). Ethnic inequality cannot be analyzed outside the class context (Li 1988, 141). For example, Nakhaie (1999; 2000) has adopted a Marxian model of class and has examined the class composition of ethnic groups. Using data from the 1973 *Canadian mobility survey* and the 1989 *General social survey*, he has demonstrated that there were significant changes to the class composition of ethnic groups between 1973 and 1989 for both men and women. During this period, the English were not overrepresented in the ownership class categories (bourgeoisie, petty bourgeoisie, self-employed) compared to other ethnic groups. Ethnic differences in the managerial classes declined, especially for the French. The British, however, still dominated the business elite and were overrepresented in the managerial classes. The French and Italians were persistently overrepresented in the working class (2000, 168, table 11.4, 170, table 11.5). Nakhaie (2000, 174) concluded that the effect of ethnicity in determining class position has declined. The relationship between ethnicity and class is in flux, and no ethnic group dominates the top of the Canadian class structure. But his analysis also shows that ethnic groups are not homogeneous. They are internally stratified in terms of class, and they are also stratified in terms of gender and place of birth. We are not suggesting that the choice is between class or ethnic analyses. We rather encourage the use of a multi-dimensional model in which the internal differences of ethnic groups are taken into account.

A third problematic issue in the analysis of social inequality in Canada is that there is sometimes a lack of definitional parsimony in the colour-coded mosaic thesis. As mentioned above, many researchers argue that there is a clear-cut division in Canadian society along 'racial' lines. More often than not, the groups under examination, ethnic or 'racial', are defined in terms of Statistics Canada census categories. Categories such as 'visible minorities', 'racialized groups', 'non-racialized groups', or even 'whites' do not always have a clear social referent. This may be explained in part by two factors. First, over time, increased rates of exogamy among groups that immigrated to Canada before the 1980s has led to a decrease in the number of census respondents who report single ethnic origins. In addition, since the 1980s, the number of visible minority immigrants has increased. These two trends make it increasingly difficult to compare single origin, multiple origin, and visible minority respondents when analyzing census data. Second, the classifications used by Statistics Canada in the census tend to lump together groups from different ethnic backgrounds, often based on 'racial' markers like skin colour. This makes it easier (both theoretically and statistically) to construct a dichotomy between visible and non-visible groups by adding their 'constituent' parts together irrespective of their ethnic or cultural differences. For example, the category 'Caribbean' includes people from various parts of that geographical area, from countries such as Cuba, Jamaica, Trinidad and Tobago, and the Dominican Republic. The category 'Latin American' includes people from Brazil, Argentina, Uruguay, Colombia, Venezuela, and so on. 'Arabs' could come from numerous countries across four continents. In 1996, Statistics Canada (1996, 2–44) defined the following groups as part of the 'collectivity' of 'visible minorities': black, south Asian, Chinese, Korean, Japanese, southeast Asian, Filipino, Arab/west Asian, Latin American, 'visible minority' not included elsewhere, and multiple 'visible minority'. For the

2006 census, the variable 'visible minority' contained the categories Chinese, south Asian, black, and 'other visible minority'.

This taxonomy creates categories so broadly defined that the considerable internal socio-economic heterogeneity within groups is concealed (Boyd 1992, 281; Liodakis 2002). The term 'visible minority' emerged in the 1970s in response to the use of pejorative terms such as 'coloured' or 'non-white' and was used by activists and scholars who were fighting social inequality. The term is now embedded not only in census questions but also in state policies of employment equity and multiculturalism (Synnott and Howes 1996, 137) and by extension in the language of social scientists and non-academics. A person is officially a member of a 'visible minority' group if s/he is 'non-white' in 'colour' or 'non-Caucasian' in 'race', other than Aboriginal. The problem with this social construction of the concept of 'visible minority', according to Synnott and Howes, is that when attempts are made to refer the concept of 'visible minority' back to the social reality it is supposed to describe, 'it falls apart' (1996, 138). It does not have a social referent. It tends to homogenize and racialize diverse groups of people. As we note in more detail in chapter 5, census-taking is not an innocent exercise of simply counting people. As Melissa Nobles (2000) has argued, censuses help to shape and reproduce a 'racial' discourse that in turn affects public policies that either restrict or protect the rights, the privileges, and the experiences we commonly associate with citizenship. Statistics Canada is not necessarily a politically neutral institution that simply 'counts' Canadians in an objective sort of way. It creates the conditions under which people will identify themselves so that Statistics Canada can count them afterwards. The terms 'ethnicity', 'visible minority', 'whites'/'non-whites' are, to paraphrase Goldberg, 'irreducibly political categories' that construct 'racial' and ethnic groups (Nobles 2000).

The term also homogenizes the non-visible category. Synnott and Howes argue that visible minorities are diverse in terms of their place of birth and place of residence as well as their length of residence in Canada, not to mention their age, class, and gender composition. This is also true, of course, of non-visible groups. Such divisions, however, have important implications for their employment and level and type of education as well as earnings. For example, there are different unemployment rates within the category of 'visible minority'. In 1991, the unemployment rate of people who reported Japanese ancestry was only 6 per cent—below the national average—whereas that of Latin Americans was 20 per cent, almost double the national average (Synnott and Howes 1996, 139, table I).

There are also important differences in types and levels of education. If we aggregate members of diverse groups under the category 'visible minorities', their internal differences are often concealed. For example, Davies and Guppy (1998) have shown that as a group, visible minorities are better educated than non-visible minorities. And some members of the visible minority category are better educated overall than others. Filipinos, Koreans, Japanese, west Asians and Arabs are more likely to have completed university than blacks, southeast Asians, and Latin Americans. The former groups are also more likely than the latter to be found in managerial and professional occupations (Kelly 1995, 5–7). As some of the studies reviewed above have shown, they have different earnings as well. In addition, not all members of the above-mentioned groups are visible or equally visible. Combining them in order to produce statistics on employment, educational attainment, or earnings is problematic. In other words, who is the 'average' south Asian, black, or Filipino person? Who is the average southern European? In fact, Synnott and Howes argue that it is better to separate the various groups from one another and analyze their socio-economic conditions separately than it is to treat them all as 'manifestations of a single (spurious) category' (1996, 142–3). Yet researchers who subscribe to the 'visibility' thesis include them all in the dichotomy of statistical categories (see Li 1998b; Lian and Matthews 1998; Hou and Balakrishnan 1999). In terms of the analysis of stratification, when we use racializing, homogenizing terms like 'visible'/ 'non-visible' minority or 'white'/'non-white', we tend to conceal their internal differences along class, gender, and nativity lines as well as the cultural and ethnic differences among them.

Fourth, the colour-coded vertical mosaic thesis does not fully explain the patterns of earnings inequality in Canada[4]. In fact, the racialized vertical mosaic thesis seems to overlook anomalies that undermine the thesis. In much of the literature on social inequality (see, for example, Li 1988) southern European groups—the Greeks, the Portuguese, and to a lesser extent the Italians—are not as well-educated as the rest of the European groups and do not earn as much; in some studies, they have been identified as not as educated and as earning less than some visible minorities (Li 1988, 76, table 5.1, 78, table 5.2, 82, table 5.3, 84, table 5.4, 88, table 5.5). In Boyd's (1992) research, it was also evident that in the case of non-visible minority women, Greek, Italian, Portuguese, other European, and Dutch women made less than the average earnings of all women. In fact, in terms of earnings ranking, Greek and Italian women ranked lower than Chinese women. Portuguese women ranked lower than Chinese, Filipino, Southeast Asian, and black women. And Dutch and eastern European women ranked lower than most visible minority women (1992, table 5). In the case of men, Greeks ranked lower than visible minority people of British descent, west Asians, south Asians, the Chinese, southeast Asians, and blacks. Greek men had the second lowest level of average earnings among all men (1992, table 5).

Lian and Matthews (1998) also found that individuals of Greek, Portuguese, Italian, and Spanish background do not receive equal rewards for their educational levels. They are, in fact, also disadvantaged and may be more disadvantaged than some visible minorities at most educational levels. For example, Greeks make less at all educational levels except in the category of 'trades certificate'. In the 'degree in medicine' category, they make 50 per cent less than the British base group. This is the lowest percentage among all groups, visible and non-visible. In the category 'earned doctorate', Greek-origin individuals make 26 per cent less, which is lower than west and south Asians, the Vietnamese, blacks, and other east and southeast Asians. And in the category 'university certificate above Bachelor level', they make 15.7 per cent less than the British, a percentage that is, again, much lower than that of visible minorities like west and south Asians, the Chinese, Filipinos, blacks, and other east and southeast Asians. Similar patterns hold for other southern European groups. In short, the poor socio-economic performance of southern European groups raises hard questions about the validity of the new racialized vertical mosaic image of Canada. There is no clear 'visible'/'non-visible' division in earnings inequality. Indeed, the examples cited above may render the colour-coded vertical mosaic thesis as only partially accurate.

BRINGING CLASS BACK IN

Central to the analysis of social inequality presented in this final section is the understanding that the production and reproduction of the conditions of people's existence is social. Individuals are interacting social subjects, situated in class, gender, and ethnic social locations (Satzewich and Wotherspoon 1993, 13). Social inequality is a social reality. In most advanced, liberal-democratic societies like ours, all social relations have class, gender, and 'race'/ethnic elements. The class analysis in this section relies upon E.O. Wright's work on social class (1983). We do not claim that class is the only or the most important dimension of social inequality. We do claim, however, that along with gender, it accounts more for the earnings differentials among and within ethnic and 'racial' groups than any of the other dimensions. Ethnicity or visibility alone are not good 'predictors' of earnings inequality in Canada (Li 1988; 1992).

According to Wright (1983, 61–83, 76, table 2.9), there are three main classes in capitalist societies (bourgeoisie, petty bourgeoisie, and proletariat) and three contradictory class locations between them. These classes are defined by:

a) economic ownership of money capital (control over investments and resources);
b) control of the physical means of production;
c) control of the labour power of others.

According to this model, the bourgeoisie (big employers) has economic ownership and possession in all three areas: money capital, physical capital, and labour. The petty bourgeoisie does not have control of labour. The proletariat (workers) have no control of money or physical capital either but unlike the petty bourgeoisie must sell labour power in exchange for wages. Small employers, a contradictory location between the petty bourgeoisie and the bourgeoisie, have only minimal control over the labour power of others and not a lot of money and physical capital. Managers and supervisors occupy a contradictory location between the proletariat and the bourgeoisie since although they exchange labour power for wages, they do have a lot of control over physical capital, as well as over the labour power and process of workers, but less control over money capital than big employers do. Finally, semi-autonomous workers (often called professionals) occupy a contradictory location between the proletariat and the petty bourgeoisie because although they do not control the labour power of others and they sell theirs, they do have minimal control over money and physical capital and considerable control of their own labour process (Wright 1983, 76). We do, however, recognize that this is a general analytical schema and in actual societies, these class locations contain sets of real people: men and women who come from different ethnic backgrounds and whose actual lives do not fit neatly into one exclusive category.

Whereas earlier traditions have tended to emphasize the 'mosaic' dimension of inequality and to examine the earnings inequalities *among* ethnic groups, in this section we emphasize the 'vertical' dimension and examine the earnings inequalities both among and *within* these ethnic groups. These ethnic inequalities do not occur in a social vacuum but take place within a class society. The approach proposed here suggests that within each structural locational basis of inequality (ethnicity, gender, or class), the other two coexist. All classes have gender and ethnic segments. Gender groups have class and ethnic segments. All ethnic groups are permeated by class and gender differences.

In the remainder of this chapter, we address two interrelated issues: First, we examine whether ethnic groups are homogeneous or heterogeneous in terms of class composition. Second, we examine the earnings differentials not only among but also within ethnic groups in terms of class, gender and nativity.

Evidence of ethnic heterogeneity

The data used in this section come from the 'Public use microdata file on individuals' from the 2001 Canadian census. The total number of people in the entire sample is 347,020. It includes persons of single ethnic origins from Ontario, Quebec, Saskatchewan, Manitoba, Alberta, and British Columbia, 25 to 60 years of age, who had worked at least one week in 2000. The ethnic adjectives in the tables that appear below do not denote the subjective ethnic or cultural identity of the respondents but that of their ancestors and the categories used by Statistics Canada. They simply indicate ethnic or cultural origin.

To simplify our argument, we do not examine the class structure of every ethnic group in Canada. Instead, we selectively examine the social class composition of the following groups: Aboriginal (not considered a 'visible minority' by Statistics Canada), British, Caribbean, Chinese, Filipino, French, Greek, Italian, Jewish, Portuguese, and south Asian. These choices are based on the fact that the British and the French are the so-called charter groups, were part of the original vertical mosaic thesis, and feature prominently in all subsequent analyses of ethnicity. They have conventionally constituted the frame of reference for all comparisons. Jews, on the other hand, albeit accorded an 'entrance status', have tended to outperform both charter and all other groups in terms of educational attainment and earnings. They represent an 'anomalous' case for proponents of the vertical mosaic thesis and/or its assimilationist versions. The three southern European groups—Greek, Italian, and Portuguese—are undoubtedly the least studied European groups. Some evidence indicates that Greeks may represent an anomalous case as well, which poses problems for the proponents of the racialized vertical mosaic argument (Liodakis 2002). Often, because of their poor socio-economic performance, they do not very well fit the 'visible'/'non-visible' dichotomy proposed by some researchers (see Li 1988; Hou and Balakrishnan 1999; Lian and Matthews 1998). The four 'visible' groups we have chosen represent the most populous of all other single-origin 'visible' groups in Canada.

As Porter argued (1965), ethnic groups are not homogeneous; they differ in terms of their internal class structure. Table 4.4 provides further contemporary confirmation of this in that it presents the percentage distribution of the selected ethnic and 'racial' groups among social classes.

Table 4.4   The Class Composition of Groups (%), 2001

Ethnic group (n)	Workers	Semi-autonomous workers	Managers, supervisors	Petty bourgeoisie	Employers
Aboriginal (3,856)	68.2	17.0	8.8	4.0	2.0
British (32,895)	51.3	21.2	14.5	7.8	5.3
Caribbean (2,348)	63.4	21.0	9.5	4.6	1.5
Chinese (10,740)	47.8	28.2	10.0	6.9	7.1
Filipino (2,811)	68.8	19.6	7.3	2.5	1.8
French (13,750)	51.7	24.4	12.1	7.2	4.5
Greek (1,801)	48.8	19.2	13.4	7.2	11.4
Italian (9,179)	51.7	20.0	15.2	6.2	6.8
Jewish (1,958)	27.2	32.5	15.6	11.5	13.2
Portuguese (3,241)	67.4	11.5	11.8	4.7	4.6
South Asian (2,106)	64.2	18.7	8.5	3.8	4.8
Canada (347,020)	52.9	22.0	12.5	7.5	5.1

Source: Statistics Canada. 2001. 'Public use microdata on individuals', 2001 census.

If we look at social inequality from the perspective of class composition, it appears that in the case of the proletariat, there is no clear-cut 'visible'/'non-visible' distinction. The Chinese, for example, are less proletarianized than the Portuguese, the Italians, the Greeks, the British, and the French. The Portuguese are more proletarianized than the Chinese, the Caribbean, and the south Asian. Aboriginal Canadians are more likely to be found in the working class and less likely to be found in the other classes. Aboriginal, British, Caribbean, Filipino, French, and Portuguese individuals are under-represented in the ranks of employers, while Chinese, Greek, and Jewish individuals are variously overrepresented among the ranks of the petty bourgeoisie. In the semi-autonomous worker category, the Chinese are well above the national average, second only to Jewish-descent respondents. In the employer category, the Chinese are overrepresented, but all other visible groups are under-represented, along with the Portuguese, the French, and Aboriginals.

Despite these patterns of over and under-representation, two important points stand out in table 4.4. First, as one should expect, members of each of the 11 ethnic groups are distributed across the range of class sites. No single group is *exclusively* one class or another. Second, the dividing line is muddied between groups traditionally conceived as 'visible minorities' and those traditionally conceived as 'non-visible' minorities. In short, there is great diversity within ethnic groups in terms of their class compositions. There is no consistent pattern of distribution across class locations. There is considerable class heterogeneity both among and within the ethnic groups under examination. If analytical primacy is given to only one of the three dimensions we have examined, the important internal, within-group class divisions that affect their earnings are obfuscated. In addition, ethnic groups have different gender and nativity compositions. For example, in terms of gender, the Caribbean and Filipino categories have more women than men in the labour market. In all visible groups, the percentage of foreign-born members exceeds 90 per cent, whereas in the non-visible category, the percentage is much lower (less than 50 per cent). These differences do affect their earnings but are concealed if we only look at them as homogeneous entities.

Earnings inequalities among and within ethnic groups

If, as we have shown above, ethnic groups differ in their class composition, do they also differ in the rewards they receive from participating in the economy? In other words, is there variation in their earnings? And if so, are the differences among them greater than the differences within them? Table 4.5 shows that there are considerable differences in the earnings of classes.

In Table 4.5, it is clear that the petty bourgeois and the proletarians have mean earnings below the sample mean. The petty bourgeois make $11,012.17 less than the mean,[6] and the proletarians make $6,538.98 less. Employers make $8,710.73 more, semi-autonomous workers $7,742.17 more, and managers and supervisors $16,726.68 more. These results are consistent with the findings of similar research using 1986, 1991, and 1996 Canadian census data (Li 1988, 1992; Liodakis 2002). In percentage terms, the petty bourgeois make 29.34 per cent less, and workers make 18.64 per cent less than the sample mean. On the other hand, employers make 24.83 per cent more than the mean, semi-autonomous workers 22.07 per cent more, and managers and supervisors 47.68 per cent more. The latter group represents the highest-paid class. These patterns also hold when we examine median earnings. Class differences are greater than differences between 'visible' and 'non-visible' groups. For example, in the same year, visible minorities made $6,156 less than non-visible minorities. Gender differences are also greater: women made $14,895 less than men, more than double the visibility difference. Foreign-born respondents made $2,110 less than the native-born. In all ethnic groups, the class, gender, and nativity patterns of earnings inequalities hold.

If we understand ethnic groups as being fractured by class, gender, and nativity divisions, a more varied pattern of earnings inequality emerges. The overall class/gender/nativity differentials are greater than the ethnic ones, especially if we exclude

Table 4.5   Gross Earnings by Class, 2000

Class	N	Mean earnings $	Std. deviation	Median earnings $	±% of National average
Workers	183,493	$28,540.82	20,857.01	$26,000.00	−18.64
Semi-autonomous workers	76,461	$42,821.97	27,941.85	$40,000.00	+22.07
Managers, supervisors	43,205	$51,806.48	36,264.33	$45,000.00	+47.68
Petty bourgeoisie	26,144	$24,785.83	29,262.01	$17,000.00	−29.34
Employers	17,717	$43,790.53	43,112.93	$30,000.00	+24.83
Canada	347,020	$35,079.80	28,419.77	$30,000.00	

Source: Statistics Canada. 2001. 'Public use microdata on individuals', 2001 census.

the top earners (Jewish-origin respondents) and the bottom ones (Aboriginals). Even within the top-earning ethnic category of Jewish-origin people, for example, male, native-born employers made $105,539, compared to female, foreign-born petty bourgeois members, who made only $27,315, a difference of $78,224. In the category of South Asian-origin respondents, the top group of male, native-born managers and supervisors made $55,500, whereas foreign-born petty bourgeois women made only $19,220, a difference of $36,280. In the group of Filipino-origin respondents, male, native-born managers and supervisors made $46,830, whereas the bottom group of female, native-born petty bourgeois made only $12,509, a difference of $34,321. In the Greek-origin group, male, native-born managers and supervisors made $57,064, whereas female, foreign-born petty bourgeois made $15,695, a difference of $41,369. In the case of Aboriginals, male employers (their highest-paid segment) made $35,802, whereas female, petty bourgeois (their lowest-paid segment) made only $14,300, or $21,502 less.

SUMMARY

In this chapter, we have reviewed whether the vertical mosaic thesis continues to be an accurate way of describing Canadian society. We began by discussing John Porter's conception of Canada as a vertical mosaic. We then reviewed occupational attainment and earnings data to assess whether the vertical mosaic metaphor continues to have relevance for Canada today. We argued that while there is a progressive convergence among ethnic groups, some differences continue to be important in discussions of social inequality.

In particular, we noted that some sociologists argue that colour has become the new dividing line such that there is now a new colour-coded vertical mosaic, with racialized minorities at the bottom of the socio-economic structure and non-racialized, white Canadians at the top. We also reviewed evidence for earnings differences between immigrants and the Canadian-born and suggested that part of the reason that some immigrants earn less than the Canadian-born, even when other possible sources of variation in earnings are accounted for, is that Canadian society devalues the educational credentials and job experience of non-Western-trained individuals.

Finally, the picture of social inequality that we presented in the last section of this chapter offers an alternative prism for the examination of social inequality. Canada may be a 'racially'/ethnically stratified society, but it remains a capitalist, patriarchal society divided along class and gender lines.

Questions for Critical Thought

1. What evidence is there to conclude that Canada is presently characterized by a colour-coded vertical mosaic? What are the problems with this kind of portrait of Canadian society?
2. Does a focus on social class offer a better picture of social inequality than a focus on ethnic/'racial' differences?
3. Does a focus on gender offer a better picture of social inequality than a focus on ethnic/'racial' differences?

4. How do you explain the earnings differences between immigrants and the Canadian-born and between visible minority and non-visible minority immigrants?
5. Assume that you are working for a telemarketing company and you are asked to place a call to people chosen randomly in order to guess their earnings. You are not allowed to ask them directly about their earnings. You can only ask three questions. What would those questions be?

Annotated Additional Readings

Galabuzi, Grace-Edward. 2006. *Canada's economic apartheid: The social exclusion of racialized groups in the new century*. Toronto: Canadian Scholars Press. A powerful and controversial argument in support of the view that Canada is characterized by a new colour-coded vertical mosaic.

Porter, John. 1965. *The vertical mosaic: An analysis of social class and power in Canada*. Toronto: University of Toronto Press. This is the book that set the intellectual context for much of the discussion of social inequality in Canada over the past four decades.

Synnott, Anthony, and David Howes. 1996. 'Canada's visible minorities: Identity and representation'. In V. Amit-Talai and C. Knowles (Eds), *Re-situating identities: The politics of race, ethnicity and culture*. Peterborough: Broadview Press. A well-thought through critique of the concept of 'visible minority'. Synnott and Howes question whether it makes sense to lump together so many different groups, with different immigration histories and backgrounds, into a single analytical category.

Related Websites

Canadian Multicultural Council: http://www.ethnocultural.ca/.
Canadian Race Relations Foundation: http://www.crr.ca/.
The Maytree Foundation: http://ftpd.maytree.com/.
Statistics Canada: http://www.statcan.ca/.
Human Resources and Social Development Canada: http://www.hrsdc.gc.ca/.

Chapter 5

Identity and Multiculturalism[1]

Learning objectives

In this chapter you will learn that:

- Ethnic and 'racial' identities are contested terrains. They are social constructions, specific to time and place, and always in flux.
- Social processes and institutions influence how ethnic identities are formed, maintained, and transformed over time. History, the economy, and our political system—but also ethnic and cultural organizations—play an especially crucial role in these processes.
- Canadian state policies and census groupings tend to produce and reproduce 'divisions' among the Canadian population based partly on people's ancestral origins but also on antiquated 'racial' categories, combined with geography.
- These categories do not always have a social referent. The 'racial'/geographical combinations are statistical categories that are reproduced by social scientists and have come to dominate popular parlance.
- Multiculturalism is part of pluralist ideology, a Canadian demographic reality, a set of government policies and programs, and an arena for ethnic competition for government funding and other resources—but also a controversial policy.
- The federal government claims that it assists in the development of cultural groups, in overcoming cultural barriers to their full participation in Canadian society, and in promoting creative encounters and exchanges among them in the interest of national unity.
- Quebec has pursued a policy of interculturalism that promotes cultural interchanges and citizenship within the context of French unilingualism.

• There exist both progressive and conservative critiques of multiculturalism. Some critics see the policy as ineffective since it does not address the economic and political inequalities among and within dominant groups and minorities, undermines the special claims of Aboriginals and francophones, marginalizes ethnic and cultural issues, and hardens ethnic stereotypes. Others argue that the policy is too effective: i.e., it promotes cultural relativism so that the Canadian identity is threatened.

INTRODUCTION

What do apples, bananas, coconuts, and Oreos have in common? Aside from being tasty snacks, these terms all speak to issues of ethnic and 'racial' identity. In particular, they represent derogatory labels that have been applied by some members of visible minority communities to describe other members of the same group. An 'apple' is an Aboriginal individual who is 'red' on the outside but 'white' on the inside; coconuts are south Asian-origin individuals who are 'brown' on the outside but 'white' on the inside; bananas are individuals of Chinese or Japanese origin who are 'yellow' on the outside and 'white' on the inside; and Oreos (if you have not figured it out by now) are individuals who are 'black' on the outside but 'white' on the inside.

What would make someone consider another person a banana, apple, Oreo, or coconut? It depends. Within Aboriginal communities, an 'apple' can be a young person who goes on to university to achieve a higher education. In this case, the implication is that achieving a higher education is incompatible with an authentic Aboriginal identity. Among black youth, Oreos are sell-outs to 'white' society. Usually, these terms represent negative labels and identities that have been applied to minority individuals seen to have assimilated into the dominant 'white' culture and who, through their attitudes and behaviour, have become less authentic members of their own communities.

These derogatory terms touch on a number of questions about the nature of ethnic and 'racial' identity. What does it mean to be south Asian, black, 'white', Ukrainian, Latvian, or Palestinian in Canada today? How do we understand the nature of ethnic and 'racial' identities? Are Canadians an ethnic group? What is assimilation, and does it occur in multicultural Canada? Is there a 'white' Canadian culture or identity? What is the meaning of the federal government's policy of multiculturalism? Does multiculturalism undermine Canadian unity, and in the post-11 September world, does it encourage the formation of 'un-Canadian', threatening identities?

This chapter examines a number of interrelated concepts and issues related to ethnic and 'racial' identity and multiculturalism. First, we begin with a discussion of the formation, maintenance, and transformation of ethnic identities. Second, we examine some of the problems and dilemmas associated with measuring and defining ethnic and 'racial' identities. Finally, we turn to a discussion of some of the more political questions associated with the discussion of the relationship between multiculturalism and ethnic identity formation and reproduction.

UNDERSTANDING IDENTITY

In chapter 1, we argued that the link between ethnicity and culture is tenuous at best and that ethnicity cannot be equated with culture (Li 1988). There is no simple, one-to-one correspondence between individual people, culture, and ethnicity or 'nation'. Culture is not monolithic, static, uniform, or homogeneous. It is rather a set of dynamic social processes and practices; it is a collective response of socially consti-tuted individuals to their ever-changing external conditions, largely determined by social structures. Assimilation, as we discussed earlier, is the process by which mem-bers of ethnic groups are incorporated into the dominant culture of a society (Isajiw 1999). Isajiw actually calls it *in*culturation (1999, 170). It is assumed that the off-spring of immigrants who assimilate are more likely to enjoy upward social and eco-nomic mobility. But how are ethnic identities acquired to begin with? What are the processes and practices whereby, and the sites or social spaces where, individuals acquire their ethnic identity, especially in societies like Canada that are multicultural?

Kallen has argued that ethnic identity contains both subjective (micro-individ-ual) and objective (macro-structural) factors. We can distinguish between individ-ual and collective ethnic identity. Collective ethnic identity refers to the existence of a certain consensus within the group about what constitutes it as such and differen-tiates it from other groups, whereas individual ethnic identity refers to the relation-ship of individuals to their own ethnic collectivity—that is, the strength and scope of the group characteristics with which they identify (Kallen 1995, 83–4). Ethnic identity is 'seen as an outcome of the impact upon the individual or the ethnic col-lectivity of the interrelationship between the diachronic and synchronic dimensions of ethnicity' (1995, 79). Diachronic dimensions include the ancestry, homeland, and culture associated with one's ethnic group. They constitute the core of one's ethnic identity. Endogamy and processes of enculturation (learning your own culture) transmit over time the distinctive culture of ethnic group members from one gen-eration to the next. Synchronic dimensions, on the other hand, are those dimensions that refer to the ways in which an individual or ethnic collectivity is defined, evalu-ated, and treated by outsiders—by others. Ethnic identity, then, is a reciprocal process that varies according to time and place, since its diachronic, core dimensions must be reproduced over time in any given place and are contingent on the syn-chronic social construction of ethnic identity by ethnic outsiders (1995, 79–80).

Driedger (1989; 1996) has identified six factors as the basic building blocks of ethnic identity: ecological territory, ethnic culture, ethnic institutions, historical symbols, ideology, and charismatic leadership. Religion and language are, of course, part of ethnic culture. Briefly put, ethnic groups are associated with specific ecolog-ical territories within different parts of the world or a specific country or parts thereof. For example, most francophones in Canada identify with Quebec and the Acadian region, most anglophones with the rest of Canada. Jewish people identify with Israel, Persians with Iran, most Arabs with the Middle East. The ecological territories may or may not be actual countries or nation-states. For example, Palestinians and Kurds may not have nation-states to call their own, but they do identify with their corresponding geographical regions. In addition, members of ethnic groups share a common legacy of history and historical symbols and religious and social ideologies as well as historical leadership. In terms of religious ideologies, for example, some ethnic groups may identify with the teachings of Jesus, Mohammad, or Buddha. These identifications, in turn, may determine the ideological and political positions of ethnic group members on a variety of social issues, such as abortion, same-sex marriage, colonization, capitalism, and globalization. In terms of political movements or resistance, ethnic group members may identify with their historical leadership. For example, Canadians may identify with Sir John A. Macdonald and Pierre Elliot Trudeau, Americans with Thomas Jefferson and Abraham Lincoln, Cubans with Che Guevara and Fidel Castro, Serbians with Marshal Tito before the destruction of Yugoslavia and with Slobodan Milosevic during and after its destruction. Indians may identify with Gandhi, Vietnamese with Ho Chi Minh, Chinese with Mao Tse-tung, black South Africans with Steve Biko and Nelson Mandela. It can be argued that charismatic leaders, over time, often create ethnic group cohesion, which is crucial in the production of ethnic identity and its reproduction and maintenance through ethnic institutions.

Ethnic institutions are sites or social spaces within which ethnic identity is produced and maintained over time. It has been argued that ethnic group identity may be evaluated in terms of the expressive, organizational, and instrumental strengths of the groups (Kallen 1995, 88–90). By expressive strengths, we refer to ethnic group folk customs like music, costumes and dances, values and activities, religion, language use, and perceived socio-economic 'performance', as well as demographic characteristics, such as size and potential for endogamy (age and sex ratios). In addition, ethnic closure may be seen as part of the expressive strengths of a group—i.e., the ability to 'enforce the rules' and sustain ethnic boundaries over time (inclusion and exclusion), either through behaviour (regulation, endogamy, segregation) or ideology (sense of peoplehood, criteria for group membership, ethnocentrism). Organizational strengths refer to the actual institutions that ethnic groups create and include their range and scope (provincial, national, international, political, economic, social, religious), ethnic communications (print and electronic news media, the Internet, and so on), and credible ethnic leadership and its ability to mobilize the group around issues pertaining to individual or group rights and/or economic demands on governments. Instrumental strengths refer to a group's relative collective political power (size, voting patterns, political party membership, positions of power and authority), the relationship of the ethnic leadership to political and economic powers and institutions in Canada, and the collective economic resources of the group.

Institutional completeness

A key concept in the understanding and analysis of ethnic identity is that of institutional completeness (Breton 1964). It refers to the extent to which an ethnic group in a particular place and time forms organizations by and for its members (Herberg 1989, 208–9). These voluntary organizations and institutions, be they educational, religious, economic, or social, cater to the needs of the ethnic group members. It is argued that 'the presence of many institutions and organizations within an ethnic community generates a social life in the community, not only among the members of these [ethnic] organizations themselves, but one that extends beyond them to persons in the community who are not members of [the ethnic] organization' (Isajiw 1999, 200).

Large numbers of organizations within an ethnic community imply high levels of institutional completeness for the ethnic group. They tend to minimize 'unnecessary' contact with non-group members. The higher the degree of institutional completeness an ethnic group enjoys, the higher the likelihood that its members will retain their ethnic identity. The role of institutions is crucial to the development of ethnic group consciousness (Kallen 1995, 86–7). First-generation members of ethnic groups—that is, those born outside Canada—endeavour to transfer their ethnic identity to subsequent generations. Second-generation Canadians are those with at least one parent who was born outside the country. Third-generation Canadians are those whose parents were both born in Canada, and so on.[2] Reitz (1980, 23) has argued that the participation of first-generation parents in ethnic organizations serves as a model of socialization for their offspring, who may be susceptible to rejecting their ethnic background or assimilating to the dominant culture. Their ethnic organizations and institutions may be alternatives to those of the dominant culture or complementary and parallel to them. For example, although individuals who identify with a specific ethnic group send their children to public school, they may also send them to an ethnic educational institution where they learn their own ethnic language, history, and culture as well. Jewish, Greek, Armenian, and Muslim day schools in Toronto and Montreal serve that purpose.

Although members of an ethnic group may do their banking with the big Canadian banks, they may also do it at their ethnic credit union. Ethnic organizations may also provide services to their members outside of the mainstream institutions and organizations of the larger Canadian society. For example, many ethnic communities have their own social services organizations that care for their youth, the elderly, newcomers, women, the unemployed, and other members in need. These services are often not available to non-group members. Furthermore, in many large cities, ethnic group members have access to professional services offered by co-ethnic members. Dentists, lawyers, real estate agents, immigration consultants, and other professionals often advertise their services in ethnic languages on the radio or television or in ethnic newspapers. They do this to expand their clientele and their business, but in doing so they further add to the institutional completeness of the community because they provide another venue for individuals to express and reaffirm their sense of identity and attachment to the community.

As Breton has argued, ethnic organizations are political entities. They are 'encapsulated political systems' embedded in the larger Canadian socio-political and economic conditions. Ethnic groups have both external and domestic 'affairs', and their institutions provide material and symbolic services to their members (Breton 1991). The domestic affairs of ethnic organizations ordinarily include the provision of material services, such as accommodating new immigrants and the elderly, as well as symbolic services, such as activities that pertain to the maintenance and development of the group's dominant cultural norms and values. Examples of such activities are celebrations of historical events and heroes, commemorations of community victimization either in the home country or in Canada, language instruction, dances, theatrical performances, and musical concerts. The external affairs of ethnic organizations relate to: (a) matters of government policies on immigration, multiculturalism, public education, human rights, the economy, and so on; (b) issues of discrimination and prejudice; (c) relations with broader societal institutions (e.g., mainstream mass media, unions, the police); and (d) relations with the country of origin and its representatives (Breton 1991, 3).

Today, most people assume that the provision of material and symbolic services to members of ethnic groups by their respective ethnic organizations and institutions exists because of the Canadian policy of multiculturalism. This is not necessarily true. Historically, such provision predates both the policy and the ideology of multiculturalism in Canada. Even during the years of anglo- and/or franco-conformity before 1971, many ethnic organizations provided ethnic language instruction, assisted new immigrants to Canada, fought against prejudice and discrimination, and struggled to maintain elements of their own culture in Canada and transmit them to the new generations. Multiculturalism, then, is not a prerequisite for community action in these areas. Many ethnic communities, even in countries without an official policy of multiculturalism (e.g., Germany, France, Italy, Greece, South Africa, Argentina) engage in similar activities (Liodakis 1998).

In Canada, ethnic organizations have tended to emerge first as mutual benefit associations to meet the symbolic needs of their members, to contribute to group cohesion, and to assist newcomers in coping with the new social and economic conditions—often of hardship—that their members face on arriving in Canada. Herberg (1989) has gone as far as arguing that ethnic institutional completeness is 'the most essential influence on a group's cohesion because it includes all the . . . arenas within which ethnic culture must be utilized and applied if it is to survive. . . . [E]thnic culture must be practised in public situations, be relevant to these public and 'formal' interactions, and even be necessary for their conduct as something more than arbitrary personal norms if ethnoculture is to survive in Canada' (1989, 213).

In Canada, interesting (but dated and limited in number and scope) research projects on the institutional completeness of ethnic groups have been undertaken, beginning with Breton's (1964) study on Montreal's ethnic groups. He found that the French, Germans, Greeks, Italians, and Ukrainians exhibited high degrees of institutional development, whereas the Dutch, English, Portuguese, Swedish, and West Indian did not. Driedger and Church in 1974 and Driedger in 1975 replicated Breton's findings (Reitz 1980). Using national data that excluded the charter groups and the Jewish, Reitz (1980) found that the participation of southern Europeans in their respective ethnic institutions was highest, followed by the Chinese, eastern Europeans, and northern Europeans. Isajiw (1981) has studied the retention of ethnic identity among Torontonian blacks, the British, the Chinese, Germans, Italians, the Jewish, the Portuguese, and Ukrainians. He examined, among many things, four dimensions of ethnic identity: (a) the extent to which ethnic group members attend ethnic functions (parties, dances, picnics, concerts); (b) the use of ethnic group-sponsored vacation facilities (resorts, summer camps) by members of the group; (c) the existence and use of ethnic group television and radio programming; and (d) the reading of ethnic newspapers and magazines. In addition, Isajiw compared results among three generations, although his data did not provide much information on groups that were recent arrivals to Toronto at the time. Even though there was a lack of information on the second and third generations for some groups (blacks, the Chinese, and the Portuguese), it became evident that the longer the history of ethnic groups in Canada, the lower the retention of ethnic identity by second and third-generation members of the group. This is arguably an open secret within ethnic organizations; many struggle to find ways of engaging the second and subsequent generations in the ethnic community, hence their efforts to transmit their language and culture to native-born members of their group.

Segmented assimilation

Ethnic organizations are agents of socialization for members. The social attachment of individuals to their ethnic group takes place within the organizations through the reproduction of ideologies of common ancestry, social and cultural attributes, and corresponding social practices. But the process of ethnic enculturation is not as linear or successful as it may appear if we merely look at the 'achievements' of certain groups with institutional completeness. As Boyd has suggested (in Kalbach and Kalbach 2000), few studies have been done on immigrant offspring and how their fate is shaped by their attachment to an ethnic community.

In general, when we examine the relationship between class and ethnicity, it can be argued that three outcomes are possible for immigrant children: (a) they become assimilated to the dominant culture (measured by their economic success); (b) they are integrated into ethnic enclaves (measured by their retention of ethnic identity); and (c) lower-social class immigrant children may develop marginalized identities and positions in the labour market (Boyd in Kalbach and Kalbach 2000, 140–1). Immigrant children with higher economic resources tend to follow the first path; those with low or no resources tend to fall within the other two. In the US, Portes (1995), Portes and Zhou (1993), and Zhou (1999), doing research on black, Chinese, and Hispanic inner-city youth, have shown that immigrant offspring of Caribbean descent may reject their parents' culture, which may emphasize education and hard work as mobility mechanisms; they tend to be absorbed into the inner-city racialized underclass and eventually end up living in poverty. They call this 'segmented' or 'truncated' assimilation (Portes and Zhou 1993). In contrast, the offspring of Cuban and Chinese immigrants, who tend to emphasize both the preservation of ethnic identity and economic advancement, are more likely to succeed within the ethnic enclave, if not in the mainstream (Portes and Zhou 1993; Portes 1995). This, of course, depends on the size of the ethnic economic enclaves and their capacity to employ large numbers of immigrant children.

While their argument is persuasive, the pattern may not be general. As Alba and Nee (1999) have argued, the vast majority of immigrants and their offspring are found in the larger, non-ethnic economy, and youth experiences—cultural and economic—may not necessarily carry over into adulthood. Mary Waters (2000) has analyzed the experiences of Jamaican, Barbadian, Trinidadian, and Guyanese immigrants in New York and compared them to Irish and Italian immigrants of the turn of the twentieth century. She has also examined relationships and differences among and within American blacks and black Caribbean immigrants. Drawing from 202 interviews with several generations of immigrants, she has found that the Caribbean immigrants who resist 'Americanization' are the most likely to succeed. By preserving their own cultural identity and by resisting the African-American label, they have done well in education and earnings. For example, when analyzing food service workers, she demonstrated that having a transnational or Caribbean identity helps them to adapt more easily to the American reality of racialization and racism. Thus, attachment to an ethnic identity is not necessarily a barrier to assimilation. One of the groups she analyzed, the 'ethnically identified', emphasized their Caribbean roots in order to differentiate and distance themselves from black Americans. They were predominantly middle-class suburban and performed well in school. They strongly believed that 'whites' treat them as Afro-Caribbeans, which they perceived as better treatment than that meted out to 'blacks'. They also felt that their ethnic values provided them with more opportunities for success. Thus, resisting assimilation into some aspects of American culture, particularly the underclass culture, provides better opportunities to the second generation (Louie 2004, 197). In fact, Louie (326–9) argues that in the US, 'becoming American' is now associated with less economic success. Often, then, the retention of ethnic identity may promote rather than hinder socio-economic advancement and help immigrant groups to combat discrimination and racism.

In Canada, Boyd has shown that results for ethnic groups tend to vary but that 'visible minority' youth from low-resource homes, especially lone-parent families, tend to be disadvantaged and display the potential of segmented assimilation. They are likely either to be found in the ethnic economic enclave or to experience downward social mobility (Kalbach and Kalbach 2000, 151). Arguing along the lines of Porter's 1965 blocked mobility thesis (see chapter 4), Kalbach and Kalbach (2000) maintain that ethnic connectedness impedes the educational and economic achievement of individuals. Using 1991 census data, they show that individuals 'in the more traditional ethnoreligious groups, who exhibit their greater ethnic commitment or connectedness through greater use of their ethnic language in the home, tend to report lower levels of educational and economic-status attainment than those who are less ethnically connected' (Kalbach and Kalbach 2000, 199–200). In addition, those who immigrated to Canada at less than 13 years of age tend to exhibit better educational and economic status attainment than those who came later. Ethnic identity, then, may hold back economic advancement or the structural integration of ethnic group members.

Ethnicity, 'Race', and the Canadian Census

Most Canadians have few qualms about answering questions on the census. For many of us, filling out the census questionnaire is a routine if somewhat invasive ritual that we have to go through every five years. Some Canadians actually look forward to receiving the 'long form' of the census in the mail because they love to detail their family history and structure.

In other countries, census-taking is neither routine nor uncontested. In Nigeria, a census enumerator was killed, and several others quit their jobs because of intimidation in the days leading up to the March 2006 census. Some ethnic group leaders in Nigeria boycotted the census, and leaders of other ethnic groups warned census-takers not to even try to enumerate members of their community. Much of the controversy about the 2006 Nigerian census was not about the kinds of questions that were asked but rather about the kinds of questions that were not asked. Specifically, the Nigerian census did not ask questions about an individual's ethnic origin or religious affiliation. Critics of the Nigerian census allege that this was a deliberate decision on the part of the federal government to maintain the traditional balance of power in the country and to continue to allocate resources disproportionately (Odunfa 2006). The Nigerian constitution provides assurances that the 'federal character' of the country must be reflected in every government appointment. According to Odunfa (2006, 2), 'this means that the relative strengths of every ethnic and religious group must be taken into consideration in determining appointments in the civil service, the armed forces and political institutions'. Muslim groups, who have traditionally been regarded as making up the majority of the population, were opposed to questions about ethnic origin and religion because the true facts about population size might undermine their claim to more state resources. On the other hand, Christian groups, traditionally regarded as a numerical minority but now believed to be a numerical majority, wanted to have ethnicity and religion included in the census in order to justify their claims for more resources. They regarded the census without questions about ethnicity and religion as a sham.

Even though few Canadians get worked about the census to the point where they kill or threaten census enumerators or turn to violence to make sure that some questions are either asked or not asked, Canada and Nigeria are not that different when it comes to some of the underlying politics surrounding census-taking and the political construction of ethnicity. In the 2001 census, several First Nations communities refused to allow Statistics Canada to collect information about individuals. Their argument was that the collection of this kind of data rarely does their communities any good, so they question why they should participate in such exercises. Furthermore, state resources are distributed on the basis of claims about the relative size of particular segments of the Canadian population. Canada has tracked the origins of Canadians since well before Confederation. Statistics Canada justifies questions about ethnic and 'racial' origin on the grounds that this information is useful and important for purposes of policy development and policy monitoring and the fair distribution of government resources. In this section, we want to examine some of the dilemmas and controversies over the measurement of ethnicity and 'race' in the Canadian census. These controversies demonstrate that ethnicity and ethnic identity are not simply matters of individual choice, ancestry, and heritage but are also constructs shaped by larger political relationships and structures (Curtis 2001).

The current census asks a number of questions in order to understand the family structure, economic position, demographic status, and 'origins' of Canadians.

The long form of the census contains questions about (among other things) education, marital status, age, occupation, income, linguistic ability, religion, nativity, Aboriginal origin, ethnic origin, and 'racial' origin.

Ethnic origin

In attempting to measure the ethnic origins of Canadians, the census asks the following question:

> Q17: While most people in Canada view themselves as Canadians, information on their ancestral origins has been collected since the 1901 Census to capture the changing composition of Canada's diverse population. Therefore this question refers to the **origins of the person's ancestors**. To which ethnic or cultural group (s) did this person's ancestors belong? **Specify as many groups as applicable** [four blank spaces]: For example, Canadian, French, English, Chinese, Italian, German, Scottish, Irish, Cree, Micmac, Métis, Inuit (Eskimo), East Indian, Ukrainian, Dutch, Polish, Portuguese, Filipino, Jewish, Greek, Jamaican, Vietnamese, Lebanese, Chilean, Somali, etc.

Starting with the 1981 census, individuals have been allowed to identify more than one ancestral origin, and as a result, responses to the ethnic origin question have resulted in two categories of individuals: individuals who identify a single ethnic origin (for persons whose ancestors are of presumably the same origin) and individuals who identify themselves as having multiple origins (for persons acknowledging ancestors of different origins). There is, of course, a third category of individual: people who have ancestors of different origins but only indicate one ancestry because they identify most with one component of their heritage. People who respond this way are not necessarily captured as a separate social category in the census. Table 5.1 provides information on single and multiple ethnic origins of Canadians in 2001.

It is evident that Statistics Canada uses a definition of ethnicity based on a person's understanding of their 'objective' ancestry or roots (Kordan 2000). This definition does not take account of how individuals feel about their ancestry or their origins or how attached or connected they feel to their ethnicity. Nor does it measure what components of their ethnicity are important to them. As a result, the information in this table needs to be interpreted with care. For example, what does it mean when data from the 2001 census in table 5.1 tell us that there are 91,795 single-origin Hungarians in Canada? At best, it means that nearly 92,000 Canadians identify their sole ethnic roots as Hungarian. However, this does not necessarily mean that there are 91,795 Hungarians in Canada. After all, not all Hungarian-origin individuals currently think of themselves as Hungarian, have a Hungarian ethnic identity, do things that represent their Hungarian origins, speak or understand Hungarian, eat traditional Hungarian food, follow traditional Hungarian religions or customs, or think that their Hungarian origins are important to their lives in Canada today. Furthermore, only a fraction of the individuals who identify their ancestry as Hungarian belong to Hungarian ethnic organizations. Clearly, the

Table 5.1   Top 25 Ethnic Origins in Canada, 2001

Ethnic origin	Single and multiple responses	Single responses	Multiple responses
CANADIAN	11,682,680	6,748,135	4 ,934,550
English	5,978,875	1,479,520	4,499,355
French	4,668 410	1,060,755	3,607,655
Scottish	4,157,210	607,235	3,549,975
Irish	3,822,660	496,865	3,325,800
German	2,742,765	705,595	2,037,170
Italian	1,270,370	726,275	544,090
Chinese	1,094,700	936,210	158,490
Ukrainian	1,071,060	326,200	744,860
North American Indian	1,000,890	455,805	545,085
Dutch	923,310	316,220	607,090
Polish	817,085	260,415	556,670
East Indian	713,330	581,665	131,665
Norwegian	363,760	47,230	316,530
Portuguese	357,690	252,835	104,855
Welsh	350,365	28,445	321,925
Jewish	348,605	186,475	162,130
Russian	337,960	70,890	267,070
Filipino	327,545	266,140	61,410
Métis	307,845	72,210	235,635
Swedish	282,760	30,440	252,320
Hungarian	267,255	91,795	175,460
American	250,010	25,200	224,805
Greek	215,105	143,780	71,320
Spanish	213,100	66,545	146,555

Source: Statistics Canada. 2005. *Ethnocultural portrait of Canada*, table 1.
<http://www12.statcan.ca/english/census01/products/highlights?ETO/Table1>.

Statistics Canada measure of ethnicity tells us nothing about the subjective attachments that individuals have to their ethnic ancestry (Isajiw 1999, 47). This is not necessarily a critique of the census but rather an indication of the limitations of this kind of question.

Furthermore, many sociologists and ethnic community leaders have trouble knowing what to do with or how to interpret the ethnic attachments of individuals who say that they have more than one ethnic ancestry (Bourhis 2003, 15). Are multiple-origin individuals less authentic members of ethnic communities? To what extent do community organizations accommodate themselves to individuals who are not fluent in the heritage language, and to what extent do religious and community leaders encourage or discourage intermarriage?

Another controversial aspect of the current ethnic origin question in the Canadian census is how to interpret the 'Canadian' response to the question. Before

'Canadian' was specifically identified as a legitimate response identity to the ethnic origin question in the 1996 census, few people in Canada identified their ethnic origin as Canadian. In 1991, just 4 per cent of individuals reported 'Canadian' as their ethnic origin. However, in the 2001 census, more than 6.7 million individuals (23.7 per cent of the population) identified themselves as having a single Canadian origin.

Some dismiss the growth of the 'Canadian' response between 1991 and 2001 as just a wording effect: that is, simply listing it as an option on the census questionnaire leads more people to mark it. As a result, it does not reflect any meaningful change in how Canadians identify their ancestry. On the other hand, some do consider this shift as a reflection of something more tangible than simply a recall or wording effect. Indeed, this has prompted some scholars to argue that Canadians are a newly emergent ethnic group not unlike other more traditional ethnic groups (Howard-Hassmann 1999). As Howard-Hassmann (1999, 531) explains, English-speaking Canadians are an ethnic group because they share many customs, desires and ambitions, norms, and common values. In her view:

> An English-Canadian may be of any ethnic or racial background; he may have Ukrainian or Ghanaian rather than British-Protestant ancestry. While the parents' sense of place may be Ukraine or Ghana, the English-Canadians' sense of place will be his immediate environment, the town or city that he knows well enough to get around—the personal map of schools, shops, offices, relatives, friends. . . . His personal life history will have taken place in Canada, not abroad. Though he may eat foods different from other Canadians and worship at a mosque or a temple rather than a church, he will have attended the same schools, learned the same Canadian history and geography, and been present at the same lessons in family studies and sex education (Howard-Hassmann 1999, 531).

Not everyone agrees that the increasing proclivity on the part of Canadians to report 'Canadian' as their ancestral roots represents the emergence of a new, pan-Canadian ethnicity that transcends old-world ethnicities and identities (Bourhis 2003; Jedwab 2003). In their analysis of the 1996 census, Boyd and Norris (2001) argue that it was mainly 'old stock' Canadians of British and French ancestry who were more likely to adopt 'Canadian' as one of their ancestries. They also found that only 1 per cent of first-generation immigrants and 2 per cent of visible minorities reported 'Canadian' as one of their ethnic origins. Furthermore, given that 54 per cent of Quebecers reported Canadian origins only on the census, some have suggested that the category conflates the French-Canadian notion of a '*canadien*' with the English-Canadian notion of an ethnic Canadian. In other words, the term 'Canadian' in the census seems to mean different things to different people (Jedwab 2003).

'Race'

After a 50-year hiatus, the measurement of 'racial origin' is once again an important part of the Canadian census. In 1951, the Canadian government stopped attempting to measure the 'racial origin' of Canadians, in part because of the widespread discredit that the term 'race' had after the Second World War (Bourhis 2003, 17). The introduction of a 'racial origin' question in the Canadian census in 1996 was justified in part on the grounds that such data was needed to better monitor the success of policies like the federal government's employment equity policy. The aim of federal employment equity legislation, introduced in 1986, is to improve the employment opportunities of women, visible minorities, Aboriginal people, and the disabled. It seeks to correct the systemic discrimination that exists in the workplace by forcing federally regulated employers and federal contractors to develop employment equity plans and reports that outline the positive measures they intend to undertake to improve employment opportunities for the four target groups. In order to monitor whether the policy is successful, the government claims that it needs baseline data on 'racial origins' so that it can track progress (Bourhis 2003, 20).

On that basis, the 'race' question in the 2006 census was as follows:

> Q19: This information is collected to support programs that promote equal opportunity for everyone to share in the social, cultural and economic life of Canada. Is this person: Mark 'X' more than once or specify, if applicable: White, Chinese, South Asian (e.g. East Indian, Pakistani, Sri Lankan, etc.), Black, Filipino, Latin American, Southeast Asian (e.g. Cambodian, Indonesian, Laotian, Vietnamese, etc.), Arab, West Asian (e.g. Afghan, Iranian, etc.), Japanese, Korean, Other–Specify [one blank space].

The inclusion of a measure of 'race' in the census has been controversial. Some argue that it contributes to the further reification of 'race'. As noted in chapter 1, 'race' is not a biologically real category but rather a socially constructed label used to describe and explain certain kinds of human difference. By attempting to measure the 'racial' makeup of the Canadian population, Statistics Canada is helping to reproduce old and outmoded biologically based understandings of 'race'. Moreover, to the extent that the idea of fixed, biologically distinct 'races' is a cornerstone of racist thinking, critics have suggested that the federal government is inadvertently promoting the racialization of public policy. As explained by Yehudi Webster, a professor of Pan-African Studies at California State University and author of *The racialization of America* (1994), Statistics Canada's effort to measure the 'racial' makeup of the country is an 'act of promiscuous stupidity' in that

> Politics are simply putting into law the racial concepts developed by 18th and 19th century racial theorists. The Canadian government clearly does not realize that when they put race in policy, they are helping to create the race consciousness that is the bane of American society. They are putting the stamp of officialdom of race consciousness. Canada will pay a heavy price down the road (cited in Bourhis 2003, 18).

Those who defend the collection of 'race'-based statistics in the census, or in other areas such as the criminal justice system, argue that such data are necessary for the pursuit of social justice.

MEANINGS OF MULTICULTURALISM

As mentioned above, ethnic organizations—and by extension the processes and practices of ethnic enculturation that take place within them—do not operate in a political, economic, or social vacuum. In Canada, an ethnically diverse liberal society, they operate within the context of multiculturalism. Multiculturalism, as we will see below, encourages the maintenance of the ethnic and cultural identities of Canadians. Multiculturalism usually has four interrelated meanings. It is a demographic reality; it is part of pluralist ideology; it is a form of struggle among groups for access to economic and political resources; and it is a set of government policies and accompanying programs (Fleras 1993, 385; Fleras and Elliott 1996, 325). It can be defined as an ideology, based on Canadian social reality, that gives rise to sets of economic, political, and social practices, which in turn define boundaries and set limits to ethnic and 'racial' group relations in order either to maintain social order or to manage social change (Liodakis and Satzewich 2003, 147).

First, when we say that multiculturalism is a fact in Canadian society, this means that demographically, the Canadian population comprises members of more than 100 ethnic groups (Fleras and Elliott 1996, 326). Canadian society has never been ethnically homogeneous, although it might have appeared as such because of the dominance of the British and the French. Canada was certainly a multicultural country long before the implementation of multiculturalism as policy. Simply put, until the introduction of the 1971 policy, Canada, although a multicultural society in terms of demography, was dominated by the hegemonic British and the French cultural norms, and the Canadian state actively promoted conformity to these norms by the rest of the population.

Second, as an ideology, multiculturalism includes normative descriptions about how Canadian society ought to be in terms of social organization based on ethnicity. The cornerstone of multiculturalism is the idea of pluralism. Pluralism, in its cultural interpretation, advocates tolerance of cultural diversity and, most important, promotes the idea that such diversity is compatible with national goals, especially those of national unity and socio-economic progress (Fleras and Elliot 1996, 326). The basic principles of multiculturalism rest on the notion of cultural relativism. It prescribes tolerance and exalts diversity to achieve peaceful coexistence in ethnically heterogeneous societies. Cultural relativism, as opposed to ethnocentrism, holds that the evaluative criteria of culture should be drawn from within the culture in question and that no external standards are applicable. In other words, we should not judge any culture by our dominant norms. In short, if we recognize individuals' right to self-identification and promotion of their own culture, then, it is hoped, those individuals will extend the same courtesy to individuals who share different cultural norms and values. We should note, however, that ethnocentrism and prejudice are not synonymous: we can differentiate between enlightened and pernicious forms of ethnocentrism. The first seeks the self-interest of the in-group but respects the rights and interests of the out-group; the second seeks it at the expense of the out-group (Kallen 1995, 43). Pernicious ethnocentrism is often called ethnic chauvinism, especially when it is associated with hostility toward other ethnic groups.

Third, multiculturalism is also a process of competition among and between ethnocultural groups for the acquisition of valuable economic and political resources. As sociologist Karl Peter has reminded us, multiculturalism 'is first and foremost a political program with very defined political aims along with the means to accomplish these aims' (in Fleras and Elliott 1996, 335). As such, it is a mechanism for conflict resolution. In Canada, it emerged out of social and demographic pressures and from the need to counterbalance western alienation and Quebec nationalism, as well as for the Liberals to acquire ethnic electoral support in urban centres (Fleras and Elliott 1996, 335).

Fourth, multiculturalism refers to all government initiatives and programs that seek to realize multiculturalism as ideology and transform it into a concrete form of social intervention and organization. As policy, it is a relatively recent aspect of Canadian state activity, introduced by the Liberals under Pierre Elliot Trudeau in 1971. Ironically, it was not the historical legacy of racism, discrimination, and prejudice in Canada that multicultural policy initially aimed to address. In fact, these issues did not figure much into the framework for the development of multicultural policy. Instead, the policy was introduced in part as a response to Canada's 'other' ethnic groups (non-English and non-French), who were dissatisfied with the terms of reference of the Royal Commission on Bilingualism and Biculturalism of the 1960s. Groups like Ukrainian Canadians were concerned that the federal government had failed to recognize that they too had made significant contributions to Canadian nation-building. The policy was also an effort on the part of the Liberals to capture the increasingly large non-English and non-French vote in this country (Hawkins 1989, 218) and a strategy on the part of Trudeau and the federal Liberal Party to undermine French Canada's claims for equality with English within the Canadian confederation (Abu-Laban and Stasiulis 1992). In short, multiculturalism seeks to accommodate social cleavages, maintain the existing social order, and manage social change, all in the context of a culturally diverse society.

The evolution of the policy of multiculturalism

Three stages of multicultural policy development have been identified by Fleras and Elliott (1996). First, from 1971 to 1980, emphasis was placed on folkloric multiculturalism, or on 'celebrating our differences'—that is, on the idea that cultural diversity is the heart of Canadian identity. We no longer had an 'official' culture. At that time, four principles guided federal multiculturalism:

1.   The federal government would support all of Canada's cultures and seek to assist the development of those cultural groups that had demonstrated a desire and effort to continue developing a capacity to grow and contribute to Canada as well as a clear need for assistance.
2.   The government would assist all cultural groups to overcome the cultural barriers to full participation in Canadian society.
3.   The government would promote creative encounters and interchange among all Canadian cultural groups in the interest of national unity.

4. The government would continue to assist immigrants in acquiring at least one of Canada's two official languages in order that they would become full participants in Canadian society (Hawkins 1989, 220).

In other words, the years of anglo-conformity had passed. All cultures were seen as equal. Culture had become an issue of personal choice, and there was no shortage in the Canadian ethnic supermarket. In this light, individuals were protected against any discrimination stemming from their cultural choices and were strongly encouraged to cultivate and promote their cultures and to participate fully in all aspects of Canadian life.

During the 1980s, the second phase of multicultural policy—the process of institutionalization—was developed. This phase entailed a number of new developments. First, an explicit concern over 'race relations' emerged. Second, an upsurge in Quebec nationalism was countered by repatriation of the Constitution (1982), including adoption of the Charter of Rights and Freedoms, both of which were subject to interpretations consistent with the notion of multiculturalism as a fundamental characteristic of Canadian society. Third, the Progressive Conservative government passed the Multiculturalism Act (1988), which essentially turned a de facto policy into a de jure, legal framework, thus elevating multiculturalism to a position of equality with the principle of bilingualism.

Finally, multiculturalism was increasingly cast in an economic dimension. Consistent with neo-conservative economic doctrine was the attempt to justify the 1988 Multiculturalism Act not only in terms of pluralist ideology but also in terms of potential economic benefits to the country. This involved a shift in emphasis away from a 'culture for culture's sake' perspective toward a more instrumentalist view of the benefits of multicultural policy. One of the most explicit signals of this shift was the Multiculturalism Means Business Conference in Toronto in 1986, which pointed to the beginning of a more market-driven approach to multiculturalism. In his opening address to the conference, Otto Jelinek, the Conservative minister of state for multiculturalism, told delegates that

> The competition is fierce; we need every edge we can get and one is knowledge of foreign languages. . . . The new mercantilism calls for a new type of corporate manager, a flexible cosmopolitan aware of cultural sensitivities . . . , who can cut costs and waste by knowing how culture affects behaviour, who can motivate workers with differing standards, read between the lines of reports from abroad, and pinpoint the pitfalls of overseas selling, what is or is not acceptable (Jelinek 1986, 5).

He went on to suggest that

> Simply expressed, this government believes emphatically that multiculturalism can and does mean business. Increased business. More business. And from this newly tapped resource will flow a prosperity which will generate greater social mobility and open even more doors to opportunity in all avenues of endeavour (Jelinek 1986, 5).

Cultural pluralism, and the image of Canada as an equal, tolerant, and fair society, was therefore defined by the 1980s Conservative government as an asset within the emerging global economy (Moodley 1983). In neo-liberal terms, the plethora of cultures and languages of Canadian society would lead to increased international trade and improve the comparative advantage of the country vis-à-vis our supposedly unilingual and monocultural competitors (Abu Laban and Gabriel 2002). What the Canadian government failed to recognize was that most countries in the world are now multicultural in de facto if not in policy terms, so Canada's multicultural nature might not be as much of an economic advantage as they thought.

In the 1990s, a third stage of policy development arose—civic multiculturalism. It can be defined as a stage during which folkloric and institutional multiculturalism are coupled with citizenship, which temporarily assumed institutional expression in the Department of Multiculturalism and Citizenship, under Canadian Heritage umbrella. The focus of civic multiculturalism is society-building: fostering a common sense of identity and belonging is considered essential for the participation and inclusion of all Canadians in national institutions (see Fleras and Elliott 1996, 334–5, table 10.2). It can be argued that in this stage, multiculturalism moves away from the folkloric focus and that this can be interpreted as a withdrawal from programs associated with that focus (e.g., funding for cultural festivals).

CONTESTING MULTICULTURALISM

Since its inception in the early 1970s, multicultural policy has been a contested terrain. There has never been agreement about the wisdom, desirability, or necessity of the federal government's multicultural policies and programs. Putting it in rather stark terms, some say that multiculturalism is what makes Canada a unique and great country, while others say that multiculturalism will lead to our eventual downfall. In the new millennium, particularly in the context of the attacks on the World Trade Center and the Pentagon on 11 September 2001, the bombing of the London transit system on 7 July 2005, and the recent arrest in Toronto of 17 Muslims allegedly plotting terrorist attacks around the country, debates about multiculturalism have taken on renewed importance and a sense of political urgency.

Box 5.1 Immigrant Integration in Canada and the United States: Does Multicultural Policy Make a Difference?

You have no doubt heard the claim that one of the things that distinguishes Canada from the United States is that we promote multiculturalism and they promote a 'melting pot', which is a form of assimilation. The following excerpt from an article by John C. Harles calls into question the view that immigrants are better integrated here than in the United States. In particular, Harles questions Canadian philosopher Will Kymlicka's view that Canada does a better job than almost any other country in the world in integrating immigrants and that our success in this regard is due to our policy of multiculturalism.

In Will Kymlicka's spirited defense of Canadian multiculturalism, *Finding Our Way: Rethinking Ethnocultural Relations in Canada* (1998), the author writes:

> Canada does better than virtually any other country in the world in the integration of immigrants. The only comparable country is Australia, which has its own multicultural policy—one largely inspired by Canada's, although of course it has been adapted to Australian circumstances. The two countries that lead the world in the integration of immigrants are countries with official multiculturalism policies. They are much more successful than any country that has rejected multiculturalism.

The observation is but one slice of a broad and intriguing discussion of the prospects for multiculturalism among national minorities—Aboriginals and Quebecois—as well as immigrants. Yet Kymlicka is not alone among social theorists in his belief that multiculturalism is a Canadian distinctive. . . . Even the Canadian government endorses his reading of official multiculturalism as the source of Canada's superiority in immigrant integration. . . .

Given that the United States is a parallel North American settler society, one subject to similar waves of immigration as Canada, Kymlicka refers to the American experience more than that of any other country in support of his thesis that Canadian multiculturalism is responsible for high levels of immigrant integration. He cites growing rates of naturalization, the lack of ethnically-based political parties, expanding immigrant demand for courses in English and/or French as a second language, ethnic residential dispersion, and an increasing incidence of ethnic intermarriage since the advent of multicultural policy in 1971 as among the principal evidence of the Canadian advantage. In Kymlicka's view, Canada is more successful on almost all of these measures than countries, the United States prime among them, which have not made an official commitment to multiculturalism. . . . Indeed, he asserts that 'Canada fares better than the United States on virtually every dimension of integration.' . . .

If one accepts Kymlicka's premise that a commitment to multiculturalism distinguishes Canada and the US, and that immigrants to Canada have higher levels of institutional integration than their American counterparts, then one must also expect that immigrants to the US will have lower levels of psychological integration to their host country than do Canadian immigrants. In fact, there is reason to believe otherwise. Qualitative data gleaned from oral histories as well as the testimony of immigrants in open-ended interviews, when supplemented by a consideration of the political behavior of immigrants in America—their overwhelming readiness to support the US in times of war, to use a most dramatic example—indicates that the majority are eager to assume the rights and responsibilities of an American identity and understand themselves as solidly part of the American nation. . . .

The quantitative evidence necessary to generalize such insights is in shorter supply. Few opinion surveys are designed specifically with an immigrant constituency in mind. An important exception is a 2002 poll of more than one thousand foreign-born US residents undertaken by Public Agenda, a nonpartisan, nonprofit public opinion research organization. . . . In this survey, the affective commitment of immigrant interviewees for America is clear. Eighty percent of respondents allow that they consider the US 'to be a unique country that stands for something special in the world.' Impressive majorities say they are happy with life in the United States (96 percent), that if given the chance they would emigrate to America again (80 percent), and find it improbable that their children would wish to live in the country of origin of their parents (70 percent). As Table 1 reveals, over three-quarters of the immigrants polled attest that they have assumed, fully or in part, an American identity. . . .

In light of the multicultural concerns of the present essay, it is especially interesting that immigrant interviewees in the 2002 Public Agenda survey feel little pressure to jettison traditional ways of life in return for becoming American. Whereas 42 percent of respondents maintain that 'I have become an American,' almost the same percentage (41 percent) say that, 'I act like an American on the outside, but at home I keep my own culture and traditions.' Only 14 percent maintain that although they live in the United States, they don't consider themselves to be American. Indeed, over 80 percent of those surveyed concurred with the statement (55 percent strongly so) that 'It is easy for me to hold on to my culture and traditions in the US'. . . . Contrary to Kymlicka, there is little in the testimony of such immigrants to suggest that the US 'repudiates' multiculturalism. . . .

If in the case of the United States the causal connection that Kymlicka makes between multiculturalism and psychological integration is suspect, so, too, with respect to Canada. To explore that relationship, I draw on a sample survey of 2001 immigrant and native-born Canadians that I co-authored with Environics Canada and which Environics administered in the summer of 1997 as part of its quarterly Focus Canada report. . . .

Immigrants to Canada who were canvassed for the Focus Canada study clearly display signs of psychological integration. Most say that they have assumed a Canadian identity. Almost half describe themselves as 'mainly Canadian,' including 32 percent of those immigrants of non-European and non-North American origin, subsequently referred to as 'Others' (Table 7). Given that the policy of official multiculturalism affirms and legitimates ethnic distinctions and that many immigrants, especially the more recent arrivals, may still view themselves as guests of a host society, one would not expect immigrants to identify exclusively with Canada. As opposed to individuals who were born in Canada, immigrant interviewees are more likely to think of themselves first and foremost in ethnic terms—33 percent of all immigrants and 45 percent of Others do so. Yet such perspectives are not much different than those given by immigrants in the US as related in Table 1. In both cases a majority of respondents say that when compared to their ethnic identity, their national identity, Canadian or American, is of equal or greater psychological importance. . . .

TABLE 1:   American Identity: Which of These Statements is True for You?

Statement	Total immigrant	Mexican	Non-Mexican Latino	European	East Asian	Caribbean
I mostly think of myself as an American	54%	45%	55%	67%	53%	49%
I mostly think of myself in terms of the country where I was born	22	28	21	13	20	24
Both equally	23	26	22	18	26	28
Don't know	2	1	3	2	2	—

Source: Public Agenda. November 2002.

TABLE 7:   Ethnic/Canadian Identity

	Mainly Ethnicity, then Canadian	Mainly Canadian	Both equally	DK/NA	N
Birthplace:					1960
Canada	16.7%	78.1%	3.7%	1.5%	
Foreign-born	33.3	48.6	12.8	5.3	
Birthplace:					1937
Canada	16.7	78.1	3.7	1.5	
Europe	29.7	55.5	11.0	3.9	
Other	45.2	31.7	17.3	5.8	

Source: Focus Canada. 1997–2. The author has re-coded the Focus Canada variables so that (1) the Canadian-born category does not encompass US-born respondents, as in the original Focus Canada report; and (2) British-born and other European-born respondents, considered separately in the Focus Canada report, are now collapsed into a single European cohort.

Source: John C. Harles. 2004. 'Immigrant integration in Canada and the United States'. *American Review of Canadian Studies* 34.2 (summer): 223–58.

In this section, we want to review the three phases of criticism that multicultural policy has gone through.

Multiculturalism as ineffective

The early criticisms of the cultural emphasis within multiculturalism in the 1970s and early 1980s were that the policy only promoted those aspects of ethnic cultures that did not challenge Anglo-Saxon assumptions about the way society should be organized and that multiculturalism was an ideology (Roberts and Clifton 1982;

Lewycky 1992). Critics suggested that there was too great an emphasis on depoliti-cized 'song and dance' activities that were non-threatening to British economic, political, and cultural hegemony and that the policy mystified social reality by cre-ating the appearance of change without actually changing the fundamental bases of ethnic and 'racial' inequality within Canada (Bolaria and Li 1988; Moodley 1983). Furthermore, it was argued that identifying 'cultural barriers' to full participation precluded a definition of the structural barriers that legitimize and indeed prioritize racism and discrimination (Bolaria and Li 1988).

Along the same lines, Stasiulis (1980, 34) argued that in line with the state's role in legitimizing the existing social order, these interventions (multiculturalism, bilin-gualism) have a depoliticizing effect. By overemphasizing 'cultural' and linguistic barriers to equality, they conceal other, perhaps more fundamental social inequali-ties based on people's property rights, position in the labour market, education, gen-der, and age. In fact, Canadian society is characterized by a clear ethnically (and gender)-based class hierarchy and struggle, which of course is not addressed by mul-ticulturalism because such struggle is challenging, if not threatening, to the existing social order. Multiculturalism obfuscates these antagonisms and shifts the struggle to the 'cultural' realm.

Finally, in practical terms, many commentators were skeptical about how an average $60 million allotted to multicultural programs annually could possibly address the range of problems and issues involving such things as: assistance to cul-tural groups in their quest to identify, preserve, and promote their cultural identi-ties; cultural interchanges with other groups; official language(s) acquisition programs; and removal of the vaguely defined cultural barriers to social equality and full participation in Canadian society. Thus, early criticisms of multiculturalism focused around the policy's inherent inability to deliver the goods and solve the problems that it set out to address.

Multiculturalism as too effective

In the 1990s, a number of new criticisms began to be levelled against multicultural policy by a combination of academics, social commentators, and political parties (Fleras and Elliott 1996, 348, table 10.3). These criticisms claim that multicultural policy helps to reproduce stereotypes of ethnic groups, undermines Canadian unity, ghettoizes minority issues, takes away from the special claims that francophones and Aboriginal peoples have within Canadian society, and depoliticizes social inequality. These criticisms differ from earlier criticism in that the emphasis is now on the neg-ative social consequences that multicultural policy has produced. It is implied that the 'problem' with multiculturalism is that it is too successful as a social policy. A policy that had as one of its underlying intentions the improvement of inter-group relations is now defined as a policy that leads to deteriorating inter-group relations and as a threat to the coherence and stability of Canada.

The hardening of stereotypes. The first criticism of multiculturalism as too effective is that it leads to the hardening of ethnic and 'racial' stereotypes. In his 1994 book *Selling illusions: The cult of multiculturalism in Canada*, novelist Neil Bissoondath argues that multiculturalism reduces people to the lowest common denominator. By reinforcing stereotypes, it simplifies and thus devalues culture. This is a potent argument against folkloric multiculturalism. 'Caravans', 'folk fests', and other multicultural festivals do not promote serious cultural exchanges; instead, they are superficial and have the effect of commodifying and 'Disneyfying' culture. According to Bissoondath (1994, 83), culture becomes 'a thing that can be displayed, performed, admired, bought, sold, or forgotten'. We have ended up, then, with no culture but theatre, no history but fantasy. Multiculturalism, therefore, is seen to encourage the devaluation of the very thing that it is intended to protect and promote. Manipulated to social and political utility, culture becomes folklore (Bissoondath 1994, 83–4, 88). For Bissoondath,

> Multiculturalism, with all its festivals and its celebrations, has done, and can do, little to foster a factual and clear-minded vision of our neighbours. Depending on stereotype, ensuring that the ethnic groups will preserve their distinctiveness in a gentle and insidious form of cultural apartheid, multiculturalism has done little more than lead an already divided country down the path of social divisiveness (1994, 89–90).

Moreover, by placing individuals into preconceived stereotypes (*what* people are, not *who* they are), multiculturalism diminishes the autonomy and role of the individual. We have become a nation of cultural hybrids, according to Bissoondath (1994, 224). 'We are, as it were, of so many colours, that we are essentially colourless' (1994, 73).

On this point, Bissoondath is probably correct. There is no evidence to suggest that intercultural exchanges take place or have indeed assisted in the 'harmonization' of 'racial' and ethnic relations in Canada. Not only have the 'problems' of minority relations not been defined, but the little intercultural exchanges that do take place are superficial and folkloric at best (Fleras and Elliott 1996, 330–1). In fact, as Mullard argued in 1982, multiculturalism appears to focus on 'saris, samosas and steel-bands' in order to diffuse 'resistance, rebellion and rejection' (in Henry and Tator 1999, 98).

The promotion of cultural relativism. The second criticism of multiculturalism is that it promotes cultural relativism and hence undermines Canadian values and social cohesion. This criticism has been developed by Reg Bibby, a sociologist at the University of Lethbridge, and is echoed by Bissoondath, the Reform Party of Canada in the 1990s, and even today in some sections of the Conservative Party of Canada. In *Mosaic madness*, Bibby (1990) argued that one of the main social trends of our post-modern time is to increasingly value collective and individual freedom. While freedom is a good in and of itself, Bibby argued that the consequence of this increasing emphasis on freedom is to promote individualism, pluralism, and relativism. Individualism, according to Bibby (1990, 1–2), leads to pluralism, and pluralism legitimizes diversity and in turn reinforces the values of both collective and individual freedom. Relativism, then, is the logical consequence of freedom, individualism, and pluralism. But what is relativism?

Bibby defines relativism in terms of the suspension of value judgments about how people live. He writes:

Truth and best are not listed in the pluralism dictionary. The only truth is that everything is relative. 'Cultural relativism' is accepted as a given; those who dare to assert that their culture is best are dubbed ethnocentric; those who dare to assert that they have the truth are labelled bigots. Truth has been replaced by personal viewpoint (1990, 2).

Mosaic madness suggests that pluralism does emancipate individuals and groups. Contrary to absolutist views about truth, which transcend cultures and individuals, cultural relativism argues that the truth is socially constructed and it thus 'erases agreement on the norms that are essential to social life' (Bibby 1990, 14). Cultural relativism, which is seen to be promoted by multicultural policy, leads to the undermining of social cohesion. We have enshrined into law our 'good intentions' of bilingualism, multiculturalism, and anti-racism by institutionalizing appropriate policies. But in consequence, we have become a fractious nation that lacks a sense of community (Bibby 1990, 15). Canada, in attempting to promote (peaceful) coexistence, is indeed promoting the breakdown of group life.

Bibby further argues that individual freedom coupled with pluralism leads to the construction of 'mosaics within mosaics' (individuals and smaller groups within groups) (Bibby 1990, 7–8). This, Bibby claims, is 'too much of a good thing'. Excessive individualism stresses individual rights over social rules. There is no 'team spirit', no social spirit. We confuse choice with 'the best' (98), and we give everything an 'A' (176). Indeed, we are abandoning the 'pursuit of the best' and slowly slipping into a state of multicultural mediocrity. Bibby does not suggest what 'the best' is, who deserves an 'A', or who should decide these issues and how.

So, according to Bibby, Canadian society has changed as a result of multiculturalism but not in entirely positive ways. There appears to be a reversal of emphasis: whereas up to the 1950s, Canadians had placed emphasis on community, on the collectivity, since then we have been emphasizing the individual. Pluralism, although imperative for coexistence, does not offer a subsequent vision of the country, does not set national goals, and does not pursue a cause. According to Bibby (1990, 103–4), we have ended up with a value system that contains nothing exclusively Canadian.

Bissoondath (1994, 71), in a similar vein, argues that multiculturalism has failed because it has eradicated the centre: 'it has diminished all sense of Canadian values, of what is a Canadian'. Most importantly, multiculturalism does not include an ultimate vision of the kind of society it wishes to create (42): it is vague. Although Bissoondath does not advocate a return to the years of anglo-conformity, he argues that multiculturalism does not offer a vision of unity and encourages division by ghettoizing people into ethnic groups. It has imposed social controls and employs 'divide and conquer' strategy and tactics. It is a myopic view of the present that ignores the future (Bissoondath 1994, 44).

In the late 1980s and early 1990s, the Reform Party of Canada, a considerable conservative political force in those days that has found its way into today's

Conservative Party of Canada, called repeatedly for the abolition of multicultural programs and the Department of Multiculturalism as a whole on the same kind of grounds expressed by both Bibby and Bissoondath. According to the party, cultural preservation is a matter of private choice, and the state has no place in promoting diversity. Instead, the government should be preserving and promoting our national culture and should encourage ethnic cultures to integrate into it (Reform Party of Canada, in Abu-Laban and Stasiulis 1992, 373). Similarly, in Bissoondath's (1994, 219) terms, public policy has no place in personal culture and ethnicity. It has to be returned to individuals, who do not need to be defined culturally by Ottawa bureaucrats. Our ultimate goal should be a cohesive, effective society with cultural diversity. If our aim is reasonable diversity within rigorous unity, we must diminish the former to achieve the latter (Bissoondath 1994, 224).

Influenced by the relative electoral appeal of Reform, the Progressive Conservative Party (which has now merged with Reform to form the Conservative party of Canada) passed a number of resolutions at its 1991 annual convention that pointed clearly to a right-wing shift in their immigration and multicultural policies. With respect to multiculturalism, it was resolved that they should abandon the policy and its department altogether and should instead 'try to foster a common national identity for the people living together in harmony as equal citizens, loyal to the Canadian ideal' (cited in Abu-Laban and Stasiulis 1992, 374). When this resolution was passed, the governing Conservatives were in an awkward position having to defend a policy that their membership no longer supported. Gerry Weiner, then the minister of state for multiculturalism, defended the policy and argued that the convention's resolutions did not represent the majority of party members since there was not enough representation of ethnic and 'racial' minorities in the body of delegates. This justification was an indirect admission that the Progressive Conservatives did not have an ethnic base and that those in government were trying hard to break into the ethnic vote. It is interesting that no one mentioned the lack of ethnic representation with respect to resolutions not related to multiculturalism (e.g., on the economy or on social programs).

What is common in criticism of this type is an appeal to the 'national' character of Canada. The implication is that the current system is biased in favour of 'non-whites' and 'non-Europeans' and it should not be. In addition, people expressing such views are always silent or purposefully vague in describing what constitutes Canadian culture (most of the time they mean anglo-tradition) or defining what is Canadian or what Canadian values are. It is unclear exactly what ethnic subcultures or countercultures are to be integrated into. Notice that there is no definition of what constitutes 'the best', whose community it is, who defines it, whose interests it serves, and so on. These critics of multiculturalism have faced at least two sets of responses. Howard-Hassmann (1999) has pointed to a basic fault in the criticisms: they assume that Canadian multiculturalism calls for individuals to retain their ancestral identities. But the Canadian policy is 'liberal', not 'illiberal': that is, it does not impose the idea of maintaining ethnic differences, nor does it force individuals to identify with ancestral cultural groups. In Howard-Hassmann's view:

> Multiculturalism 'normalizes' a wide range of customs and makes the enjoyment of such customs part of what it means to be a Canadian. . . . Liberal multiculturalism acknowledges the social need for difference, for smaller, more close-knit communities separated from the Canadian mainstream. But it does not mandate such difference (Howard-Hassmann 1999, 533)

She has also argued that far from promoting disloyalty to Canada and things Canadian, multicultural policy has the seemingly ironic consequences of integrating immigrants to the dominant society, promoting national unity, and encouraging 'a sense of connection with other Canadians' (1999, 534).

A second response to criticisms of multicultural policy is the argument that pluralism does not inevitably lead to relativism. Multiculturalism, as we experience it in our daily lives, does not encourage an 'everything goes' mentality, although it does help to create some ambiguity about the lines between what is acceptable and what is not, lines that are usually contested in the courts and other public domain places of political struggle. According to Fleras and Elliot (1996, 354), multiculturalism operates within limits: 'it rejects any customs that violate Canadian laws, interferes with the rights of others, offends the moral sensibilities of most Canadians, or disturbs central institutions or core values.' For example, female circumcision is a cultural practice in parts of Africa and Asia and presumably part of the cultural heritage of some Canadians. In May 1997, an amendment to the Criminal Code of Canada outlawed female genital mutilation precisely because that practice violates the human rights of young women and offends notions of equality, human integrity, and other core values prevalent in Canada and internationally. This legislation was based in part on the United Nations Declaration against Violence against Women (1993) as well as the Declaration of the Beijing Conference on Women (1995). The Canadian legislation links the practice to criminal harassment and regards it as a threat to the life, liberty, and security of Canadian women.

The marginalization of ethnocultural issues. The third criticism of multiculturalism is that it promotes the ghettoization of ethnic issues. Ironically, this criticism was most forcefully developed within the ranks of the federal Liberal Party. The Liberals have historically been the party that has most identified with multiculturalism. It developed the non-discriminatory immigration policy, as well as the official policy of multiculturalism, and it has also been the party most rewarded by the ethnic vote. It too, however, harbours people opposed to the policy of multiculturalism. As Abu-Laban and Stasiulis write (1992, 375), a number of 'ethnic' MPs were critical of multiculturalism's ghettoizing effects in the early 1990s. John Nunziata, then a Liberal MP, was the most vocal opponent of the policy, arguing that it no longer served a constructive purpose in Canadian society. When he ran and won as an Independent in the 1997 federal election, a number of his supporters raised the issue of the Liberals' grip on the Italian community in Canada, vowing to put an end to it.

One of Nunziata's criticisms is of particular interest: that the case of the internment and confiscation of property of Japanese Canadians during the Second World War was handled by the Department of Multiculturalism, not by the Ministry of

Justice. These were justice issues, he argued, not ethnic ones (Abu-Laban and Stasiulis 1992, 376). Subsequently, the Liberal Party, after reaffirming its support for multiculturalism at its 1992 convention, has proceeded to incorporate some of these criticisms into its platform. Specifically, it has recognized that multiculturalism may indeed have ghettoizing effects and that a single cultural policy may be a more appropriate course of action, accompanied by a single department of culture and communications. This was a clear shift toward society-building—civic multiculturalism—which involved facilitating the inclusion and participation of all citizens by pursuing anti-racist policies and by promoting 'citizenship' (Abu-Laban and Stasiulis 1992, 376). When the Liberals assumed power in 1993, they established the Ministry of Canadian Heritage, and multiculturalism was once again relegated to a branch of a larger federal department.

Multiculturalism and the undermining of special claims. The fourth criticism of multiculturalism is that it undermines the special claims that francophones and Aboriginal peoples have in Canadian society. As noted above, the inception of multicultural policy had an ulterior motive: namely, the undermining of the legitimacy of Quebec nationalism by reducing the Quebec factor to an ethnic phenomenon (Bissoondath 1994, 40, 62). Initially, multiculturalism was seen as an attempt by the federal government to undermine the legitimate Quebec aspirations for 'nationhood'. 'By severing culture from language, multiculturalism policy rejected the "two nations" thesis about Canada's development, and reduced the status of French Canadians and/or the Québécois from that of "founding people" to the same rank as the "other ethnic groups"' (Abu-Laban and Stasiulis 1992, 367).

This interpretation of multiculturalism was, of course, shared by René Lévesque and by many Quebec academics (Abu-Laban and Stasiulis 1992, 367–8). Lévesque, for example, was dismissive of multiculturalism from the beginning because it obscured the Quebec issue (Bissoondath 1994, 40). As Christian Dufour (1992) argued in *Le défi québécois*, multiculturalism was a mechanism to buy allophone votes and reduce the Quebec factor to an ethnic phenomenon: i.e., reduce the francophone majority to just another ethnic group and undermine its historical claim to 'nationhood'. Harvey (1985, cited in Abu Laban and Stasiulis 1992) and Labelle (1990, cited in Abu Laban and Stasiulis 1992) argued that multiculturalism had an adverse effect on the Quebec collectivity by minoritizing it (similar to the process of 'racialization') (Bissoondath 1994, 40). Quebec's assimilationist policies towards allophones (immigrants whose first language is neither French nor English) can be understood in this context.

Aboriginal people and organizations have expressed similar criticisms and have related reservations about multiculturalism. They argue that multiculturalism reduces them to 'just another minority' and undermines their aspirations for self-government (Abu-Laban and Stasiulis 1992, 376). They claim that they possess a distinct and unique set of rights that stem from being the first occupants of the land in Canada. Since Aboriginal people do not consider themselves part of a pluralist society but as distinct peoples, multiculturalism is seen as an actual threat to their survival. They prefer to negotiate their future in a binational framework (as the

Québécois do) that recognizes their collective rights to special status and distinctiveness (Fleras and Elliott 1996, 343).

QUEBEC'S RESPONSE: INTERCULTURALISM

The Quebec government has pursued a policy of interculturalism (which is also
prominent in Europe) instead of multiculturalism. Interculturalism recognizes cultural diversity within Quebec but does not reduce the 'national question' in Quebec
to an ethnic phenomenon; it discourages ethnic enclaves and promotes *linguistic
assimilation* (Abu-Laban and Stasiulis 1992, 368). Interculturalism promotes cultural exchanges in the hope that as people of different cultures are exposed to various elements of other cultures, the ensuing dialogue may lead not only to tolerance
but to an understanding of the Other. That, in turn, should lead to a fusion of all
commonalities of cultures within a francophone framework. Historically, Quebec
governments have been preoccupied with the protection of the French language,
which has been the main tool for the preservation and development of Québécois
identity and culture. The concern with language stems from two Quebec realities:
first, the alarming decline of the birth rate in the province over the past 30 years;
second, the fact that allophone communities in Quebec tend to 'gravitate linguisti-
cally towards the anglophone community' (Gagnon 2004, 374). Immigration to
Quebec and the integration of immigrants became the preoccupation of successive
Quebec governments since the creation of the Quebec Ministry of Immigration in
1968. The Quebec Liberal government passed the Official Language Act (Bill 22) in
1974, making Quebec officially a unilingual French province. In 1977, with the Parti
Québécois in power, René Lévesque introduced the Charter of the French Language,
commonly known as Bill 101. Although ethnically diverse, Quebec pushed for the
creation of a unilingual (political) community. In 1981, in response to the federal
policy of multiculturalism, the Quebec Ministry of Communications launched an
action plan in a document entitled *Autant de façons d'être québécois* (1981), or 'the
many ways of being Québécois', which spelled out the parameters within which
immigration and immigrant integration would take place in Quebec. Unlike the federal government with its multiculturalism policy, Quebec would pursue a policy of
'convergence' through interculturalism (Gagnon 2004, 374–5).

Some researchers have argued that interculturalism is the most advanced form of
pluralism today (Karmis 2004, 79). It is claimed that it combines multiculturalism and
multinationalism, with three interrelated features. First, it is more inclusive than either
multiculturalism or multinationalism. It does not apply only to ethnic groups or
nations but also applies to 'lifestyle' cultures and world views associated with new
social movements. For example, it is inclusive of cultural gay, punk, ecologist, feminist,
and other non-ethnically based identities. Thus, it includes nations, ethnocultural
groups, and non-ethnic cultural groups. No cultural community is excluded from
Québécois identity. Second, whereas multiculturalism is believed to undermine the
national claims of peoples within Canada by juxtaposing communities composing the
Canadian mosaic, interculturalism seeks to intertwine them. Third, interculturalism
recognizes that most individuals do have multiple identities and that none of them is
so dominant as to subordinate others (Karmis 2004, 79–80).

In 1990, the Quebec ministère des Communautés culturelles et de l'Immigration made the intentions of interculturalism more explicit. Pushing for *citoyenneté québécoise* (Quebec citizenship), it spoke of a 'moral contract' between the host society (Quebec) and immigrants in order to empower all citizens and create a 'common public culture'. The bases on which this moral contract is 'signed' are: (a) a recognition of French as the language of public life; (b) respect for liberal democratic values, including civil and political rights and equality of opportunity; and (c) respect for pluralism, including openness to and tolerance of others' differences (Kymlicka 1998, 7).

In this setting, the French language would be the common language of public life and institutions. In such a society, the active participation of all is expected and encouraged. There exist not only rights but also reciprocal obligations among the participants in the 'moral contract'. Intercommunity exchanges are encouraged, but limits are imposed based on respect for principles of fundamental democratic rights (Gagnon 2004, 375). As Carens (2000, 131) has suggested, '[i]mmigrants can be full members of Quebec's society even if they look and act differently from the substantial segment of the population whose ancestors inhabited Quebec and even if they do not in any way alter their own customs and cultural patterns with respect to work and play, diet and dress, sleep and sex, celebration and mourning, so long as they act within the confines of the law.' In this respect, then, it may appear that there is not much difference between federal multiculturalism and Quebec interculturalism. The 'centre of convergence' for different cultural groups in Quebec, however, is the 'collective good' of the French language, which is seen as an indispensable condition for the creation of the *culture publique commune* (common public culture) and the cohesion of Quebec society. The French language needs to be protected and promoted. It constitutes the basis for the self-definition of Quebec as a political community—indeed, as a nation. Particular emphasis is thus placed on the educational system. As Stéphane Lévesque (1999, 4) has argued, 'common blood or ethnicity hardly creates social cohesion or nationhood, but an education system with a common language do make a "homeland". . . . [I]t is language more than land and history, that provides the essential form of belonging.' Federal multiculturalism promotes individualist approaches to culture, whereas interculturalism focuses on the collectivity. Former prime minister Pierre Elliot Trudeau had argued that there cannot be an official Canadian culture. Interculturalism stresses that the French language is crucial to the development of Québécois culture and citizenship and an instrument of democracy. Without the existence of a community of language, there cannot be democratic debate or decision-making (Giroux 1997, 137). Immigrants can maintain their language of origin, but at a minimum it is their obligation to learn French for use in public space and in order to exercise their citizenship rights. There are no clear 'rules' on what constitutes public space, but common civic norms exist and they form the basis for social cohesion. The goal of interculturalism is 'to achieve the largest possible consensus regarding the limits and possibilities of expressions of *collective* differences based on identity, weighed against the requirements of social cohesion and individual rights in a *common* public context' (Gagnon 2004, 378; emphasis ours).

In 1984, the National Assembly of Quebec established the Conseil des Communautés culturelles et de l'Immigration, a permanent and autonomous body that advises the minister on issues relevant to the integration of immigrants and on intercultural relations (Juteau 2002). In 1996, following the 1995 referendum, the creation of the ministère des Relations avec les citoyens et de l'Immigration signalled a shift away from references to cultural communities, who were displaced to the margins, toward Quebecois citizenship (Juteau 2002, 447). The ministère de l'Immigration et des Communautés culturelles established the program 'Québec interculturel', which promotes the policy of Québécois citizenship by holding the annual Semaine québécoise des rencontres interculturelles, or a week of intercultural exchanges among Quebec's cultural communities. The theme in October 2006 was 'Mille visages, notre avenir', or 'a thousand faces, our future'. Despite the good intentions and efforts of successive Quebec governments, there is no evidence that immigrants in Quebec integrate better than immigrants in the rest of Canada. In addition, there is evidence that immigrants in Quebec were not yet imagined as true Québécois, and large segments have remained outside the Quebec community, as demonstrated by the controversy over the *hijab* (headscarf) that some Muslim women wear (Juteau 2002, 444, 447). In Quebec, the position of Aboriginals—another 'segment' with equally rightful claims to nationhood—abundantly demonstrates this. In short, Quebec nationalism is more in tune with the 'two founding nations' (British and French) image of Canada. Dualism has always been cherished in Quebec but usually resisted by anglophones (Stevenson 2005). But dualism is no longer possible. Quebec has moved away from an ethnic definition of nation toward a cultural definition—away from the French-Canadian, Catholic 'race' notion, toward a francophone common public culture and more recently Québécois citizenship (Juteau 2002, 445).

MULTICULTURALISM AS A RECIPE FOR TERRORISM AND INTOLERANCE?

Many other countries around the world now officially celebrate their multicultural character, and some, like Canada, have polices designed to promote multiculturalism. However, a number of events around the world over the past few years have provided a context for renewed questions about and attacks on multiculturalism policies, both here in Canada and abroad. Certainly, the attacks on the World Trade Center in New York and the Pentagon on 11 September 2001 put many Western governments on alert about the threats that cultural and religious Others posed to the peace and security of their countries. Other, less spectacular events have contributed to even more anxiety about the wisdom of multiculturalism policies: the 2006 controversy about the publication in Denmark of cartoons depicting the Muslim prophet Mohammed; the attacks on the London transit system undertaken by so-called 'home-grown' terrorists; the riots in Paris by immigrant youth in the fall of 2005; and the arrest of 17 Muslims in Toronto on the grounds that they were plotting terrorist attacks.

The two most trenchant post-9/11 criticisms of multiculturalism are that such policies encourage and tolerate the promotion of cultures and religions that are decidedly intolerant and that multiculturalism is a recipe for home-grown terrorism. Robert Fulford, in a *National Post* article, summarizes these two themes and describes the Canadian policy of multiculturalism as a 'grave mistake'. According to Fulford:

> Multiculturalism has become a way of putting people in narrow categories. Some groups have decided to live in ghettos of their own making, apart from the rest of us. While living apart temporarily often is a necessary part of the immigration process, if only because of language, those who see cultural isolation as a permanent way of life tend to cripple their own possibilities, limit their ability to contribute to Canada, and create impregnable communities in which they can nourish their imported grievances and generate hatred for democracy and the West (2006, A19).

Critics of multiculturalism like Fulford go overboard when they claim that multiculturalism promotes the formation of entire ethnic communities in Canada that are closed, insulated, and opposed to everything that Canada stands for. At the same time, questions about the relationship between multicultural policy and the role it plays in the preservation of ethnic cultures that are seemingly at odds with Canadian values need to be asked. It is probably fair to say that no country has arrived at an ideal solution to the issue of managing ethnic and 'racial' diversity. Canada's multicultural approach to managing issues of diversity may not be perfect, but there are many far more problematic approaches to managing diversity that we should take pride in having avoided.

SUMMARY

For historical reasons related to colonization, conquest, and immigration, Canada is, and will remain for the foreseeable future, a diverse society. In recent debates about multiculturalism, however, the social value of this diversity has been increasingly called into question. For some, multiculturalism and our accompanying diversity are what makes our country both strong and unique. For others, to rephrase the immortal words of Jacques Parizeau, former leader of the Parti Québécois, our 'racial' and ethnic diversity is like the toothache that just will not go away. As we have seen in this chapter, multiculturalism and the diversity that it claims to celebrate and promote are seen by some as a deleterious social policy that has produced far more serious problems than it has resolved. Whereas previous criticisms focused on its relative weakness in effecting social change, more recent criticisms have assumed that the problem with multiculturalism is that it has been too successful in promoting difference and diversity and hence has led to an undermining of Canadian values, attitudes, and culture. As we have seen in this chapter, while some of the critics are probably correct in their assessment that multiculturalism fails to change the underlying structural conditions that produce inequality, racism, and discrimination, other criticisms attribute too much power and significance to an underfunded and beleaguered policy.

It has been argued, however, that multiculturalism is not only a 'strategy of containment rather than change' (Henry and Tator 1999, 95) but a means by which minority communities can resist racism. As Allahar (1998, 342) has suggested, multiculturalism may be seen as a strategic retreat on the part of ethnic groups. It has a triple function, for both minority individuals and communities: '(1) it enhances their self-esteem and cultivates a favourable predisposition to the society and its institutions; (2) through exposure it promotes greater understanding of difference in the minds of others, thus reducing tension and the possibility of conflict; (3) it holds out the promise of equality to members of minorities both new and old.' At the same time, in recent years there has been a call for a new kind of critical/radical multicultural paradigm (Henry and Tator 1999), one that capitalizes on the civic aspects of multiculturalism and in which ethnic and cultural communities are not seen simply as another type of interest group but as

> active and full participants in the state . . . [and] part of its shared history. This paradigm represents a different axis, moving away from tolerance and accommodation and towards equity and justice. Critical multiculturalism rejects a unified and static concept of identities and communities as fixed sets of experiences, meanings, and practices. Instead, it focuses on identities as dynamic, fluid, multiple, and historically situated. Multiculturalism, in this context, moves beyond the narrow understanding of identity politics to make way for alliances and affiliations based on mutual needs and shared objectives (1999, 99).

Critical/radical multiculturalism could then provide new possibilities for the restructuring and reconceptualization of power and power relations both among and within cultural communities. We cannot understand diversity outside of the context of social justice (Henry and Tator 1999, 99).

Questions for Critical Thought

1. Would you prefer to live in a country where there is no official policy of multiculturalism? What would be some of the advantages and disadvantages of living in a monocultural society?
2. Which is a better framework for accomplishing the full participation of Canada's minorities in the political, social, and economic institutions of the country? One based on the notion that Canada is constituted by two founding nations (British and French) or one that includes First Nations as well as other ethnic and cultural groups that migrated to Canada later? Why?
3. Does multiculturalism undermine the special claims of Aboriginal peoples in Canada? Are they just another ethnic/cultural group? Can the policy and the programs associated with multiculturalism address social, economic, and political conditions of Natives in Canada?
4. Why have Quebec governments resisted the federal policy of multiculturalism?
5. Should the Canadian policy of multiculturalism be adopted by other multi-ethnic countries? Why? Think of France, Belgium, Australia, and the US. What about countries that have been historically more culturally homogeneous, like Italy, Greece, Spain, or Ireland?
6. In September/October 2006, there was a debate in the United Kingdom about the right of Muslim women to wear a veil. Both Prime Minister Tony Blair and Jack Straw,

ex-minister of foreign affairs, had asked Muslim women to remove their veils in their presence in order to improve communication, as they claimed. Also, a Muslim teacher was required by law to remove her veil when in the classroom because it supposedly hindered student learning. Who do you think is right and why?

Annotated Additional Readings

Abu-Laban, Yasmeen, and Christina Gabriel. 2002. *Selling diversity: Immigration, multiculturalism, employment equity and globalization*. Peterborough: Broadview Press. A critical introduction to immigration, globalization, and the policies of multiculturalism and employment equity. It explores the interconnections of citizenship, nation-building, and the commodification of diversity in the global era.

Fedorak, Shirley. 2006. *Windows on the world*. Toronto: Thomson-Nelson. An anthropological approach that contains 15 synopses of ethnic and cultural group histories. The book has sections on Chinese Canadians, Sikhs, Acadians, the Cree, the Utku Inuit, and the Jewish diaspora, among others.

Henry, Frances, and Carol Tator. 2005. *The colour of democracy: Racism in Canada*. 3rd ed. Toronto: Thomson-Nelson. The authors examine racism in the context of multiculturalism by examining public institutions (justice system, policing, human services), educational organizations, the arts, media, and other cultural institutions. They argue that multiculturalism is an inadequate policy instrument for fighting racism in Canadian society.

Kymlicka, Will, and Wayne Norman. 2000. *Citizenship in diverse societies*. Toronto: Oxford University Press. A collection of articles by international scholars, who deal primarily with citizenship, education, religious and ethnic diversity, political participation, immigration, identity and multiculturalism, gender issues, and the rights of indigenous peoples, as well as federalism and nationalism, from a liberal perspective.

Related Websites

Multiculturalism: http://www.canadianheritage.gc.ca/progs/multi/index_e.cfm.
Québec interculturel: http://www.quebecinterculturel.gouv.qc.ca/fr/index.html.
Intercultural Institute of Montréal: http://www.iim.qc.ca/.
Toronto Chinese Community Services Association: http://www.tccsa.on.ca/.
Greek Community of Toronto: http://www.greekcommunity.org/.
Ukrainian-Canadian Congress: http://www.ucc.ca/.
The Weekly Voice (south Asian news in Canada): http://www.weeklyvoice.com/.
National Consultative Committee on Racism and Interculturalism, Ireland:
    http://www.nccri.ie/.

Chapter 6

Racism

Learning objectives

In this chapter you will learn:

- About different sociological definitions of racism;
- About the evolution of racism as a scientific doctrine;
- About different folk versions of racism and 'race' thinking;
- That racism is not necessarily a 'whites only' phenomenon;
- That scholars in Canada and in many other countries argue that racism has taken on new forms and new meanings; some suggest that Islamophobia is one of the new forms of racism that has emerged in many Western societies in the aftermath of the attacks in the United States on 11 September 2001;
- That some scholars claim that racism remains pervasive in Canadian society;
- That there are different ways that social scientists have tried to measure racism;
- That there are three forms that institutional racism can take;
- That critics claim that zero-tolerance polices are racist;
- That critics also claim that the over-policing and under-policing of minority communities further reflects the racist nature of Canadian society.

Introduction

Few words in the English language carry the same negative connotations as the word racism. Racism has been identified as a cause of a number of the world's historical and current social evils, including slavery, genocide, human rights violations, environmental degradation, and social inequality. In many cases, racism is also an epithet. To call someone a racist is to label a person as not only outside of polite society but also beyond the pale of civilization itself (Banton 1970, 18–19). Indeed, a rather telling indicator that most people do not wear the term 'racist' as a badge of honour is that even members of the Ku Klux Klan in the United States resist this label as a description of themselves (Reitz and Breton 1994, 68).

Even though 'racist' is a highly charged and emotionally laden term, it is routine to hear allegations that individuals, organizations, and social institutions are racist. In the United States, some commentators called the Bush administration racist because of the way it handled Hurricane Katrina in New Orleans in September 2005. Some commentators explained the lack of planning and effective response in the aftermath of the hurricane as the result of the federal government's lack of interest in the suffering of black people in the city. In Canada over the past decade, various police forces, school boards, employers, media outlets, cultural productions, government policies, and private individuals have also been labelled 'racist' (Henry and Tator 2005).

Michael Banton (2002, 54) cautions that words like racism have 'high rhetorical value' and can be often 'over employed' in their characterization of individuals, organizations, or ideas. The problem is that using the term loosely and uncritically to describe a wide variety of phenomena or social situations can inadvertently lead to the undermining of its analytical and political power. In other words, if it is used too cavalierly to describe too wide a range of phenomena, then there is a danger that people become desensitized to the issue. It also becomes too easy to dismiss genuine instances of racism simply in terms of a sarcastic 'here we go again' response.

One of the difficulties associated with analyzing racism is that there is no single agreed-upon definition of the term. Some might approach the definition of racism in much the same way as the definition of the proverbial duck: namely, that 'if it walks like a racist, and it talks like a racist, then it is a racist.' This approach, however, is not necessarily good enough for social scientists. Since the term is used in so many different ways and in so many different contexts to describe everything from individual actions and beliefs, to conscious and unconscious governmental and organizational practices and policies, to media images and discourses, we should not easily dismiss the question of definition. In this chapter, we want to examine the variety of definitions of racism and some of the debates about contemporary forms of racism.

'RACE' AND RACISM

As we noted in chapter 1, 'race' is an empty biological concept. Even though people believe that 'races' of people exist as distinct biological groups, it is clear that 'race' is better seen as a concept that has been used to describe, categorize, and explain certain patterns of physical or genetic differentiation (Miles and Brown 2003; Nagel 2003). While physical and genetic differences among people exist, these are not 'racial' differences. Even though we have serious reservations about the analytical utility of the concept of 'race', this does not mean that racism is of equally questionable status as a social scientific concept. After all, people hold negative beliefs and act in discriminatory ways about other people on the basis of the belief that individuals are of a different 'race' and/or that they are members of a biologically or culturally inferior social group. Even though those beliefs and actions are based on question-able assumptions about the biological reality of 'race', the beliefs and actions are nevertheless real, as are their social consequences. Thus, questioning the existence of biologically based 'races' should never be taken to imply that racism is not a prob-lem (Satzewich 1998b).

What, then, is racism, and why does it exist? A number of sociologists have attempted to offer both definitions of and explanations for racism. There are many specific approaches to the problem of defining and analyzing racism, and we started to flag some of them in earlier chapters. In this chapter, we want to examine a num-ber of different approaches to understanding racism critically and more systemati-cally. We argue that a distinction should be made between racism as science and racism as a folk concept. We further suggest that there are at least four ways of understanding racism as a folk concept: white racism, new racism, racism and class relations, and racism as a way of making sense of the world.

RACISM AS A SCIENTIFIC DOCTRINE

Sociologist Michael Banton argues that the term racism should properly be confined to the world of scientific ideas. He also warns us against extending the term to situ-ations in which racial referents are absent and to the world of folk or everyday beliefs. The term 'race' has obscure origins. Banton (2002) traces its first usage to Old Norse in which it referred to running or rushing water. Since then, its meaning has changed. Ideas about the ranking of different 'races' in a hierarchy of biological superiority and inferiority are of more recent origin. Banton defines racism as 'the doctrine that a man's behaviour is determined by stable inherited characteristics deriving from separate racial stocks having distinctive attributes and usually consid-ered to stand to one another in relations of superiority and inferiority' (Banton 1970, 18). Banton argues that the first systematic expressions of biologically informed racism appeared in the form of the doctrine of racial typology that was advanced by certain European scientists in the mid to late nineteenth century. By his definition, one of the first true racists was Robert Knox, the Edinburgh anatomist who published *The races of men* in 1850. Knox's work signified a change in the social meaning of 'race': away from vertical lines of individual and collective descent to basic 'horizontal' differences between discrete groups of people. European scientists who held to the doctrine of racial typology believed that much of human history and many of the variations in human culture could be explained by reference to innate biological differences between groups and that 'races' could be arranged along a continuum of superiority and inferiority. Although the scientific theories that advanced the doctrine of racial typology took different forms depending on the scientist and the context, they had certain basic assumptions in common. That doctrine held that (1) there exist distinct and permanent types of *Homo sapiens*; (2) the physical appearance and behaviour of individuals is an expression of a discrete biological type that is permanent; (3) cultural variation is determined by differences in biological type; (4) biological variation is the origin of conflict both between individuals and between nations; and (5) 'races' are differentially endowed such that some are inherently inferior to others (Banton 1977).

Banton argues that racism was a scientific mistake. Scientists in fact made a number of mistakes, not least of which was equating biological difference with cultural difference. Banton cautions us to be wary of explanations that attribute such theories and their scientific errors to the scientists' personality traits: 'the inductivist explanation of scientific error is not only wrong but dangerous. It implies that men like . . . Knox . . . made mistakes because their hearts were not in the right place and that all we need today in order to avoid or combat racism is a pure heart. I believe that we also need a clear head' (Banton 1970, 27).

Although some scientists began to have serious reservations about racially based theories of human development in the 1920s, scientific racism reached its zenith in Nazi Germany. Nazi 'race' scientists were determined to prove the racial superiority of the Aryan 'race' and the racial inferiority of Jews, blacks, Gypsies, and a wide range of others. According to Nazi sympathizer and physical anthropologist Alfred Baeumler, 'race' is 'a definite psycho-physical type which is common to a larger national and tribal circle of men, and maintains itself by hereditary descent. . . . Race is the alpha and omega of the life of nations in its entirety' (quoted in Montagu 1964, 33).

It is important to recognize that theories linking 'race', history, culture, and 'national destiny' in the years that bracketed World War II were by no means confined to Nazi Germany. In 1948, a Greek anthropologist wrote that the Greek 'race' 'has almost uniform physical characteristics, physical and psychical, inherited in its descendants; it has all the characteristics of the basic elements, which are all Greek and indigenous in spite of the variety of types. . . . The Greek race, as all others, has to preserve its own "fluid constancy" by avoiding mixture with foreign elements' (quoted in Montagu 1964, 31). It is also important to recognize that these kinds of ideas were not confined to the level of scientific discourse. Politicians, captains of industry, and members of the general public in many countries believed in and articulated racist doctrines that explained the past and possible futures of different communities. As we saw in chapter 2, racial theories of human development and human capacities guided Canadian immigration policy until the early 1960s.

In the middle of the twentieth century, 'race' thinking was ubiquitous. At the same time, many people understood that horrible atrocities had been committed during the war, in part in the name of 'race'. Individuals and organizations began to develop deep reservations about racial thinking, and the period after World War II produced some notable attempts at challenging racist thinking, both on the level of science and on the level of public discourse. After the war, the United Nations Educational, Scientific and Cultural Organization (UNESCO) played a leading role in challenging scientific racism by sponsoring a series of conferences where the aim was, among other things, to discredit Nazi-style racial ideology. Held in 1950, 1952, 1964, and 1967, these conferences were variously attended by internationally recognized scholars in the fields of anthropology, biology, population genetics, sociology, and zoology. After each conference, UNESCO published a series of 'statements' summarizing what 'race' was, what it was not, and why rankings of groups along continuums of biological superiority and inferiority were wrong. The statements vary in their approaches and are subtly different from each other, but the common thread in these UNESCO-inspired conferences was that theories about the biological inferiority or superiority of groups of people and theories that claimed there was a deterministic relationship between biological and genetic characteristics and human culture were without scientific foundation. The 1950 *Statement on race*, for example, explained that:

> 15 (2) According to present knowledge there is no proof that the groups of mankind differ in their innate mental characteristics, whether in respect to intelligence or temperament. The scientific evidence indicates that the range of mental capacities in all ethnic groups is much the same.
>
> (3) Historical and sociological studies support the view that genetic differences are not of importance in determining the social and cultural differences between groups of Homo sapiens, and that the social and cultural changes in different groups have, in the main, been independent of changes in inborn constitution. Vast social changes have occurred which were not in any way connected with changes in racial type.
>
> (4) There is no evidence that race mixture as such produces bad results from the biological point of view. The social results of race mixture whether for good or ill are to be traced to social results (Montagu 1964, 365–6).

The scientists associated with the various UNESCO conferences worked hard to try to discredit scientific racism. Though by no means naive enough to think that racism could be eliminated simply by presenting and popularizing the true 'facts' surrounding the nature of 'race' and 'race difference', the scientists involved in these projects nevertheless believed that a key part of challenging racism was to undermine its status as a scientific concept. However, one of the contradictions inherent in the efforts of scientists who participated in the conferences was that they did not effectively undermine the idea of 'race' itself. They challenged notions of racial hierarchy and the idea that 'race' determined cultural and historical development, but at the same time they left the concept of 'race' intact. That is, they continued to endorse the idea that there was something out there that could legitimately and objectively be called 'race'. As a result, critics have argued that the UNESCO conferences did not go as far as they should have in undermining the scientific grounding of 'race'-based thinking.

Modern versions of 'race' science
Even though many of the experts brought together by UNESCO after World War II thought that they were well on the way to putting nails in the coffin of racism and racial science, some scholars have continued the elusive search for biologically based racial differences in intelligence and social and sexual behaviour. In the mid-1990s in the United States, Richard Herrnstein and Charles Murray (1994) published *The bell curve: Intelligence and class structure in American life*. This was a wide-ranging book that considered a number of complicated issues surrounding the relationship between environment, genetic makeup, intelligence, social inequality, and social behaviour. Hernnstein and Murray (1994) argue that human beings differ in what psychologists call the general factor of intelligence. Referred to as g, it is defined as

'a general capacity for inferring and applying relationships drawn from experience' (Herrnstein and Murray 1994, 4). As Hernnstein and Murray explain:

> being able to grasp, for example, the relationship between a pair of words like harvest and yield, or to recite a list of digits in reverse order, or to see what a geometrical pattern would look like upside down, are examples of tasks . . . that draw on g (1944, 4).

They argue that American society is becoming increasingly stratified along differences in cognitive ability and that a cognitive elite is increasingly occupying positions of social, political, and economic power. In their view, cognitive ability is also related to a number of social problems, such as crime, vice, welfare dependency, unemployment, poverty, workplace injuries, and poor parenting styles. They argue that individuals with less g display more pathological forms of social behaviour than individuals with more general intelligence.

They also argue, however, that general intelligence not only varies among individuals but also varies according to ethnicity and 'race'. Generally, they claim to have detected a pattern showing basic differences in intelligence among Asians, whites, and blacks such that Asians on average have marginally higher levels of general intelligence than whites. Asians and whites display on average significantly higher levels of intelligence than blacks. According to Herrnstein and Murray (1994), these racial differences in intelligence are the result of a combination of genetic and environmental differences.

Canadian psychologist Philippe Rushton has taken this line of thinking a step further and places even more emphasis on the biological basis for racial differences in behaviour than Herrnstein and Murray do. He argues, for example, that, 'Orientals, whites and blacks' differ in terms of sexual behaviour. In particular, these three groups differ in relation to what he calls 'sexual restraint'. Sexual restraint is a composite variable made up of things like rate of premarital sex, frequency of sex after marriage, and general level of interest in sex. He argues that blacks display less sexual restraint than whites, while 'Orientals' display more sexual restraint than both whites and blacks. Whites are in between blacks and 'Orientals' in their degree of sexual restraint (Rushton and Bogaert 1987, 535–6). Rushton and Bogaert (1987) then go on to argue that blacks, whites, and 'Orientals' also differ in their sexual anatomies. Black men have larger average penis sizes than white men, who in turn have larger average penis sizes than 'Orientals'. Women vary in similar ways. Black women have larger vaginas and longer clitorises than white women, who in turn have larger vaginas and longer clitorises than 'Oriental' women (Rushton and Bogaert 1987, 536). Though Rushton and Bogaert (1987, 543) admit that environmental differences might explain some of the differences in degrees of 'sexual restraint' among the three groups, they argue that the correlation between dimensions of sexual anatomy and sexual restraint is likely biologically driven. These patterns, they argue, are the result of the 'variegated complex of human life history characteristics resulting from a tradeoff between egg production and other adaptive behaviour such as parental care and social organization' (Rushton and Bogaert 1987, 545). In short, blacks are less sexually restrained than whites. 'Orientals' are most restrained because of supposed differences in their sexual anatomy. In other work, Rushton argues that blacks, whites, and 'Orientals' differ in their cranial capacities and brain sizes, which accounts for differences in intelligence (Rushton 1988). As Rushton once stated in an interview with *Rolling Stone* magazine, 'Even if you take things like athletic ability or sexuality—not to reinforce stereotypes—but it's a trade-off: more brain or more penis' (cited in Rosen and Lane 1995, 60).

The work of Rushton and Herrnstein and Murray has been subject to intense critical attack. Rosen and Lane (1995, 58) dismiss it as the work of 'disreputable race theorists and eccentric eugenicists'. Others question the data and methods they use to arrive at their conclusions and their understanding of the fields of intelligence testing and genetics (Devlin et al. 1997; Fraser 1995). While the criticisms are both complex and involved, critics of this type of research argue that Herrnstein and Murray and Rushton considerably overstate the degree to which intelligence is an inherited as opposed to environmental characteristic (Daniels, Devlin, and Roeder 1997; Wahlsten 1997) and considerably understate the degree to which socio-economic achievement is more conditioned by education, family background, and where one lives than by the notion of general intelligence (Cawley et al. 1997). Rushton's work on 'race' differences in sexual behaviour is based on problematic data and on poorly grounded and stereotypical understandings of the diverse nature of human sexuality. Sexual practices, preferences, and identities vary as much within as they do between groups, and Rushton seems to equate certain patterns of physical difference with inherent 'race' difference.

The Human Genome Project

The debate about the existence and meaning of 'race' differences has been undertaken with renewed vigour and respectability in the context of the Human Genome Project. With funding from a wide range of sources, the Human Genome Project began in 1987 as an attempt to trace the human genome and involved mapping the three billion nucleotides that make up the human DNA. Particular sequences of nucleotides combine to form the approximately 25,000 genes. Our genes provide the proteins to help produce human traits, such as the length of a person's index finger and the way the lungs work (Abraham 2005). The project found, among other things, that humans were far more alike than they are different. In fact, the project found that humans share as much as 99.9 per cent of genetic material. Put simply, this means that individuals from different parts of the world are 99.9 per cent alike genetically speaking. This means that only 0.1 per cent of genetic material accounts for differences among humans. This 0.1 per cent genetic variation is the basis for differences in skin colour, head shape, and disposition toward certain diseases.

Scholars are divided on how to interpret the results of the Human Genome Project. Some scientists focus on the big picture and argue that the 99.9 per cent of genetic similarity that was discovered in the project confirms that 'race' is an empty biological concept. Conversely, others suggest that even though the 0.1 per cent of difference in human genetic material appears small, it is nevertheless significant and further proof that there is something biologically real and relevant about 'race'. Indeed, a second research project, known as the Haplotype Project, has begun to draw out the significance of this 0.1 per cent difference. The project involves the mapping of genetic combinations in four populations: Utah residents with European descent, the Yoruba people in Nigeria, Han Chinese in Beijing, and Japanese inhabitants of Tokyo.

The advances associated with genetic mapping of the human genome raise a number of ethical questions about so-called 'race'-based research. Ethicists are concerned about the long-term social consequences. Will insurance companies, employers, and others make decisions about individuals based on their genetic profile? To what extent will individuals with predispositions to particular types of disease be subject to unequal and discriminatory treatment?

These are not easy questions to answer. However, the other issue that needs to be raised is whether genetic mapping really undermines the view that 'race' is a socially constructed label. The same observations about the socially constructed nature of 'race' that were relevant in pre-genetic mapping days are still relevant today. There may in fact be a small proportion of human genetic difference from individual to individual. But they are precisely that—genetic differences. As a society, we still choose to label those genetic differences as 'race' differences, but they are really genetic differences pure and simple.

RACISM AS A FOLK CONCEPT

Critics argue that simply discrediting the scientific evidence surrounding the existence of biologically based 'races' of people is not enough to put an end to racism. Racism, after all, is not just articulated in laboratories, at academic conferences, and in scientific journals. It may have originated as a scientific error, but it has taken on a life of its own and has filtered down into popular consciousness and institutional practices. Thus, sociologists need to understand the reasons that racism and 'race' thinking more generally have become folk or everyday concepts that individuals hold and believe in. The battle against racism should be fought not only in labs and scientific journals but also in the everyday world and within the social conditions that produce racism. In this section, we consider four approaches in the way that social scientists have defined and analyzed racism.

White racism: the only racism?

One social scientific approach to defining racism suggests that racism is something that plagues only white people. American sociologists Joel Feagin and Hernan Vera (1995) suggest that because of their power and privilege, white people in the United States are uniquely placed as both beneficiaries and defenders of racial hierarchies. Members of other communities may express negative attitudes about white people and even other minority groups. However, according to Feagin and Vera (1995, x), 'what is often referred to as "black racism" consists of judgments made about whites by some black leaders or commentators to the effect that "no white people can be trusted" or "the white man is the devil"'. Feagin and Vera dismiss these ideas as not equivalent to 'modern white racism' because unlike white people, black people in the United States are powerless to act on the basis of those ideas and deny privileges to whites or to other groups. They argue that in the United States, 'black racism does not exist' (Feagin and Vera 1995, x) because racism 'is more than a matter of individual prejudice and scattered episodes of discrimination'. 'There is no black racism,' they further claim, 'because there is no centuries-old system of racialized subordination and discrimination designed by African Americans to exclude white Americans from full participation in the rights, privileges and benefits of this society' (Feagin and Vera 1995, ix).

In their view, 'white racism can be viewed as the socially constructed set of attitudes, ideas, and practices that deny African Americans and other people of color the dignity, opportunities, freedoms, and rewards that this nation offers white Americans' (Feagin and Vera 1995, 7).

Though they are correct to point out that racism has both individual and institutional dimensions, there are problems with their view that racism is the exclusive domain of white people. One problem is that this view assumes that all black people, or members of minority communities more generally, are powerless in the face of an insurmountable white power structure. However, black and other minorities are not entirely devoid of power in American or Canadian society. Depending on the context, members of minority communities do hold positions of power within the social, economic, and political structures of society. Black people and other minority group members own businesses, run corporations, make decisions about hiring, and occupy positions of political influence. To assume, as do Feagin and Vera (1995), that black people are economically and politically powerless assumes, in stereotypical fashion, that black people form an underclass within American and Canadian society and that all black people or members of other minority communities are alike and occupy disadvantaged, socially marginal positions in political and economic relations. Not all blacks live in ghetto-like or working-class environments. As we suggested in chapter 4, individuals within ethnic and racialized communities occupy a variety of class positions.

Furthermore, individuals within minority communities are not uniquely immune to racism or powerless to act on the basis of those beliefs. For example, surveys in the United States show that whites, blacks, Asians, and Hispanics display complicated negative stereotypes about each other. For example, in one survey, members of each of the four groups were asked to rate the other groups on three dimensions: perceptions of intelligence, perceptions of welfare dependency, and perceptions of their difficulty to get along with. In the survey, nearly two-thirds of Asian respondents thought that blacks were less intelligent than members of their own group. Forty per cent of white respondents and thirty per cent of Hispanic respondents believed that blacks were less intelligent than members of their own groups. On the other hand, nearly one-third of black respondents and 15 per cent of white and Hispanic respondents believed that Asians were less intelligent than members of their own group. Between 40 and 50 per cent of each of the three groups believed that Asians were hard to get along with (Johnson, Farrell, and Guinn 1999, 395–6).

Arguably, the racism expressed by minority group members against other people is just as socially consequential as white racism directed against blacks and other minority groups. Perhaps the best documented example of inter-minority group racism and associated conflict and hostility comes from Los Angeles. The Los Angeles riots in the 1990s were telling in that the conflicts and hostilities did not have clear and simple 'racial' dividing lines (Feagin and Vera 1995, 1). Though Feagin and Vera (1995, 1) argue that the conflicts in Los Angeles in 1992 were the result of 'anger and rage at white racism', there is evidence that they were not just white versus black conflicts. For instance, black and Hispanic rioters purposely targeted Korean-owned businesses, not just enterprises owned by individuals with 'white' privilege. As explained by Johnson, Farrell, and Guinn, in Los Angeles, New York, and other major immigrant-receiving cities in the United States:

> Disadvantaged blacks in these communities see the Korean merchants as 'foreigners' who are taking advantage of them by charging high prices, by refusing to invest any of the profits they earn either by employing local black residents or otherwise aiding the community, and by being rude and discourteous in their treatment of black customers. On the other hand, many of the stereotypic views that Koreans have of blacks are confirmed in their daily interaction with some of the most disadvantaged residents of inner-city communities (1999, 406).

Furthermore, in the aftermath of the 1992 Los Angeles riots, research indicated that

> By looting and destroying Korean-owned businesses in Koreatown, Hispanics vented their anger and frustration about the disrespectful treatment and exploitation to which they were routinely subject as customers and as employees in Korean-owned and -operated establishments (Johnson, Farrell, and Guinn 1999, 406).

The black and Latino attacks against Korean-owned small businesses were rooted in shifting power and economic dynamics in Los Angeles. Latino immigrants are defined by some blacks as competitors for jobs in the local labour market. Some black people in the city feel that immigrants and illegal aliens from Mexico and Latin America are contributing to lower wages and taking away 'their' jobs. Korean immigrants, who face different forms of exclusion in American society, have been able to carve out an economic niche for themselves as corner store operators. As major grocery store chains vacate inner-city American neighbourhoods, Korean-owned corner stores are filling the gap. Since these corner stores tend to be the only shopping option in many neighbourhoods, they become the focus of conflicts surrounding pricing, the lack of jobs, and other community issues.

It would be a mistake to dismiss these kinds of events and issues as not relevant to Canada because they happen south of the border. In Vancouver in 2003, a Filipino-Canadian teen was beaten to death by a group of Indo-Canadian youths in what the police describe as a 'racially' motivated attack. According to a *Globe and Mail* report on the incident:

> The attack heightened tensions between Indo-Canadian and Filipino-Canadian youths. At [the teen's] . . . funeral dozens of Indo-Canadian youths, many who didn't know the victim, attended as a demonstration of their respect and commitment to peace between the two ethnic groups. Police and community leaders urged calm amidst rumours that Filipino-Canadian youths were planning retaliation (Fong 2005, A11).

Some Filipino-Canadian community leaders were reluctant to blame other ethnic communities as the source of the problem and instead argued that systemic racism was to blame because it created 'artificial conflicts' between racialized minorities. One commentator suggested that 'if Indo-Canadian, Vietnamese-Canadian and Filipino-Canadian contributions are taught in school, we will have a better understanding of each other' (Fong 2005, A11).

Even though it might be reasonable on one level to assume that groups that are the object of racism and discriminatory treatment might be more sympathetic to other groups that experience the same thing, it is clear that this does not always happen (Noivo 1998). In many ways, there is surprisingly little 'transfer sympathy' among groups with common experiences of racism and discrimination. Nor is it clear that the responsibility for such incidents should be shouldered by 'white society'. Some immigrant groups bring their old-world prejudices to Canada. Even though these pre-existing prejudices may not fully explain why hostilities emerge among groups in Canada, they do form part of the context for these kinds of events. The conflicts and hostilities can only be understood if racism is not assumed to be a 'white only' phenomenon.

New racisms

In the early 1980s, British philosopher Martin Barker (1981) published a book titled *The new racism*. In it, Barker argued that old, biologically informed expressions of racism were a thing of the past and that negative evaluations of racially defined groups were being masked in racially neutral language and rearticulated to make them more politically acceptable in public discourse. Since then, analysts in a number of countries have taken up this argument and elaborated on the new ways that racism is being expressed less overtly in different contexts and in different countries.

Britain. Barker argued that in Britain, new ideologies, which emphasized that social problems were caused by people of different cultures coming into contact and living in close proximity to each other, had come to replace previous views that 'race relations' problems were caused by biologically distinct 'races' coming into contact. He suggested that because of the general abhorrence in Britain of biologically based understandings of the link between 'race' and social problems and conflict, certain conservative segments of British society developed a code language that allowed them to talk about 'race' but in a way that would allow them to deny that they were being racist. This code language used politically neutral terms that played on racial themes, but it did so in ways that allowed individuals who expressed these ideas to avoid the racist label because they did not suggest racial inferiority. One of the most famous expressions of the new racism in Britain came in a speech by prime minister Margaret Thatcher in 1978 in which she argued that

> If we went on as we are, then by the end of the century there would be 4 million people of the New Commonwealth of Pakistan here. Now that is an awful lot and I think it means that people are really rather afraid that this country might be

swamped by people with a different culture. And, you know, the British character has done so much for democracy, for law, and done so much throughout the world, that if there is a fear that it might be swamped, people are going to react and be rather hostile to those coming in (cited in Barker 1981, 15).

Thatcher, expressing sentiments that were quite widespread among conservative segments of British society in the late 1970s and the 1980s, was deeply ambivalent about immigration from India, the Caribbean, and Pakistan and the negative consequences that such immigration was causing in Britain. Her speech, however, was devoid of biological referents and instead focused on a negative evaluation of cultural differences. In Barker's view, these kinds of ideas were no less pernicious or racist than the old versions of racism based on biological notions of the racial inferiority of certain groups of people.

France. This kind of new racism is also present in France. According to Taguieff (1999), the New Right in France, represented by the National Front, has rearticulated racism to emphasize the notion of natural cultural differences between 'race' and ethnic groups. Rather than expressing hostility toward non-European immigrants on the grounds of biological inferiority, they have appropriated much of the language of anti-racism by emphasizing their apparent respect for maintaining the cultural differences of both French people and new immigrants. For the National Front, immigrants from North Africa are bad for France not because they are biologically inferior. Instead, immigration from North Africa is allegedly bad for France—and for North Africans themselves—because it results in ethnic and racial mixing. Taguieff (1999, 209), quoting from texts published by radical right wing groups in France, suggests that they have successfully turned the discourse of difference on its head. Taguieff cites claims like the following to demonstrate that notions of difference have replaced notions of inferiority as the rationale for maintaining a separation of the 'races':

'The truth is that the people must preserve and cultivate their differences.... Immigration merits condemnation because it strikes a blow at the identity of the host culture as well as at the immigrants' identity'; 'It is because we respect ourselves and others, that we refuse to see our country transformed into a multi-racial society in which each one loses one's specificity'; 'Peoples cannot be summarily qualified as superior or inferior, they are different, and one must keep in mind these physical or cultural differences' (quoted in Taguieff 1999, 209).

In Taguieff's view, the creation of group boundaries around notions of cultural difference is no less pernicious that the creation of group boundaries around notions of biological superiority or inferiority. The objectives of so-called old racism and new racism in France are the same—to exclude North African immigrants, either by voluntary return or involuntary repatriation. This would be for the good both of France and of the immigrants themselves because they would lose their distinctive differences by assimilating into French society.

The United States. A number of American analysts have also argued that there are new forms of racism in the US, which are replacing older, biologically informed expressions of racism. Sociologist Nestor Rodriguez (1999, 373; see also Sanchez 1999) argues that increased immigration from Asia and Latin America has led to the emergence of a new American racism. This new racism, according to Rodriguez (1999, 376), is closely linked to the concept of *nativism,* which can be defined as a fear of 'foreignness'. Rodriguez outlines three anti-foreign sentiments that have characterized the new racialized American nativism in recent times. First, there is a fear of non-English languages based on the suspicion that the linguistic differences of immigrants will undermine the American nation. Second, there is a fear that racialized immigrants take advantage of multicultural ideology and affirmative action entitlements to strengthen their ability to retain distinct ethnic and racial identities. Many Americans feel that multiculturalism and affirmative action are 'un-American' because they seem to contradict America's commitment to equality of opportunity and favour 'non-Americans'. Third, racialized anti-immigrant attitudes are informed by the fear that immigrants are a drain on public resources, particularly welfare, education, and health care services (Rodriguez 1999, 377–8). According to Rodriguez (1999, 373), this new racialized nativism transcends both political divisions between liberals and conservatives and historical divisions between blacks and whites. Rodriguez suggests that the violence in Los Angeles in 1992, which we discussed in the previous section, is only one of many examples of the ways that racialized anti-immigrant sentiments are transcending the historical black/white divide in that country.

Other American analysts do not necessarily disagree with Rodriguez but suggest that anti-black racism continues to be a powerful force in American society. Some suggest that this new form of racism is a 'kinder, gentler form of racism' (Shull 1993) or a form of 'symbolic racism' (Kinder and Sears 1981). Shull (1993) argues that in the 1980s and early 1990s, negative attitudes towards blacks were evident in the Reagan and Bush administrations' offensive against civil rights. Their attack on affirmative action, the appointment of conservatives to key administrative posts in the civil rights field, and budget cuts to the Civil Rights Commission, the Equal Employment Opportunity Commission, and the Fair Housing and Equal Opportunity Program were couched in non-racist language: promoting equality, freedom, and less government intervention in the lives of Americans. Although these measures were never politically framed or justified in old-style racist, anti-black terms, according to Shull (1993) they had particularly severe consequences for the income, employment, and housing conditions of poor black Americans. Rather than promoting the development of a 'kinder and gentler society', these initiatives promoted a 'kinder and gentler racism' (Shull 1993).

Framing the issue more broadly than Shull, Kinder and Sears (1981) and McConahay (1986) suggest that the core of symbolic racism is the perceived value conflict between programs and philosophies that attempt to improve the conditions of minority groups in society and universal Western values of freedom and equality. As explained by Brown (1995, 219), in the United States:

it is thought that what upsets modern racists is not so much that Blacks may be going to the same school as their (White) children, but that the educational policy of enforced bussing to achieve better ethnic balances within city schools contradicts parents' 'right' to choose the school for their children.

Canada. Henry and Tator (2005) build on the work of Barker (1981) and Kinder and Sears (1981) to argue that there is a peculiarly Canadian form of racism, which they term 'democratic racism'. Like Barker, they argue that new forms of racism do not necessarily rely on or make reference to notions of inherent biological difference and/or inferiority. However, their definition of racism is even more inflated than that of Barker in that they broaden the understanding of racism to include a wide variety of beliefs about the way that society does and should operate. Racism, in their view, is not simply about the negative evaluation of cultural difference. They argue instead that democratic racism is more about value conflicts in Canadian society. Democratic racism is:

> an ideology in which two conflicting sets of values are made congruent to each other. Commitments to democratic principles such as justice, equality, and fairness conflict but coexist with attitudes and behaviours that include negative feelings about minority groups, differential treatment, and discrimination against them (Henry and Tator 2005, 22).

Democratic racism is expressed mainly through a variety of discourses of domination, which are 'myths, explanations, codes of meaning, and rationalizations that have the effect of establishing, sustaining, and reinforcing democratic racism' (Henry and Tator 2005, 24). They identify a number of discourses of democratic racism that aim to undermine claims about the existence and seriousness of racism in Canadian society. While their list of examples of democratic racism is exhaustive, these are some of the main forms it takes:

- The discourse of colour blindness. This discourse involves white people insisting that they do not notice the skin colour of a racial minority person. In Henry and Tator's view, this is racist because it involves a 'refusal to recognize that race is part of the "baggage" that people of colour carry with them, and the refusal to recognize that race is part of the everyday values, policies, programs, and practices, is part of the psychological and cultural power of racial constructions' (2005, 25).
- The discourse of equal opportunity. This refers to ideas that suggest that 'all we need to do is treat everyone the same, and fairness will be ensured' (2006, 25). This discourse is racist because it is premised on the belief that 'White institutional power' does not have to be dismantled in order for Canadian society to become fair and equal.
- The discourse of blaming the victim. This discourse suggests that minorities themselves are the source of their own 'problems'. That is, the failure of certain

groups to succeed in Canadian society is explained either in terms of inherent cultural differences with the dominant society or in terms of the lack of motivation to succeed.

- The discourse of multiculturalism. This discourse involves the belief that tolerance and harmony can be achieved through accommodating diversity into society in general and into organizations in particular. It is premised on the notion that the idiosyncrasies of others must be tolerated but that the dominant ways of doing things are ultimately superior. This is a form of democratic racism, in Henry and Tator's (2005, 28) view, because 'declarations of the need for tolerance and harmony tend to conceal the messy business of structural and systemic inequality and the unequal relations of power that continue to exist in a democratic liberal society'.
- The discourse of national identity. The discourse of national identity in Canada is racist because it tends to erase, omit, and silence the contributions of ethno-racial minorities. Canadian national identity, Henry and Tator (2005, 28) suggest, is characterized by democratic racism to the extent that Canadian national culture and identity continue to place emphasis on the two founding nations myth, ignoring the fact that there was a third founding nation, First Nations, and that racial minorities have also contributed to the nation-building project.

Henry and Tator (2005, 29) argue that many Canadians regard themselves as egalitarian and have little difficulty in rejecting the more overt, 'in-your-face' expressions of racism. However, even though symbolic gestures are made toward inclusion and respect, these gestures are largely token efforts that mask a continued adherence to white supremacy.

Henry and Tator (2005) and researchers in other societies who espouse the notion that new forms of racism have emerged to replace old, biologically informed forms offer a powerful condemnation of modern Western societies. However, we should not accept these inflated conceptions of racism uncritically. First, this kind of argument attaches simple motivations to complex ideas and discourses. For example, some people may genuinely believe that Canadian multicultural policy is an appropriate tool for the promotion of ethno-racial equity in this country. They may be naive or misguided in their belief, but this does not necessarily mean that they are opposed to the concerns of people of colour. Further, in the United States, some liberal objections to policies like affirmative action may be grounded in the belief that such policies are 'patronizing to minority groups and undermine their subsequent academic or professional achievements' (Brown 1995, 226). Second, these arguments tend to homogenize the category of ethno-racial communities. They assume that all members of ethnic/racial communities think the same way—that racism is a fundamental problem in Canadian society. Yet, as we show in more detail later in this chapter, the majority of visible minority Canadians report that they have had few if any experiences of racism in the recent past. Third, there is no clear dividing line between 'old' and 'new' versions of racism (Brown 1995, 225; Miles and Brown 2003, 63). Many supposedly 'old' versions of racism that were prevalent in the late nineteenth and early twentieth centuries also involved negative evaluations of cultural and religious differences. These differences were not necessarily understood as biologically grounded but rather as socially and contextually formed. For example, the Canadian federal government's policy of assimilating Indian people in the late nineteenth and early twentieth centuries was not exclusively grounded in a biologically based understanding of their supposed inferiority. Rather, both the general assimilation policy and the programs that were designed to carry it out, such as residential schools, were grounded in the assumption that Indian people could change and become culturally more like Europeans in their attitudes, beliefs, and values. Had Indian difference been defined in purely biological terms, policies of assimilation would have made no sense.

Islamophobia. The attacks on the World Trade Center in New York and the Pentagon in Washington on 11 September 2001 have provided the fodder for the emergence of yet another new form of hostility in Western societies—Islamophobia. Contemporary fears about Islam tend to transcend national boundaries, particularly in the developed Western world, and have added yet another layer of complexity to debates about forms of new racism. According to the British-based Runnymede Trust, Islamophobia is present when some of the following conditions are met:

- Islam is seen as a single monolithic bloc, static and unresponsive to new realities.
- Islam is seen as separate and other: (a) not having any aims or values in common with other cultures; (b) not affected by them; (c) not influencing them.
- Islam is seen as violent, aggressive, threatening, supportive of terrorism, engaged in a 'clash of civilizations'.
- Islam is seen as a political ideology, used for political or military advantage.
- Criticisms made by Islam of 'the West' are rejected out of hand.
- Hostility toward Islam is used to justify discriminatory practices toward Muslims and exclusion of Muslims from mainstream society.
- Anti-Muslim hostility is accepted as natural and 'normal' (cited in Miles and Brown 2003, 164).

Concrete manifestations of Islamophobia are legion and can be drawn from a variety of countries. In Britain in the fall of 2006, Labour MP Jack Straw provoked controversy when he wrote in a local newspaper that veils worn by Muslim women were barriers to good community relations in the country. British Prime Minister Tony Blair echoed this concern when he suggested that the *niqab* (a piece of cloth that covers the lower face, leaving the eyes exposed) worn by some Muslim women was a 'mark of separation' that makes British non-Muslims 'uncomfortable' (Valpy 2006, A16). In Canada, Arab and Muslim Canadians reported that immediately after 11 September 2001, they faced harassment, intimidation, and violence (Arat-Koc 2006, 220–1). Arat-Koc (2006, 227) argues that Islamophobia informs much of the new security agenda within Canada and the United States (and elsewhere) and as a result Muslim and Arab Canadians are increasingly concerned about how their travel patterns, their charitable donations, and their remittances to friends and family members overseas will be interpreted by other Canadians and by police and security forces.

The question of whether Islamophobia is a new form of racism is a matter of debate. Arat-Koc (2006, 220) argues that

> What has been new for Arab and Muslim Canadians since 11 September, 2001 is not the experience of racism but its growing public legitimacy, spread, and main-streaming in all major institutions, from the media to law and policy.

Opposing Arat-Koc, Miles and Brown (2003, 164) argue that since the 'other-ness' of Muslims tends to be constructed in religious rather than biological or phys-ical terms, Islamophobia should not necessarily be regarded as an instance of racism. They do, however, recognize that this form of religious othering interacts with racism in that in some cases, the negative evaluation of religious differences is accompanied by the negative evaluation of presumed physical differences. They also suggest that Islamophobia has many of the same consequences as racism, particu-larly in terms of social exclusion from jobs, border crossing difficulties, and concep-tions of who constitutes a 'good' Western citizen (Miles and Brown 2003, 167).

Racism, capitalism, and class relations

Karl Marx had little to say about racism in his analysis of the origins of capitalism and of the way that capitalist societies operated in the late nineteenth century. How-ever, subsequent generations of political economists have devoted considerable attention to the issue of racism and ethnic antagonisms. Political economists tend to argue that people do not hate each other simply because of the colour of their skin; rather, in situations of conflict, 'racial' and ethnic symbols are used to represent 'some other, more fundamental reality' (Bonacich 1979, 19). Another common thread in different versions of political economy's analysis of 'race' and racism is the view that 'race problems begin as labour problems' (Bolaria and Li 1988, 7). Politi-cal economists argue that contacts between different groups of people are structured not simply by the 'innocent' mixing of populations but rather by economic imper-atives associated with trade, colonization, and the search for production sites and labour power. These economically inspired contacts form an important part of the basis for racial hostility and racism.

Some early versions of political economy focused on the specific issue of the relationship between racism and slavery. Slavery emerged not because of the belief in the existence of a superior 'white' race and inferior 'black' but rather because of the need for cheap, unfree labour. The construction of racial ideologies served as a justification for the allocation of one group of people—Africans—to positions of unfree labour in the system. According American sociologist Oliver Cromwell Cox:

> Sometimes, probably because of its very obviousness, it is not realized that the slave trade was simply a way of recruiting labour for the purpose of exploiting the great natural resources of America. This trade did not develop because Indians and Negroes were red and black . . . but because they were the best workers to be found for the heavy labour in the mines and plantations across the Atlantic (1948, 23).

For plantation owners and slave traders in search of ever-cheaper sources of labour, racism operated to dehumanize Africans. Racism served as a justification for their exploitation and for their unequal treatment. According to political economists, defining certain groups of people as biologically inferior is a useful justification for poor pay and poor treatment.

Ashley Montagu (1964, 50), in a slightly different version of this argument, contended that racism emerged just as serious moral and ethical questions were being raised about slavery—when calls for the abolition of slavery were starting to be made more regularly in the United States and Europe. According to Montagu:

> It was only when voices began to make themselves heard against the inhuman traffic in slaves, and when these voices assumed the shape of influential men and organizations, that, on the defensive, the supporters of slavery were forced to look about them for reasons of a new kind to controvert the dangerous arguments of their opponents (1964, 39).

Supporters of slavery, according to Montagu (1964), latched onto the idea of 'race' and propagated the idea that blacks and whites were inherently different in their mental and physical capacities and that Negroes were inferior to whites: 'the idea of "race" was, in fact, the deliberate creation of an exploiting class which was seeking to maintain and defend its privileges against what was profitably regarded as an inferior social caste' (Montagu 1964, 50).

Obviously, racism did not end with the demise of slavery. Political economists used broadly similar arguments in order to understand more modern forms of racism. Although the context was different, the underlying forces that sustained racism were the same. For some political economists, racism was employed as a weapon in the super-exploitation of certain groups of workers and as a strategy developed by employers to divide and conquer the working class (Castles and Kosack 1973). Racist ideas were propagated by capitalists as a way of creating artificial distinctions between different groups of workers. By perpetuating ideas of racial superiority and inferiority, capitalists were able to sow discontent within the working class, reduce the unity of workers, and as a result better control them. Racism, according to this approach, deflects workers' attention away from the true source of their socio-economic problems—the capitalist system—and instead encourages them to focus on each other as the source of their problems. Racism, in other words, is a red herring that workers and others have bought into. As described by Bolaria and Li:

> Race provides a convenient basis for generating low-cost labour, and racial discrimination serves as an effective barrier in preventing non-white workers from moving away from undesirable jobs. . . . Advanced capitalist countries rely on immigration as a means to recruit and to regulate the supply of cheap labour. Within the flow of immigration to industrialized nations are non-white workers from ex-colonies, who are recruited as guest workers, refugees and illegal immigrants, in addition to being

admitted as regular immigrants. Their tenuous status, partly resulting from the political and legal conditions under which these immigrants are admitted, makes them exceptionally vulnerable to exploitation (1988, 36).

One of the problems with this argument is that there is little evidence that racism is a capitalist conspiracy. It also wrongly assumes that workers and the working-class movement are empty vessels that are then filled with capitalist-inspired ideology.

Other researchers within the political economy tradition have tried to address these problems by focusing on the other side of the capital/labour dynamic. They focus on the dynamics of class conflict, and the other culprit in the search for the origins and development of racism is the white working class (Bonacich 1972; 1976). In capitalist societies, racism and ethnic antagonism emerge out of the dynamics of the relationships between capitalist employers, higher-paid labour, and cheap labour According to split labour market theory, ethnic and racial conflict are rooted in differences in the price of labour (Bonacich 1979, 19). Employers try to hire workers at the cheapest price possible. For historical reasons, workers who move from rural to urban areas or from other countries have often been prepared to offer their labour power for a price below that of native-born and more established workers. For reasons connected more to accidents of history than to biology, non-white people have played the role of cheap labour, while white workers have tended to be higher-priced (Bonacich 1979, 20). The existence of these low-wage workers constitutes a threat to the social and economic position of higher-priced workers because employers try to replace expensive labour with cheap labour. According to this theory, higher-priced workers seek to reduce competition by imposing restrictions on where and under what conditions lower-priced workers can work. Racial hostility and exclusionary movements arise and attempt to limit job opportunities for cheaper, usually 'non-white' labour. Racism and ethnic prejudices are the by-products of these kinds of competitive labour market dynamics.

Although the split labour market has existed in a variety of forms and places, perhaps the most extreme form was evident in South Africa during the period of apartheid (1948–94). Apartheid was characterized by a strict segregation of 'races' in all spheres of life—education, work, leisure, and place of residence. While the origins of the apartheid system are complex, it came about when white workers sought protection from the competition of lower-priced black workers and were able to convince the governing authorities and employers that it was in all white people's interest to maintain a strict separation of 'races'. In the employment sphere, apartheid policies guaranteed more prestigious and better-paid jobs to whites and also dictated highly discrepant wages between blacks and whites. The job reservation system meant that no black could advance above a white in the same occupational area, and in some cases blacks were completely excluded from certain occupations (Marger 1997, 406). One of the consequences of this policy was the virtual elimination of the class of poor whites from South African society: apartheid was essentially a policy by which black people subsidized white wages and white lifestyles. Drawing on notions of biological and cultural superiority, many whites believed that because they constituted 'the civilized, Christian race', it was their duty 'to use their control of the state to prevent racial friction and racial bastardization by ensuring that the races would be separated from one another' (Thompson 1985, quoted in Marger 1997, 409). According to Bonacich, the racial ideologies that accompanied the system of apartheid were essentially justification for the unequal treatment that black Africans experienced at the hands of whites.

Canada has also seen versions of the split labour market (Makabe 1981), though less extreme than in South Africa. Agnes Calliste has documented the formation and reproduction of a split labour market on Canadian railways in the early and mid-twentieth century. She argues that black men were confined to lower-paying jobs such as sleeping car porter, while better-paying jobs such as sleeping car conductor were reserved for white men. According to Calliste, white union members and employers collaborated to keep black men out of better-paying jobs on railways. Black workers were kept in their inferior positions because they were desperately poor and needed the work and because it was a sign of status among whites to be served by black people. Furthermore, because of the social distance that existed between white and black people in Canada at the time, white people could commit indiscretions on trains without fear of social repercussion (Calliste 1987, 3).

Though more compelling than earlier versions of political economy's analysis of racism, split labour market theory is limited in its historical scope. While it is useful for understanding and analyzing forms of racism in the past, racially based forms of employment discrimination are now very difficult to create and enforce in countries like Canada, where both domestic and international human rights norms prevent the development of polices or practices that explicitly put one particular ethnic or racial group at a disadvantage. Indeed, according to Calliste (1987, 11), black workers used the 1953 Fair Employment Practices Act to challenge the discriminatory practices of both railway unions and railway employers.

Political economy lite

Though traditional versions of political economy that draw deterministic connections between the interests of workers and/or capitalists and the maintenance of patterns of social inequality no longer seem suitable for explaining contemporary forms of racism, softer versions of political economy that focus on the broad links between the expression of racism and wider materially based class relations and social conflicts remain relevant to the contemporary world. Economically driven contacts between different groups of people and struggles over markets, jobs, housing, and other resources often produce tensions and hostility (Mitchell 2004). For example, Peter Li (1998a) argues that the controversies that occasionally arise in large Canadian cities over the development of 'ethnic malls' reflect underlying class dynamics and class-based resentments. In Markham, Ontario, in 1995, the deputy mayor warned that the growing concentration of Chinese people in the city and the growth of malls catering to the Chinese community were causing social tensions and contributing to an exodus of white people from the city. Among other things, the deputy mayor called for restrictions on non-English language signs in the city. According to Li (1998a, 147), the hostility directed toward Chinese businesses had little to do with primordial and supposed 'natural' hostilities between white and Chinese residents. Instead, it mainly had to do with the success that Chinese business-owners were experiencing in suburban shopping areas where other small businesses were unable to survive. Part of the hostility, then, reflected the fear and concern of white business-owners that they might not be able to survive in a competitive and changing marketplace.

From this perspective, racism is not simply an idea that floats free and independent of wider social relations and conflicts. Rather, racism constitutes one of the ways that individuals interpret and give meaning to their lives, to their experiences and relationships, and to the tensions and contradictions that they face in the everyday world. In other words, people use 'race' or biological and cultural attributes of themselves and others to explain and provide meaning to events in a complex and changing world.

This approach allows us to take the issue of racism seriously but without necessarily prejudging either the motives for or the consequences of racism. If ideas about the biological and cultural superiority of groups of people are used to make sense of the world, then we need to understand the motives and perspectives of those who articulate those ideas. We also need to recognize that there is no a priori social consequence associated with such ideas. Racism has a variety of consequences, and these consequences depend on context, the power that individuals and organizations have to impose their ideas on others, and the degree of resistance that groups of people can mount to racism.

RACISM, SURVEYS, AND PUBLIC OPINION

One way that social scientists have attempted to measure the significance of racism in Canadian society is by collecting data through surveys. In this section, we briefly discuss three kinds of surveys: surveys that tap into an individual's sense of being a victim of racism; surveys that try to uncover the existence of explicitly racist attitudes among Canadians; and social distance surveys that serve as proxy or indirect measures of racial prejudices.

Victimization surveys show that visible minority Canadians perceive that they have been discriminated against or have experienced unfair treatment because of their skin colour. The *Ethnic diversity survey* conducted by Statistics Canada in 2003 found, for example, that 32 per cent of black respondents had sometimes or often experienced discrimination in the previous five years. Twenty-one per cent of south Asian respondents and 18 per cent of Chinese respondents also reported experiencing discrimination sometimes or often during the previous five-year period. Conversely, only five per cent of non-visible minority respondents indicated that they had experienced discrimination sometimes or often during the previous five years (see table 6.1.)

Other research shows that proportionately more Aboriginal people than other visible minorities claim that they have experienced discrimination. A 2003 survey conducted by Ekos Research showed, for example, that 46 per cent of Aboriginal people living off-reserve indicated that they had been victims of racism or discrimination over the previous two-year period.

Table 6.1   Perceptions of Discrimination by Generation and Visible Minority Status, Canada, 2002 (in per cent)

	Frequency of Discrimination			
	Total population '000s	Sometimes or often %	Rarely %	Did not experience discrimination %
Total population	22,444	7	6	86
Not a visible minority	19,252	5	5	90
Visible minority	3,000	20	15	64
First generation	5,272	13	10	77
Not a visible minority	2,674	5	6	89
Visible minority	2,516	21	14	65
Second generation or more	16,929	6	5	89
Not a visible minority	16,349	5	5	90
Visible minority	480	18	23	59

Source: Statistics Canada. 2003. Ethnic diversity survey: Portrait of a multicultural society. Ottawa: Minister of Industry. Catalogue no. 89-593-XIE

Is the glass half empty or half full? Depending on one's perspective, these figures are either a cause for concern or a sign that racism is not particularly widespread in Canadian society. Canada's Action Plan against Racism (2005) uses the results of the *Ethnic diversity survey* and the Ekos poll to justify its argument that racism is a serious problem in Canadian society and that active measures need to be taken to combat it. Read differently, however, the *Ethnic diversity survey* points to some signs of optimism. While nearly half of the Aboriginal people in the Ekos survey felt that they had been victims of racism or discrimination (and these feelings have to be taken seriously), the *Ethnic diversity survey* shows that 68 per cent of black respondents, 79 per cent of south Asian respondents, and 82 per cent of Chinese respondents rarely or never experienced discrimination over the previous five years.

Victimization surveys provide valuable information, but they are not particularly good measures of the existence of racism in Canadian society. For one thing, individuals may experience discrimination but may not define it as such. For example, it is difficult for individuals to know the real reasons that they were not hired for a particular job or denied housing. The stated, non-racist reasons may be plausible, and an individual may accept those reasons as valid, but there may been deeper, racially based reasons for not hiring or providing housing to the person that never come to light. Institutional authorities sometimes dismiss the results of victimization surveys on the grounds that some visible minorities are not objective, have 'chips on their shoulders', and are too eager to identify racism as a problem in Canadian society (Henry and Tator 2005, 59).

This is part of the reason that Frances Henry and Effie Ginzberg (1985) conducted an experiment that involved sending black and white applicants to employers advertising job vacancies. Black and white actors were hired to play the role of job applicants and were given resumés that reflected similar levels of training and experience for particular jobs. Black applicants approached employers first, followed several minutes later by white applicants. After repeated trials, Henry and Ginzberg (1985) found that white applicants were offered jobs three times more often than black applicants. This was powerful evidence that 'race' played a role in the Toronto job market in the early 1980s. Unfortunately, few studies have followed up and replicated this kind of research.

A third way that social scientists and others have tried to measure the existence of racism is through the use of social distance surveys. As noted above, being a racist is not a socially desirable character trait. As a result, individuals who hold negative attitudes about minority groups may be reluctant to admit to those feelings in surveys. Social distance surveys vary in terms of the kinds of questions they ask. Some ask how 'happy' or how 'concerned' respondents would be if a member of a specific minority group married their son or daughter, joined their social club, moved into their neighbourhood, and the like. Other surveys ask how 'comfortable' individuals are 'being around' different minority groups. For example, a 1991 survey conducted on behalf of the federal government's multiculturalism program examined the comfort level of Canadians towards a variety of immigrant and Canadian-born groups. The results of this survey are given in table 6.2. It shows that Canadians in general are more comfortable around Canadian-born members of ethnic groups than around their immigrant counterparts. The survey also shows considerable variation in comfort toward different ethnic groups, regardless of whether they are Canadian-born or immigrants. For example, while 83 per cent and 86 per cent of respondents indicated that they had a high level of comfort around British immigrants and Canadian-born British, only 43 per cent and 55 per cent of respondents respectively indicated that they had high levels of comfort around Sikh immigrants and Canadian-born Sikhs (Angus Reid Group 1991, 51). More recently, a 2000 survey asked individuals to indicate how they felt about someone from another country moving into their neighbourhood. The survey found that the individuals surveyed were more positive toward people from Britain and France than they were toward people from China, Jamaica, or Somalia (cited in Li 2003, 175).

Peter Li (2003, 172–6), in a stinging critique of academic and polling company survey research on anti-immigrant attitudes and racism, argues that this kind of research unwittingly lends legitimacy to racist ways of thinking. By asking Canadians to rank groups in terms of 'comfort level' and 'social distance' or by asking people to express preferences for white as opposed to 'visible minority' immigrants, this research creates a space for individuals to think about and problematize 'race'. Referring to the issue of survey research on attitudes toward immigrants, Li argues that

> The immigration discourse in Canada has a strong racial dimension, in part because of the changing racial composition of immigrants to Canada, but also in part because academic research has contributed to racializing immigrants and

Table 6.2   Ranking of Selected Immigrant Ethnic Groups and Canadian-born Ethnic Groups according to the Per Cent of Respondents Who Indicated Having the Highest Comfort Levels Being around Individuals from Each Group

| | Respondents indicating the highest comfort levels toward: | |
Origin being evaluated	Immigrant ethnic group (%)	Canadian-born ethnic group (%)
British	83	86
Italian	77	83
French	74	82
Jewish	74	78
Ukrainian	73	79
German	72	79
Portuguese	70	76
Chinese	69	77
Native Canadian	—	77
West Indian black	61	69
Moslem	49	59
Arab	52	63
Indo-Pakistani	48	59
Sikh	43	55

Source: Angus Reid Group. 1991. *Multiculturalism and Canadians: Attitude study.* National survey report submitted to Multiculturalism and Citizenship Canada, August.

minority groups by encouraging the public to articulate their racial preferences and then legitimizing such preferences as harmless and democratic choices (2003, 176).

INSTITUTIONAL RACISM

Racism, as should be clear from the previous discussion, is not only about ideas and individual-level expressions of behaviour. Racism can also be reflected in the ways that social institutions operate by denying groups of people fair and equitable treatment. Institutional racism can take three forms.

First, racist ideas and assumptions about the social capacities and incapacities of groups of people can explicitly inform the development of social policies, programs, or institutional practices. At present, there are few, if any, examples of this form of institutional racism in Canada. As noted in chapter 2, however, many aspects of the pre-1967 Canadian immigration system were informed by racist assumptions about the relative capacities and capabilities of groups of people; racist ideas were used to shape and justify various forms of exclusion from Canada. The head tax on Chinese workers and the Chinese Immigration Act of 1923 are good examples of this kind of institutional racism since in both cases, government policies were explicitly informed by negative, racist stereotypes about the harm that

Chinese immigrants were causing Canadian society. The other two forms of institutional racism are far more relevant to contemporary Canadian society, although they are not entirely uncontested.

The second form of institutional racism occurs when ideas about the racial inferiority of groups of people inform the initial development of specific policies or programs but no longer sustain those policies and programs. In other words, certain policies and programs are racist in origin, and even though racism may no longer sustain them, the policies and practices continue to exist. Discussed in chapter 2, the Indian Act is probably the best example of this form of institutional racism in Canada. The Act and its various nineteenth-century precursors explicitly assumed that Indian people were inferior to Europeans and that Indians needed the guiding hand of racially superior Europeans in order to have a future in Canada.

Another relevant example of this form of institutional racism is the Caribbean and Mexican Seasonal Agricultural Workers Program. In chapter 3, we explained that the program originated because there was a shortage of labour to fill seasonal farm jobs in Ontario in the mid-1960s. Some government officials believed that black workers were racially suited for backbreaking labour under the hot sun and so justified the program in part on the basis of racist beliefs about the innate capacities of black people. Further, government officials thought that while black workers were useful as sources of temporary labour, they were not good as potential Canadian citizens because their presence in Canada would cause the emergence of a 'race relations' problem (Satzewich 1991; Basok 2002). Although these racist ideas no longer explicitly sustain or justify the program, it is arguably a continuing example of institutional racism in Canada because it had its origins in racism.

The third form of institutional racism appears in certain policies or programs that may seem ethnically or racially neutral but either intentionally or unintentionally put minority group members at a disadvantage. This form of institutional racism has generated the most heated debates in Canada because its existence is difficult to prove conclusively and there is ambiguity surrounding the true motives behind the policies and programs in question. In the remainder of this chapter, we consider two policies and practices that have been the subject of the most consistent controversies about institutional racism: 'zero tolerance' policies in schools and racial profiling by police.

Zero tolerance policies in schools

A number of Canadian provinces have versions of so-called zero tolerance policies toward students who misbehave in schools. In Ontario, the Safe Schools Act, introduced in 2001, incorporates provisions for zero tolerance (Henry and Tator 2005, 211). In Toronto, the zero tolerance policy provides for the automatic suspension or expulsion of students who commit violent or aggressive acts, such as assault, drug trafficking, or selling or carrying weapons. Children who threaten to harm other students, engage in vandalism, swear, or are in possession of or under the influence of drugs or alcohol also face automatic suspension (Leslie 2005).

Though initially designed to deal with apparently growing levels of violence and aggression in schools, zero tolerance provisions are often characterized as a reflection of institutional racism because either by design or by circumstance, they have resulted in the disproportionate targeting of black and other racialized youth. Critics argue that while the Act appears to be ethnically and racially neutral, its weight disproportionately falls on black youth. According to one black youth, 'something can't be right about a policy that winds up aimed at a single racial group' (Valpy 2005, A1, A15).

Although it does not specifically examine zero tolerance policies, a recent Canadian study showed that perceptions of differential and discriminatory treatment by schools vary in part on the basis of the background of students. Ruck and Wortley (2002) argue that there is a skin colour hierarchy when it comes to student perceptions of differential treatment within schools in Toronto. In their research, they studied perceptions of white, black, Asian, south Asian, and 'other' (Aboriginal and Latin American) high school students about a range of issues surrounding teacher and police treatment at school, school suspensions, and the general school environment. According to Ruck and Wortley, student perceptions of differential treatment in schools vary, with

> Black students generally being the most likely to perceive bias followed by South Asian students, students from 'other' racial/ethnic backgrounds, Asian students, and finally White students. This is consistent with the view that the darker the skin color the greater the social penalties that exist (2002, 194).

Critics of zero tolerance policies argue that these perceptions are in fact a reflection of reality. Schools are obliged to follow certain procedures regardless of the reason for or context of misbehaviour. Because teachers and principals have no discretionary power, the policy comes down hardest on students who are the most disadvantaged and have the greatest need to stay in school. Some characterize zero tolerance policies as culturally insensitive because they are based on 'white' models of appropriate behaviour that are at odds with black models of appropriate behaviour. As Jull argues:

> School discipline policies based on the principles of zero tolerance reinforce Anglo-Eurocentric sensibilities of right and wrong and the authoritative structures within public education. . . . To claim that social justice can be achieved through the implementation of a so-called unbiased zero tolerance school discipline policy is to believe that discriminatory practice can be eradicated by implementing policies that are blind to personal or individual and/or cultural contexts. . . . Equal treatment in an unequal social and academic environment is discriminatory (2000, 4).

Finally, some critics also argue that zero tolerance policies help create a 'school-prison pipeline' for black youth (Solomon and Palmer 2004). Ontario NDP leader Howard Hampton argues that the Safe Schools Act should really be called a 'gang recruitment act' because the provisions end up putting youth who most need to stay in school on the street. By kicking black youths out of school, school boards are throwing them into the welcoming arms of gangs, who are more than happy to recruit youth disaffected with school. As explained by the Ontario Human Rights

Commission in its report, *Disproportionate impact of 'zero tolerance' discipline,* 'Once kids are out of the mainline and expelled, then they are on a different path. . . . If you put anti-social kids together it escalates their anti-social behaviour' (Ontario Human Rights Commission 2005a).

The controversy over zero tolerance policies raises complicated issues about the appropriate balance between the exercise of discretion and the use of a strict, rules-based approach to dealing with social problems or other kinds of issues. As we saw in chapter 3 on immigration, some critics claim that the exercise of discretionary power on the part of immigration officers is racially biased and puts racialized minority individuals at a disadvantage in the immigration process. At the other end of the spectrum, zero tolerance polices in schools, which are aimed at curtailing the exercise of discretionary power by principals, vice-principals, and the police, are criticized for being racially biased because they do not take into consideration the social and personal contexts within which youth infractions of rules take place in schools. In other words, critics suggest that the lack of discretion is racist and call for a more sensitive and contextual approach to the problem of dealing with youth mis-behaviour in school. In short, one system is alleged to be institutionally racist because it allows too much discretion, and another system is alleged to be institutionally racist because it does not allow for discretion. Perhaps the lesson to be learned is that there is no 'one size fits all' approach to dealing with allegations of institutional racism within Canadian society. This policy and program dilemma is obviously not easily resolved.

Racial profiling and policing

Arguably, the way that the justice system deals with minority groups captures the most headlines and generates the most concern in Canada when it comes to accusations of institutional racism. Police forces across the country have been accused of various acts of institutional racism, and allegations that the police engage in institutional racism are an almost weekly occurrence. Two of the most frequent accusations are that the police *under-police* minority communities when their members are the victims of crime and that they simultaneously *over-police* those communities when their members are suspected as the perpetrators of crime (Royal Commission on Aboriginal Peoples 1996, 37–9).

Regarding under-policing, it is alleged that the police do not take crimes as seriously or do not conduct thorough investigations when minorities are the victims of crime. The case of Robert Pickton (the Surrey, BC, pig farmer accused of murdering several dozen women, many of whom were Aboriginal and working in the prostitution industry) has raised concerns about under-policing. That is, the Vancouver police department has been accused of institutional racism because it allegedly did not take the disappearance of these women from Vancouver streets as seriously as it would have had the missing women been white and middle-class. Because they were members of marginalized racial and socio-economic groups, they were regarded as disposable people undeserving of full police protection.

The November 2005 shooting of Amon Beckles has also been defined as a case of under-policing. Beckles, a black teenager, was shot and killed outside a church

Box 6.1 Officers make racist remarks on tape

Members of Ontario Provincial Police slag natives
before protester killed in 1995

By Jeff Gray

Ontario Provincial Police involved in the 1995 standoff with Aboriginals occupying Ipperwash Provincial Park made 'racial' slurs and joked about luring native people out using beer, according to a newly released recording.

The tape, obtained in a Freedom of Information request by CBC News, appears to have been made just before an OPP officer shot and killed unarmed native protester Dudley George, an incident that dogged the previous Ontario government and is the subject of a public inquiry.

According to the CBC, the recording is on a videotape made by OPP officers posing as a television crew outside the park. The lens was covered, so the tape offers only an audio track.

On a portion broadcast by the CBC yesterday, a voice responding to a question about whether members of the news media are in the area says: 'No, there's no one down there. Just a big fat-fuck Indian.'

Another voice warns: 'The camera's rolling.' But the only response is, 'Yeah.'

Then, another voice says: 'We had this plan, you know. We thought if we could get five or six cases of Labatt's 50, we could bait them. And we would have this big net and a pit.'

People are heard laughing, and the officer dubs his plan 'creative thinking.'

Then, he adds: 'Works in the South with watermelons,' in reference to a stereotype regarding black Americans.

Murray Klippenstein, a lawyer for the George family, said he was stunned by the language on the tape, appearing to have been spoken just before an OPP officer killed the protester.

'To hear that kind of talk come up in Ontario at all—there's some murky toxins beneath the surface,' Mr. Klippenstein said.

'The references to baiting Indians with alcohol and the reference to the South and the watermelon are the kind of poisonous, racist talk I thought we had put behind us in Ontario,' Mr. Klippenstein said.

'The reference to blacks in the South is the kind of talk you would hear when people are dehumanizing someone, and that attitude makes it easy to lynch or shoot them.'

Mr. Klippenstein said the tape likely would broaden the scope of the inquiry, called by the Ontario Liberal government after years of Conservative-government refusals.

Sam George, brother of the slain man, said he hopes the inquiry will reveal which officers made the remarks, as well as address attitudes toward native people among OPP officers in general.

'It's very disturbing. . . . This is before my brother was shot,' Mr. George said last night. He called the remarks the 'mental mud' of the officers involved in the confrontation. 'I am sitting around wondering what other kind of remarks were made. It just opens a whole flood of questions in your mind.'

He said he also is disturbed by the reference to racism in the U.S. South. 'They not only took a shot at the first-nations people . . . but in the same sentence they also did that to some more people.

'So that just shows you that they're not only thinking that way about our people but other races, as well.'

OPP officials could not be reached last night for comment. But the Ontario Provincial Police Association, which represents the 7,500 uniformed and civilian members of the OPP, issued an apology for what it said were racist remarks.

'The association and its members, past and present, deeply regret both the tone and content of the remarks on this tape made by two of our members. We do not condone the remarks and we do not accept them as being representative of the views of the vast majority of men and women who are members of the OPPA,' association vice-president Ed Kinnear said in a statement.

'On behalf of all our members, we are very sorry and offer our apologies for these hurtful remarks.'

The association said it plans to co-operate fully with the government's Ipperwash inquiry.

The recently elected Ontario government made good on its campaign promise to call a public inquiry into the Ipperwash incident after the election. It appointed Mr. Justice Sidney Linden, a former Toronto police complaints commissioner, to head the probe.

The George family dropped a civil suit against the government on election day, confident that the Liberals would take power. Members of the family had accused the former government of pushing the provincial police toward a strategy of confrontation with the protesters.

Among those named as defendants were former premier Mike Harris and former solicitor-general Bob Runciman.

Dudley George was shot to death on Sept. 6, 1995, after he and two dozen other natives occupied Ipperwash Provincial Park on the shores of Lake Huron to protest against what they considered the desecration of ancestral burial grounds.

The Ontario government rejected the claim eight years ago, then had to accept it when its files showed that the Stoney Point Reserve had a legitimate claim to the land.

Former OPP Sergeant Kenneth Deane was convicted of criminal negligence causing death.

Source: The Globe and Mail. 2004. 21 January: A7

where he was attending the funeral of his friend Jamal Hemmings, who had been murdered a week earlier. Beckles had witnessed Hemmings's murder, and police believe that the same person shot both Beckles and Hemmings. Some suggest that the police should have anticipated the possibility of violence at Hemmings's funeral and ensured that they had a presence at the service. Since Hemmings's murder was a case of so-called 'black on black' violence, critics suggest that the police did not take the case as seriously as they would have had white people been involved. Some further suggest that the lack of a police presence at Hemmings's funeral contributed to Beckles's death and was an example of the under-policing of the black community in Toronto (Friesen 2005, A11).

The other side of the policing coin—the over-policing of minority communities when members are suspected of perpetrating crime—has also raised allegations of racial profiling and institutional racism. Over-policing refers to situations in which police resources and energies are targeted against groups based on the stereotype that they are over-involved in criminal behaviour. There is an old adage in criminology circles that the police find crime where they look for crime. As a result, a group's overrepresentation in the justice system may be as much a reflection of over-policing as it is of real group differences in criminal behaviour.

In western Canada, Aboriginal peoples have been the main targets of over-policing. A number of inquiries and research reports have detailed over-policing issues related to Aboriginal peoples (see Royal Commission on Aboriginal Peoples 1996 for a summary of these reports). Quigley describes the way that over-policing works and its consequences for Aboriginal people in the following terms:

> Police use race as an indicator for patrols, arrests, detentions. . . . For instance, police in cities tend to patrol bars and streets where Aboriginal people congregate, rather than the private clubs frequented by white business people. . . . This does not necessarily indicate that the police are invariably racist (although some are) since there is some empirical basis for the police view that proportionately more Aboriginal people are involved in criminality. But to operate patrols or to allocate police on . . . [this] basis . . . can become a self-fulfilling prophecy: patrols in areas frequented by the groups that they believe are involved in crimes will undoubtedly discover some criminality; when more police are assigned to detachments where there is a high Aboriginal population, their added presence will most assuredly detect more criminality (Quigley 1994, cited in Royal Commission on Aboriginal Peoples 1996, 25–36).

In eastern Canada, the issue of over-policing has been framed by specific concerns about police engaging in racial profiling of the black community. Racial profiling in policing can be defined as 'investigative or enforcement activity initiated by an individual officer based on his or her stereotypical, prejudicial or racist perceptions of who is likely to be involved in wrong doing or criminal activity. This conduct is systemically facilitated when there is ineffective policy, training, monitoring and control mechanisms in the system' (Association of Black Law Enforcers 2003, 2).

One of the main sources of evidence about 'racial' profiling comes from personal accounts of minority group members who feel that they have been unfairly stereotyped and targeted by police. A number of task force reports, newspaper articles, and scholarly research studies contain the accounts of individuals who feel that they have been racially profiled by police or by other institutions in Canadian society. According to the Ontario Human Rights Commission, these reports have conclusively shown that racial profiling occurs in a wide variety of social institutions in Canada. In 2005, the commission published its own study of racial profiling in order to move the debate a step forward. In their study, they invited individuals to submit their experiences of racial profiling to highlight its negative social, economic, and community consequences. One person suggested that

> Even if I am standing in a MTHA [Metro Toronto Housing Authority] area with another university student and cops pass I always stop and look to make sure that I am not being challenged by the cops. It's a feeling of fear, and of being less than them as they are in an authoritative position. We shouldn't be afraid of people who are supposed to be protecting our rights (Ontario Human Rights Commission 2005b, 6).

The commission documented some of the negative social and individual consequences associated with the experience of being racially profiled. Among other things, the commission found that individuals felt alienated from police and other social institutions and had a diminished sense of citizenship and of being part of a community as a result of having been racially profiled. The commission also found that members of racialized communities described themselves as 'living within a perpetual state of crisis due to the effects of racism'. It suggested that the

> African Canadian community in particular stressed that racial profiling is having an overwhelming impact in their community. The sense of injustice that develops among individuals in these communities creates a state of psychological imbalance and inner conflict and reinforces their concern that racism exists and that they may be subjected to it at any time (2005b, 12).

Part of the further unseen toll of racial profiling includes: individuals change their behaviour to avoid situations that might lead them to be stopped and profiled by police; individuals feel ashamed of themselves and their backgrounds; individuals lack trust in relationships; and individuals feel helplessness, hopelessness, fear, and anxiety.

The report also argued that there are larger social costs associated with racial profiling. Individuals who felt that they were racially profiled in stores and malls by security personnel reported that one of their responses was to boycott the establishments. The morale of employees who work in organizations believed to engage in racial profiling is also damaged.

One of the limitations of reports based on personal experiences of racial profiling is that they rely on anecdotal evidence that does not present a full, accurate, and objective picture of the problem. As a result, efforts have been made to collect more systematic information, and a second kind of evidence about racial profiling has come from data collected by police. Some of the police data had been purposefully collected to shed light on the problem of racial profiling, but other data had been compiled from information that police routinely collect on stops and searches.

In 2002, *The Toronto Star* published a series of articles alleging that statistics collected by the Toronto Police Services confirmed what many black residents of Toronto had believed for many years: namely, that the Toronto police force practised racial profiling. The newspaper used the Ontario Freedom of Information and Protection of Privacy Act to gain access to Toronto police arrest data for the period 1996 to 2002. It analyzed data on 480,000 cases in which individuals were arrested or ticketed for an offence and 800,000 cases in which criminal charges were laid. The analysis showed that black people are overrepresented in certain charge categories, treated more harshly than whites after they were arrested, and much more likely to be held in custody for bail hearings than their white counterparts (Rankin et al. 2002). The findings of this study were widely contested in the press as well as by academics (Wortley and Tanner 2003).

It was partly in response to allegations of racial profiling in Toronto that William Closs, chief of police in Kingston, Ontario, committed the organization to transparency and agreed to undertake a study to examine whether racial profiling was being practised in Kingston. The chief felt that the debate about racial profiling needed to move beyond accusations and denials. Concrete, purposefully collected data was needed in order to shed light on whether racial profiling was being practised by his force. Data collection for the project began in October 2003. Kingston police officers were required to complete 'contact cards' every time they stopped and questioned a civilian in any manner. Between 1 October 2003 and 30 September 2004, officers recorded the age, gender, and 'race' of the person stopped as well as the location of the stop, the reason for the stop, and the final disposition of the case (Wortley 2005).

The information on police stops was analyzed by University of Toronto criminologist Scot Wortley, and a preliminary report was issued in the summer of 2005. Described as one of the first of its kind in Canada, the study found that even though black residents of Kingston represented only 0.6 per cent of the total population of the city, they experienced 2.1 per cent of all police stops during the study period. Native people were also over-policed in that they made up 1.6 per cent of the population of the city but experienced 2.4 per cent of all police stops during the study period (Wortley 2005).

When the results were announced, Chief Closs tearfully apologized to members of Kingston's black and Aboriginal communities, saying that

> especially to the Black and the Aboriginal community where there are disparities, we apologize. I apologize. I'm not asking any police officer to apologize in this room . . . my police officers have the right to leave this room and walk with pride. What we're doing wrong, if we're doing anything wrong, is systemic and that's my problem. So, I apologize to the Black community, the Aboriginal community and we'll do better (Farmer 2005).

The police community is divided on its position on racial profiling. The Association of Black Law Enforcers (ABLE), in their *Official position on racial profiling in Canada* (2003), argues that a distinction needs to be made between legitimate 'criminal profiling' and illegitimate 'racial profiling'. They argue that criminal profiling is a legitimate law enforcement tool and that there is a distinction between inductive and deductive criminal profiling. Inductive criminal profiling refers to generalizations about an individual criminal based on initial behavioural and demographic characteristics shared by other criminals who have been studied in the past. Deductive criminal profiling refers to the processes of interpreting evidence such as crime scene photographs, autopsy reports, and other information to deduce specific offender characteristics. ABLE argues that legitimate criminal profiling may rely on 'race' as a descriptor within a profile. However, legitimate criminal profiling turns into illegitimate 'racial' profiling when 'race' is construed as a factor leading to criminal behaviour. They explain the distinction in the following terms:

> ABLE is troubled by the connection being made between acts of violence being perpetrated by the criminal element within the Black community and racial profiling. We reject the notion of 'Black on Black' crime in that the term is pejorative and appears only to be reserved for use when young Black men take the lives of other young Black men. Race based terms are not used to describe violent crime that occurred in other racial or ethnic communities. For example when members of the Hells Angels and Rock Machine were killing each other in Quebec the situation was not referred to as 'White on White' crime, it was called a 'Biker War' (2003, 3).

The Kingston police chief's apology for racial profiling has not met with a great deal of enthusiasm from other police organizations or police boards. Indeed, other jurisdictions have been reluctant to embrace the allegation that racial profiling is routinely practised and widespread among the police in Canada. Like the Association of Black Law Enforcers, police forces make a distinction between legitimate criminal profiling and racial profiling. They argue that while criminal profiling is a necessary part of police work, racial profiling 'does not exist' (Henry and Tator 2005, 157).

Summary

Racism is both a sociological concept and an epithet. The fact that few people admit to being racist makes it particularly hard to study sociologically. This chapter critically reviewed a number of debates about how to define the concept of racism and how to explain its existence. Racism is more than a scientific doctrine. It is also a folk concept. Negative ideas about minority groups are not inherent in white people, but rather they appear to help some people make sense of their changing circumstances and material surroundings. Many individuals, organizations, and practices in Canada have been charged with racism. This chapter provided a number of examples of what sociologists refer to as institutional racism. Finally, the chapter analyzed some of the major concerns about racism in Canadian schools as expressed in so-called zero-tolerance policies and about racism in the justice system as expressed in the controversy over racial profiling.

Questions for Critical Thought

1. To what extent is white racism similar to and different from racism expressed by minority groups?
2. The police argue that there is a difference between racial profiling and criminal profiling. They admit that they do criminal profiling but deny that they engage in racial profiling. To what extent is this a valid difference when it comes to the debate about the differential treatment of minority groups?
3. Given what you have learned about racism in this chapter, what are some of the appropriate methods and strategies for dealing with racism?
4. What are the forms of new racism? Historically speaking, is new racism all that new? Does the concept of new racism define racism too broadly?
5. How do seemingly neutral policies and procedures work to the disadvantage of some racialized groups? Are these forms of institutional racism?

Annotated Additional Readings

Banton, Michael. 2002. *The international politics of race*. Cambridge: Cambridge University Press. A thoughtful account of the role that the United Nations has played in efforts to eliminate 'racial' discrimination.

Miles, Robert, and Malcolm Brown. 2003. *Racism*. 2nd edn. London: Routledge. A comprehensive discussion and analysis of the concepts of 'race' and racism. This book is essential reading on the topic.

Henry, Frances, and Carol Tator. 2005. *The colour of democracy: Racism in Canada*. 3rd edn. Toronto: Thomson Nelson. A hard-hitting and unsettling discussion of the pervasiveness of racism in Canadian society.

Reitz, Jeffrey, and Raymond Breton. 1994. *The illusion of difference: Realities of ethnicity in Canada and the United States*. Toronto: C.D. Howe Institute. A detailed discussion, supported by extensive empirical evidence, of the similarities and differences between the United States and Canada in their treatment of minority issues. To the discomfort of some Canadians, the authors show that Canada and the United States are not all that different when it comes to these issues.

Related Websites

Association of Black Law Enforcers: http://www.ablenet.ca/.
Canadian Race Relations Foundation: http://www.crr.ca/.
Human Genome Project: http://www.ornl.gov/sci/techresources/Human_Genome/home.shtml.
Slavery reparations: http://www.nationalcenter.org/Reparations.html.

Chapter 7

Aboriginal and Non-Aboriginal Relations

Learning objectives
In this chapter you will learn that:
- Debates about Aboriginal identities are not simply matters of political correctness. They are important because these identities carry certain rights and because they try to express more authentic ways of being.
- There are four categories of Aboriginal peoples in Canada: Inuit, Métis, First Nations, and non-status Indians. These categories are based on a combination of self-definition and socio-legal definition.
- Measures taken by the federal government in the 1980s to correct gender discrimination in the Indian Act have been controversial.
- Some Aboriginal leaders claim that the federal government is continuing to pursue a policy of assimilation through the way that it defines First Nations.
- There are controversies within First Nations communities about how to define who is a band member.
- There are stubborn disparities between the health and socio-economic conditions of Aboriginal and those of non-Aboriginal peoples.
- There are four main explanations for the disparities between Aboriginal and non-Aboriginal peoples: biological, cultural, structural, and historical.
- First Nations communities are not internally homogeneous. There are gender divisions and divisions between leaders and the led.

INTRODUCTION

What's in a name? Sometimes this question is used as a way of trivializing issues of individual and collective identity. Sociologically speaking, however, the question of naming is far from trivial, and it is certainly not just a matter of political correctness. Ethnic and other identity labels can be externally imposed on groups of people, or they can be internally adopted. They can be sources of pride or terms of derision. They can also define social and political priorities, provide bases for political mobilization and rationales for social inclusion and exclusion, and provide the basis for claims to certain rights. As Kim Anderson (2000, 23) notes, 'naming is politically and emotionally loaded' in the area of Aboriginal and non-Aboriginal relations (see also Alfred 1999, 84–5).

Take, for example, the term 'Indian'. Thinking he had discovered a sea route to India, Christopher Columbus mistakenly applied the label to the Arawak people on the present-day San Salvador Island in the Bahamas in 1492. Even though he and other Europeans quickly realized that he had not in fact discovered a sea route to India, the term 'Indian' nevertheless took hold and came to generally describe the original inhabitants of the Americas. While Aboriginal peoples in the Americas have maintained certain pre-contact collective names and identities, the externally imposed label of 'Indian' eventually became quite widely accepted, if not entirely uncontested, both by European and Aboriginal societies.

This historical mistake did not start to be systematically challenged for more than 450 years. While 'Indian' is still a popular term in social discourse and is invested with certain legal meanings that continue to sustain its lifespan, individuals and organizations once defined as 'Indian' have now started to use the term 'First Nation' as a more accurate description of themselves and their identities. Other Aboriginal groups have been equally concerned about their names and how to define their identities.

This chapter is divided into three parts. First, it examines in more detail some of the current social and legal controversies about labels and identities of Aboriginal peoples in Canada. Second, it discusses inequalities between Aboriginal and non-Aboriginal peoples, and third, it discusses inequalities within Aboriginal communities.

LABELS, IDENTITIES, AND GROUP BOUNDARIES

In the spring of 1939, after a lengthy court battle involving the federal government and the government of Quebec, the Supreme Court of Canada ruled that 'Eskimos' were 'Indians' within the constitutional framework of the day (Backhouse 1999, 18). At the time, this decision was important both for the quality of reasoning that led to the conclusion and its social consequences. In coming to this conclusion, the Supreme Court avoided the testimony of influential anthropologists who provided evidence about the cultural, religious, linguistic, and 'racial' differences between 'Eskimos' and 'Indians'. Instead of taking this testimony into account, the Court based its decision on historical precedent. It argued that since the Fathers of Confederation thought that 'Eskimos' were akin to Indians when the British North

America Act came into force in 1867, then from a legal perspective, 'Eskimos' were 'Indians'. At the time, the ruling was also significant for the way that it resolved a decades-old dispute about whether the provincial or federal government should be financially responsible for the provision of social support to the people indigenous to Canada's North. In defining 'Eskimos' as 'Indians', the Supreme Court decided in favour of the province of Quebec and ruled that 'Eskimos' were in fact a financial responsibility of the federal government (Backhouse 1999, 53–5).

This case highlights some of the historical and contemporary complexities associated with defining Aboriginal peoples. The definitions of Inuit, status Indians, non-status Indians, First Nations, and Métis, and the formation of group boundaries around these identities, reflect a combination of self-definitions, externally imposed categories, historical precedent, and biological and cultural lines of descent. In this section, we try to untangle some of the complexities associated with these definitions and also to draw out some of the social, legal, and political implications of the ways that group boundaries have been drawn around these categories.

One, albeit imperfect, way to begin to approach issues of naming and group boundaries is to start with the 1982 Constitution of Canada. The Constitution recognizes 'the existing Aboriginal rights of the Aboriginal peoples of Canada'. While the specific nature of these rights is subject to ongoing political and legal negotiation, the Constitution specifies that three groups fall within the general category of Aboriginal people: status Indians, Inuit, and Métis. One of the groups falling outside of this list of Aboriginal peoples with Aboriginal rights are 'non-status Indians'. The size of these groups is given in table 7.1. How are they defined?

Inuit

In 1941, the federal government conducted a special census in an effort to determine the exact number of Inuit in the country. Before then, trading post managers, missionaries, and police officers carried out federal government enumerations of the Inuit population. These early efforts were problematic, in part because of the lack of a clear definition of who should be counted as Inuit. In conducting the 1941 census, the Royal Canadian Mounted Police allotted a 'disc' number to each individual Inuk. Initially, these were four-digit numbers that were inscribed on thin discs the size of a Canadian quarter and were supposed to be worn around the neck. Later discs

Table 7.1   Aboriginal Population of Canada, 2001

Status Indians	690,101	
Métis	300,000–800,000	(estimate)
Inuit	55,700	(estimate)
Non-status Indians	440,000	(estimate)

Sources: Congress of Aboriginal Peoples. 2006. *Distribution of non-status Indian population of Canada*; Canada. Indian and Northern Affairs Canada. 2003. *Basic departmental data*; Métis National Council. 2006. *Who are the Métis?*; Canada. Indian and Northern Affairs Canada. 2000. *Inuit*.

contained code numbers for family names and for the district of residence (Mitchell 1996, 112). Before disc numbers were discontinued in 1971, only those individuals with a government-provided identity number were officially defined as Inuit. Even though the institution of the disc number system implied that the government saw them as a distinct group of people, the 1939 Supreme Court decision (discussed earlier) ran counter to this approach when it ruled that for constitutional purposes, the Inuit should be considered 'Indians'. Matters of defining the Inuit remain vitally important, particularly when it comes to the determination of who is eligible for the benefits associated with land claims settlements. For example, in the 1975 James Bay Agreement, an Inuk was defined as 'any individual who possesses a disc number, or has one-quarter Inuit blood, or is considered an Inuk by the local community, and such other persons as may be agreed upon' (Frideres and Gadacz 2004, 46).

Politically, the Inuit of Canada continue to work to overcome the consequences of the 1939 Supreme Court decision that equated them with Indians and eventually brought them under the purview of the Indian Act and the federal Department of Indian Affairs. While the Inuit are no longer under the thumb of the Indian Act, the Inuit Tapiriit Kanatami, which is the main umbrella organization representing the Inuit of Canada, has argued for greater government recognition of their specific issues and concerns (Inuit Tapiriit Kanatami 2004b). The organization claims that the Inuit are generally invisible and ignored within federal policy and within Indian and Northern Affairs Canada. In seeking to address this invisibility, they have called for a name change for the department to better reflect its responsibilities to all indigenous people of Canada. Furthermore, they argue that the government's 'First Nations on reserve' policy carries little relevance for them and that the amount spent on Inuit as opposed to 'First Nations' or status Indian issues is grossly inadequate (Inuit Tapiriit Kanatami 2004a, 3).

Métis

The term 'Métis' is the French word for 'half caste'. In the sixteenth and seventeenth centuries, the term was used for the descendants of unions between French-Canadian fur traders and Indian women. Later, it was extended to the descendants of English fur traders and Indian women living in and around Hudson Bay. By the nineteenth century, the term came to be used more generally to refer to the 'mixed blood' descendants of European (regardless of their specific origins) and Indian relationships who were living in Western Canada in the vicinity of Hudson Bay and the Red River Valley in present-day Manitoba and in parts of Saskatchewan and Alberta.

At present, however, there are two approaches to the definition of Métis. One is a fairly narrow and exclusive definition with relatively well-defined group boundaries. The other is a looser definition with more fluid and flexible boundaries. These competing definitions are reflected in the two main organizations that currently claim to represent the interests of Métis people in Canada: The Métis National Council (MNC) and the Congress of Aboriginal Peoples of Canada. In September 2002, The MNC became the first Métis organization in Canada to adopt a formal definition of the Métis. In their rather narrow definition 'Métis means a person who self-identifies as Métis, is of historic Métis Nation Ancestry, is distinct from other

Aboriginal Peoples, and is accepted by the Métis Nation' (see Box 7.1). While self-definition is an important aspect of this approach (i.e., a person has to believe themselves to be a Métis person), a number of other important conditions apply. One of the key elements in this definition is the concept of 'historic Métis Nation'. This refers to people 'known as Métis or Half-Breeds who resided in the Historic Métis Nation Homeland' in 'west central North America'. In effect, this provides for a definition of Métis that is limited to individuals recognized as descendants of 'the original' Métis people who lived in northern Ontario, Manitoba, Saskatchewan, and Alberta. The MNC adopted this narrow approach to the definition of their group boundaries in part because they felt that they had to have a distinct national content for rights recognized under the Constitution (Congress of Aboriginal Peoples 1998). In other words, they wanted to present themselves as a nation and not simply an agglomeration of individuals united simply by their ancestors' choice of marriage partners.

Box 7.1 National Definition of Métis

Métis means a person who self-identifies as Métis, is of historic Métis Nation Ancestry, is distinct from other Aboriginal Peoples and is accepted by the Métis Nation.

Moved: David Chartrand, MB Second: Al Rivard, SK CARRIED UNANIMOUSLY

Defined Terms in National Definition of Métis

WHEREAS on September 27, 2002 the Métis Nation adopted a national definition of Métis; and

WHEREAS within the definition there are defined terms;

THEREFORE BE IT RESOLVED that the Métis Nation adopts the following defined terms for its national definition of Métis;

'Historic Métis Nation' means the Aboriginal people then known as Métis or Half-Breeds who resided in Historic Métis Nation Homeland;

'Historic Métis Nation Homeland' means the area of land in west central North America used and occupied as the traditional territory of the Métis or Half-Breeds as they were then known;

'Métis Nation' means the Aboriginal people descended from the Historic Métis Nation, which is now comprised of all Métis Nation citizens and is one of the 'aboriginal peoples of Canada' within s.35 of the Constitution Act of 1982;

'Distinct from other Aboriginal Peoples' means distinct for cultural and nationhood purposes.

Moved: Al Rivard, SK Second: David Chartrand, MB Carried

Source: Métis National Council. 2004. *National definition of Métis*. http://metisnation.ca/who/definition.html.

On the other hand, the Congress of Aboriginal Peoples does not use a formal/ legal definition of a Métis person. In their view, Métis are more broadly defined as 'mixed populations' who include but are not limited to the historic Métis as defined by the Métis National Council (Congress of Aboriginal Peoples 1998). That is, for the congress, Métis ancestral origins need not be rooted in the historic Métis homeland in western Canada, and the Métis can include, for example, the more recent descendants of 'mixed' European/Indian ancestry in places like Nova Scotia, British Columbia, and southern Ontario.

First Nations

The term 'First Nations' is now commonly used to describe status Indians. It is not necessarily an ethnic identity, since many people use it instead of the concept of status Indians, and it can include individuals who have older linguistic and tribal identities. The term 'First Nation' came into widespread use in the early 1980s with the transformation of the National Indian Brotherhood into the Assembly of First Nations (AFN). This was more than just a name change in that the organization underwent a major reorganization of its structure (Assembly of First Nations 2001). However, part of the reason for the name change was the desire on the part of some leaders to rid themselves of both masculinist and colonial definitions of their identity. The notion of a 'brotherhood' seemed to exclude women from participation, and the term 'First Nations', leaders argued, better reflected their unique social and legal status in this country: namely, that they had special rights because they were the first occupants of the land. Despite the growing popularity of the term First Nation, the terms 'Indian' or 'status Indian' are still occasionally also used.

Historically, the federal government's need to define precisely who was an 'Indian' stemmed in part from the way that powers between the federal and provincial governments were divided in the 1867 British North America Act. Within the Act, many aspects of policy-making, such as matters pertaining to education, health care, and social services, were defined as responsibilities of provincial governments. However, 'Indians and lands reserved for Indians' were defined as responsibilities of the federal government. In taking on this responsibility, the federal government was forced to figure out and define exactly who were the people that they were responsible for (Satzewich and Wotherspoon 2000).

As noted in chapter 2, Indian policy was articulated in the Indian Act, which was the basic framework for the federal government's approach to dealing with Indian matters. A major preoccupation of the various incarnations of the Indian Act was therefore the question of who the government defined as an 'Indian' person.

The early historical definitions of who was an Indian were based on a mix of blood, line of descent, and community acceptance. While the definitions of 'Indian' contained in the various incarnations of the Indian Act are complex and full of complex legal/bureaucratic jargon, in the Indian Act of 1876, an 'Indian' basically was any male person of Indian blood reputed to belong to a particular band, any child of such person, and any woman who is or was lawfully married to such a person (Ponting and Gibbins 1980, 9). This definition allowed the Department of Indian Affairs to create a 'register' or list of individuals in Canada whom they considered to be Indians under Indian Act legislation. Hence, the term registered, or status, Indian came to be applied to people who were officially recognized as Indian persons by the federal government. Self-definition became less important than an externally imposed legal definition and social acceptance.

In defining who was an Indian, the Indian Act also defined how someone could lose their Indian status or stop being an Indian, at least from the perspective of the federal government. The concept of *enfranchisement* referred to the processes whereby an individual could forcibly lose or voluntarily give up their legal status as an Indian. For a time, Indians who earned a university degree, lived outside of the country for five years or more, or became lawyers, doctors, or Christian ministers were forced to give up their Indian status (Furi and Wherrett 2003, 2). This policy essentially meant that being an Indian person was incompatible with being highly educated, a respected professional, or a clergyman. In fact, it created a disincentive for Indian persons to get a higher education, which they might need to improve their socio-economic status.

The other, more common way that individuals lost their status as Indians was through intermarriage (Frideres and Gadacz 2001, 31). Under the pre-1985 provisions of the Indian Act, Indian men who married non-Indian women were allowed to retain their Indian status; their children and their non-Indian spouses also acquired Indian status. On the other hand, Indian women who married non-Indian men lost their Indian status, as did their children. Non-Indian men who married Indian women were not granted Indian status. Between 1876 and 1985, approximately 70 per cent of the 20,738 Indians who were enfranchised were Indian women who had married non-Indian men (Frideres and Gadacz 2001, 31).

Non-status Indians

These enfranchisement provisions led to the creation of the social category and political identity of 'non-status Indians'. Generally, the term 'non-status Indian' refers to individuals who lost their legal status as Indians through one of the enfranchisement provisions, which have since been eliminated from the Indian Act. The differences between non-status Indians and the Métis are sometimes difficult to untangle. Some individuals who lost their Indian status because their mother or grandmother married a non-Indian man define themselves and are socially accepted as 'Métis'. Yet others reject the label of Métis or are not accepted as Métis by virtue of the more narrow definition of the Métis National Council and therefore define themselves as non-status Indians. Non-status Indians are different from other Aboriginal groups in that even though they define themselves as 'Indian' or 'Aboriginal', they are not specifically included in the constitutional definition of Aboriginal peoples in Canada.

The blatantly obvious sexual discrimination built into the pre-1985 versions of the Indian Act, which forced Indian women to give up their Indian status if they married non-Indian men but did not require Indian men to give up their status if they married non-Indian women, became the object of political struggle in the 1960s and 1970s. In being forced to give up their Indian status, Indian women were no longer eligible for reserve-based benefits such as housing or support for higher education. Further, even if their marriages to their non-Indian male partners broke down, there were no provisions for women to regain their Indian status, return to their communities, and claim rights and resources as band members.

The momentum for change built up in the early 1970s as Jeannette Lavell and Yvonne Bédard challenged the sexual discrimination inherent in the enfranchizement provisions of the Indian Act. The Supreme Court of Canada ruled against Lavell and Bédard in 1973 on the grounds that the Indian Act was exempt from the equality protections of the Canadian Bill of Rights. However, further challenges to the law followed. In 1977, Sandra Lovelace filed a complaint against Canada with the United Nations Human Rights Committee in Geneva, and four years later the Canadian government was embarrassed by the committee's finding that the Indian Act was in breach of the International Covenant on Civil and Political Rights because it denied Lovelace and other women in the same circumstance the legal right to live in the communities of their birth (Silman 1987, 176). After continued lobbying by Indian women, the federal government amended the Indian Act in 1985 by passing Bill C-31.

The terms of the amendment to the Indian Act are complex, but at its simplest, Bill C-31 provided for:

a) elimination of the 'enfranchisement' provisions of the Indian Act and the reinstatement of certain individuals who had lost their Indian status as a result of the previous enfranchisement provisions;

b) elimination of patrilineal definitions of eligibility for Indian status;

c) the opportunity for bands to develop membership codes and to assume control over the definition of who was a band member;

d) the opportunity for bands to deny membership to certain individuals even though they had legal Indian status. (Daniels 1998, 1)

The fallout from Bill C-31: a case of 'abocide'?

The changes to the Indian Act introduced under Bill C-31 attempted to correct a legitimate historical injustice. However, as sometimes happens when governments try to correct historical wrongs, Bill C-31 resulted in the creation of further controversies and social divisions.

First, in enabling individuals to regain their Indian status, the legislation has led to a significant increase in the status Indian population of Canada. As can be see in table 7.2, the status Indian population of Canada has nearly doubled since it was introduced. In 1985, the status Indian population stood at 360,241, while in 2002 it was 704,851 (Canada. Indian and Northern Affairs Canada 2004, 8). While some of the recent increase in the Indian population is due to natural population growth among non-Bill C-31 Indians, much of the growth in the status Indian population in the late 1980s and early 1990s was the result of the reinstatement of individuals who had earlier lost their Indian status. Since many of the individuals who have had their status reinstated live in urban areas, there has also been a dramatic increase in the number of urban-based status Indians. In 2002, 42.8 per cent of status Indians lived off-reserve, compared to 29.1 per cent twenty years earlier (Canada. Indian and Northern Affairs Canada 2004, 10). In this context, controversies have surrounded the appropriate focus of the main national umbrella organization that in theory is

Table 7.2   Percentage Change in Registered Indian and Bill C-31 Population, Canada, 1985 to 2003

Year	Total registered Indians		Bill C-31		Non-Bill C-31	
	No.	% change	No.	% change	No.	% change
1985	360,241	—	—	—	358,636	—
1986	387,829	7.7	16,252	—	369,972	3.2
1987	415,898	7.2	37,056	128.0	378,842	2.4
1988	443,884	6.7	54,774	47.8	389,110	2.7
1989	466,337	5.1	66,904	22.1	399,433	2.7
1990	490,178	5.1	73,990	10.6	416,188	4.2
1991	511,791	4.4	79,639	7.6	432,152	3.8
1992	533,461	4.2	85,947	7.9	447,514	3.6
1993	553,316	3.7	91,439	6.4	461,877	3.2
1994	573,657	3.7	96,148	5.1	477,509	3.4
1995	593,050	3.4	100,958	5.0	492,092	3.1
1996	610,874	3.0	104,869	3.9	506,005	2.8
1997	627,435	2.7	107,577	2.6	519,858	2.7
1998	642,414	2.4	108,924	1.3	533,490	2.6
1999	659,890	2.7	109,913	0.9	549,977	3.1
2000	675,499	2.4	111,476	1.4	564,023	2.6
2001	690,101	2.2	112,306	0.7	577,795	2.4
2002	704,851	2.1	113,254	0.8	591,597	2.4
2003	719,496	2.1	113,354	0.1	606,142	2.5

Note: The slow growth rate of the Bill C-31 population between 1997 and 1998 is partly due to a backlog of files, which were cleaned up in 1999.
Sources: 1985–2003: Canada. Indian and Northern Affairs Canada. Indian register; 1985–2003: Canada. Indian and Northern Affairs Canada. Membership and entitlement.

supposed to represent all status Indians in Canada—the Assembly of First Nations. The AFN has been accused of ignoring the interests of Bill C-31 and other status Indians who live in urban areas. Arguably, the assembly is more concerned with reserve-based issues and issues surrounding treaty rights—issues that have little resonance for individuals struggling to make a life in cities.

Second, some argue that 'abocide' was in fact part of the hidden agenda in the government's 1985 solution to the problem of sexual discrimination in the Indian Act. In defining what he means by 'abocide', Harry Daniels, former president of the Congress of Aboriginal Peoples, argues that the

> Bill not only continues but will actually accelerate the extermination policies—the integration of Canada's Indian population into mainstream society—that have always been at the heart of the federal Indian Act regime. So serious are the Bill's implications in this regard that, within a few generations, there may no longer be any status Indians left in Canada (Daniels 1998).

Although Daniels may exaggerate the rate at which status Indians might drop off the political landscape of Canada, he does identity a legitimate long-range issue. While the rules are complex, essentially if two consecutive generations of status Indians marry non-Indians, the children of the second-generation relationships will no longer be eligible for Indian status. That is, to qualify for Indian status in the future, a grandchild of individuals who are currently status Indians has to have either both parents as status Indians or one parent as a status Indian, both of whose parents (the grandparents) were status Indians. Daniels argues that as time goes on, many individuals will not be able to meet this test, and he predicts that even though there has been a temporary increase in the size of the status Indian population and a temporary decline in the non-status Indian population, in 20 years' time, the trend will reverse: there will be an explosion in the number of non-status Indians and a decrease in the number of status Indians. Because status Indians have special rights in the Constitution and non-status Indians do not, this potential trend is identified as yet another way that the federal government is trying to rid itself of the so-called 'Indian problem' (Dyck 1991). Indeed, Bonita Lawrence (2004, 67) suggests that 'intermarriage now represents a "ticking time bomb" in Native communities' because it will eventually reduce the size of the status Indian population that can claim special rights. While conspiracies are easier to dream up than they are to implement or prove, given that the government chose to exclude non-status Indians from the definition of Aboriginal peoples in the 1982 Constitution of Canada, Daniels's allegation of continued government 'abocide' may not be that far off the mark. In his view, this new policy plays into the long-term objectives of the federal government, which has always been to eliminate the special status of Aboriginal people in Canada (Daniels 1998).

Third, even though Bill C-31 made it possible for individuals to have their Indian status reinstated, this has not necessarily meant that people have been socially accepted as part of their former ancestral communities. In other words, legal definitions of identity continue to clash with self-definitions and community acceptance. As part of the amendments included under Bill C-31, bands were invited to develop rules that defined whom they considered a band member. Between 1985 and 1999, 236 of 610 First Nations had developed their own band membership codes. These codes are not necessarily the same as the rules that the federal government uses to determine Indian status (Furi and Wherrett 2003, 10). This has created cases in which individuals have had their Indian status reinstated by the federal government but have not been reinstated as band members with the right to access band resources, participate in band elections, and live and own property on reserves.

According to some commentators, Bill C-31 has in fact led to the creation of an increasingly complex 'caste system' under the Indian Act (Daniels 1998, 5). Research has begun to document some of the tensions in reserve communities surrounding the reinstatement of Bill C-31 Indians (Lawrence 2004, 70–3). According to one study conducted in British Columbia, some women who have been reinstated report that they have been treated as second-class citizens in their communities and that bands are reluctant to share resources with those who are reinstated (Huntley and Blainey 1999). In Alberta, Bill C-31 Indians have been characterized as 'strangers who would bring conflict, stress, and problems' to reserves.

Alfred, in summarizing what needs to be done to address the conflicts and tensions surrounding the social consequences of Bill C-31, expresses a rather harsh assessment of those who have sought reinstatement as a result of Bill C-31:

> ... white society must do something to address the concerns of individuals who have been incorrectly associated with our nations. This issue is particularly relevant in Canada, where tens of thousands of self-identifying and minimal-blood persons who are excluded from membership in Indian communities are recognized as 'Aboriginal' by Canadian governments, receiving benefits and legal entitlement to the resources of indigenous nations. It seems that white society feels some obligation to these people—probably because they are actually white, and therefore likely to cooperate with government efforts to eliminate indigenous nations as political forces. In any case, the problem can be resolved by recognizing that non-Indian 'Aboriginals' are a strictly state defined community, with rights and obligations deriving only from their membership in that community, and having nothing to do with the treaty and political rights of indigenous nations. The state would then have one set of relationships with indigenous nations, premised on their right to self determination, and a completely separate, presumably different set with the communities that it created and sponsors (1999, 86).

Although it is difficult to know how widespread such opinions and conflicts are, in part because positive experiences of being accepted into a community do not 'make the news', the existence of such tensions continues to speak to the continued importance of clashes between externally imposed definitions of identity, individual identity choices, and the social recognition of those identity choices. While many ethnic groups have formal and informal debates about group membership, who belongs and who does not belong, and what makes a particular individual 'Hungarian' or 'Yoruba', the political debate about who is an 'authentic Indian' is more heated because there is more at stake.

Fourth, there are controversies over the nature of membership codes that have been developed by some bands. According to Furi and Wherrett, First Nations bands have developed four main types of membership codes:

1) one-parent descent rules whereby a person is eligible for membership based on the membership eligibility of one parent;
2) two-parent descent rules, which declare that for a person to become eligible, both of that person's parents must be members or eligible for membership;
3) blood quantum rules, which base eligibility on the amount of Indian blood a person possesses (typically 50 per cent);
4) Indian Act rules that base membership on sections of the Indian Act. (Furi and Wherrett 2003, 10).

Bands that have developed blood quantum rules have been the site of the most controversy. Daniels argues that the federal government's new rules regarding the maintenance of Indian status through the generations will place pressure on bands to 'maintain the "racial purity" of their community and to discourage unions with Non-Status partners' (Daniels 1998, 3). The Kahnawake Mohawk community's code is probably the most controversial, in part because they are the most high-profile community to have developed a blood quantum code. There are two basic elements to their code:

1) *Moratorium on mixed marriages*: Any Mohawk who married a non-Native after 22 May 1981 loses the right to residency, land holding, voting, and office-holding in Kahnawake.
2) *Kahnawake Mohawk law*: As of 11 December 1984, a biological criterion for future registrations requires a 'blood quantum' of 50 per cent or more Native blood (cited in Lawrence 2004, 78).

Culture and individual identity are also factors in Mohawk identity, but they seem to be subordinate to biological descent. As Alfred notes, 'today there are many different ideas about what constitutes a Native person. We know what does not: pure self-identification and acting the part, however diligent the research or skilful the act' (Alfred 1999, 85).

In this context, individuals in Kahnawake have lost jobs and have not been allowed to run for office because they have less than the requisite 50 per cent blood quantum. In 1995, efforts were made to bar children who were deemed to not have the requisite 50 per cent blood quantum from Kahnawake schools (Lawrence 2004, 79).

Critics have argued that these kinds of membership codes are racist and in violation of basic human rights (Lawrence 2004, 78). In defence of the code, Alfred (1995, 174–7) argues that in the absence of an easily operational set of cultural criteria to define what being a Mohawk means, 'Indian communities in the modern era have been forced to accept race-based criteria' (Alfred 1995, 174). This kind of racialized definition of group membership is 'easy to police' because once the criteria are established, it is easy to measure 'race'. Alfred further argues that the use of these criteria is the natural by-product of living in a racialist society with a racialist history. Some have pointed out that critics use a double standard when they condemn the Mohawks for developing this kind of code. According to Lawrence (2004, 78), the Canadian government regularly uses blood quantum in its determination of who is eligible for resources in land claims settlements, yet it is rarely criticized for using racist criteria in this context. Alfred admits that this is a defensive reaction on the part of Mohawks faced with threats to their identity and to the future of their community. He identifies a number of specific threats, including: intermarriage with non-Mohawks; the wider popularity of assuming an Indian identity; and that individuals who take on an Indian identity and in some cases seek formal reinstatement as Indians are after the special rights and monetary benefits associated with an Indian status.

Finally, Alfred (1995) justifies the blood quantum codes on the grounds of the right to self-determination: what is the right to self-determination if it is not a right to define your own group boundaries? In Alfred's view, 'To deny the Mohawks of

Kahnawake the right to determine for themselves what the boundaries are between theirs and other communities is itself inherently colonial.' 'Membership,' in Alfred's (1999, 85) view, 'is a matter of blood and belonging determined through the institutions governing a community at a particular time.' The problem, as we noted in chapter 1, is that 'race' is neither fixed nor obvious. In fact, it is very difficult to define 'race' from a biological or blood quantum point of view, and any definition will inevitably draw arbitrary boundaries between those who belong and those who do not belong.

COMPARING COLLECTIVITIES: BETWEEN-GROUP DIFFERENCES

A common way of trying to understand the position and experiences of Aboriginal people in Canada is to compare their social, health, educational, and economic conditions to those of non-Aboriginal people. In this section, most of the comparisons are between First Nations or status Indians living on reserves in Canada and the Canadian population as a whole. Generally, the differences between Canadians as a whole and First Nations living in urban areas or Métis people are less dramatic than the former. While most of the measures used to gauge socio-economic differences between reserve-based First Nations and other Canadians indicate that there is a declining gap between these two broad collectivities, these measures also tend to show that there are still stubborn disparities.

While the gap in average life expectancy between status Indians and the rest of Canada has decreased over the years, First Nations men can still expect to live on average 6.0 years less than other Canadian men, and First Nations women on average live 6.1 years less than other Canadian women (Canada. Indian and Northern Affairs Canada 2004, 26). Tuberculosis rates are nearly six times higher for on-reserve First Nations than they are for Canada as a whole (2004, 28). In 2000, the infant mortality rate for on-reserve First Nations was 6.4, compared to 5.5 for Canada as a whole (2004, 29). Furthermore, the age-adjusted prevalence rates for chronic conditions such as heart problems, hypertension, diabetes, arthritis, and rheumatism are between 1.5 and 5.3 times higher for First Nations people (on and off-reserve status Indians and Labrador Inuit) than they are for the general Canadian population (Frideres and Gadacz 2004, 81).

There has been a steady improvement over the years in some dimensions of housing. For example, more than 95 per cent of reserve houses have an adequate water supply and sewage disposal system, a dramatic improvement over the situation in 1963 when just over 10 per cent of the reserve-based population had adequate water and sewage facilities (Frideres and Gadacz 2004, 87). How accurate these data are is of course open to question. The October 2005 mass evacuation of the Kashechewan reserve in northern Ontario because of water supply problems shows that decent water supplies are not available to all reserve communities; indeed, 98 other reserve communities were also under boil-water advisories (Curry 2005). At the same time, however, the overall quality of housing does not appear to be getting much better: in 1999–2000, for example, 56.9 per cent of on-reserve housing was considered 'adequate' (defined as houses that do not require any minor or major renovations or replacement), but in 2002–3, this figure dropped to 53.2 per cent (Canada. Indian and Northern Affairs Canada 2004, 62). Overcrowding remains an issue. The number of Aboriginal homes with more than one person per room is 200 to 300 times higher than that of the overall Canadian population (Frideres and Gadacz 2004, 85). In Canada as a whole, the average number of persons per dwelling is less than two, but the number of Aboriginal persons per dwelling is 3.5. The average Canadian dwelling has 7.2 rooms, but the average Aboriginal dwelling has 5.8 rooms (Frideres and Gadacz 2004, 85). Overcrowding leads to deteriorating housing stock and to other social problems.

A variety of measures can be used to assess income differences, and it is not possible to provide complete documentation here. As with other measures of well-being, evidence suggests that the economic gap between First Nations and other Canadians is slowly closing but that persistent differences remain. Government transfer payments constitute a greater proportion of Aboriginal peoples' total income than that of non-Aboriginal people. Among status Indian families, 37 per cent make less than $20,000 per year, compared to 17 per cent of non-Aboriginal families (Frideres and Gadacz 2004, 101). Status Indian families have an average income of $21,800, which was 57 per cent of the average Canadian family income of $38,000 in 1995. In 1995, average individual income for all Canadians was $26,474, but average individual income for on-reserve status Indians was $14,055, for off-reserve status Indians $18,463, and for Inuit $16,378.

Differences in employment status are also evident. In 1996, the unemployment rate for Canadians as a whole was 9.0 per cent, for First Nations it was 18 per cent, and for Inuit it was 21 per cent (Frideres and Gadacz 2004, 104). Unemployment rates on reserves are even higher and in some cases reach more than 50 per cent. Labour force participation rates are correspondingly lower for status Indians than they are for non-Aboriginal people. When it comes to the kinds of jobs that people do, compared to other Canadian men, First Nations men are under-represented in management, business, finance and administration, natural science, and related occupations and overrepresented in the ranks of skilled, semi-skilled, and other manual occupations.

There are fewer variations between Aboriginal and non-Aboriginal women in Canada. Compared to Canadian women, Aboriginal women are overrepresented in service occupations and slightly under-represented in clerical occupations. At the upper end of the occupational scale, Aboriginal women are distributed in roughly the same proportion as non-Aboriginal women (Frideres and Gadacz 2004, 104–5).

Overall, the educational attainment of Aboriginal people is improving, but as with other dimensions, there remains a gap. For example, in 1996, more than half of the Aboriginal population did not have a high school diploma, compared to one-third of the non-Aboriginal population over the age of 15. Conversely, while 16 per cent of Canadians have university degrees, less than 5 per cent of Aboriginal peoples have university degrees (Frideres and Gadacz 2004, 118).

Another approach to analyzing trends and differences in the well-being of Aboriginal peoples is to use the United Nations human development index. Initially developed to examine country by country differences in human development (in

which Canada has come out near the top), the index is now being applied to populations within countries. The index is compiled by using three broad measures of
well-being: education, life expectancy, and income. Cooke, Beavon, and McHardy
(2004) examined changes in the human development index for status Indians (First
Nations) and other Canadians during the period 1981 to 2001. They show (see table
7.3) that while differences in human development between Aboriginal and non-
Aboriginal people have decreased since 1981, the gap remains substantial. Further,
they show that there are important within-group differences in the trends in human
development. They argue that the biggest improvements in human development
have been for non-reserve status Indians and for Indian women. Index scores for
Indian men on reserves have remained stagnant. Of particular concern is the level of
income, which has stagnated over the period.

Table 7.3   Human Development Index and Component Measurement Scores,
Registered Indians and Reference Population, 1981–2001

Indicator	Population	1981	1986	1991	1996	2001
Life expectancy at birth	Registered Indians	65.7	67.5	70.6	72.2	72.9
	Reference	75.6	76.2	77.9	78.5	78.7
Life expectancy index	Registered Indians	.678	.708	.760	.786	.799
	Reference	.843	.853	.881	.891	.896
Proportion completing high school or higher	Registered Indians	.330	.341	.456	.514	.567
	Reference	.597	.618	.680	.717	.754
Proportion completing grade 9 or higher	Registered Indians	.597	.628	.721	.781	.825
	Reference	.802	.829	.863	.881	.903
Educational attainment index	Registered Indians	.508	.533	.633	.692	.739
	Reference	.733	.759	.802	.826	.853
Average annual income (Year 2000 constant dollars)	Registered Indians	6,840	6,795	8,243	8,887	10,094
	Reference	16,554	18,132	20,072	19,989	22,489
Income index	Registered Indians	.694	.693	.725	.737	.759
	Reference	.841	.856	.873	.873	.892
HDI score	Registered Indians	.626	.644	.706	.739	.765
	Reference	.806	.823	.852	.863	.880

Source: Martin Cooke, Daniel Beavon, and Mindy Hardy. 2004. *Measuring the well-being of Aboriginal people:
An application of the United Nations human development index to registered Indians in Canada, 1981–2001.* Canada.
Indian and Northern Affairs Canada. Strategic Research and Analysis.

EXPLAINING ABORIGINAL CONDITIONS

How do social scientists try to explain the above-noted differences between Aboriginal and non-Aboriginal people in Canada? In this section, we review four kinds of explanations: sociobiological, cultural, structural, and historical. It should be noted that some explanations are invoked to explain more general differences while other explanations focus on specific issues.

Sociobiological explanations

As noted in chapter 1, sociobiological explanations of behaviour and of ethnic and racial relations have generally fallen out of favour in the social sciences. However, one area in which sociobiological explanations tend to remain both popular and influential is First Nations alcohol addiction. Thatcher (2004) argues that the predominant explanation for First Nations peoples' alcohol abuse problems, which he describes colloquially as 'the firewater theory', is a form of the disease model of alcoholism. At its simplest, in this model individuals who develop the disease of alcoholism are seen to be predisposed to it because of chemical dysfunction in the brain. This dysfunction is reinforced and aggravated by extensive alcohol consumption. The disease is chronic, and those who suffer from it must manage the disease through complete avoidance of alcohol. Further, it is characterized by a complete loss of control during an alcohol consumption episode (Thatcher 2004, 29–30). Thatcher argues that

> inherent in the firewater complex is the belief that aboriginal Canadians are constitutionally (genetically) incapable of moderation in the amount of alcohol they consume in drinking episodes. Drinking, moreover, is seen as a social activity, typically carried out in venues devoted wholly to group drinking. It also tends to be carried out through binges, rather than as persistent, ongoing, addictive drinking. The firewater complex also includes the popular belief that 'Indian drinking' is inevitably associated with extreme impairment and irresponsible and antisocial behaviour. The assumption is that, once a drinking episode has begun, indigenous North Americans lose their capacity to regulate their drinking behaviour, the amount they drink, as well as other behaviours during the episode. Colloquially stated, Indian drinking tends to quickly get 'out of control', a concept which is consistent with conventional notions of alcoholic behaviour described in the disease model of alcoholism (2004, 130–1).

This approach to understanding Aboriginal alcohol problems is shared by many health professionals and demonstrated in treatment programs run by and for First Nations communities. Thatcher argues that the thinking behind the 'firewater complex' has been extended to explain many other social problems in reserve communities, including gambling, co-dependency, family violence, anxiety, depression, anger, and rage (Thatcher 2004, 139).

One of the problems with this explanation is that it is based on essentialist and primordial understanding of 'race' differences. Assessing the evidence on the impact of biological factors on alcohol use, Thatcher (2004, 122) argues that there is 'no convincing evidence' that Aboriginal peoples 'are genetically prone to alcohol problems or that they are necessarily problem drinkers if they do drink'. As an alterative explanation, Thatcher suggests that problem drinking among First Nations is the result of complex sociological and historical factors. These factors include: the patterns of learning about drinking within First Nations communities; the federal government's historical encouragement of dependency on the part of First Nations; the breakdown of social controls within communities to regulate anti-social drinking; and the absence of 'stakes in sobriety' for many First Nations people (Thatcher 2004, 166–93).

Cultural explanations

A second explanation for Aboriginal conditions is cultural and focuses on presumed value, attitudinal, and behavioural differences between Aboriginal and non-Aboriginal people. There are three versions of cultural theory: the first sees culture, cultural difference, and the unwillingness and/or inability to assimilate to 'mainstream' society as the source of many of the socio-economic problems that First Nations face; the second, which tends to be articulated by some Aboriginal people themselves, uses cultural explanations less as an explanation for social inequality than as a justification for self-government; and the third, which has certain affinities with the theory of segmented assimilation as outlined in chapter 5, suggests that many of the problems in Aboriginal communities stem not from the lack of assimilation but rather from too much assimilation into 'mainstream' culture.

The first version of cultural theory tends rely on folk understandings of First Nations people and their cultures. 'Culture of poverty' arguments were popular in the United States in the 1960s and early 1970s to explain black people's poor economic conditions, and the same logic used in that context has been applied to explain Aboriginal peoples' poor economic, social, and health conditions in Canada. According to this explanation, Aboriginal peoples tend to be poor or in ill health because their culture is different from or incompatible with the dominant culture. The dominant culture values things like personal autonomy, private property, individual economic success, and individual well-being. Writing in the mid-1970s, Mark Nagler argued that Aboriginal peoples possess a cultural complex that is very different from that of non-Aboriginal people. In his view, they possess a present rather than a future time orientation; they value free mutual aid without the expectation of anything in return; they do not place a high value on the possession of wealth or material goods; they do not save for the future; they do not have an appreciation of the monetary value of time; and they do not have the same work ethic as non-Aboriginal people (Nagler 1975, 18–22). According to Nagler, this cultural complex means that large segments of the Aboriginal population refuse to take part in full-time economic pursuits and is therefore a major factor contributing to their poor economic standing.

Elements of this view are also contained in volume 1 of the report of the Royal Commission on Aboriginal Peoples, *Looking forward, looking back*. Quoting Clare Brant, a Mohawk psychiatrist, the report suggests that within Aboriginal communities, there is a 'core ethic of non-interference', which is a 'behavioural norm of North

American Native tribes that promotes positive interpersonal relations by discouraging coercion of any kind, be it physical, verbal, or psychological' (Royal Commission on Aboriginal Peoples 1996b, 9.1). Related to this core ethic are the ethics of non-competitiveness, emotional restraint, sharing, and a number of 'less influential' ethics such as: 'a concept of time that emphasizes doing things "when the time is right" rather than by the clock; shying away from public expressions of praise; ordering social relations by complex but unspoken rules; and teaching by modelling rather than shaping' (Royal Commission on Aboriginal Peoples 1996b, 9.1). The report suggests that while these interrelated behaviours were required for survival in a small society in which a high degree of cooperation was required, a person could be put at a serious disadvantage if that person's environment changed and success and survival depended on competitive achievement (1996b, 9.1).

In relation to health and health care, Indian peoples' supposed under and overuse of certain kinds of medical services is sometimes explained in terms of cultural differences (Waldram, Herring, and Young 1995, 195). According to a 1969 report cited by Waldram, Herring, and Young (1995, 195), 'Many Indians have little understanding of the meaning of good health because of cultural differences and educational deficiencies. Indians exhibit little awareness of what is meant by good health and because of this lack of awareness there is a tendency to both over and underutilize health services. . . . Indians frequently fail to recognize significant symptoms and delay seeking treatment until they are acutely ill.' In other words, because of their lack of awareness of what it means to be in good health, Indian people were said to overutilize emergency services and underutilize preventative health care serves.

More recently, economist John Richards (1995, 156) offers another version of the view that Aboriginal peoples' problems are cultural in nature. He explains the profound dilemma that Aboriginal peoples in Canada face in the following terms:

> Personal success in an industrialized society requires that people restrict voluntary sharing of their personal income and wealth essentially to those in their (extended) family; it also requires that they invest in individual training and defer consumption via financial savings. Such activities are severely at odds with the values of most traditional cultures, and realizing a workable synthesis of the traditional and the modern is far from easy (Richards 1995, 156).

Richards argues that historically, most ethnic and 'racial' groups around the world have more or less successfully confronted the problem of the transition from traditional to modern culture. Aboriginal peoples in Canada are unique, not because their traditional cultures are substantially different from other traditional non-European cultures but rather because of the relatively recent timing of their transition. According to Richards:

> For those of European or Asian origin, the cultural journey from feudal agriculture to modern industrial society has been a long and tortuous one. In an anthropological sense, however, that journey has been shorter and more direct than the one to

be undertaken by people who start from a pre-agricultural society. The cultural adjustments required of a Punjabi farmer who moves from rural India to urban Toronto may be huge, but they are less than those required of a reserve-based aboriginal who moves from northern Saskatchewan to Regina (1995, 156).

In contrast to this version of cultural theory, a second version has tended to be put forward by some Aboriginal people themselves. Emphasis on the enduring cultural differences between Aboriginal and non-Aboriginal people is used by some as a justification for self-government and as an argument for the transfer of more decision-making powers to Aboriginal peoples. Whereas the first version of cultural theory tends to cast Aboriginal culture in a negative light insofar as it is the source of 'the problem', the second is a positive portrayal of the values, beliefs, and attitudes of Aboriginal peoples and part of 'the solution'.

The latter version is reflected in the report of the Royal Commission on Aboriginal Peoples on the justice system, titled *Bridging the cultural divide* (1996a). While careful to place Aboriginal justice issues in the wider context of colonialism and economic disadvantage, the report also provided a powerful statement of the role that cultural differences play in the problem of and solution to Aboriginal peoples' overrepresentation in the justice system. One of the major findings of the commission was that

> The Canadian criminal justice system has failed the Aboriginal peoples of Canada—First Nations, Inuit and Métis people, on-reserve and off-reserve, urban and rural—in all territorial and governmental jurisdictions. The principal reason for this crushing failure is the fundamentally different world views of Aboriginal and non-Aboriginal people with respect to such elemental issues as the substantive content of justice and the process of achieving justice (1996a, 309).

Part of the solution, the report went on to suggest, stems from the constitutional right of Aboriginal peoples to self-government. In the commission's (1996a, 310) view, 'Aboriginal nations have the right to establish criminal justice systems that reflect and respect the cultural distinctiveness of their people pursuant to their inherent right to self-government.'

The third take on the role of cultural differences between Aboriginal and non-Aboriginal people suggests that many of the social problems in Aboriginal communities do not stem from a lack of assimilation but rather from the fact that too many Aboriginal people, particularly leaders of Aboriginal communities, have become too assimilated into some of the negative features of dominant Canadian society and have drifted too far away from their authentic indigenous roots. This explanation has certain affinities with the theory of segmented assimilation that we outlined in chapter 5. That theory, initially developed in the United States, suggests that some immigrants to the US become integrated into the existing American underclass (Zhou 1999). As a result, the economic problems that some immigrants face do not stem from their supposed lack of assimilation into American society but rather from their assimilation into the wrong segment of American society—an underclass subculture that rejects economic success. While not directly applicable to Canada, this theory does have similarities to the third version of cultural explanation for First Nations conditions in Canada. According to Alfred:

> The only way we can survive is to recover our strength, our wisdom, and our solidarity by honouring and revitalizing our traditional teachings. Only by heeding the voices of our ancestors can we restore our nations and put peace, power and righteousness back into the hearts and minds of our people (1999, xii).

In this kind of formulation, 'white society' and various 'white man's diseases' have persistently 'eaten away at the purity of the First Nation person or culture' (Thatcher 2004, 139).

What are we to make of cultural explanations for Aboriginal conditions? As the above discussion indicates, notions of 'cultural difference' and 'traditional culture' are rather like flexible friends: cultural differences can variously be seen as both the problem with and the solution to Aboriginal conditions. On their own, cultural explanations are problematic for a number of reasons. First, some versions of cultural theory, particularly the first version outlined above, tend to portray Aboriginal peoples as cultural cripples who despite centuries of contact with European society have been unable or unwilling to make the transition to a dominant society that is fast-paced, competitive, and individualistic.

Second, within each of the approaches, the definition of what constitutes authentic Aboriginal culture is often vague and sometimes relies on unsubstantiated stereotypes. These explanations also make use of an uncritical essentialism that tends to portray both Aboriginal culture and the dominant 'Euro-Canadian' culture as monolithic, all-encompassing, and inherently ingrained. In other words, all individuals within these broad groups have or should have these particular world views if they are to be authentic group members. This is particularly evident in Alfred's (1999, 42) characterization of 'Western' and 'indigenous' understandings of justice. Furthermore, according to anthropologist Noel Dyck:

> The 'culturalist' arguments advanced by Indian leaders in support of aboriginal claims, effective though these may be, run the risk of encapsulating Indians' political initiatives within . . . a straightjacket. The danger is that the honouring of static images of Indian culture may run counter to development of critical support for the less culturally 'colourful' but, nonetheless, pragmatic aspirations of Indians (1991, 151).

Third, cultural explanations tend to overgeneralize and assume that because an individual has a certain background or origin, that individual must automatically believe in certain things (Crawley 1995, 76). According to Crawley (1995, 76) 'one can assume nothing about how real flesh-and-blood individuals feel or what they believe or the sort of life they want to live simply because they are aboriginal'. It is just as dangerous to generalize about what 'white' people think and believe as it is to generalize about what Aboriginal people believe.

Fourth, some critics challenge the excessive assimilation into 'white society' thesis on the grounds that it is a form of 'reverse racism'. Thatcher argues that

> A broad-brush stroke of blame is painted over both irresponsible corporate direc-
> tors and unsympathetic politicians and those who are seriously and demonstrably
> concerned about and victimized by the same influences as those which cause great
> concern among aboriginal people. Ordinary, struggling workers and parents of non-
> aboriginal ancestry are placed on the same plane as the big shareholders and man-
> agers of corporations that produce and sell such potentially corrupting products as
> violent Hollywood movies, fatty hamburgers, cigarettes, or alcohol (2004, 139).

As Thatcher notes, the assimilation into 'white society' thesis assumes that all white people, regardless of the amount of power they have or do not have, are implicated in the problems facing First Nations people.

Structural explanations

Structural explanations locate the cause of Aboriginal peoples' poor socio-economic conditions in racism, discrimination, and economic disparities within the wider society. Structural explanations focus on the historical and contemporary obstacles that are both deliberately and accidentally placed in the way of Aboriginal peoples. There are many historical examples showing how social and economic opportunities and basic human rights were denied to First Nations (status Indians). Let us take only a few examples. Aboriginal veterans of World War II were cheated out of entitlements given to other war veterans. First Nations on reserves faced restrictions on the marketing of commodities produced on reserve. And First Nations were denied the right to vote in elections in many jurisdictions in Canada until the 1960s. Stereotypes about 'lazy Indians' are still powerful in some parts of Canada (Ponting 1998). These stereotypes form part of a self-fulfilling prophecy whereby managers and business-owners believe that Aboriginal people do not work hard and therefore do not hire them for certain jobs, which further contributes to their precarious economic status.

Some researchers focus on economic disadvantage as the source of Aboriginal peoples' over-involvement in certain aspects of the justice system (see Royal Commission on Aboriginal Peoples 1996a, 42–4, for a good summary). According to this approach, Aboriginal peoples are disproportionately impoverished, and their over-representation in the justice system simply reflects the wider correlation that exists between economic disadvantage and criminality. A related version of this argument is that many Aboriginal offenders end up in jail because they default on the payment of fines. As a number of inquiries into the operation of the justice system have noted, many Aboriginal males are currently serving time in jail simply because they cannot afford to pay fines. Thus, their over-incarceration is not due to any inherent cultural difference but rather a direct reflection of their poverty.

The weight of history

The fourth explanation for Aboriginal socio-economic conditions is what we refer to here as 'the weight of history' argument. We review two versions of this argument, one liberal and one conservative. Whereas liberal versions of the weight of history argument place blame on colonial oppression, conservative versions place the blame on the current supposed generosity of the Canadian government.

Liberal versions of the weight of history argument are perhaps the most popular of the current explanations of Aboriginal conditions. Generally, they suggest that many of the particular maladies found within Aboriginal communities can be attributed to past government policies and practices (Waldram, Herring, and Young 1995, 270). 'Colonialism', and its attendant ideologies, practices, policies, and controls, is the most frequently cited culprit. Noel Dyck, for example, argues that the cumulative weight of historical coercive tutelage has produced negative consequences both for First Nations peoples and their communities and for non-Aboriginal people. Dyck argues that coercive tutelage has been premised on the stated and unstated assumption that the personal and/or cultural deficiencies of Indians are the source of the Indian problem (Dyck 1991, 107). According to Dyck:

> Although the difficulties that Indians, like all human beings, suffer are many and various, the 'problem' that has dictated their lives for so long and with such sad consequences has resulted from the usually well-intentioned but, nonetheless, coercive and arbitrary rule to which they have been subjected (1991, 162).

Colonialism is also blamed for the creation of complex psychological problems for Aboriginal people. In some formulations of this argument, First Nations are a group of people who have been profoundly damaged on a basic psychological level by the racism, discrimination, and disempowerment that has characterized Euro-Canadian/Aboriginal relations in Canada. According to Alfred:

> Long-term subjugation has a series of effects on both the mind and the soul. We must recognize and take seriously the effects of colonial oppression on both individual and collective levels. In many people's view, political and economic problems are less urgent than the damage to our psychological health. As the psychologist Eduardo Duran has characterized the problem: 'Once a group of people have been assaulted in a genocidal fashion, there are psychological ramifications. With the victim's complete loss of power comes despair, and the psyche reacts by internalizing what appears to be genuine power—the power of the oppressor. The internalizing process begins when Native American people internalize the oppressor, which is merely a caricature of the power actually taken from Native American people. At this point, the self-worth of the individual and/or group has sunk to a level of despair tantamount to self-hatred. This self-hatred can be either internalized or externalized' (1999, 34–5).

Alfred argues that 'denied, medicated, rationalized, ignored, or hated, this is a reality that affects all indigenous people to one degree or another' (Alfred 1999, 35).

Other versions of this argument focus on the negative consequences of specific aspects of colonialism. For example, policies that did not allow Indians to participate fully in electoral processes in Canada until the 1960s are said to be responsible for the political indifference that some Aboriginal people appear to display toward improving themselves and their communities. Another frequently articulated version of this perspective is that there is a 'residential school' mentality or syndrome that continues to plague individual Aboriginal people and wider Aboriginal communities (Thatcher 2004, 161). Even though residential schools began to be phased out in the 1950s, one of the long-term negative consequences of the system was that it did not allow for a normal family life. In this context, parents did not have the opportunity to raise their children independently of government intervention, and children did not learn normal parenting skills when they were being raised. According to Kim Anderson:

> For a full century, native children were removed from biological parents and placed in residential schools where they often learned negative behaviours related to sex, intimacy and love. Many learned their dysfunction in foster homes where they were abused. We are seeing the effects of history pass down through the generations. . . . Many of our families have no means to teach intimacy and love because they were not party to these lessons themselves (2000, 200).

There are, however, conservative versions of the 'weight of history' argument as well. For example, according to economist John Richards (1995), one of the main reasons for the continuing high rate of Aboriginal poverty is the historical generosity that the Canadian welfare state has displayed toward Aboriginal peoples. In his view:

> Whatever the historical injustices [that Aboriginal people have experienced], the relative generosity of transfer programs available to aboriginals has become part of the explanation for—not the solution to—aboriginal poverty. . . . Whether they be aboriginals or not, the psychological effect on people from long-term dependence on transfer income is damaging. . . . Among men, particularly, long-term welfare induces a loss of self-respect, increased rates of depression, and a tendency towards self-destructive activities (such as substance abuse and family violence) (1995, 161).

Political scientist Thomas Flanagan shares this view of the negative effects of government policy and government financial support of various Aboriginal programs. In Flanagan's view, by providing what he sees as overly generous and virtually unlimited support through a variety of social assistance measures, the government is part of the problem. According to Flanagan, the 'problem' is that Aboriginal peoples

> have little sense of real-world trade-offs because everything their governments do for them is paid for by other people. They never have to give up anything in order to get additional programs. If they had to make the same claims that other Canadians routinely make, they would, I predict, take the axe to many of the government programs proliferating luxuriantly in their communities (2000, 197–8).

Whereas liberal versions of the weight of history argument see 'compensation', more government intervention, and better policies and programs as the solution to many of the problems facing First Nations and Aboriginal communities (Thatcher 2004, 134–7), conservative versions see the solution as lying in less government intervention.

Clearly, history matters. Historical conditions and past policies and practices, as we have seen in chapter 1, have long-lasting consequences and shape current policies, practices, and institutions. At the same time, care needs to be taken in invoking historical factors as explanations for contemporary maladies and conditions. Some historical explanations lack specificity, and broad generalizations about historical policies are sometimes used as a substitute for concrete analysis of the specific connections between particular social behaviours and historical conditions. For example, while many individuals were undoubtedly damaged by the residential school system, at its zenith in the 1940s and 1950s, less than one-half of school-age First Nations children were enrolled in residential schools; a larger number were enrolled in some type of day school run either by the federal government or a provincial school board. Furthermore, are people simply victims of history? Some individuals have succumbed to the weight of negativity stemming from historical forces and have internalized the prejudices of wider society by losing respect for themselves, their families, and their communities, yet others have overcome those forces (Anderson 2000). According to Thatcher:

> . . . the temptation of this metaphorical thinking is understandable, originating as it does in a knowledge of the actual historical record. However, in a fundamental way it also assumes and reinforces a sense of powerlessness and it can thus serve as a self-defeating prophecy. This singular blame attribution, however, completely ignores external and internal social class differences, treating all levels of reserve society in a unitary, blame-free fashion, and all levels of non-aboriginal society as being equally responsible for causing reserve problems (2004, 135).

As Thatcher suggests, it is not enough sociologically speaking to simply invoke abstract, metaphorical notions of 'history' as the explanation for current social conditions and social relations. While 'history' is without question highly relevant to the present, concrete connections need to be made between those historical conditions and individual biographies.

STRATIFICATION AND DIFFERENCES WITHIN ABORIGINAL COMMUNITIES

One of the problems involved in comparing Aboriginal and non-Aboriginal people along traditional dimensions of income, education, and occupation and then offering broad explanations of those differences is that such comparisons tend to homogenize both the category of 'Aboriginal' and the category of 'non-Aboriginal'. That is, by focusing on differences in average rates of educational achievement, income, labour force participation, incarceration, health status, and other variables between Aboriginal and non-Aboriginal people, there is a tendency to blur differences within the Aboriginal population of Canada. This kind of statistical bench marking (Li 2003) can also unwittingly contribute to reinforcing outmoded stereotypes, which the comparisons are often meant to undermine. These comparisons are usually made with good intentions in that they are intended as a way of demonstrating how bad the situation is for Aboriginal peoples and asserting that it can improve through the provision of more resources, better policies, and better government treatment. However, the comparison and a constant focus on the negative aspects of Aboriginal peoples' lives and conditions tend to imply that Aboriginal peoples and communities rarely if ever do anything right and that all Aboriginal peoples occupy the same decrepit positions in Canadian society.

An alternative way of looking at Aboriginal conditions is to look more closely at group differences. Many scholars have called for analysis of the links between gender, 'race', and class. For us, Aboriginal peoples represent one of the instances in which such intersectional analysis has the potential to be most fruitful. Often, Aboriginal scholars are most aware of social, political, and economic differences and conflicts within Aboriginal communities and as a result are the most articulate advocates of intersectional analysis. A number of social divisions within Aboriginal communities have been identified (between urban and reserve-based First Nations; between different socio-legal categories of 'status Indian'; between the interests of Métis, Inuit, and Indians), and we have already touched on some of these divisions in earlier sections of this chapter. In the remainder of the chapter, we want to focus on two main axes of difference: gender differences and differences between 'leaders and led'.

Gender

Aboriginal communities are no different from other minority and 'mainstream' communities to the extent that gender divisions and politics are increasingly important lines of difference.

One of the first public manifestations of gender divisions within First Nations communities came in the 1970s in the context of Indian women challenging the sexually discriminatory nature of the enfranchisement provisions of the Indian Act. Ironically, some of the male leadership of the Assembly of First Nations and other Aboriginal organizations were originally against changing the Indian Act to address the issue of sexual discrimination. Some argue that their resistance was rooted in continuing sexist attitudes within a largely male leadership (Silman 1987, 200). Others suggest that the AFN leaders opposed the changes because they were lobbying for a complete rewriting of the Indian Act and not just piecemeal changes. This issue, they argue, needed to be negotiated in the context of a wider re-evaluation of the Indian Act. Furthermore, the largely male leadership of the organization were also concerned about the financial implications of large numbers of individuals having their Indian status reinstated; without corresponding increases in funding, an already small pie would have to be cut into ever smaller pieces. Whatever the explanation for the male leadership's opposition to reforming a clearly unjust situation, one of the long-term consequences of that opposition was the creation of a more politicized attitude among First Nations women and a recognition that the interests of male First Nations leaders were not the same as the interests of women.

Gender divisions within Aboriginal communities arguably also played a key role in the defeat of the 1992 Charlottetown Accord in a national referendum. In the accord, the federal and provincial governments were prepared to entrench the right to Aboriginal self-government in the Constitution. The accord further provided that the form that self-government took in Aboriginal communities would not necessarily have to be constrained by the sexual equality provisions of the Charter of Rights and Freedoms. While the male leadership of the national Aboriginal organizations regarded these provisions as a victory and reason enough to support the accord in the referendum, many Aboriginal women opposed the accord precisely because they would lose the protection of the Charter of Rights and Freedoms in their fight for equality within Aboriginal communities. The Native Women's Association of Canada lobbied against the accord, and when it was defeated in a national referendum, many male leaders of Aboriginal organizations felt a profound sense of betrayal and disappointment.

The small number of female chiefs is, according to Anderson (2000, 218), 'largely due to the imposed Euro-Canadian political system that only validates the voices of men by handing them exclusive authority over the governance of our nations'. According to Anderson (2000, 239), the colonial system played a fundamental role not only in reorganizing gender relations within Aboriginal communities but also in undermining certain aspects of Aboriginal male existence and power. While elevating men politically, the system also disempowered and emasculated them:

> Native women acknowledge the suffering of Native men, interpreting those who engage in dysfunctional behaviour as products of colonization. Many Native women have been able to continue their traditional responsibilities of creation and nurturing, but many men's responsibilities have been greatly obscured by the colonial process. It is more difficult for men than it is for women to define their responsibilities in the contemporary setting and reclaim their dignity and sense of purpose. . . . Our communities moved away from the land where men could hunt and provide into a more urban, industrialized society where men had to 'find jobs' to provide. And of course, racist barriers kept Native men out of jobs. The introduction of the social welfare system intensified dependency that Native men had never experienced before. These are the things that pushed the men further away from their roles (Anderson 2000, 239).

Leaders and led

Aboriginal leadership has recently come under attack from a variety of quarters. Sadly, stories of alleged corruption and the mismanagement of band funds are quite common in the media. On occasion, band chiefs and council members are accused of corruption and not acting in the interest of their communities. At the same time, it is possible that these sensational cases are overblown and only attract attention because they cast a negative light on Aboriginal communities. Communities that are run honestly, efficiently, and with the collective good in mind are simply not newsworthy and so attract less attention.

Menno Boldt (1993) argues that the main division within Indian communities is between 'elite' Indians who control Indian governments and the mass of Indians who are outside of the small circles that control political and economic resources on reserves.

Others cast the divisions between leaders and led within Aboriginal communities more in terms of the concept of social class, sometimes inspired by a political economy perspective. A number of versions of class-based theory have been used to understand the position of Aboriginal peoples in Canadian society. Some are more nuanced than others.

Howard Adams (1999), a Métis academic, has put forward a two-class model. For Adams, there is an Aboriginal bourgeoisie and an Aboriginal underclass. Even though they face certain common issues and are both subject to the racism of the larger white society (Adams 1999, 111), these two classes have complex relationships with each other and with elements of white society.

Adams further divides the Aboriginal bourgeoisie into three segments. The first is broadly defined as 'elite leaders' of national Aboriginal organizations such as the Assembly of First Nations, the Métis National Council, and the Congress of Aboriginal Peoples. In a rather uncomplimentary manner, he describes them as 'Uncle Tomahawks' because they collaborate with white society to maintain the larger structure of racial and class privilege. The second segment consists of Aboriginal professionals and intellectuals such as lawyers, academics, teachers, and social workers. And the third consists of small business owners, government administrators, and directors of various training programs. According to Adams (1999, 118–19), the common feature among these three segments of the Aboriginal bourgeoisie is that 'driven by the need to establish social status, this group strives to achieve mastery of the colonizer's cultural practices and language, while appearing authentically Aboriginal'.

The Aboriginal bourgeoisie, in Adams's view, stands in opposition to the rest of the Aboriginal population, who occupy an underclass position in Canada. Their underclass position stems from their relationship to the means of production; they are the people who 'do the unskilled, menial work' within a capitalist society (Adams 1999, 111). According to Adams, the classification of the majority of Aboriginal people as part of the underclass 'has no relationship to intelligence, skill, or personal qualities, rather it has to do with race and oppression'.

Within Aboriginal communities, the relationship between these two classes is characterized by a combination of economic exploitation of the underclass by the bourgeoisie and a colonized psychological relationship between the two. Adams argues that Aboriginal business-owners and those who control the large development corporations that have arisen in the context of land claim settlements have increasingly injected Aboriginal communities with traditional class-based conflicts that many Marxists originally thought were only endemic to white society. Adams applies the notion of a 'comprador capitalist' class to the situation of the Aboriginal bourgeoisie. This comprador class acts as a go-between for 'white capitalists' and government and the larger mass of the Aboriginal underclass. They owe their positions to the power of white society, and their main role is to act as agents of social control on behalf of the larger capitalist structure. In Adams's view:

Aboriginal workers are kept in rigid control through the capitalist class structure. They are confined to the bottom of the occupational ladder; as a result, few are unionized. Within the last ten years, class divisions have developed within Native communities which have resulted in even greater exploitation and control. The La Ronge Indian Band created the Kitsaki Development Corporation, a private enterprise which is heavily dependent on external corporate capitalism and government support. It is one of the large employers on the reserve and includes a large range of business activities that claim sixteen million dollars worth of business annually. The band hires members for trainee and entry positions that pay extremely low wages. Such Indian entrepreneurship does not take into consideration the system of domination and exploitation of its own people, and serves to contain any class struggle within Native communities. The results are no different than corporate capitalism in mainstream society. (Adams 1999, 124–5).

In Adams's view, this economic exploitation is supplemented by complex relations of psychological exploitation:

Since the Indian/Métis bourgeoisie live largely in the white middle-class society of make-believe, the masks which they wear give them a sham life-style, and conceal the feelings of inferiority and hypocrisy that haunt their inner lives. Although they loudly proclaim their Indian heritage, they desperately attempt to escape from the Aboriginal under-class.... In attempting to evade identification with the Indian/Métis under-class they have developed self-hatred. These Aboriginal bourgeois try to shield themselves from racial discrimination and the contempt of the white people as they struggle for assimilation (Adams 1999, 119).

Marybelle Mitchell's (1996) analysis of the class structure within the Inuit population is somewhat more nuanced than that of Adams. Working within a political economy framework, Mitchell argues that what is important about the definition of social class is not so much ownership of but rather control over the means of production. She argues that the economic development corporations that have arisen as a consequence of land claim settlements are vehicles by which capitalist class relations are creeping into Inuit and other Aboriginal communities in the North. Since 1973, when the comprehensive claims process was instituted, 15 comprehensive land claims agreements have been completed, with dozens of other communities currently involved in various stages of negotiation (Frideres and Gadacz 2004, 215). While land claim settlements are complicated, they generally involve the exchange of vast tracts of land in return for cash payments, control over smaller allocations of land, control over wildlife management, protection of the environment, and resource royalty-sharing arrangements.

Not unlike the land surrender treaties that were agreed to between Indians and the federal government 100 years ago, contemporary comprehensive land claim settlements are also mainly about clearing away political/legal obstacles to development and capitalist expansion. As the search for oil and gas, diamonds, gold, and other precious metals and minerals in the North intensifies, so too does the need to ensure that development takes place on a firm legal footing. As a result, since many Aboriginal communities, including the Inuit, have never formally ceded land to the Canadian state, the federal government has taken the lead in negotiating land claim settlements with Aboriginal peoples, including the Inuit, as a way of clearing away these potential political/legal obstacles to exploration and development.

Even though land claim settlements are meant, in theory, to benefit all Aboriginals who fall within the terms of reference of the settlement and are sometimes framed in terms of the need to preserve and maintain Aboriginal cultural identity and values, in practice the chief beneficiaries of the settlements are those in position to control the development corporations. In a well-developed analysis, Mitchell argues that patterns of ethnic relations overlap with class relations. The Inuit ruling class is a creation of the Canadian state. As a result, this ruling class lacks certain features of other capitalist classes that have more autonomy from the state. At the same time, they are also an ethnically subordinate ruling class:

> Inuit have many interests in common with the working class, and we can begin to talk about Inuit participation in the ruling class as one effect of the institution of development corporations. There is within the political structures available to Inuit and the development corporation an element or 'class' that controls labour, means of production, allocation of resources, and investments *in alliance* with an outside ruling class; but to reiterate, *because* they are Inuit, it is an unequal alliance. All Inuit are shareholders in the development corporations, but a class of people is benefiting disproportionately. They do not own the corporations, but they control them (Mitchell 1996, 404).

This approach has promise. It emphasizes the importance of historical conditions, but at the same time it does not portray Aboriginal peoples as victims of historical forces over which they have no control. Some have access to resources, power, and influence; some have different values, and so on. A focus on class and other inequalities within Aboriginal communities is not meant to foment divisions and discontent within these communities. Divisions and discontent already exist, and what is needed are the tools to better understand those divisions.

SUMMARY

In this chapter, we have focused on three main issues. First, we sought to understand the complexity of Aboriginal identity and the interrelationship among externally imposed labels, internally adopted identities, and the social conflicts arising from different ways of understanding Aboriginal identity. Second, we provided documentation on some of the main socio-economic differences between Aboriginal and non-Aboriginal people and critically reviewed some of the main explanations for those differences. Finally, we considered the problem of divisions within Aboriginal communities in Canada and focused on emergent gender and leadership-related concerns.

Questions for Critical Thought

1. What evidence is there that the federal government continues to pursue a policy of assimilation in relation to First Nations? Is it accurate to call Bill C-31 an 'abocide' bill?
2. Why are debates about Aboriginal identity important? Are these debates simply matters of 'political correctness'?
3. What are the strengths and weaknesses of the four explanations that have been offered to explain the socio-economic and health status differences between Aboriginal peoples and non-Aboriginal people?
4. What are some of the ways that First Nations communities are internally stratified? Are these differences less important than collective differences between First Nations and non-First Nations?

Annotated Additional Readings

Dyck, Noel. 1991. *What is the Indian 'problem': Tutelage and resistance in Canadian Indian administration*. St. John's: Institute of Social and Economic Research. This book examines past and present relations between First Nations and governments in Canada, tracing the many negative effects of federal government policy on First Nations.

Frideres, James, and René Gadacz. 2004. *Aboriginal peoples* in Canada. 7th edn. Toronto: Pearson Educational Canada. A detailed and comprehensive summary and analysis of contemporary conditions and controversies within First Nations communities. The book contains up-to-date statistical material, the latest court decisions, and current legislation as it affects Aboriginal peoples.

Lawrence, Bonita. 2004. *'Real' Indians and others: Mixed-blood urban Native peoples and indigenous nationhood*. Lincoln, NE: University of Nebraska Press. An excellent discussion of the political dimensions of Aboriginal identity. The book focuses on how Aboriginal people with 'Indian status' react and respond to 'non-status' Aboriginals and how federally recognized Aboriginal peoples attempt to impose an identity on urban natives.

Mitchell, Marybelle. 1996. *From talking chiefs to a Native corporate elite: The birth of class and nationalism among Canadian Inuit*. Montreal: McGill-Queen's University Press. This highly detailed and theoretically informed book traces the development of class relations and collective identity among Canadian Inuit over several centuries of contact with Western capitalism.

Related Websites

Assembly of First Nations: http://www.afn.ca/.
Indian and Northern Affairs Canada: http://www.ainc-inac.gc.ca/.
Indian Residential Schools Resolution Canada: http://www.irsr-rqpi.gc.ca/.
Ipperwash Inquiry: http://www.ipperwashinquiry.ca/.
Métis National Council: http://www.metisnation.ca/.

Chapter 8

Transnationals or Diasporas? Ethnicity and Identity in a Globalized Context

Learning objectives

In this chapter you will learn:

• About the rationales that have been offered to support the concepts of diaspora and transnationalism;
• How the concept of transnationalism is defined;
• How the concept of diaspora is defined;
• That some of the rationales advanced in favour of the concepts of diaspora and transnationalism are problematic;
• That transnationalism among immigrants is not historically new;
• That legal distinctions between 'immigrants' and 'migrant workers' are still very important;
• That there are numerous examples of transnational practices among immigrants and ethnic community members.

INTRODUCTION

In the first seven chapters of this book, we have offered a number of important conceptual distinctions and sociological perspectives in the field of 'race' and ethnic relations. Some chapters have spoken of the differences between immigrants, migrants, refugees, and illegal immigrants. Other chapters have spoken of ethnicity, visible minorities, non-visible minorities, and 'race' and racism. In much of our discussion, these concepts have overlapped.

Over the past 20 years, a number of social scientists have expressed dissatisfaction with the kinds of approaches to understanding ethnicity, 'race', and immigration that we have outlined so far. Put simply, their argument is that in this new age of globalization, we need new theories and new concepts in order to truly understand the complexities of migration, ethnic group formation, and identity maintenance and change. As a result, the concepts of 'diaspora' and 'transnational' have become popular alternatives to many of the terms we have used so far to describe people who have moved abroad, their patterns of settlement, their identities, and their communities. Many scholars now talk about 'transmigrants' (Basch et al. 1994), 'transnational immigrants' (Glick Schiller 1999), 'transnational communities' (Van Hear 1998), 'ethno-national diasporas' (Sheffer 2003), 'ethnic diasporas' (Tatla 1999), or 'transnational ethnic diasporas'.

A number of efforts have recently been undertaken to define, operationalize, theorize, and critique the two concepts (Akenson 1995; Brubaker 2005; Cohen 1995, 1997; Vertovec 1999; Glick Schiller 1999; Reis 2004; Satzewich and Wong 2006). However, there has been less interest in systematically analyzing the relationship between the concepts of 'diaspora' and 'transnationalism'. While Brubaker (2005, 6) notes in passing that there has been a fusing of the literature on transnationalism and diaspora in recent years, he does not systematically analyze this trend. Do these concepts describe the same social reality, or do they try to capture different aspects of social life? If there is a difference, then how should researchers conceptualize the relationship between the terms diaspora and transnational? What are some of the strengths and weaknesses of diaspora and transnational studies? And do these approaches really constitute effective alternatives to the approaches and concepts that we have outlined so far in this book? This chapter aims to provide a critical appreciation of both concepts. First, we delineate some of the main similarities and differences between the concepts of diaspora and transnationalism and assess their relative strengths and weaknesses. Second, we try to offer a way of thinking about the links between the two concepts and approaches.

THE GENEALOGY OF DIASPORA AND TRANSNATIONALISM

The concepts of diaspora and transnationalism have had remarkably similar careers in recent times. Even though the concept of diaspora has a much longer historical pedigree in the social sciences (see Cohen 1997; Safran 1991), there are two important points of convergence in their more recent histories. First, the two concepts became popular in scholarly circles at about the same time. A search of *Sociological Abstracts* reveals that in 1980–1, the term 'diaspora' appeared in the title of only one academic article; the term 'transnational' appeared in the title of 13 articles. None of these articles was about immigrants; instead, they dealt with either transnational state politics or transnational corporations. In 2000–1, 'diaspora' appeared in 78 article titles (see also Brubaker 2005) and 'transnational' in 183 article titles in *Sociological Abstracts*; the vast majority of the latter references dealt with immigrants, ethnic groups, or related phenomena.

Second, contemporary advocates for both concepts ground the justification for their use in a sense of dissatisfaction with 'traditional' studies of immigration and ethnic relations: namely, that traditional concepts of and approaches to studying immigrants, immigration, and ethnicity are ill-equipped to understand new trends and realities. Cohen (1997), in advancing the concept of diaspora, argues that the static terms of migration theory, with their emphasis on the binary process of 'travel from' and 'return to', are no longer particularly useful (see also Anthias 1998, 562). Immigrants, Cohen argues, are hyper-mobile: they no longer permanently leave their countries of origin, nor do they permanently remain in their countries of destination.

The perceived failures of so-called ethnicity and 'race' paradigms include their primary focus on processes such as 'assimilation, integration and accommodation or ethnic conflict and exclusion' within the nation-state (Anthias 1998, 559). According to Anthias (559), 'the terms "ethnicity" and "race" turn the analytical gaze to processes of inter-group relations within particular territorial boundaries' rather than on the ways that inter-group relations are shaped by forces and conditions outside of particular national borders (see also Brubaker 2005). In other words, Anthias would argue that in order to truly understand the structure and dynamics of a group like the Ismailis in Canada, one needs to understand their diverse countries of origin, their links with Ismailis in other countries, and the wider global context in which people who believe in this particular branch of Islam are regarded.

In justifying the use of the concept of transnationalism, Basch et al. (1994) similarly argue that the traditional terms in the sociology of migration that are used to understand individuals who have moved abroad, which include 'immigrant' and 'migrant', no longer capture a complex social reality. In their view,

> The word 'immigrant' evokes images of permanent rupture, of the abandonment of old patterns of life and the painful learning of a new culture and often a new language. . . . The popular image of immigrant is one of people who have come to stay, having uprooted themselves from their old society in order to make for themselves a new home and adopt a new country to which they will pledge allegiance. Migrants, on the other hand, are conceived of as transients who have come only to work; their stay is temporary and eventually they will return home or move on. Yet it has become increasingly obvious that our present conceptions of 'immigrant' and 'migrant', anchored in the circumstances of earlier historical moments, no longer suffice. Today, immigrants develop networks, activities, patterns of living, and ideologies that span their home and host society (Basch et al. 1994, 3–4).

Clearly, the intellectual justifications for both the concept of diaspora and the concept of transnationalism point in the same direction. Both concepts, proponents argue, better capture the importance of real and imagined places of origin in immigrant and ethnic groups lives and identities as well as the complex interactions between 'here' and 'there' for individuals, families, and communities that have moved abroad.

Even though the two concepts emerged out of similar critiques, one major difference between them is the extent to which they have permeated popular consciousness and wider public discourse. The concept of diaspora has become so popular—and elastic—that groups outside of an immigrant or ethnic nexus have adopted the label or have been described as such (Brubaker 2005). A search of the Internet will find references to a 'gay and lesbian diaspora', a US 'pro-war' biker diaspora, and a 'mountain biker diaspora' in White Plains, New York, that until recently 'wandered nomadically from shop to shop looking for good, friendly advice without attitude, fair prices without a bargain-basement atmosphere, and a fine selection of merchandise'. Indeed, the concept has even been extended to our fine feathered friends: a feral pigeon colony at the edge of human civilization, depicted in a certain work of art, is 'more accurately described as a diaspora', according to the Saskatchewan Arts Board (http://www.artsboard.sk.ca/SCAM/s_curator.shtml).

Many immigrant and ethnic groups now define themselves as a diaspora (Brubaker 2005). Furthermore, groups that once rejected the label now routinely use the term to describe their larger community of co-ethnics who have settled abroad. For example, in the 1970s, Ukrainians in North America generally avoided use of the term diaspora. At that time, the concept had negative connotations in that it was seen as a Soviet-originated term meant to discredit Ukrainian and other émigré nationalists living abroad who were awaiting and in some cases working for the overthrow of the Soviet Union. As an alternative, Ukrainians at the time tended to define themselves as being 'in the emigration' rather than a 'diaspora'. Now, however, the concept is embraced, and many Ukrainians and their organizations in North America wrap themselves in a diaspora flag (Satzewich 2002).

In contrast, the concept of transnationalism has generally not filtered down into the vocabulary of the non-scholarly community or into immigrant and ethnic community organizations. Indeed, it is difficult to find any statements by leaders of ethnic or immigrant organizations or communities that describe their collectivity as 'transnational'.

This begs the question as to why there is a difference in the way that the two concepts have filtered down into the individuals, communities, and organizations that academics study. In other words, why have ethnic, immigrant, and a range of other groups adopted the diaspora label, and conversely, why does the 'transnational' label seem to carry less political currency than the term 'diaspora'?

There are a number of hypotheses. Robin Cohen (1997, x) provides one hypothesis, arguing (without systematically developing the point) that adoption of the label 'diaspora' may be 'functional' for groups in the sense that it allows for 'a certain degree of social distance to displace a high degree of psychological alienation' that immigrants experience in their countries of settlement. In other words, groups like the Sikhs may define themselves as a diaspora community because they do not feel as though they are full and equal members of Canadian society.

A second possible reason why the concept of diaspora has been widely adopted by ethnic and immigrant groups is that it carries certain *positive* connotations that derive from the Jewish historical experience. As many have noted, Jews have been defined as the 'classic' diaspora (Mandelbaum 2000; Cohen 1997). Despite the Jews' history of persecution and suffering, some ethnic elites outside of Jewish communities may perceive them as having cracked the problem of successfully maintaining group boundaries, ties to their ancestral homeland(s), and a relatively viable religious, educational, and community life in various countries of settlement. Arguably, for at least some leaders of ethnic communities, Jews are akin to a 'model minority' whose real and apparent success in maintaining a vibrant community life outside of Israel should be emulated.

Third, it may be that the concept of diaspora, with its emphasis on different forms of traumatic dispersal and the actual and potential victimization faced by earlier generations of co-ethnics, may play a role in helping contemporary community leaders and elites to maintain boundaries and cultivate solidarity within the larger imagined community. That is, the promotion and cultivation of victim narratives, along with adopting the diaspora label itself, may be strategies that elites employ to develop and sustain community solidarity, collective identities, and group boundaries (Brubaker 2005).

In contrast, the concept of transnationalism is not saturated with the same deep historical and contemporary narratives about trauma, victimization, and survival despite the odds. Because of this, 'transnationalism' may have less political resonance within immigrant and ethnic communities and wider publics, and this may account for its relative absence in the claims-making process.

The various efforts undertaken to define and theorize the two concepts have a number of nuances. The next section of this chapter will not review all of the subtleties of the different definitions and approaches (see, for example, Anthias 1998; Vertovec 1999; Smith 1999). Instead, we focus on what we think are good representative definitions of each concept and provide relevant examples to highlight how the approaches and concepts are used to better understand the world.

Diasporas

Robin Cohen (1997) offers one of the most comprehensive and influential definitions of diaspora and an extensive argument elaborating how and why the concept can be helpful in understanding immigrants and their descendants. Cohen uses the cases of the Afro-Caribbean, British, Armenian, Chinese, Jewish, Lebanese, and Sikh communities to construct both an ideal type of diaspora and a typology of different kinds of diaspora. He suggests that diasporas 'normally' exhibit several of the following features:

- dispersal from an original homeland, often traumatic;
- alternatively, expansion from a homeland in search of work, in pursuit of trade, or to further colonial ambitions;
- a collective memory and myth about the homeland;
- idealization of the supposed ancestral home;
- a return movement;
- strong ethnic group consciousness sustained over time;
- a troubled relationship with host societies;
- a sense of solidarity with co-ethnic members in other societies;
- the possibility of a distinctive creative, enriching life in tolerant host countries (Cohen 1997, 180).

Though an important element in Cohen's (1997) definition is forcible and traumatic dispersal from an ancestral home, diasporas can also be made up of mass movements of people who move for economic reasons, such as a search for work or trading partners. Political persecution is therefore not the only precondition for diaspora formation.

According to Cohen, the type of diaspora a group becomes depends largely on their initial reasons for leaving. *Victim diasporas*, such as the Jews and Armenians, are formed as a result of the traumatic events that occurred in their homeland and resulted in large-scale and widespread dispersal. *Imperial diasporas* are formed out of the colonial or military ambitions of world powers. Despite the cultural differences between the Scots, English, and Irish, Cohen argues that people from the United Kingdom who moved overseas to places like Canada formed a larger British imperial diaspora. *Labour diasporas* consist of groups who move mainly in search of wage labour. They include the Turks who after World War II emigrated to a variety of countries in Europe, North America, and the Middle East. *Trade diasporas*, like those formed by the Chinese merchants who emigrated to southeast Asia in the nineteenth and early twentieth centuries, consist of people who left their homelands to pursue opportunities as movers of goods and services in the emerging system of international trade. And finally, Cohen develops the notion of a *cultural diaspora* to characterize the migration and settlement experiences of migrants of African descent from the Caribbean after the Second World War. Cohen (1997, 127–53) considers these migrants as the paradigmatic case of people who have developed a unique culture and identity out of the influences of Africa, the Caribbean, and their new countries of settlement.

One of the reasons that Cohen's delineation of an ideal type of diaspora is useful is that it provides social scientists with a conceptual framework to study ethnic communities in their totality. It is possible to use this approach to sociologically analyze the extent to which communities conform to or deviate from the ideal type and to offer theoretical explanations for these patterns. This ultimately helps to illuminate and understand the dynamics of ethnic community life. As we discussed in the previous section, Jewish communities outside of Israel are often considered to be 'classic' victim diasporas. Thus, it is not surprising that Cohen (1997) argues that Jews display many of the features of his ideal type. Let us take a few examples from their experience.

Regarding the place of return movements within diasporas, Cohen suggests that they are the product of a complicated sense of attachment to ancestral homelands. Return movements can take many forms. The Israeli Law of Return, for example, provides that Jews from anywhere in the world have a right to move to Israel to live and work. Many Jews have taken advantage of this, particularly when incidents of anti-Semitism erupt in the countries where they live (Schoenfeld, Shaffir, and Weinfeld 2006). Jews in Russia and other former Soviet countries have also taken advantage of the Law of Return to move to Israel; it is estimated that in the 1990s, some 800,000 Jews left countries in the former Soviet Union and moved to Israel. Many other Jews return to Israel to visit family and friends or to discover their roots. Some Jewish organizations encourage temporary return to help individuals sustain a Jewish identity, learn about Jewish history, and maintain contacts with an ancestral homeland. Other countries around the world have also encouraged members of their respective diasporas to return 'home'. Sometimes, return is envisioned as only temporary and is simply meant to increase tourist revenue. At other times, as we see in box 8.1, states encourage skilled professionals like doctors and nurses who have emigrated abroad to return 'home' to help staff hospitals and medical clinics temporarily. In yet other cases, states encourage the permanent return of co-ethnics who have settled abroad because their population growth rates are low and/or declining or because they value their business or political acumen.

Box 8.1   Scientific Diaspora Could Ease Brain Drain

Stephen Leahy

BROOKLIN, Canada, Jun 15 (IPS) – Many expatriate scientists and medical professionals who work in Canada want to contribute their skills to their native developing countries—all that is lacking are mechanisms to help them do so without permanently returning to their country of origin, reports a study to appear Friday in Science magazine.

For many years, industrialised countries have been attracting scientists, engineers, information technology experts and talented university students from poorer countries in what's called 'a global brain drain'.

'The brain drain is a very big problem for developing countries. In sub-Saharan African countries, the majority of medical doctors have left,' said report co-author Abdallah Daar, director of ethics and policy at the R. Samuel McLaughlin Centre for Molecular Medicine at the University of Toronto.

'They leave to find a better future for their families, for better salaries and improved research or career opportunities,' Daar told IPS.

But there was a strong desire to help their country of origin among the 60 scientists from developing countries who now live and work in Canada and were interviewed for the study, he said.

'Although we didn't investigate their motivation, it seems to be a sense of obligation and altruism,' Daar said.

The full extent of the global shift of highly skilled people from the south to north is not known. One US estimate suggests 900,000 information technology (IT) professionals entered the US labour market between 1990 and 2000 under the H-1B temporary visa programme.

The Organisation for Economic Cooperation and Development (OECD) estimates that skilled IT workers from poor countries, especially in Asia, now account for one-sixth of the US total IT workforce. Indeed IT entrepreneurs who created highly successful companies like Intel and Ebay were not US citizens.

Other countries that rely heavily on such workers include Australia, Canada and Britain, and to a lesser extent in Denmark, Finland and Italy, the OECD reported.

In Canada, it is estimated that 15,000 science and health-related experts alone immigrated from developing countries. It could be at least 10 times that number in the US, Daar says as a rough guess.

Not surprisingly, these countries have aggressive marketing, lucrative incentive plans and long-term visas designed to attract the best and the brightest from around the world.

'The loss of highly skilled health workers has a big impact on many countries, including those in Latin America,' says co-author Béatrice Séguin of the University of Toronto Joint Centre for Bioethics.

Although some of those who are part of this 'scientific diaspora' return to their country of origin, particularly India and China, most do not want to return permanently, Séguin said in an interview.

'This is not about permanent return, it is about creating mechanisms to enable collaborations, training, skills exchanges on a short or medium-term basis or virtually,' she said.

One creative example is an expatriate Kenyan who is a professor of engineering in the US and who teaches students in Kenya via computer. The Kenyan students can control and do experiments using expensive research equipment located in the US through computers located at their Kenyan school, she says.

Industrialised countries should promote this kind of exchange with a 'National Science Corps' to fund the direct interaction between diaspora scientists and science and technology institutions in their countries of origin, the report recommends.

Another approach is a 'Diaspora Business Initiative' that would offer support and funding for partnerships between business, research and educational institutions and professionals in industrialised and developing countries.

'These mechanisms needn't cost very much and would benefit industrialised countries like Canada,' says Daar

The scientific diaspora represents an untapped resource for their countries of origin. And since industrialised countries greatly benefit from the brain drain, they should help enable those expatriates who are willing and able. If the Group of Eight countries make 'brain circulation' a priority it would foster innovation in developing countries, which could create long-term health and economic benefits, the report said.

Industrialised countries will also benefit from expanded networks and partnerships with emerging markets and related commercial opportunities, enhancing their own international competitiveness and productivity, the report concludes.

'If the Canadian government created an organisation, provided us with a nucleus, made the initial effort, I think there would be so many people who would join,' said one participant in the study.

Currently Canada is developing a government agency to assess the credentials of professionals immigrating to Canada to ease their entry. That would be excellent starting point from which to gather information and to create formal mechanisms to 'enable diaspora scientists in Canada to give back to their countries of origin', says Séguin.

There are many ways this can be done but the next step is to convene a conference or pilot project with one country to work out some of the ways this might be accomplished, she says: 'It's a very exciting initiative with tremendous potential.'

Source: Stephen Leahy. 2006. 'Scientific diaspora could ease brain drain'. 15 June. Inter Press News Agency. http://ipsnews.net/news.asp?idnews=33642.

Cohen's ideal type of diaspora often has a troubled relationship with otherwise tolerant and accepting 'host' societies. This is relevant for Jews in the diaspora: many Jews are concerned about declining levels of tolerance in countries of settlement. For example, while traditional forms and expressions of anti-Semitism in Canada appear to be declining, Schoenfeld, Shaffir, and Weinfeld (2006, 291) argue that a new globalized form of anti-Semitism has emerged. As with the arguments about new racism that we discussed in chapter 6, they argue that this new form of anti-Semitism tends to be politically framed in terms of opposition to Israeli government policy. As they explain, 'it is often hard to tell when "protests" against Israel are criticisms of policy, part of a campaign of delegitimation [of the existence of the state of Israel], or part of a war against "the Jews".' For some anti-Semites, opposing Israeli government policies (which became particularly sharp in the summer of 2006 in the context of the Israeli military response to Hezbollah rocket attacks staged from Lebanon) is a politically acceptable mask to cover their deeper anti-Jewish sentiments and actions. Schoenfeld, Shaffir, and Weinfeld (2006) take care to suggest, however, that criticism of policies of the government of Israel should not always and automatically be equated with anti-Semitism. After all, many Jews in North America who see themselves as Zionists have themselves been critical of Israeli government policy (Schoenfeld, Shaffir, and Weinfeld 2006, 293).

Another feature of Cohen's (1997) definition that is useful in understanding Jewish communities outside of Israel is the idea that the diaspora can also be a site of creativity. Cohen argues that even though many diaspora communities have histories of traumatic dispersal from original homelands, the places where they eventually settle can also provide the basis for a vibrant and creative cultural life. Jews in the diaspora have made important contributions to education, art, music, medicine, science, and commerce around the world. Cohen (1997, 198) notes that in the early 1990s, Ali Mazrui (1990) pointed out that even though the 15 million Jews worldwide were just 0.2 per cent of the world's population, they accounted for about 25 per cent of the Nobel Prize winners. Researchers interested in other diaspora communities have also noted this seemingly paradoxical feature of diaspora life. Lebanese scholar Albert Hourani (1992, cited in Cohen 1997, 98) noted that the descendants of Lebanese migrants around the world 'boasted a President of Colombia, a prime minister of Jamaica, a majority leader in the US Senate, a Nobel Prize winner for medicine, a president of the [United Kingdom] Royal Society, a world famous heart surgeon and a prizewinning Lebanese-Australian novelist'. Cohen (1997, 24) argues that the creativity found in many ethnic diasporas may be the result of the inevitable tensions between ethnic, national, and transnational identities.

TRANSNATIONALISM

Transnationalism is defined by Basch et al. as a way of describing certain practices in which immigrants appear to be increasingly engaged. In their view, transnationalism refers to:

> the processes by which immigrants forge and sustain multi-stranded social relations that link together their societies of origin and settlement. We call these processes transnationalism to emphasize that many immigrants today build social fields that cross geographic, cultural and political borders. Immigrants who develop and maintain multiple relationships—familial, economic, social, organizational, religious, and political—that span borders we call 'transmigrants'. . . .

Transmigrants take actions, make decisions, and develop subjectivities and identities embedded in networks of relationships that connect them simultaneously to two or more nation-states (1994, 7).

Since the publication of *Nations unbound* by Basch, Glick Schiller, and Szanton Blanc (1994), several empirical studies have been undertaken under the banner of transnationalism, and others have reflected on wider conceptual and theoretical points (Levitt and de la Dehesa 2003; Portes 1999; Satzewich and Wong 2003). Vertovec summarizes this literature by suggesting that there are a number of different ways that transnationalism is defined and analyzed within social science literature. These forms include: transnationalism as social morphology or a kind of new community; transnationalism as a type of consciousness; transnationalism as a mode of cultural reproduction; transnationalism as an avenue of capital; and transnationalism as a site of political engagement (Vertovec 1999, 455).

Transnationalism as social morphology refers to the formation of new kinds of ethnic communities. In some ways, these communities are similar to what Cohen describes as diasporas. In Vertovec's view, transnational ethnic communities are made up out of a triadic relationship between globally dispersed but collectively self-identified ethnic groups, the territorial states where these groups live, and the homeland states where they or their ancestors came from (Vertovec 1999, 449). For example, Italians who have settled outside of Italy can be characterized as a transnational community. They have a strong ethnic group identity that is sustained independently of the specific countries where they live; they have bonds of solidarity with Italians around the world; and they have complicated ties to Italy. Nicholas Harney evocatively describes the transnational connections of the Italian community in Canada in the following terms:

> [These connections] also include the personal travels of Italian Canadians to visit kin or to explore Italy with Italian-Canadian tour groups, sports teams, and student exchange programs sponsored by ethnic voluntary organizations. Some hardworking Italian Canadians who laboured, for example, in construction in Canada for thirty years, invest in land and build new homes in their village of birth (1998,7).

Moreover, Italians living abroad are now able to vote in national elections in Italy and can elect their own legislators to represent their particular interests as a transnational community.

Transnationalism as a type of consciousness refers to the multiple and overlapping identities that individuals now possess. Simmons and Plaza (2006, 142–3) argue that in Canada, many of the children of immigrants from various countries in the Caribbean have developed co-ethnic transnational identities. These hybrid identities are reflected in their 'engagement with Caribbean art, music, food, dress, religion, social norms, myths, customs and "language"' (Simmons and Plaza 2006, 143). At the same time, these identities are also reflected in things like language code-switching, which involves conversing in 'proper' English when talking to authority figures but slipping into patois when talking to close friends. This kind of hybrid identity allows youth whose parents came from the Caribbean to engage both with Canadian society and with the real and imagined societies of their parents or grandparents. Simmons and Plaza (2006, 143) argue further that code-switching is a new form of transnational social incorporation: 'one code facilitates better incorporation in mainstream Canadian institutions, jobs, and lifestyles, while the other code facilitates the development of networks of friendship and support within the community'.

Some scholars within the field of transnational studies argue that this kind of code-switching, along with the broader development of hybrid, transnational identities, has its social origins in social exclusion in the country of settlement. That is, some argue that experiences of racism, social exclusion, and non-acceptance in countries like Canada, the United States, and Britain, are factors that encourage members of some groups to retain their ancestral origin identities. If people are made to feel unwelcome or as not truly belonging to the imagined community of the nation, then they seek social and psychological protection and find a sense of belonging in their ethnic communities and ancestral identities (Simmons and Plaza 2006; Faist 2000).

Transnationalism as a mode of cultural reproduction, according to Vertovec (1999, 451), refers to the contemporary fluidity of constructed styles, social institutions, and everyday practices. The intermingling of cultures that is reflected in fashion, music, and films involves a complex process of give-and-take between various national and international traditions. In the area of transnational fashions, for example, scholars are interested in how forms, styles, and materials associated with nationally based heritage intersect with international styles of dress and how these new transnational styles reflect shifting identities and power relations in society (Bryden and Niessen 1998).

The 'Bollywood' film industry is a good example of what authors like Vertovec mean when they refer to transnationalism as a mode of cultural production. Though originally intended for Indian audiences, films produced in India are now widely available in North America and Europe, reflecting the ability of members of Indian communities outside of India to have access to film entertainment. This internationalization of the Bollywood film industry is also leading to changes in film styles. As more Indians in Britain and North America consume this form of entertainment, new 'Western' themes, issues, and styles are being introduced into the Bollywood film industry. Musical forms and tastes are also being reconfigured as a result of complex interactions between places of origin and places of settlement. According to Tatla (1999, 68), bhangra music, which was originally a form of Punjabi folk dancing, has become a 'byword for Asian music, especially in Britain'. Tatla argues that

> Although it had a humble beginning in the 1960s, several bhangra groups became quite prominent by the 1980s . . . while maintaining their regional roots in Punjabi lyrics, bhangra bands are trying to 'cross over' into Western music. British bhangra groups perform in places as far apart as Los Angeles, Frankfurt, and Singapore, whereas Punjab's pop singers make regular appearances in the diaspora (1999, 68).

When Vertovec speaks of transnationalism as an avenue of capital, he is refer-ring to the increasing international movement of money and resources. The move-ment of money and resources can take many forms. There are, for example, transnational capitalists who both live their lives and make their investment deci-sions in the context of networks that not only span their country of origin and their country of settlement but also the globe. Wong and Ho (2006, 249–52) describe Vic-tor Li, the eldest son of Li Ka-Shing (the 19th richest person in the world in 2004, according to *Forbes* magazine) as one of a growing number of transnational capital-ists. Li came to Canada in the 1980s and is a Canadian citizen. His migration to Canada was motivated in part by his family's desire to pursue dispersal as a way of protecting their business interests in the context of the British government's han-dover of Hong Kong to China in 1999. Li's business interests are both massive and diverse. His companies invest in Canada, Hong Kong, and the global marketplace. One of his conglomerates, Cheung Hong, is involved in property development, real estate, hotels, telecommunications, e-commerce, ports and related services, and energy, to name only a few. It has operations in 40 countries, employs over 175,000 people, and is ranked among the top 100 corporations in the world (Wong and Ho 2006, 250). While the case of Victor Li may be exceptional in terms of the vast amount of wealth he controls, Wong and Ho (2006) argue that smaller-scale transnational investments on the part of other Chinese Canadians are also an important aspect of capital flows between Canada and Hong Kong.

The transnational movement of money and capital is not just confined to large corporations that invest around the world but also includes the money and resources that flow around the world from 'ordinary' individuals in support of their families and friends. For many developing countries around the world, remittances are an increasingly important part of their respective Gross Domestic Product. In 1994 alone, for example, Pakistani workers around the world sent US $1.4 billion to Pakistan; Indians remitted US $5 billion to India and Bangladeshis US $1.1 billion to Bangladesh (Castles and Miller 2003, 170). The US $9 billion in remittances that is sent every year by Mexicans living in the United States to family members in Mex-ico (Castles and Miller 2003, 152) is the Mexican economy's biggest source of for-eign income; remittances provide more foreign income to Mexico than oil, tourism, or foreign investment (Lugo 2003). The International Monetary Fund estimates that in 2001, US $28.4 billion was sent out of the United States alone to other countries in the form of remittances (Wong and Ho 2006, 258).

Many ethnic and religious communities encourage individuals who have moved abroad to invest in not-for-profit projects in their ancestral homelands. These investments constitute yet another form of the transnational movement of money and resources. For example, over the past 30 years, Sikhs in North America, Britain, and Malaysia have helped to fund a variety of schools, shrines, health cen-tres, and community welfare agencies, all of which are intended to promote the well-being of communities in the Punjab (Tatla 1999, 64–5). Since 1991, Ukrainians in North America have helped to fund the construction of churches, stock libraries, and provide resources for medical aid as a result of the Chernobyl nuclear accident in Ukraine (Satzewich 2002). Many other ethnic communities around the world support similar projects in their respective ancestral homelands. The scale of funding for these kinds of transnationally funded, non-profit projects in various ancestral homelands appears to be substantial but is difficult to quantify precisely because much of the funding goes through informal channels and is not necessarily recorded in government statistics.

Transnationalism as a site of political engagement refers in part to the ways that immigrants and members of ethnic communities continue to engage in the political processes in their respective homelands. As noted above in the case of Italians, this form of transnationalism can involve formal involvement in homeland elections. A related dimension to transnationalism as a site of political engagement is the existence of dual citizenship. Approximately 90 countries around the world currently allow dual citizenship, and it is estimated that 500,000 Canadians currently living in Canada possess dual citizenship (Fong 2006, A1). Dual citizenship provides certain individuals with citizenship rights and obligations in two countries. For some individuals, the desire for dual citizenship pertains mainly to symbolic ethnicity. Political attachment to an ancestral homeland through the possession of citizenship is simply used to reaffirm a sense of roots or identity, with little or no formal involvement in the homeland. In other cases, however, there are more instrumental reasons for individuals wishing to have and retain dual citizenship. In an age of globalization, dual citizenship can not only facilitate travel but also make investing and doing business easier in both an ancestral and an adopted homeland. Individuals who possess dual citizenship and have business interests in two or more countries may be able to use their multiple citizenships to negotiate more favourable tax policies or to gain access to state subsidies not available to non-citizens.

Political engagement with an ancestral homeland can also occur in the absence of dual citizenship. It can involve support for specific political parties in the homeland, lobbying government officials in countries of settlement, and support for the democratic process more generally. The Ukrainian Canadian Congress, with the financial support of the Canadian government, helped to organize and send individuals of Ukrainian heritage to Ukraine to help monitor the fairness of the parliamentary elections there in 2004 and again in 2006. In the 1990s, Croatians in Canada, the United States, Germany, and Australia raised nearly US $4 million in support of the Hrvatska Democratska Zajednica, one of the main political parties in Croatia (Winland 2006, 266). And many ethnic groups lobby government officials in their countries of settlement to help support the development of favourable foreign policies toward ancestral homeland governments. For example, the Canadian government was one of the first countries to recognize an independent Ukrainian state in 1991 in part because of lobbying by the Ukrainian Canadian community in Canada.

A number of important questions have arisen about dual citizenship and transnational political ties. First, the conflict between Israel and Lebanon in the summer of 2006 raised the question of what kinds of obligations countries like Canada have toward their citizens who have citizenship in another country if they appear to have moved away from Canada relatively permanently and have rather thin connections to this country. It is estimated that before the conflict began, approximately 50,000 Lebanese Canadians lived in Lebanon. During the conflict, 15,000 Lebanese Canadians were evacuated from Lebanon at a cost to the Canadian government of about $85 million; as many as one-half of those evacuated have since returned to Lebanon (Fong 2006). The issues arising out of the evacuation led Citizenship and Immigration Canada to begin a review of the rights and responsibilities associated with dual citizenship (Fong 2006).

Second, what do these kinds of transnational political engagements mean with regard to where political loyalties truly lie? That is, when Italian Canadians vote in the election of representatives to the Italian parliament or when Ukrainian Canadians lobby the Canadian government on an issue related to Ukraine, does this mean that members of these communities are less loyal to Canada? And what happens if conflicts arise between the Canadian government and the ancestral homeland that an ethnic or immigrant community politically supports or is simply from?

In chapter 2, we saw that on occasions when Canada was in conflict with another country, immigrants and ethnic community members who maintained real and imagined political or social relationships with that country were defined as threats to Canada. Perceptions about divided loyalties created concern on the part of Canadian government officials, who feared that some groups' homeland-related activities and identities undermined social and political stability in this country. For example, Japanese Canadians were interned and/or put into prisoner of war camps during the Second World War for their real and imagined transnational political ties and identities (Sugiman 2006). Nearly 8,600 Ukrainians and other peoples were interned in labour camps during the First World War. These were people unlucky enough to have come from the Austro-Hungarian Empire who had yet to take out Canadian citizenship when war broke out with the Triple Alliance in 1914. Ukrainians and others were interned in part because of their perceived political loyalties to the Austro-Hungarian Empire and in part because they were perceived as a potential fifth column, ready to surreptitiously undermine the war effort in this country (Kordan 2002). In both cases, real and imagined ties to ancestral homelands put immigrants in political jeopardy and resulted in harsh treatment by the federal government.

It is important to note that these kinds of fears have not necessarily dissipated in the early twenty-first century. As we noted in chapter 6, some Muslim and Arab Canadians worry that their real and imagined interest in maintaining social and political ties with their countries of origin makes them targets of special state surveillance because they are suspected of supporting terrorist organizations and causes (Arat-Koc 2006). Members of other ethnic and religious communities have also been labelled as terrorists or as supporters of terrorist causes by the media or by governments for their real and imagined support of political causes in their homelands. In North America and Britain, Sikh support for independence for Punjab has historically been of special concern to governments, and the bombing of an Air India flight from Vancouver in 1985 placed segments of the Sikh community in Vancouver under even more scrutiny for its suspected links to terrorist activity (Tatla 1999, 174–5).

The irony of targeting and putting immigrants and ethnic community members under special surveillance because they maintain either real or imagined interests in the politics of their respective homelands and may lobby the Canadian government for favourable political and economic relationships with their countries of origin is that these interests and this lobbying might actually lead to better social and political integration in Canada. Clearly, there is a difference between support for terrorist causes or the use of violence to achieve political ends in an ancestral home-land and legitimate ethnic mobilization around foreign policy issues. The latter can benefit social and political culture in Canada and other countries of settlement because it helps groups to learn the political ropes and how to make political com-promises and it reinforces the values of democracy and pluralism (Wayland 2006).

FIVE CRITICAL COMMENTS

The concepts of diaspora and transnationalism have pointed social scientists in use-ful directions. As we have seen, it is true that some immigrants return to their coun-tries of origin or move on to other locations. Vaira Vike-Frieberga came to Canada as a child from Latvia after the Second World War. She spent most of her adult life as a professor of psychology at the University of Montreal, but she returned to Latvia after her retirement and in 1999 became its president (Wayland 2006, 27). Many other individuals who left their countries of origin are now returning to participate in the social, economic, and political affairs of those countries. It is also true that some migrant populations eventually become permanent residents and citizens of the state where they settled. Many undocumented Mexican workers who originally entered the United States temporarily have lived in the country for dozens of years. Clearly, where people come from undoubtedly plays a critical role in identity and group formation. Thus, advocates of both concepts have identified a number of important aspects of immigrant and ethnic group life. At the same time, however, a number of notes of caution should be raised about some of the wider conceptual claims that these approaches make. In the concluding part of this chapter, we want to highlight five particular reservations.

Are 'old' distinctions passé?

First, the distinction between 'immigrants', 'migrants', 'refugees', and other categories of people who cross international borders is not simply relevant to an earlier phase of migration within the world system. As we pointed out in chapter 3, the socio-legal distinctions between immigrants, migrants, and illegal immigrants have real conse-quences, particularly at the level of state policy, citizenship, and access to public resources. In many countries, the distinction between 'migrants' (who only have the right of temporary entry and settlement), 'immigrants' (who have the right of per-manent residence in their country of destination), and 'illegal immigrants' is still an important point of differentiation in citizenship rights and associated claims to access to certain public resources (Satzewich 2006). Moreover, these socio-legal con-siderations have an impact on processes of community formation and associated transnational practices—issues that are obviously dear to scholars working within both the diaspora and the transnational frameworks. To state the obvious, migrant workers, like those who come to Canada every year from Mexico and have the right of temporary entry but face restrictions on their ability to circulate within particu-lar national labour markets, are forced into being 'transnational' and at the same time face serious external constraints on their ability to become or form part of a relatively permanent 'diaspora' community in the countries where they work. Immigrants, with the right to permanent settlement, have more options and face different sets of constraints and concerns.

Is transnationalism historically new?

Second, while Basch et al. (1994) may have been correct in their assumption that 'the popular' image of immigrants was one of 'uprootedness' and 'permanent rupture from their ancestral homelands', earlier research on immigrant and migrant incorporation did in fact recognize the complexity of migratory flows, the fluidity of international boundaries, and migrants' complicated attachment to and relationship with their ancestral homelands. Some authors were in fact silent on transnationalism and the significance of homeland ties and identities, but others did pay attention to 'transnationalism', although they may not necessarily have labelled the activities and behaviour as such (Winland 1998). As some historians have been at pains to point out, immigrants have always had a transnational orientation, although the forms and intensity of transnationalism may have become more complex (Gabaccia 2000).

For example, American historian Marcus Lee Hansen, author of *The immigrant in American history* (1940) and *The Atlantic migration: 1607–1860* (1961) was well aware of transnational connections, the fluidity of international boundaries, and the influence of 'home countries' on the lives, experiences, and practices of immigrants in North America. In an essay titled 'Migration across the northern border', published in 1936, Hansen argued that

> . . . no population study of historical interest is complete if it ignores the fact that the Canadian-American boundary, which meant so much to the diplomat, legislator and tradesman, was non-existent in the consciousness of the unnumbered hundreds of thousands who were doing the principal jobs of the century—turning the wilderness into farms and homes (1940, 177).

Hansen's early recognition of the fluidity of international borders and identities was not just relevant to his analysis of Canada/US patterns of migration. In an overview of the field titled 'Immigration as a field for historical research', originally published in 1926, Hansen was acutely aware that European immigrants to the United States had complicated identities and relationships with their ancestral homelands. According to Hansen, immigrants and their descendants had

> . . . on occasion, . . . been more interested in fighting the battles of the old country than in participating in the affairs of the new. . . . Research will probably reveal that the emergence of the new nations of Eastern and Central Europe in consequence of the World War was possible only because there had existed in America, for a generation or two, active colonies of those nationalities, which had kept alive the ideal of independence and could offer financial support and political pressure at the critical moment (1940, 211–12).

Furthermore, in a rather prescient observation made in 1967, Anthony Richmond concludes his book *Post-war immigrants in Canada* with the following observation:

Nationalism, and questions of political allegiance, are likely to remain important social issues in Canada, as in may other parts of the world, in the foreseeable future. Nevertheless, if migration, like other forms of occupational and social mobility, is functionally necessary in industrialized societies, concepts such as 'absorption', 'assimilation', and 'integration' may no longer have any sociological significance. Instead it will be necessary to focus attention upon specific social processes such as group formation, socialization, occupational mobility, and the changing reference models of migrants and non-migrants respectively. It becomes anachronistic to assume that migrants will settle permanently in a particular country or locality. It will be important to make the optimum use of their occupational skills for the duration of their stay and to facilitate the rapid assumption and relinquishment of social ties. The political and social institutions of urban societies will have to be adapted to the needs of *transilient* rather than sedentary populations (Richmond 1967, 278; emphasis ours).

Clearly, earlier work in the field did recognize the fluidity of boundaries and borders, the transitory nature of identity, and the impact of the 'homeland' on the lives, consciousness, and social and political organization of immigrants and ethnic groups (Brubaker 2005). In some ways, criticisms of the so-called 'traditional' work are based on the construction of a straw man.

The usual rejoinder to this historical critique of the concept of transnationalism is that new communications and transportation technologies have made transnational practices more intense, more immediate, and more systematic than in the past. Portes et al. (1999, 225) argue that while previous generations of immigrants engaged in practices that reinforced bonds between their country of origin and their country of settlement, these activities lacked the 'regularity, routine involvement, and critical mass characterizing contemporary examples of transnationalism'. While they recognize that there are some legitimate examples of transnationalism in the past—particularly 'elite-type' transnationalism and long-distance trading relationships—they are largely exceptional cases that are not relevant for the vast majority of Europeans who left their ancestral homelands in the first half of the twentieth century. In their view, 'contemporary transnationalism corresponds to a different period in the evolution of the world economy and to a different set of responses and strategies by people in a condition of disadvantage to its dominant logic. Herein lies the import of its emergence' (Portes et al. 1999, 227).

However, few have *systematically* compared the similarities and differences between the 'old' ways that immigrants maintained ties with their homelands through letters, telexes, trains, and ships and the new forms of transnationalism facilitated by faxes, e-mail, and fast airplanes (but see Glick Schiller 1999). While it is obvious that communications and transportation technologies have evolved, it is not obvious that these technologies have produced *qualitatively* different kinds of communities, patterns of settlement, and adjustment. In other words, differences between then and now have tended to be asserted rather than demonstrated.

Are nation-states irrelevant?

Third, are nation-states really irrelevant in a supposedly transnational world? How important are states versus international norms and conventions in shaping the lives and rights of immigrants? Christian Joppke (1999; Soysal 2000) argues that within liberal democracies, the main source of immigrant rights still tend to be domestic in nature. While not discounting the role of international human rights norms, regimes, and conventions, Joppke argues that in states with a 'robust liberal infra-structure and tradition, there is no need to resort to international norms'. In contrast, he suggests that international human rights norms matter mostly in 'illiberal or newly liberalizing states'. Perhaps the most telling example of Joppke's point is the United Nations Convention on the Protection of the Rights of Migrant Workers, which came into force in July 2003. The convention has generated far more interest in 'liberalizing states' than in the 'developed world'. The 32 states that had adopted the convention as of 1 January 2004 include: Azerbaijan, Bangladesh, Belize, Bolivia, Bosnia and Herzegovina, Burkina Faso, Cape Verde, Chile, Colombia, Comoros, Ecuador, Egypt, El Salvador, Ghana, Guatemala, Guinea-Bissau, Kyrgyzstan, Mali, Mexico, Morocco, Paraguay, Philippines, Sao Tome and Principe, Senegal, Seychelles, Sierra Leone, Sri Lanka, Tajikistan, Togo, Turkey, Uganda, and Uruguay. There are a number of notable absences from this list: Australia, Canada, the United States, and all of the European Union countries (Satzewich 2006). Clearly, one common denominator in the list above is that it is made up of immigrant-sending countries. The question of why advanced, industrialized, immigrant-receiving countries have not signed on to the convention needs to be the subject of further research (Weisbrodt 1999). However, their failure to do so points to the limited role that this particular international charter plays in migrant-receiving countries and the continuing relevance of state-based charters, human rights codes, and legislation in shaping the rights that migrants and immigrants have and claim.

Clearly, states and nations still weigh heavily on diaspora and transnational politics and identity. As Anthias (1998, 570) notes, diasporas may finance various kinds of national struggles and projects, and nation-states see their respective diasporas as resources and use real and imagined bonds of ethnicity to secure capital, financial aid, and political influence. States, particularly in the aftermath of 11 September 2001, also continue to spend considerable resources on border control to protect the integrity of the nation-state. Canada and the United States are taking active and cooperative measures to beef up border control and border security, including the sharing of more information.

Is assimilation irrelevant?

Fourth, some of the previous work on immigrants and ethnic relations was more relational and nuanced than contemporary critics give it credit for. That is, before the 'discovery' of transnationalism, earlier generations of scholars studied how immigrants settled into their new country, their occupational careers, their educational adjustment, their attitudinal, cultural, and structural assimilation, *and* the extent to which they lost or maintained their old-world identities and ties (Alba and Nee 1999). Some conceptualized the immigrant settlement process as a trade-off between integration and ethnic maintenance. Ironically, however, in searching for evidence of transnational practices, some present-day scholars seem to have forgotten that immigrants and members of ethnic groups who engage in transnational activities or practices have jobs or run businesses in their country of settlement, join trade unions or business associations, vote in and occasionally run in elections, send their children to school, watch television, buy groceries, and take visiting relatives to see Niagara Falls. That is, at the same time that immigrants maintain their transnational or diaspora identities and practices, they also reproduce their conditions of existence in their country of residence and settlement. These routine and everyday non-transnational activities are just as important to understand as voting in an election back home, sending money to relatives, and spending time in the old country. Some contemporary studies of transnationalism leave the impression that all immigrants or ethnic groups do is 'be' transnational (Roberts, Frank, and Lozano-Ascencio 1999).

The concept of diaspora is somewhat insulated from this shortcoming in that it recognizes the dialectical nature of immigrant and ethnic group incorporation. Cohen's (1997) approach recognizes that the material conditions that propel people to leave their countries of origin have an impact on the formation of diaspora consciousness, although he does not systematically examine how the conditions that led people to leave shapes their adjustment to their new homeland. Cohen also recognizes that diasporas often have an uneasy relationship with the host society and that the diaspora can be a site of creativity. Thus, the concept of diaspora may be more useful for recognizing the relational aspects of settlement and continued engagement with a distant homeland than the concept of transnationalism.

Marginality and exclusion a driving force of transnationalism?

Fifth, is marginality and exclusion, in both the country of origin and the country of settlement, responsible for transnationalism? Some scholars seem to be unaware of the contradictions inherent in their own work. That is, while marginalization, exclusion, and blocked mobility are important themes in the analysis of transnationalism, many of the same researchers also acknowledge that there is an 'elite'-level transnationalism in which relatively privileged groups participate in the international circulation of capital, commodities, and services. Faist's (2000, 196) example of this kind of transnationalism is 'the hypermobile Chinese businessmen in North America'. He argues that 'these "astronauts" establish a business, say, in Singapore, but locate their families in Los Angeles, New York or Toronto to maximize the educational opportunities for their children or as a safe haven in the event of political unrest'. While it is true that this group of business immigrants in Canada and elsewhere have been racialized, and while the children of the 'astronauts' may face a certain amount of everyday racism in North America (Li 1994), it is difficult to argue that these wealthy capitalists and their families face serious economic disadvantages, deprivation, and blocked mobility in Canadian society and that their 'disadvantage' in Canada contributes to their transnational identities or practices.

Other research suggests that socially marginal communities are not the only ones engaged in transnational activities (Matthews and Satzewich 2006). For instance, immigrants from the United States in Canada, while generally economically privileged, appear to engage in many of the same individual and institutional-level transnational practices that other less advantaged immigrants do. According to research conducted by John Hagan (2001) on American war resisters in Canada, many Americans in Canada regularly travel to the United States to visit friends and family or on vacation. Many have gone back to live in the United States for periods of time and then return to Canada. Furthermore, research shows that American immigrants in Toronto have a lower than average rate of home ownership in the city, and Murdie and Teixeira (2003, 177) argue that this is due in part to the fact that 'Americans employed by US-owned firms view their stay in Toronto as transitory'. Furthermore, Americans have one of the lowest rates of citizenship acquisition of all immigrant groups in Canada. It is not implausible to suggest that this is in part because they continue to identify at some level with their ancestral homeland and because like other transnational immigrants, they want to keep their options open both for themselves and for their children. Americans in Canada have plenty of access to information about their ancestral homeland and can easily follow American economic, political, cultural, and sporting events. Both Democrats Abroad and Republicans Abroad encourage continued political participation in the US by American citizens who have moved abroad (Matthews and Satzewich 2006). In short, marginality, blocked mobility, and socio-economic deprivation are not the only forces driving transnationalism.

SUMMARY

Over the past 20 years, the concepts of 'diaspora' and 'transnationalism' have become central to scholarly scripts about immigrant and ethnic community life. The concepts share similar critiques of existing literature and display similar concerns about the changing nature of immigrant and ethnic group activities, practices, and community life. For example, when Alejandro Portes et al. (1999, 221) talk about the transnational practices of immigrants that include 'the manifold socio-cultural enterprises oriented toward the reinforcement of a national identity abroad or the collective enjoyment of cultural goods', they seem to be talking about the same thing that Robin Cohen (1997) describes as a diaspora's effort to maintain a strong ethnic group consciousness over time.

Despite their common recent histories and common analytical concerns, the concept of diaspora has been more sharply criticized than the concept of transnationalism. Further, each concept has been developed largely within its own problematic. While there have been some efforts to delineate the proper relationship between the concepts of diaspora and transnational, this chapter has suggested that solutions proposing that 'diaspora' should be thought of as one particular form of transnational community are problematic. The chapter has offered an alternative way of thinking about the relationship between these two important concepts. It has suggested that the two are more compatible than some who work within the transnational perspective imply and that one way to reconcile them is to define transnationalism as a set of practices in which diasporas, immigrants, and others engage.

Questions for Critical Thought

1. According to Cohen, what are the main characteristic features of diasporas? Think of a group that you are familiar with and see if it fits his ideal type.
2. What arguments have scholars used to justify their use of the concepts of diaspora and transnationalism? How convincing are these arguments?
3. What kinds of transnational ties do immigrants have with their various countries of origin? Does transnationalism undermine a commitment to Canada?
4. What, if anything, is historically new about modern forms of transnationalism?
5. How do sociologists explain the apparent growth in transnational activities over the past 20 years?

Annotated Additional Readings

Cohen, Robin. 1997. *Global diasporas: An introduction*. Seattle: University of Washington Press. Cohen makes a comprehensive case for the utility of the concept of diaspora. The book is wide-ranging in scope and examines various forms of diasporas around the world.

Basch, Linda, Nina Glick Schiller, and Christine Szanton Blanc. 1994. *Nations unbound: Transnational projects, postcolonial predicaments and deterritorialized nation-states*. Amsterdam: Gordon and Breach. A highly influential early statement of the transnational approach. Most of the examples are taken from the American context.

Satzewich, Vic, and Lloyd Wong (Eds). 2006. *Transnational communities in Canada*. Vancouver: University of British Columbia Press. An edited collection containing articles on transnationalism in Canada by some of this country's leading historians, anthropologists, sociologists, geographers, and political scientists.

Related Websites

African Diaspora Policy Center: http://www.diaspora-centre.org/.
Global Networks Journal: http://www.globalnetworksjournal.com/.
International Organization for Migration: http://www.iom.ch/.
Scottish Diaspora Project—The Tartan Transformation Project: http://tartan.communitiesofthefuture.org/scottish-diaspora.html.
Transnational Communities Program, Oxford University: http://www.transcomm.ox.ac.uk/.

Notes

CHAPTER 4

1. It should be mentioned that elite theorists of the Porter tradition have looked at the class composition of ethnic groups (Clement 1975). However, they have only looked at their upper echelons, which comprise a very small group of people in elite positions. They have not examined the entire class structure of ethnic groups. See Nakhaie (2000) for an updated exchange between Nakhaie and Ogmundson and McLaughlin on the dominant position of the British in the Canadian elite.

2. Winn (1988) uses income, not earnings, in his analysis of inequality. Income as a measure includes investments and government transfers, along with wages, salaries, and self-employment income. As Boyd suggests, it is not a very good indicator of labour market inequalities (1992, 281). We have chosen earnings for our analysis. We have also chosen not to exclude those with negative earnings, unlike some researchers (Lian and Matthews 1998). See Li (1988, 1992) and Hou and Balakrishnan (1999), among others, for earnings used as an appropriate measure of inequality.

3. Thomas Sowell (1989) makes a similar and more theoretically informed argument against affirmative action programs in the United States and other countries.

4. It should be made clear that this chapter is not about racism in general or discrimination in the labour market. It is about earnings differentials and the internal stratification of ethnic groups in terms of their class, gender, and nativity dimensions. Unfortunately, there are not many studies or much preponderant evidence to support claims about discrimination in the Canadian labour market. See Henry and Ginzberg (1988) for a 1985 study of 201 jobs offers showing evidence of discrimination based on 'race'. See also an unpublished 1989 restudy of the Economic Council of Canada (1991), which claims that 'no discrimination was discernable' (Henry 1999, 233). Others, like de Silva (1992), argue that once immigrants are hired 'there is no significant discrimination against immigrants in general. . . . More important, there is no detectable general tendency to discriminate against immigrants originating from the Third World' (1992, 37). Levitt (1994) puts forward the issue of relativity and the historical specificity of racism. He provides evidence that racism and discrimination are diminishing and argues that Canada today is not, in fact, a racist country, compared to earlier periods of time and other countries. This, of course, does not diminish the importance of combating racism. No 'degree' of racism is acceptable.

5. In our class model, the category 'employers' refers to small employers. We suggest that since Statistics Canada does not ask employers how many people they actually employ and for confidentiality reasons places limits on reported earnings ($250,000), people in this category are small employers. In all probability, big employers make a lot more than this per annum.

6. This result should not be considered unusual. Consistently, across censuses from 1986 to 2006, the petty bourgeoisie has been the lowest-earning class and the proletariat the second lowest. Nikos Poulantzas has also claimed that the petty bourgeoisie shares an affinity with the working class (see Li 1992). Marx might have been right after all.

CHAPTER 5

1. Parts of this chapter first appeared in: Nikolaos Liodakis and Vic Satzewich. 1998, 2003. 'From solution to problem: Multiculturalism and 'race relations' as new social problems'. In Wayne Antony and Les Samuelson (Eds), *Power and resistance: Critical thinking about Canadian social issues*, 2nd edn, 95–114, 3rd edn, 145–68. Halifax: Fernwood Press.

2. The definition provided here is the one adopted by Statistics Canada (2001). In the litera-ture, and often in popular parlance, first generation refers to the immigrant parents, born outside Canada, whereas immigrant offspring who were foreign-born but were raised or became adults in Canada are called 'the 1.5 generation' or second generation. Third and all subsequent generations refer to offspring who were born and raised in Canada.

References

Abraham, Carolyn. 2005. 'Race: Five years ago, the Human Genome Project said race didn't exist. Now, huge scientific projects are studying the genetic traits of ethnic groups. What happened?' *The Globe and Mail* 18 June: F1.

Abu-Laban, Yasmeen, and Christina Gabriel. 2002. *Selling diversity: Immigration, multiculturalism, employment equity and globalization.* Peterborough: Broadview Press.

————, and Daiva Stasiulis. 1992. 'Ethnic pluralism under siege: Popular and partisan opposition to multiculturalism'. *Canadian Public Policy* 27 (4):365–86.

Adams, Howard. 1999. *Tortured people: The politics of colonization.* Penticton: Theytus Books.

Agnew, Vijay. 1996. *Resisting discrimination: Women from Asia, Africa, and the Caribbean and the women's movement in Canada.* Toronto: University of Toronto Press.

Agocs, Carol, and Monica Boyd. 1993. 'The Canadian ethnic mosaic recast for the 90s'. In James Curtis, Edward Grabb, and Neil Guppy (Eds), *Social inequality in Canada: Patterns, problems, policies,* 2nd edn, 330–52. Scarborough: Prentice Hall Canada.

Akenson, Donald. 1995. 'The historiography of English speaking Canada and the concept of diaspora: A sceptical appreciation'. *Canadian Historical Review* 76 (3):377–410.

Alba, Richard, and Victor Nee. 1999. 'Rethinking assimilation theory for a new era of immigration'. In Charles Hirschman et al. (Eds), *The handbook of international migration: The American experience.* New York: Russell Sage Foundation.

Alfred, Gerald. 1995. *Heeding the voices of our ancestors: Kahnawake Mohawk politics and the rise of Native nationalism.* Toronto: Oxford University Press.

Alfred, Taiaiake. 1999. *Peace, power and righteousness: An indigenous manifesto.* Toronto: Oxford University Press.

Allahar, Anton. 1998. 'Race and Racism: Strategies of Resistance'. In Vic Satzewich (Ed.). *Racism and Social Inequality in Canada.* Toronto: Thompson Educational Publishers.

Allen, Robert. 1993. *His Majesty's Indian allies: British Indian policy in the defence of Canada, 1774–1815.* Toronto: Dundurn Press.

Amit-Talai, V., and C. Knowles (Eds). 1996. *Re-situating identities: The politics of race, ethnicity and culture.* Peterborough: Broadview Press.

Andersen, Kay. 1991. *Vancouver's Chinatown: Racial discourse in Canada, 1875–1980.* Montreal and Kingston: McGill-Queen's University Press.

Anderson, Alan, and James Frideres. 1980. *Ethnicity in Canada: Theoretical perspectives.* Toronto: Butterworths.

Anderson, Kim. 2000. *A recognition of being: Reconstructing Native womanhood.* Toronto: Sumach Press.

Angus Reid Group, Inc. 1991. *Multiculturalism and Canadians: Attitude study 1991.* Submitted to Multiculturalism and Citizenship Canada.

Anthias, Floya. 1998. 'Evaluating "diaspora": Beyond ethnicity?' *Sociology* 32 (3):557–80.

Arat-Koc, Sedef. 2006. 'Whose transnationalism? Canada: Clash of civilizations discourse, and Arab and Muslim Canadians'. In Vic Satzewich and Lloyd Wong (Eds), *Transnational identities and practices in Canada*. Vancouver: University of British Columbia Press.

Assembly of First Nations. 2001. 'Assembly of First Nations—The story'.

———. 2006. 'Key elements of the Indian residential schools settlement agreement'.

Association of Black Law Enforcers. 2003. 'Official position on "racial profiling" in Canada'. Toronto: Association of Black Law Enforcers.

Avery, Donald. 1995. *Reluctant host: Canada's response to immigrant workers, 1896–1994*. Toronto: McClelland and Stewart.

Backhouse, Constance. 1999. *Colour-coded: A legal history of racism in Canada, 1900–1950*. Toronto: University of Toronto Press.

Bakan, Abigail, and Daiva Stasiulis (Eds). 1997. *Not one of the family: Foreign domestic workers in Canada*. Toronto: University of Toronto Press.

Bansak, Cynthia, and Steven Raphael. 2001. 'Immigration reform and the earnings of Latino workers: Do employer sanctions cause discrimination?' *Industrial and Labour Relations Review* 54 (2):275–95.

Banton, Michael. 1970. 'The concept of racism'. In S. Zubaida (Ed.), *Race and racialism*. London: Tavistock.

———. 1977. *The idea of race*. London: Tavistock.

———. 1979. 'Analytical and folk concepts of race and ethnicity'. *Ethnic and Racial Studies* 2:12–38.

———. 1987. *Racial theories*. London: Cambridge University Press.

———. 2002. *The international politics of race*. Cambridge: Cambridge University Press.

Barker, Martin. 1981. *The new racism*. London: Junction Books.

Basch, Linda, Nina Glick Schiller, and Christina Szanton Blanc. 1994. *Nations unbound: Transnational projects, postcolonial predicaments and deterritorialized nation-states*. Amsterdam: Gordon and Breach Publishers.

Basok, Tanya. 2002. *Tortillas and tomatoes: Transmigrant Mexican harvesters in Canada*. Montreal and Kingston: McGill-Queen's University Press.

Basran, Gurcharn, and B. Singh Bolaria. 2003. *The Sikhs in Canada: Migration, race, class and gender*. New Delhi: Oxford University Press.

———, and Li Zong. 1998. 'Devaluation of foreign credentials as perceived by non-white professional immigrants'. *Canadian Ethnic Studies* 30:6–23.

Beaujot, Roderic, and Kevin McQuillan. 1982. *Growth and dualism: The demographic development of Canadian society*. Toronto: Gage.

Bibby, Reginald. 1990. *Mosaic madness*. Toronto: Stoddart.

Bissoondath, Neil. 1994. *Selling illusions: The cult of multiculturalism*. Toronto: Penguin.

Black, Jerome, and David Hagen. 1993. 'Quebec immigration politics and policy: Historical and contemporary perspectives'. In Alain-G. Gagnon (Ed.), *Québec: State and society*, 2nd edn. Toronto: Nelson Canada.

Bolaria, B. Singh, and Peter Li. 1988. *Racial oppression in Canada*. 2nd edn. Toronto: Garamond Press.

Boldt, Menno. 1993. *Surviving as Indians: The challenge of self-government*. Toronto: University of Toronto Press.

Bonacich, Edna. 1972. 'A theory of ethnic antagonism: The split labour market'. *American Sociological Review* 37:547–59.

———. 1976. 'Advanced capitalism and black-white relations in the United States: A split labour market interpretation'. *American Sociological Review* 41:34–51.

———. 1979. 'The past, present and future of split labour market theory'. In Cora Bagley Marrett and Cheryl Leggon (Eds), *Research in race and ethnic relations: A research annual,* vol. 1:17–64. Greenwich, CT: JAI Press.

Borjas, George. 1999. *Heaven's door: Immigration policy and the American economy.* Princeton: Princeton University Press.

Borowski, Allan, and Alan Nash. 1994. 'Business immigration'. In Howard Adelman et al. (Eds), *Immigration and refugee policy: Australia and Canada compared,* vol. 1. Carleton, Victoria: Melbourne University Press.

Borrows, John. 1997. 'Wampum at Niagara: The Royal Proclamation, Canadian legal history, and self-government'. In Michael Asch (Ed.), *Aboriginal and treaty rights in Canada.* Vancouver: University of British Columbia Press.

Bouchard, Genevieve, and Barbara Wake Carroll. 2002. 'Policy-making and administrative discretion: The case of immigration in Canada'. *Canadian Public Administration* 45 (2):239–57.

Bourhis, Richard. 2003. 'Measuring ethnocultural diversity using the Canadian census'. *Canadian Ethnic Studies* 35 (1):9–32.

Boyd, Monica. 1992. 'Gender, visible minority, and immigrant earnings inequality: Reassessing an employment equity premise'. In Vic Satzewich (Ed.), *Deconstructing a nation: Immigration, multiculturalism and racism in '90s Canada,* 279–321. Halifax: Fernwood Press.

———, John Goyder, Frank E. Jones, Hugh A. McRoberts, Peter C. Pineo, and John Porter. 1981. 'Status attainment in Canada: Findings of the Canadian Mobility Study'. *Canadian Review of Sociology and Anthropology* 18 (5):657–73.

———, and Doug Norris. 2001. 'Who are the "Canadians"? Changing census responses, 1986–1996'. *Canadian Ethnic Studies* 33 (1):1–24.

Breton, Raymond. 1964. 'Institutional completeness of ethnic communities and the personal relations of immigrants'. *American Journal of Sociology* 70:193–205.

———. 1991. *The governance of ethnic communities: Political structures and processes in Canada.* New York: Greenwood Press.

———, Wsevolod Isajiw, Warren W. Kalbach, and Jeffrey G. Reitz. 1990. *Ethnic identity and equality: Varieties of experience in a Canadian city.* Toronto: University of Toronto Press.

———, and Howard Roseborough. 1971. 'Ethnic differences in status'. In Bernard R. Blishen, Frank E. Jones, Kaspar D. Naegele, and John Porter (Eds), *Canadian society: Sociological perspectives,* 540–68. Toronto: MacMillan Canada.

Brimelow, Peter. 1995. *Alien nation: Common sense about America's immigration disaster.* New York: Random House.

Brown, Rupert. 1995. *Prejudice: Its social psychology.* Oxford: Blackwell Publishers.

Brubaker, Rogers. 2005. 'The "diaspora" diaspora'. *Ethnic and Racial Studies* 28 (1):1–19.

Bryden, Anne, and Sandra Niessen (Eds). 1998. *Consuming fashion: Adorning the transnational body.* Oxford: Berg Publishers.

Brym, Robert J., and Bonnie Fox. 1989. *From culture to power: The sociology of English Canada.* Toronto: Oxford University Press.

Calliste, Agnes. 1987. 'Sleeping car porters in Canada: An ethnically submerged split labour market'. *Canadian Ethnic Studies* 19 (1):1–20.

———. 1991. 'Canada's immigration policy and domestics from the Caribbean: The second domestic scheme'. In Jesse Vorst et al. (Eds), *Race, class, gender: Bonds and barriers*, 136–68. Toronto: Garamond Press.

———. 1996. 'Antiracism organizing and resistance in nursing: African Canadian women'. *Canadian Review of Sociology and Anthropology* 33 (3):361–90.

Canada. 1993. *Indian treaties and surrenders, from no. 281 to no. 483.* vol. 3. Saskatoon: Fifth House Publishers.

Canada. Citizenship and Immigration Canada. 2002a. *Business immigration program statistics.*

———. 2002b. *A look at Canada.* Ottawa: Minister of Public Works and Government Services.

———. 2003a. *Facts and figures.* http://www.cic.gc.ca/english/pub/facts2003/overview/1.html.

———. 2003b. *Sponsor a family member.* http://www.cic.gc.ca/english/sponsor/index.html.

———. 2003c. *Who is eligible for selection.* http://www.cic.gc.ca/english/refugees/resttle-2.html.

———. 2003d. *Will you qualify as a skilled worker?*

———. 2004. *Facts and figures, 2004: Immigration overview.*

———. 2005. *Facts and figures, 2005.* http://www.cic.gc.ca/english/pub/facts2005/permanent/17.html.

Canada. Department of Justice. 2002. *Immigration and refugee protection regulations.* http://laws.justice.gc.ca/en/I-2.5/SOR-2002-227/239632.html.

Canada. Indian and Northern Affairs Canada. 2004. *Basic departmental data 2003.* Ottawa: Indian and Northern Affairs Canada.

Canadian Race Relations Foundation. 2001. 'Canada's immigration polices: Contradictions and shortcomings'. *CRRF Perspectives: Focus on Immigration and Refugee Issues* autumn/winter. www.crr.ca/en/Publications/ePubHome.htm.

Carens, Joseph. 2000. *Culture, citizenship and community: A contextual exploration of justice and evenhandedness.* Oxford: Oxford University Press.

Carter, Sarah. 1990. *Lost harvests: Prairie Indian reserve farmers and government policy.* Montreal and Kingston: McGill-Queen's University Press.

Castles, Stephen, and Godula Kosack. 1973. *Immigrant workers and class structure in western Europe.* London: Oxford University Press.

———, and ———. 1984. *Immigrant workers and class structure in western Europe.* 2nd edn. Oxford: Oxford University Press.

———, and Mark Miller. 2003. *The age of migration: International population movements in the modern world.* 3rd edn. New York: Guilford.

Cawley, John, Karen Conneely, James Heckman, and Edward Vytlacil. 1997. 'Cognitive ability, wages, and meritocracy'. In Bernie Devlin et al. (Eds), *Intelligence, genes and success: Scientists respond to* The bell curve. New York: Springer-Verlag.

Chimbos, Peter, 1974. 'Ethnicity and occupational mobility: A comparative study of Greek and Slovak immigrants in Ontario city'. *International Journal of Comparative Sociology* 15:57–67.

———. 1980. *The Canadian odyssey: The Greek experience in Canada.* Toronto: McLelland and Stewart.

Clement, Wallace. 1975. *The Canadian corporate elite: An analysis of economic power.* Toronto: McClelland and Stewart.

————, and John Myles. 1994. *Relations of ruling*. Montreal: McGill-Queens University Press.

Cohen, Robin. 1995. 'Rethinking "Babylon": Iconoclastic conceptions of the diasporic experience'. *New Community* 21 (1):5–18.

————. 1997. *Global diasporas: An introduction*. Seattle: University of Washington Press.

Collins, Jock. 1988. *Migrant hands in a distant land: Australia's post-war immigration*. Sydney: Pluto Press.

Congress of Aboriginal Peoples. 1998. 'Profile—Background information'. http://www.abo-peoples.org/background/background.html.

Cooke, Martin, Daniel Beavon, and Mindy McHardy. 2004. 'Measuring the well-being of Aboriginal people: An application of the United Nations Human Development Index to registered Indians in Canada, 1981–2001'. Ottawa: Indian and Northern Affairs Canada.

Cornelius, Wayne. 2004. 'Spain: The uneasy transition from labor exporter to labor importer'. In Wayne Cornelius et al. (Eds), *Controlling immigration: A global perspective*, 2nd revised edn. Stanford: Stanford University Press.

Cox, David, and Patrick Glenn. 1994. 'Illegal immigration and refugee claims'. In Howard Adelman et al. (Eds), *Immigration and refugee policy: Australia and Canada compared*, vol. 1. Carleton, Victoria: Melbourne University Press.

Cox, Oliver Cromwell. 1948. *Caste, class and race: A study in social dynamics*. New York: Doubleday.

Creese, Gillian. 1984. 'Immigration policies and the creation of an ethnically segmented labour market'. *Alternate Routes* 7 (1):1–34.

Crowley, Brian Lee. 1995. 'Property, culture, and aboriginal self-government'. In Helmar Drost, Brian Lee Crowley, and Richard Schwindt (Eds), *Market solutions for native poverty*. Toronto: C.D. Howe Institute.

Cuneo, Carl, and James E. Curtis. 1975. 'Social ascription in the educational and occupational status attainment of urban Canadians'. *Canadian Review of Sociology and Anthropology* 12 (1):6–24.

Curry, Bill. 2005. 'The government responds: Indian Affairs minister announces plan to relocate settlement, improve sanitation'. *The Globe and Mail* 28 October: A1.

Curtis, Bruce. 2001. *The politics of population: State formation, statistics and the census of Canada, 1840–1875*. Toronto: University of Toronto Press.

Daniels, Harry. 2005. 'Bill C-31: The abocide bill'. http://abo-peoples.org/programs/dnlsc-31.html.

Daniels, Michael, Bernie Devlin, and Kathryn Roeder. 1997. 'Of genes and IQ'. In Bernie Devlin et al. (Eds), *Intelligence, genes and success: Scientists respond to* The bell curve. New York: Springer-Verlag.

Darroch, Gordon. 1979. 'Another look at ethnicity, stratification and social mobility in Canada'. *Canadian Journal of Sociology* 4 (1):1–24.

Davies, Scott, and Neil Guppy. 1998. 'Race and Canadian education'. In Vic Satzewich (Ed.), *Racism and social inequality in Canada: Concepts, controversies and strategies of resistance*, 131–55. Toronto: Thompson Educational Publishing.

Devlin, Bernie, Stephen E. Fienberg, Daniel P. Resnick, and Kathryn Roeder (Eds). 1997. *Intelligence, genes, and success: Scientists respond to* The bell curve. New York: Springer-Verlag.

de Silva, Arnold. 1992. *Earnings of immigrants: A comparative analysis*. Economic Council of Canada.

Denis, Wilfrid. 1999. 'Language policy in Canada'. In Peter Li (Ed.), *Race and ethnic relations in Canada*, 2nd edn. Toronto: Oxford University Press.

Devortez, Don, and Samuel Laryea. 1998. *Canadian human capital transfers: The USA and beyond.* Metropolis Working Paper series #98-18. Vancouver: Vancouver Centre of Excellence.

Dickason, Olive. 1992. *Canada's First Nations: A history of founding peoples from earliest times.* Toronto: McLelland and Stewart.

Driedger, Leo. 1989. *The ethnic factor: Identity in diversity.* Toronto: MacGraw-Hill Ryerson.

———. 1996. *Multi-ethnic Canada: Identities and inequalities.* Toronto: Oxford University Press.

———. 2003. *Race and ethnicity: Finding identities and inequalities.* Toronto: Oxford University Press.

Dua, Enakshi. 2004. 'Racializing imperial Canada: Indian women and the making of ethnic communities'. In Marlene Epp, Franca Iacovetta, and Frances Swyripa (Eds), *Sisters or strangers: Immigrant, ethnic, and racialized women in Canadian history*, 71–85. Toronto: University of Toronto Press.

Dufour, Christian. 1992. 'A little history'. Excerpt from *Le défi québécois*. In William Dodge (Ed.), *Boundaries of identity*. Toronto: Lester Publishing.

Dunk, Thomas. 1991. *It's a working man's town: Male working-class culture.* Montreal and Kingston: McGill–Queen's Press.

Durham, first earl of. 1963. *The Durham report.* Toronto: McClelland and Stewart.

Dyck, Noel. 1991. *What is the Indian 'problem': Tutelage and resistance in Canadian Indian administration.* St. John's: Institute of Social and Economic Research.

Economic Council of Canada. 1991. *New faces in the crowd: Economic and social impacts of immigration.* Ottawa: Ministry of Supply and Services.

Faist, Thomas. 2000. 'Transnationalism in international migration: Implications for the study of citizenship and culture'. *Ethnic and Racial Studies* 23 (2):189–222.

Farmer, Nathan. 2005. 'Kingston police chief apologizes for force's systemic racism'. http://friendsofgrassynarrows.com/item.php?427F.

Feagin, Joe, and Hernan Vera. 1995. *White racism.* New York: Routledge.

Flanagan, Thomas. 2000. *First Nations, second thoughts.* Kingston and Montreal: McGill-Queen's University Press.

Fleras, Augie. 1993. 'From "culture" to "equality": Multiculturalism as ideology and policy'. In James Curtis, Edward Grabb, and Neil Guppy (Eds), *Social inequality in Canada: patterns, problems, policies*, 2nd edn. Scarborough: Prentice Hall Canada.

———, and Jean Leonard Elliott. 1996. *Unequal relations: An introduction to race, ethnic and Aboriginal dynamics in Canada.* Toronto: Prentice Hall Canada.

———, and ———. 1999. *Unequal relations: An introduction to race, ethnic and Aboriginal dynamics in Canada.* 3rd edn. Toronto: Prentice Hall Canada.

Fong, Petti. 2005. 'B.C. teen pleads guilty in school beating death'. *The Globe and Mail* 27 October: A11

———. 2006. 'Immigrant groups fear dual-citizenship review'. *The Globe and Mail* 19 October: A1.

Forcese, Dennis. 1997. *The Canadian class structure.* 4th edn. Toronto: McGraw-Hill Ryerson.

Frances, Diane. 2002. *Immigration: The economic case.* Toronto: Key Porter Books.

Fraser, Steven. 1995. 'Introduction'. In Steven Fraser (Ed.), *The bell curve wars: Race, intelligence and the future of America.* New York: Basic Books.

Frideres, James, and René Gadacz. 2001. *Aboriginal peoples in Canada: Contemporary conflicts.* 6th edn. Toronto: Prentice-Hall Canada.

———, and ———. 2004. *Aboriginal peoples in Canada.* 7th edn. Toronto: Pearson Education Canada.

Friesen, Joe. 2005. 'Another funeral, this one well-guarded'. *The Globe and Mail* 28 November: A11.

Fulford, Robert. 2006. 'How we became a land of ghettos'. *The National Post* 12 June: A19.

Furi, Megan, and Jill Wherrett. 2003. *Indian status and band membership issues.* Ottawa: Parliamentary Research Branch, Library of Parliament.

Gabaccia, Donna. 2000. *Italy's many diasporas.* Seattle: University of Washington Press.

Gagnon, Alain-G. (Ed.). 2004. *Québec: State and society.* 3rd edn. Peterborough: Broadview Press.

Galabuzi, Grace-Edward. 2006. *Canada's economic apartheid: The social exclusion of racialized groups in the new century.* Toronto: Canadian Scholars Press.

Gibbon, Edward. 1998. *The decline and fall of the Roman Empire.* Hertfordshire: Wordsworth.

Gimpel, James, and James Edwards. 1999. *The congressional politics of immigration reform.* Boston: Allyn and Bacon.

Giroux, France. 1997. 'Le nouveau contrat nationalist: Est-il possible dans une démocratie pluraliste? Examen comparatif des situations française, canadienne et québécoise'. *Politique et société* 16 (3).

Glick Schiller, Nina. 1999. 'Transmigrants and nation-states: Something old and something new in the U.S. immigrant experience'. In Charles Hirschman et al. (Eds), *The handbook of international migration: The American experience.* New York: Russell Sage Foundation.

Goldberg, David Theo (Ed.). 1990. *Anatomy of racism.* Minneapolis: University of Minnesota Press.

———. 1993. *Racist culture: Philosophy and the politics of meaning.* Oxford: Blackwell Publishers.

Goyder, John C., and James E. Curtis. 1979. 'Occupational mobility over four generations'. In James E. Curtis and William G. Scott (Eds), *Social stratification: Canada,* 221–33. Scarborough: Prentice Hall Canada.

Guillaumin, C. 1995. *Racism, sexism, power and ideology.* London: Routledge.

Hagan, John. 2001. *Northern passage: American war resisters in Canada.* Cambridge, MA: Harvard University Press.

Hansen, Marcus Lee. 1940. *The immigrant in American history.* New York: Harper and Row.

———. 1961. *The Atlantic migration: 1607–1860.* New York: Harper and Row.

Hardcastle, Leonie, Andrew Parkin, Alan Simmons, and Nobuaki Suyama. 1994. 'The making of immigration and refugee policy: Politicians, bureaucrats and citizens'. In Howard Adelman et al. (Eds), *Immigration and refugee policy: Australia and Canada compared,* vol. 1. Carleton, Victoria: Melbourne University Press.

Harney, Nicholas. 1998. *Eh, Paesan! Being Italian in Toronto.* Toronto: University of Toronto Press.

Hawkins, Freda. 1988. *Canada and immigration: Public policy and public concern.* 2nd edn. Montreal and Kingston: McGill-Queen's University Press.

———. 1989. *Critical years in immigration: Canada and Australia compared.* Montreal: McGill-Queen's University Press.

Henry, Frances. 1999. 'Two studies of racial discrimination'. In James Curtis, Edward Grabb, and Neil Guppy (Eds), *Social inequality in Canada: Patterns, problems, and policies*, 3rd edn, 226–35. Scarborough: Prentice Hall Canada.

———, and Effie Ginzberg. 1985. *Who gets the work? A test of racial discrimination in employment*. Toronto: Urban Alliance on Race Relations and the Social Planning Council of Metropolitan Toronto.

———, and ———. 1988. 'Racial discrimination in employment'. In James Curtis, Edward Grabb, Neil Guppy, and Sid Gilbert (Eds), *Social inequality in Canada: patterns, problems, policies*, 214–20. Scarborough: Prentice-Hall Canada.

———, and Carol Tator. 1999. 'State policy and practices as racialized discourse: Multiculturalism, the Charter, and employment equity'. In Peter Li (Ed.), *Race and ethnic relations in Canada*. Toronto: Oxford University Press.

———, and ———. 2005. *The colour of democracy: Racism in Canada*. 3rd edn. Toronto: Thomson Nelson.

Herberg, Edward N. 1989. *Ethnic groups in Canada: Adaptations and transitions*. 2nd edn. Scarborough: Nelson Canada.

Herodotus. 1998. *Histories*. Hertfordshire: Wordsworth.

Herrnstein, Richard, and Charles Murray. 1994. *The bell curve: Intelligence and class structure in American life*. New York: Free Press.

Hier, Sean, and Joshua Greenberg. 2002. 'News discourse and the problematization of Chinese migration to Canada'. In Frances Henry and Carol Tator, *Discourses of domination: Racial bias in the Canadian English-language press*. Toronto: University of Toronto Press.

Hobsbawm, Eric. 1990. *Nations and nationalism since 1780: Programme, myth, reality*. Cambridge: Cambridge University Press.

Hooten, Ernest. 1946. *Up from the ape*. New York: MacMillan.

Hou, Feng, and T.R. Balakrishnan. 1999. 'The economic integration of visible minorities in contemporary Canadian society'. In James Curtis, Edward Grabb, and Neil Guppy (Eds), *Social inequality in Canada: patterns, problems, and policies*, 3rd edn, 214–25. Scarborough: Prentice Hall Canada.

Howard-Hassmann, Rhoda. 1999. '"Canadian" as an ethnic category: Implications for multiculturalism and national unity'. *Canadian Public Policy* 25 (4).

Hume, David. 1964. 'On national characters'. In T.H. Green and T.H. Grose III (Eds), *The philosophical works*. Aalen: Scientia Verlag.

Huntley, Audrey, and Fay Blaney. 1999. *Bill C-31: Its impacts, implications, and recommendations for change in British Columbia—Final report*. Vancouver: Aboriginal Women's Action Network and Vancouver Status of Women.

Iacovetta, Franca. 1992. *Such hardworking people: Italian immigrants in postwar Canada*. Toronto: University of Toronto Press.

———, and Robert Ventresca. 2000. 'Redress, collective memory and the politics of history'. In Franca Iacovetta, Roberto Perin, and Angelo Principe (Eds), *Enemies within: Italian and other internees in Canada and abroad*. Toronto: University of Toronto Press.

Inuit Tapiriit Kanatami. 2004a. 'The case for Inuit specific: Renewing the relationship between the Inuit and government of Canada'. Ottawa: Inuit Tapiriit Kanatami.

———. 2004b. 'The Inuit Tapiriit Kanatami: The origin of the ITK'. http://www.tapirisat.ca/.

Isajiw, Wsevolod W. 1981. 'Ethnic identity retention and socialization'. Paper presented at the annual meeting of the American Sociological Association, Toronto.

———. 1999. *Understanding diversity: Ethnicity and race in the Canadian context.* Toronto: Thompson Educational Publishing.

Jakubowski, Lisa. 1997. *Immigration and the legalization of racism.* Halifax: Fernwood Press.

Jedwab, Jack. 2003. 'Coming to our census: The need for continuing inquiry into Canadians' ethnic origins'. *Canadian Ethnic Studies* 35 (1):33–50.

Jelinek, Otto. 1986. 'Welcoming remarks to the Multiculturalism Means Business Conference'. Toronto, 18 May.

Jhappan, Radha. 1996. 'Post-modern race and gender essentialism or a post-mortem of scholarship'. *Studies in Political Economy* 51 (3):15–63.

Jiminez, Marina. 2003. '200,000 illegal immigrants toiling in Canada's underground economy'. *The Globe and Mail* 14 November: A1.

———. 2005. 'Broken gates: How people smugglers are beating the system'. *The Globe and Mail* 20 April: A1.

Johnson, James, Walter Farrel, and Chandra Guinn. 1999. 'Immigration reform and the browning of America: Tensions, conflicts and community instability in metropolitan Los Angeles'. In Charles Hirschman et al. (Eds), *The handbook of international migration: The American experience.* New York: Russell Sage Foundation.

Joppke, Christian. 1999. 'How immigration is changing citizenship: A comparative view'. *Ethnic and Racial Studies* 22 (4):629–52.

Juteau, Danielle. 2002. 'The citizen makes an entrée: Redefining the national community in Quebec'. *Citizenship Studies* 6 (4):441–58.

Kalbach, Madeline, and Warren Kalbach. 2000. *Perspectives on ethnicity in Canada.* Toronto: Harcourt Canada.

Kallen, Evelyn. 1995. *Ethnicity and human rights in Canada.* 2nd edn. Toronto: Oxford University Press.

———. 2003. *Ethnicity and human rights in Canada.* 3rd edn. Toronto: Oxford University Press.

Kant, Immanuel. 1960. *Observations on the feeling of the beautiful and the sublime.* Berkeley: University of California Press.

Karmis, Demetrios. 2004. 'Pluralism and national identity(ies) in contemporary Quebec: Conceptual clarifications, typology, and discourse analysis'. In Alain-G. Gagnon (Ed.), *Québec: State and society,* 3rd edn, 69–96. Peterborough: Broadview Press.

Kaye, Vladimir. 1964. *Early Ukrainian settlements in Canada: 1895–1900.* Toronto: University of Toronto Press.

———, and Frances Swyripa. 1982. 'Settlement and colonization'. In Manoly Lupul (Ed.), *A heritage in transition: Essays in the history of Ukrainians in Canada,* 32–58. Toronto: McClelland and Stewart.

Kelly, Karen. 1995. 'Visible minorities: A diverse group'. *Canadian Social Trends* 37 (summer):2–8.

Kinder, D., and D. Sears. 1981. 'Prejudice and politics: Symbolic racism versus racial threats to the good life'. *Journal of Personality and Social Psychology* 40:414–31.

Kirkham, Della. 1998. 'The Reform Party of Canada: A discourse on race, ethnicity and equality'. In Vic Satzewich (Ed.), *Racism and social inequality in Canada: Concepts, controversies and strategies of resistance.* Toronto: Thompson Educational Publishing.

Knowles, Valerie. 1992. *Strangers at our gates: Canadian immigration and immigration policy, 1540–1990.* Toronto: Dundurn Press.

Kordan, Bohdan. 2000. *Ukrainian Canadians and the Canadian census, 1981–1996.* Saskatoon: Heritage Press.

———. 2002. *Enemy aliens, prisoners of war.* Montreal and Kingston: McGill-Queen's University Press.

Koser, Khalid. 2001. 'The smuggling of asylum seekers into western Europe: Contradictions, conundrums and dilemmas'. In David Kyle and Rey Koslowski (Eds), *Global human smuggling: Comparative perspectives.* Baltimore: Johns Hopkins University Press.

Koslowski, Rey. 2001. 'Economic globalization, human smuggling, and global governance'. In David Kyle and Rey Koslowski (Eds), *Global human smuggling: Comparative perspectives.* Baltimore: Johns Hopkins University Press.

Krahn, Harvey J., and Graham S. Lowe. 1993. *Work, industry and Canadian society.* 2nd edn. Scarborough: Nelson Canada.

Kymlicka, Will. 1998. 'The theory and practice of Canadian multiculturalism'. Paper presented to the Canadian Federation of the Social Sciences and Humanities, 23 November: 1–10. http://www.fedcan.ca/english/fromold/breakfast-kymlicka1198.cfm.

Lautard, Hugh, and Neil Guppy. 1990. 'The vertical mosaic revisited: Occupational differentials among Canadian ethnic groups'. In Peter Li (Ed.), *Race and ethnic relations in Canada*, 189–208. Toronto: Oxford University Press.

———, and ———. 2007. 'Occupational inequality among Canadian ethnic groups, 1931 to 2001'. In Robert J. Brym (Ed.), *Society in question*, 5th edn. Toronto: Nelson Canada.

Lawrence, Bonita. 2004. *'Real' Indians and others: Mixed-blood urban Native peoples and indigenous nationhood.* Lincoln: University of Nebraska Press.

Lee, Yeuh-Ting, Victor Ottati, and Imtiaz Hussain. 2001. 'Attitudes toward "illegal" immigration into the United States: California Proposition 187'. *Hispanic Journal of Behavioural Sciences* 23 (4):430–43.

Lehr, John. 1991. 'Peopling the prairies with Ukrainians'. In Lubomir Luciuk and Stella Hryniuk (Eds), *Canada's Ukrainians: Negotiating an identity*, 30–52. Toronto: University of Toronto Press.

Leslie, Keith. 2005. 'NDP wants Safe Schools Act repealed: Claim it helps gangs recruit'. http://www.canada.com/components/printstory/.

Lévesque, Stéphane. 1999. 'Rethinking citizenship and citizenship education: A Canadian perspective for the 21st century'. Paper presented at the Citizenship Research Network Symposium, Fourth International Metropolis Conference, Georgetown University, Washington, DC, 1–29.

Levitt, Cyril. 1994. 'Is Canada a racist country?' In Sally F. Zerker (Ed.), *Change and impact: Essays in Canadian social sciences*, 304–16. Jerusalem: Magnes Press, Hebrew University.

Levitt, Peggy, and Raphael de la Dehesa. 2003. 'Transnational migration and the redefinition of the state: Variations and explanations'. *Ethnic and Racial Studies* 26 (4):587–611.

Lewis, Oscar. 1959. *Five families: Mexican case studies in the culture of poverty.* New York: Oxford University Press.

———. 1966. 'The culture of poverty'. *Scientific American* 215:19–25.

Lewycky, Laverne. 1992. 'Multiculturalism in the 1990s and into the 21st century: Beyond ideology and utopia'. In Vic Satzewich (Ed.), *Deconstructing a nation: Immigration, multiculturalism and racism in '90s Canada*. Halifax: Fernwood Press.

Li, Peter. 1988. *Ethnic inequality in a class society*. Toronto: Thompson Educational Publishing.

———— (Ed.). 1990. *Race and ethnic relations in Canada*. Toronto: Oxford University Press.

————. 1992. 'Race and gender as bases of class fractions and the effects on earnings'. *Canadian Review of Sociology and Anthropology* 29 (4):488–510.

————. 1994. 'Unneighbourly houses or unwelcome Chinese: The social construction of race in the battle over "monster homes" in Vancouver'. *International Journal of Comparative Race and Ethnic Studies* 1 (1):47–66.

————. 1998a. *The Chinese in Canada*. 2nd edn. Toronto: Oxford University Press.

————. 1998b. 'The market value and social value of race'. In Vic Satzewich (Ed.), *Racism and social inequality in Canada: Concepts, controversies and strategies of resistance*, 115–30. Toronto: Thompson Educational Publishing.

————(Ed.). 1999. *Race and ethnic relations in Canada*. 2nd edn. Toronto: Oxford University Press.

————. 2003. *Destination Canada: Immigration debates and issues*. Toronto: Oxford University Press.

————, and B. Singh Bolaria. 1979. 'Canadian immigration policy and assimilation theories'. In J.A. Fry (Ed.), *Economy, class and social reality*, 411–22. Toronto: Butterworths.

Lian, Jason Z., and Ralph Matthews. 1998. 'Does the vertical mosaic still exist? Ethnicity and income in Canada, 1991'. *Canadian Review of Sociology and Anthropology* 35 (4): 461–81.

Lieberson, Stanley. 1980. 'A societal theory of race and ethnic relations'. In J.E. Goldstein and Rita M. Bienvenue (Eds), *Ethnicity and ethnic relations in Canada*, 67–79. Toronto: Butterworths.

Liodakis, Nikolaos. 1998 'The activities of Hellenic-Canadian secular organizations in the context of Canadian multiculturalism'. *Études Helléniques/Hellenic Studies* 6 (1):37–58. Montreal: Centre for Hellenic Studies and Research.

————. 2002. 'The vertical mosaic within: Class, gender and nativity within ethnicity'. Unpublished Ph.D. dissertation, Department of Sociology, McMaster University, Hamilton.

————, and Vic Satzewich. 2003. 'From solution to problem: Multiculturalism and "race relations" as new social problems'. In Wayne Antony and Les Samuelson (Eds), *Power and resistance: Critical thinking about Canadian social issues*, 3rd edn, 145–68. Halifax: Fernwood Press.

Locke, John. 1960. *Two treatises on government*. New York: Mentor Books.

Louie, Vivian S. 2004. *Compelled to excel: Immigration, education, and opportunity among Chinese Americans*. Stanford: Stanford University Press.

Luciuk, Lubomir (Ed.). 1994. *Righting an injustice: The debate over redress for Canada's first national internment operations*. Toronto: Justinian Press.

Lugo, Luis. 2003. 'Remittances are Mexico's biggest source of income, says Fox'. http://www.signonsandiego.com/news/mexico/20030924-2051-us-mexico.

McAll, Christopher. 1990. *Class, ethnicity and social inequality*. Montreal: McGill-Queen's University Press.

McConahay, J. 1986. 'Modern racism, ambivalence, and the modern racism scale'. In J. Dovidio and S. Gaertner (Eds), *Prejudice, discrimination, and racism*. New York: Academic Press.

McLaren, Angus. 1990. *Our own master race: Eugenics in Canada, 1885–1945*. Toronto: McLelland and Stewart.

Makabe, Tamoko. 1981. 'The theory of the split labour market: A comparison of the Japanese experience in Brazil and Canada'. *Social Forces* 59:786–809.

Malloy, Jonathan. 2003. 'To better service Canadians: How technology is changing the relationship between members of Parliament and public servants'. *New Directions*, no. 9. Toronto: Institute of Public Administration.

Mandelbaum, Michael. 2000. 'Introduction'. In Michael Mandelbaum (Ed.), *The new European diasporas: National minorities and conflict in eastern Europe*. New York: Council on Foreign Relations Press.

Marger, Martin. 1997. *Race and ethnic relations: American and global perspectives*. Belmont, CA: Wadsworth Publishing.

Massey, Douglas. 1999. 'Why does immigration occur? A theoretical synthesis'. In Charles Hirschman et al. (Eds), *The handbook of international migration: The American experience*. New York: Russell Sage Foundation.

Matthews, Kim, and Vic Satzewich. 2006. 'The invisible transnationals: American immigrants in Canada'. In Vic Satzewich and Lloyd Wong (Eds), *Transnational identities and practices in Canada*. Vancouver: University of British Columbia Press.

Miles, Robert. 1982. *Racism and migrant labour*. London: Routledge and Kegan Paul.

———. 1984. *White man's country: Racism in British politics*. London: Pluto Press.

———. 1993. *Racism after 'race relations'*. London: Routledge.

———, and Malcolm Brown. 2003. *Racism*. 2nd edn. London: Routledge.

———, and Rudy Torres. 1996. 'Does "race" matter? Transatlantic perspectives on racism after "race relations"'. In V. Amit-Talai and C. Knowles (Eds), *Re-situating identities: The politics of race, ethnicity and culture*, 24–46. Peterborough: Broadview Press.

Mill, James. 1820. *History of British India*. 2nd edn. London.

Mitchell, Katharyne. 2004. *Crossing the neoliberal line: Pacific Rim migration and the metropolis*. Philadelphia: Temple University Press.

Mitchell, Marybelle. 1996. *From talking chiefs to a Native corporate elite: The birth of class and nationalism among Canadian Inuit*. Montreal and Kingston: McGill-Queen's University Press.

Montagu, Ashley. 1964. *Man's most dangerous myth*. New York: World Publishing.

———. 1972. *Statement on race*. Oxford: Oxford University Press.

Moodley, Kogila. 1983. 'Canadian multiculturalism as ideology'. *Ethnic and Racial Studies* 6 (3):320–31.

Murdie, Robert, and Carlos Teixeira. 2003. 'Towards a comfortable neighbourhood and appropriate housing: Immigrant experiences in Toronto'. In Paul Anisef and Michael Lanphier, *The world in a city*. Toronto: University of Toronto Press.

Nagel, Joane. 2003. *Race, ethnicity and sexuality: Intimate intersections, forbidden frontiers*. New York: Oxford University Press.

Nagler, Mark. 1975. *Natives without a home*. Toronto: Longmans.

Nakhaie, Reza (Ed.). 1999. *Debates on social inequality: Class, gender and ethnicity in Canada.* Toronto: Harcourt Canada.

———. 2000. 'Ownership and management position of Canadian ethnic groups in 1973 and 1989'. In Madeline A. Kalbach and Warren Kalbach (Eds), *Perspectives on ethnicity in Canada.* Toronto: Harcourt Canada.

Ng, Roxana. 1986. 'The social construction of immigrant women in Canada'. In R. Hamilton and M. Barrett (Eds), *The politics of diversity: feminism, Marxism and nationalism,* 169–86. Montreal: Book Centre Inc.

———. 1991. 'Sexism, racism and Canadian nationalism'. In Jesse Vorst et al. (Eds), *Race, class, gender: Bonds and barriers,* 12–26. Toronto: Garamond Press.

Nobles, Melissa. 2000. *Shades of citizenship: Race and the census in modern politics.* Stanford: Stanford University Press.

Noh, Samuel, and Violet Kaspar. 2003. 'Diversity and immigrant health'. In Paul Anisef and Michael Lanphier (Eds), *The world in a city.* Toronto: University of Toronto Press.

Noivo, Edite. 1998. 'Neither "ethnic heroes" nor "racial villains": Inter-minority group racism'. In Vic Satzewich (Ed.), *Racism and social inequality in Canada: Concepts, controversies and strategies of resistance.* Toronto: Thompson Educational Publishing.

Odunfa, Sola. 2006. 'Nigeria's counting controversy'. BBC News. http://news.bbc.co.uk/go/pr/fr/-/1/hi/world/africa/4512240.stm.

Ogmundson, Richard. 1991. 'Perspective on the class and ethnic origins of Canadian elites: A methodological critique of the Porter/Clement/Olsen tradition'. *Canadian Journal of Sociology* 15 (2):165–77.

———. 1993. 'At the top of the mosaic: Doubts about the data'. *American Review of Canadian Studies* autumn: 373–86.

———, and J. McLaughlin. 1992. 'Trends in the ethnic origins of Canadian elites: The decline of the BRITS?' *Canadian Review of Sociology and Anthropology* 29 (2):227–42.

Omatsu, Maryka. 1992. *Bittersweet passage: Redress and the Japanese Canadian experience.* Toronto: Between the Lines Press.

Ontario Human Rights Commission. 2005a. *Disproportionate impact of 'zero tolerance' discipline.* http://www.ohrc.on.ca/en_text/consultations/safe-schools-submission.

———. 2005b. *The existence of racial profiling.* Toronto: Ontario Human Rights Commission.

Ooka, Emi, and Barry Wellman. 2000. *Does social capital pay off more within or between ethnic groups? Analysing job searches in five Toronto ethnic groups.* Toronto: Centre of Excellence for Research on Immigration and Settlement. http://www.chass.utoronto.ca/~wellman/publications/ethnic14a/ooka-bw-uq-26feb03.PDF.

Ornstein, Michael. 1981. 'The occupational mobility of men in Ontario'. *Canadian Review of Sociology and Anthropology* 18 (2):181–215.

———. 1983. *Accounting for gender differentials in job income in Canada: Results from a 1981 survey.* Ottawa: Minister of Supply and Services.

Osborne, John. 1991. '"Non-preferred" people: Inter-war Ukrainian immigration to Canada'. In Lubomir Luciuk and Stella Hryniuk (Eds), *Canada's Ukrainians: Negotiating an identity,* 81–102. Toronto: University of Toronto Press.

Park, Robert. 1914. 'Racial assimilation in secondary groups'. *American Journal of Sociology* 607.

Pendakur, Krishna, and Ravi Pendakur. 1996. 'Earnings differentials among ethnic groups in Canada'. Ottawa: Strategic Research and Analysis, Department of Canadian Heritage.

Persons, Stow. 1987. *Ethnic studies at Chicago, 1905–45.* Urbana: University of Illinois Press.

Petryshyn, Jaroslav. 1991. 'Sifton's immigration policy'. In Lubomir Luciuk and Stella Hryniuk (Eds), *Canada's Ukrainians: Negotiating an identity,* 17–29. Toronto: University of Toronto Press.

Pettipas, Katherine. 1994. *Severing the ties that bind: Government repression of indigenous ceremonies on the prairies.* Winnipeg: University of Manitoba Press.

Phillips, Paul. 1967. *No power greater: A century of labour in BC.* Vancouver: BC Federation of Labour.

Poliakov, L. 1974. *The Aryan myth.* New York: Basic Books.

Ponting, J. Rick. 1998. 'Racism and stereotyping of First Nations'. In Vic Satzewich (Ed.), *Racism and social inequality in Canada: Concepts, controversies and strategies of resistance.* Toronto: Thompson Educational Publishing.

————, and Roger Gibbins. 1980. *Out of irrelevance: A Sociopolitical introduction to Indian affairs in Canada.* Scarborough: Butterworth.

Porter, John. 1965. *The vertical mosaic: An analysis of social class and power in Canada.* Toronto: University of Toronto Press.

————. 1985. 'Canada: The societal context of occupational allocation'. In Monica Boyd, John Goyder, Frank E Jones, Hugh A. McRoberts, Peter C. Pineo, and John Porter, *Ascription and achievement: Studies in mobility and status attainment in Canada,* 29–65. Ottawa: Carleton University Press.

Portes, Alejandro. 1995. 'Children of immigrants: Segmented assimilation and its determinants'. In Alejandro Portes (Ed.), *The economic sociology of immigration.* New York: Russell Sage Foundation.

————. 1999. 'Conclusion: Towards a new world—The origins and effects of transnational activities'. *Ethnic and Racial Studies* 22 (2):463–77.

————, Luis Guarnizo, and Patricia Landolt. 1999. 'The study of transnationalism: Pitfalls and promise of an emergent research field'. *Ethnic and Racial Studies* 22 (2):217–37.

————, and Min Zhou. 1993. 'The new second generation: Segmented assimilation and its variants among post-1965 American youth'. *Annals of the American Academy of Political and Social Science* 530 (November):74–96.

Pratt, Anna. 2005. *Securing borders: Detention and deportation in Canada.* Vancouver: University of British Columbia Press.

Preston, Valerie, Lucia Lo, and Shunguang Wang. 2003. 'Immigrants' economic status in Toronto; Triumph and disappointment'. In Paul Anisef and Michael Lanphier (Eds), *The world in a city.* Toronto: University of Toronto Press.

Principe, Angelo. 2000. 'A tangled knot: Prelude to 10 June, 1940'. In Franca Iacovetta et al. (Eds), *Enemies within: Italian Canadians and other internees in Canada and abroad.* Toronto: University of Toronto Press.

Quigly, Tim. 1994. 'Some issues in sentencing of Aboriginal offenders'. In Richard Goose et al. (Eds), *Continuing in Poundmaker and Riel's quest.* Saskatoon: Purich Publishing.

Ralston, Helen. 1991. 'Race, class, gender and work experience of south Asian immigrant women in Atlantic Canada'. *Canadian Ethnic Studies* (23):129–39.

Rankin, Jim, et al. 2002. 'Singled out: An investigation into race and crime'. *Toronto Star* 26 October: A6.

Reis, Michele. 2004. 'Theorizing diaspora: Perspectives on "classical" and "contemporary" diaspora'. *International Migration* 42 (2):41–60.

Reitz, Jeffrey G. 1980. *The survival of ethnic groups*. Toronto: McGraw-Hill Ryerson.

———. 2001. 'Immigrant skill utilization in the Canadian labour market: Implications of human capital research'. *Journal of International Migration and Integration* 2 (3):347–78.

———, and Raymond Breton. 1994. *The illusion of difference: Realities of ethnicity in Canada and the United States*. Toronto: C.D. Howe Institute.

Richards, John. 1995. 'A comment'. In Helmar Drost, Brian Lee Crowley, and Richard Schwindt (Eds), *Market solutions for Native poverty*. Toronto: C.D. Howe Institute.

Richmond, Anthony. 1967. *Post-war immigrants in Canada*. Toronto: University of Toronto Press.

Rivera-Batiz, Francisco. 2000. 'Underground on American soil: Undocumented workers and US immigration policy'. *Journal of International Affairs* 53 (2):485–501.

Roberts, Barbara. 1988. *Whence they came: Deportation from Canada 1900–1935*. Ottawa: University of Ottawa Press.

Roberts, Bryan, Beanne Frank, and Fernando Lozano-Acencio. 1999. 'Transnational migrant communities and Mexican migration to the US'. *Ethnic and Racial Studies* 22 (2):238–66.

Roberts, Lance, and Rodney Clifton. 1982. 'Exploring the ideology of Canadian multiculturalism'. *Canadian Public Policy* 8 (1):88–94.

Rodriguez, Nestor. 1999. 'U.S. immigration and changing relations between African Americans and Latinos'. In Charles Hirschman et al. (Eds), *The handbook of international migration: The American experience*. New York: Russell Sage Foundation.

Roediger, David. 1991. *The wages of whiteness*. New York: Verso.

Rosen, Bernard C. 1956. 'The achievement syndrome: A psychocultural dimension of social stratification'. *American Sociological Review* 21:203–11.

———. 1959. 'Race, ethnicity, and the achievement syndrome'. *American Sociological Review* 24:47–60.

Rosen, Jeffrey, and Charles Lane. 1995. 'The sources of the bell curve'. In Steven Fraser (Ed.), *The bell curve wars: Race, intelligence and the future of America*. New York: Basic Books.

Roy, Patricia. 1989. *A white man's province: British Columbia politicians and Chinese and Japanese immigrants, 1858–1914*. Vancouver: University of British Columbia Press.

Royal Commission on Aboriginal Peoples. 1996a. *Bridging the cultural divide: A report on Aboriginal people and criminal justice in Canada*. Ottawa: Supply and Services Canada.

———. 1996b. *Report, volume 1: Looking forward, looking back*. Ottawa: Supply and Services Canada.

Royal Commission on Bilingualism and Biculturalism. 1969. *Report*. vol. 3a. Ottawa: Queen's Printer.

Royal Commission on Equality in Employment. 1984. *Report*. Ottawa: Supply and Services Canada.

Ruck, Martin, and Scot Wortley. 2002. 'Racial and ethnic minority students: Perceptions of school disciplinary practices: a look at some Canadian findings'. *Journal of Youth and Adolescence* 31 (3):185–95.

Rudin, Ronald. 1993. 'English speaking Quebec: The emergence of a disillusioned minority'. In Alain-G. Gagnon (Ed.), *Québec: State and society*, 2nd edn. Toronto: Nelson Canada.

Rushton, J. Philippe. 1988. 'Race differences in behaviour: A review and evolutionary analysis'. *Personality and Individual Differences* 9:1009–24.

———, and A. Boegart. 1987. 'Race differences in sexual behavior: Testing an evolutionary hypothesis'. *Journal of Research in Personality* 21:529–51.

Safran. 1991. 'Diasporas in modern societies: Myths of homeland and return'. *Diaspora* 1 (1):83–99.

Sanchez, George. 1999. 'Face the nation: Race, immigration and the rise of nativism in late twentieth-century America'. In Charles Hirschman et al. (Eds), *The handbook of international migration: The American experience*. New York: Russell Sage Foundation.

Satzewich, Vic. 1989. 'Racisms: The reactions to Chinese migrants in Canada at the turn of the century'. *International Sociology* 4 (3):311–27.

———. 1991. *Racism and the incorporation of foreign labour: Farm labour migration to Canada since 1945*. London: Routledge.

——— (Ed.). 1998a. *Racism and social inequality in Canada: Concepts, controversies and strategies of resistance*. Toronto: Thompson Educational Publishing.

———. 1998b. 'Race, racism and racialization: Contested concepts'. In Vic Satzewich (Ed.), *Racism and social inequality in Canada: Concepts, controversies and strategies of resistance*. Toronto: Thompson Educational Publishing.

———. 1999. 'The political economy of race and ethnicity'. In Peter Li (Ed.), *Race and ethnic relations in Canada*, 2nd edn, 311–46. Toronto: Oxford University Press.

———. 2000. 'Whiteness limited: Racialization and the social construction of "peripheral Europeans"'. *Histoire sociale/Social History* 32 (66):271–90.

———. 2002. *The Ukrainian diaspora*. London: Routledge.

———. 2006. 'The economic rights of migrant and immigrant workers in Canada and the United States'. In Rhoda Howard-Hassmann and Claude Welch (Eds), *Economic rights in Canada and the United States*. Philadelphia: University of Pennsylvania Press.

———, and Linda Mahood. 1994. 'Indian affairs and band governance: Deposing Indian chiefs in western Canada'. *Canadian Ethnic Studies* 26 (1):40–58.

———, and Lloyd Wong. 2003. 'Immigration, ethnicity, and race: The transformation of transnationalism, localism, and identities'. In Wallace Clement and Leah Vosko (Eds), *Changing Canada: Political economy as transformation*. Montreal and Kingston: McGill-Queen's University Press.

———, and ———. (Eds). 2006. *Transnational communities in Canada*. Vancouver: University of British Columbia Press.

———, and Terry Wotherspoon. 2000. *First Nations: Race, class and gender relations*. Regina: Canadian Plains Research Centre.

Schissel, Bernard, and Terry Wotherspoon. 2003. *The legacy of school for Aboriginal people: Education, oppression and emancipation*. Toronto: Oxford University Press.

Sharma, Nandita. 2001. 'On being *not* Canadian: The social organization of "migrant workers" in Canada'. *Canadian Review of Sociology and Anthropology* 38 (4):415–39.

———. 2006. *Home economics: Nationalism and the making of 'migrant workers' in Canada*. Toronto: University of Toronto Press.

Sheffer, Gabriel. 2003. *Diaspora politics: At home abroad*. Cambridge: Cambridge University Press.

Shepard, R. Bruce. 1991. 'Plain racism: The reaction against Oklahoma black immigration to the Canadian plains'. In Ormond McKague (Ed.), *Racism in Canada*. Saskatoon: Fifth House Publishers.

Schoenfeld, Stewart, William Shaffir, and Morton Weinfeld. 2006. 'Canadian Jewry and transnationalism: Israel, anti-Semitism and the Jewish diaspora'. In Vic Satzewich and Lloyd Wong (Eds), *Transnational identities and practices in Canada*. Vancouver: University of British Columbia Press.

Shull, Steven. 1993. *A kinder, gentler racism? The Reagan-Bush civil rights legacy*. Armonk, NY: M.E. Sharpe.

Siegfried, André. 1966. *The race question in Canada*. Toronto: McClelland and Stewart.

Silman, Janet. 1987. *Enough is enough: Aboriginal women speak out*. Toronto: The Women's Press.

Simmons, Alan. 1998. 'Racism and immigration policy'. In Vic Satzewich (Ed.), *Racism and social inequality in Canada: Concepts, controversies and strategies of resistance*. Toronto: Thompson Educational Publishing.

———, and Dwaine Plaza. 2006. 'The Caribbean community in Canada: Transnational connections and transformations'. In Vic Satzewich and Lloyd Wong (Eds), *Transnational identities and practices in Canada*. Vancouver: University of British Columbia Press.

Smith, Graham. 1999. 'Transnational politics and the politics of the Russian diaspora. *Ethnic and Racial Studies* 22 (2):500–23.

Soave Strategy Group. 2006. *The impact of undocumented workers on the residential construction industry in the Greater Toronto Area*. Toronto: Labourers' International Union of North America.

Solomon, R. Patrick, and Howard Palmer. 2004. 'Schooling in Babylon, Babylon in school: When racial profiling and zero tolerance converge'. *Canadian Journal of Educational Administration and Policy* 33:1–16.

Sowell, Thomas. 1989. 'Affirmative action: A worldwide disaster'. *Commentary* 12:21–41.

Soysal, Yasmeen N. 2000. 'Citizenship and identity: Living in diasporas in post-war Europe?' *Ethnic and Racial Studies* 23 (1):1–15.

Spener, David. 2001. 'Smuggling migrants through south Texas: Challenges posed by Operation Rio Grande'. In David Kyle and Rey Koslowski (Eds), *Global human smuggling: Comparative perspectives*. Baltimore: Johns Hopkins University Press.

St. Germain, Jill. 2001. *Indian treaty making policy in the United States and Canada, 1867–1877*. Toronto: University of Toronto Press.

Stalker, Peter. 2000. *Workers without frontiers—The impact of globalisation on international migration*. Geneva: International Labour Organization.

Stasiulis, Daiva. 1980. 'The political structuring of ethnic community action'. *Canadian Ethnic Studies* 12 (3):19–44.

———. 1990. 'Theorizing connections: Gender, race, ethnicity, and class'. In Peter Li (Ed.), *Race and ethnic relations in Canada*, 269–305. Toronto: Oxford University Press.

———. 1999. 'Feminist intersectional theorizing'. In Peter Li (Ed.), *Race and ethnic relations in Canada*, 2nd edn, 347–97. Toronto: Oxford University Press.

Statistics Canada. 1996. 'Public use microdata file on individuals—User documentation'.

———. 2003. *Ethnic diversity survey*. Ottawa: Supply and Services Canada.

Stevenson, Garth. 2005. 'Remarks'. Panel discussion of the Institute of Intergovernmental Relations, Department of Political Science, Brock University, St Catharines, 14 May.

Stoffman, Daniel. 2002. *Who gets in: What's wrong with Canada's immigration program—and how to fix it*. Toronto: Macfarlane Walter and Ross.

Sugiman, Pamela. 2006. 'Unmaking a transnational community: Japanese Canadian families in wartime Canada'. In Vic Satzewich and Lloyd Wong (Eds), *Transnational identities and practices in Canada*. Vancouver: University of British Columbia Press.

Synnott, Anthony, and David Howes. 1996. 'Canada's visible minorities: Identity and representation'. In V. Amit-Talai and C. Knowles (Eds), *Re-situating identities: The politics of race, ethnicity and culture*. Peterborough: Broadview Press.

Taguieff, Pierre-Andre. 1999. 'The new cultural racism in France'. In Martin Bulmer and John Solomos (Eds), *Racism*. Oxford: Oxford University Press.

Tatla, Darshan Singh. 1999. *The Sikh diaspora: The search for statehood*. Seattle: University of Washington Press.

Tepperman, Lorne. 1975. *Social mobility in Canada*. Toronto: McGraw-Hill Ryerson.

Thatcher, Richard. 2004. *Fighting firewater fictions: Moving beyond the disease model of alcoholism in First Nations*. Toronto: University of Toronto Press.

Thomas, William, and Florian Znaniecki. 1920. *The Polish peasant in Europe and America*. Boston: Gorham Press.

Thompson, Leonard. 1985. *The political mythology of apartheid*. New Haven: Yale University Press.

Titley, Brian. 1986. *A narrow vision: Duncan Campbell Scott and the administration of Indian Affairs in Canada*. Vancouver: University of British Columbia Press.

Toronto Star. 2005. 'Cast aside by France'. 10 November.

Ujimoto, Victor. 1999. 'Studies of ethnic identity, ethnic relations, and citizenship'. In Peter Li (Ed.), *Race and ethnic relations in Canada*, 2nd edn, 253–90. Toronto: Oxford University Press.

US Government Accounting Office. 1990. *Immigration reform: Employer sanctions and the question of discrimination, Report to Congress*. Washington: United States Government Accounting Office.

Valentine, Charles. 1968. *Culture and poverty*. Chicago: University of Chicago Press.

Valpy, Michael. 2005. 'As riots rage across France, troubling parallels emerge among children of Canada's visible minority youth'. *The Globe and Mail* 12 November: A1, A5.

———. 2006. 'Westerners face up to their fear of the veil'. *The Globe and Mail* 23 October: A16.

van den Berghe, Pierre. 1981. *The ethnic phenomenon*. New York: Elsevier.

———. 1986. 'Ethnicity and the sociobiology debate'. In J. Rex and D. Mason (Eds), *Theories of race and ethnic relations*. Cambridge: Cambridge University Press.

Van Hear, Nicholas. 1998. *New diasporas: The mass exodus, dispersal and regrouping of migrant communities*. Seattle: University of Washington Press.

Vernon, Philip. 1984. 'Abilities and achievement of ethnic groups in Canada with special reference to Canadian Natives and Orientals'. In R.J. Samuda et al. (Eds), *Multiculturalism in Canada*, 382–95. Boston: Allyn and Bacon.

Vertovec, Stephen. 1999. 'Conceiving and researching transnationalism'. *Ethnic and Racial Studies* 22 (2):447–62.

Vlassis, George Demetrios. 1942. *The Greeks in Canada*. Ottawa.

Voyer, Jean-Pierre. 2004. 'Foreword to special issue on the role of social capital in immigrant integration'. *Journal of International Migration and Integration* 5 (2):159–64.

Wagley, Charles, and Marvin Harris. 1959. *Minorities in the New World*. New York: Columbia University Press.

Wahlsten, Douglas. 1997. 'The malleability of intelligence is not constrained by heritability'. In Bernie Devlin et al. (Eds), *Intelligence, genes and success: Scientists respond to* The bell curve. New York: Springer-Verlag.

Waldram, James, Ann Herring, and T. Kue Young. 1995. *Aboriginal health in Canada: Historical, cultural and epidemiological perspectives*. Toronto: University of Toronto Press.

Wallerstein, Immanuel. 1974. *The modern world-system I*. New York: Academic Press.

———. 1979. *The capitalist world-economy*. London: Cambridge University Press.

Ward, Peter. 2002. *White Canada forever: Popular attitudes and public policy towards Orientals in British Columbia*. 3rd edn. Montreal and Kingston: McGill-Queen's University Press.

Waters, Mary C. 2000. *Black identities: West Indian dreams and American realities*. Cambridge: Harvard University Press

Wayland, Sarah. 2006. 'The politics of transnationalism: Comparative perspectives'. In Vic Satzewich and Lloyd Wong (Eds), *Transnational identities and practices in Canada*. Vancouver: University of British Columbia Press.

Weber, Max. 1958. *The Protestant ethic and the spirit of capitalism*. New York: Scribner.

———. 1978. *Economy and society*, vol. I and II. (Guenther Roth and Claus Wittich, Eds). Berkeley: University of California Press.

Webster, Yehudi. 1994. *The racialization of America*. London: Palgrave Macmillan.

Weinfeld, Morton. 1988. 'Ethnic and race relations'. In James Curtis and Lorne Tepperman (Eds), *Understanding Canadian society*, 587–616. Toronto: McGraw-Hill Ryerson.

Weissbrodt, David. 1999. 'Comprehensive examination of thematic issues relating to the elimination of racial discrimination'. Working paper, Sub-Commission on Prevention of Discrimination and Protection of Minorities. Geneva: United Nations Commission on Human Rights.

Whitaker, Reginald. 1993. 'From the Quebec cauldron to the Canadian cauldron'. In Alain-G. Gagnon (Ed.), *Québec: State and society*. 2nd edn. Toronto: Nelson Canada.

Winland, Daphne. 1998. 'Our home and Native land? Canadian ethnic scholarship and the challenge of transnationalism'. *Canadian Review of Sociology and Anthropology* 35 (4):555–77.

———. 2006. 'Raising the iron curtain: Transnationalism and the Croatian diaspora since the collapse of 1989'. In Vic Satzewich and Lloyd Wong (Eds), *Transnational identities and practices in Canada*. Vancouver: University of British Columbia Press.

Winn, Conrad. 1985. 'Affirmative action and visible minorities: Eight premises in quest of evidence'. *Canadian Public Policy* 11 (4):684–700.

———. 1988. 'The socio-economic attainment of visible minorities: Facts and policy implications'. In James Curtis, Edward Grabb, Neil Guppy, and Sid Gilbert (Eds), *Social inequality in Canada: Patterns, problems, policies*, 195–213. Scarborough: Prentice Hall Canada.

Wong, Lloyd, and Connie Ho. 2006. 'Chinese transnationalism: Class and capital flows'. In Vic Satzewich and Lloyd Wong (Eds), *Transnational identities and practices in Canada*. Vancouver: University of British Columbia Press.

————, and Nancy Netting. 1992. 'Business immigration to Canada: Social impact and racism'. In Vic Satzewich (Ed.), *Deconstructing a nation: Immigration, multiculturalism and racism in '90s Canada*. Halifax: Fernwood Press.

————, and Vic Satzewich. 2006. 'Introduction: The meaning and significance of transnationalism'. In Vic Satzewich and Lloyd Wong (Eds), *Transnational identities and practices in Canada*. Vancouver: University of British Columbia Press.

Woodsworth, J.S. 1972. *Strangers within our gates: Or coming Canadians*. Toronto: University of Toronto Press.

Wortley, Scot. 2005. *Bias free policing: The Kingston data collection project, preliminary results*. Toronto: Centre of Excellence for Research on Immigration and Settlement.

————, and Julian Tanner. 2003. 'Data, denials and confusion: The racial profiling debate in Toronto'. *Canadian Journal of Criminology and Criminal Justice* 45 (3):1–9.

Wright, Erik Olin. 1983. *Class, crisis and the state*. 2nd impression. London: Verso.

Zhou, Min. 1999. 'Segmented assimilation: Issues, controversies and recent research on the new second generation'. In Charles Hirschman et al. (Eds), *The handbook of international migration: The American experience*. New York: Russell Sage Foundation.

Index

Page numbers in **bold** type indicate figures.